POST-CHRISTIANITY IN AFRICA

ALSO BY G. C. OOSTHUIZEN

Theological Discussions and Confessional Developments in the Churches of Asia and Africa, (Franeker, 1958)

The Theology of a South African Messiah, (Leiden/Cologne, 1967)

POST-CHRISTIANITY
IN AFRICA

*A Theological and
Anthropological Study*

BY

G. C. OOSTHUIZEN

Gerhardus Cornelis

WILLIAM B. EERDMANS PUBLISHING COMPANY,
GRAND RAPIDS, MICHIGAN

First published
in the United States of America 1968
by Wm. B. Eerdmans Publishing Co.
© *G. C. Oosthuizen*
Library of Congress Catalog Card No. 69-12489

Printed in Great Britain

ACKNOWLEDGMENTS

I should like to express my indebtedness to Dr. C. E. Hundleby, temporary lecturer in the department of English at the University College of Fort Hare, for reading the manuscript from the linguistic point of view, and to Mr. Christopher Hurst, my publisher, for his most valuable assistance in this connection; to Prof. O. F. Raum, head of the department of anthropology at Fort Hare, and Prof. B. A. Pauw of the University of South Africa for their helpful suggestions; to the Rev. Dr. A. I. Berglund and the Rev. Danie van Zyl for permission to reproduce their photographs, and to Mr. O. O. Cornhill for his help in developing the negatives. I am especially grateful to Prof. J. J. Ross, Principal of the University College of Fort Hare, for the keen interest he has taken in this study and in our research in general. This study is dedicated to him on the occasion of his retirement.

G. C. O.

Fort Hare
March 1968

CONTENTS

PLATES

INTRODUCTION

THE main object of this book is to analyse the theological challenges with which the Church is faced in Africa as a result of the vast proliferation of so-called separatist or indigenous movements in sub-Saharan Africa, where mission activities have been carried out. The main problem is the Church itself; in so many ways it is unrelated to Africa, so that it is the main instrument in the growth of the movements, some of which develop into post-Christianity.

It is estimated that not less than 6,000 of these movements exist in Africa, among 270 of its tribes (about one-third of the total number), and it constitutes over 7 million followers in thirty-three states on the Continent south of the Sahara (cf. David B. Barrett's lecture delivered at the Social Science Conference held at Makerere, Uganda, in January 1967, entitled *Two Hundred Independent Church Movements in East Africa: a Survey, Analysis and Prediction*). These schisms are taking place on a scale unparalleled in the history of Christianity. Many of them broke away from a static, unrelated, and in many ways foreign Church governed by Western power and money; others are the result of schisms from Christian sects (the term 'sect' is not used in a derogatory sense, but to indicate emphasis on Jesus Christ *plus* adult baptism or the Sabbath [Saturday] or both), while others are the result of schisms amongst themselves. Many form easy bridges back to nativism. They are neither Christian nor traditional, but a syncretism of both, and thus a new religion.

One finds here a spontaneous development of Christianity, but at the same time a concealed reaction against it. These movements have started where Christian missionary activity and/or contact with the Western culture has been intense. Before one attempts to analyse the movements, it is absolutely necessary to realise that one has to do with a great range of beliefs which vary from those of the established Churches and the so-called Christian sects to post-Christianity. This makes a typology important. One could divide them into three main categories, namely Churches, Christian sects and Nativistic movements, or simply into Churches and Nativistic movements. The well-known author on communication Eugene A. Nida, in an article entitled 'Christo-Paganism',[1] describes these movements in Latin America as the most serious challenge to the Evangelical witness in indigenous areas on that Continent. Louis J.

xi

Luzbetak describes these movements in Latin America, which Protestants often identify with Roman Catholicism, as 'a theologically untenable amalgam'.[2] Such an amalgam is not foreign to the United States. One has to expect it in a situation such as that in Africa, where a traditional religion with its ages-old background, seated in the very blood of the people, is confronted with a totally different religion and with Western culture.

To understand syncretism, one has to study the type of Christianity preached in an area, as well as the type of traditional religion of that area. But it is just as important to determine what happened to the elements selected, and how they are reinterpreted in the new context. It is important that we learn from Church history that these movements should not be dismissed as pagan; however, we should be careful also not to accept every movement as Christian, even if we detect in it Christian elements. Islam is not accepted as Christian, in spite of the place it gives to Jesus, neither is the Ahmadiyya, in spite of its use of the name of Jesus Christ. Furthermore, Church history is not too encouraging about the influence such communities exert towards the glorification of Jesus Christ as Lord and Saviour of Mankind. Montanus, for example, personified the Holy Spirit for his followers, and stood very much in the centre.

Why is the Lord's Supper pushed into the background in so many of these movements, adult baptism taking precedence? A theology with emphasis on vital force, in which power is predominant, cannot accept a Cross unless it is magically interpreted. The difficulty with what Nida calls 'Christo-Paganism' is that it is much more complex than most people, who do not study the indigenous religion, can imagine. When two cultures meet, the contact culture is blamed for breaking up what is considered to be a meaningful way of life. A reformulation of the old takes place in the light of the new, or in reaction to the new, or the new is reformulated in the light of the old. This is in many respects the essence of renascent Africa. When the outer crust is scratched off from the immediate political and social issues put forward to justify the existence of these nativistic movements the undercurrent of the traditional religion and culture will be discovered as their main attraction, because there is found the age-old security which the mission and Churches could not give. The preservation of what is meaningful to the traditional man in Africa, in face of its destruction by missionary activity and modern society, has much to do with the existence of many of these movements. In the Republic of South Africa, very few independent movements exist amongst the one-and-three quarter million Coloureds (people of mixed blood), who are westernised. There are issues at stake so fundamental that one cannot maintain they are merely due to race or denominationalism. In Japan, which has no colour problem, there are already about 600 new religions and independent movements, one of which has a membership of over ten million. Some of these have been in contact with Christianity, but have nothing to do with the Christian faith in the Scriptural sense.

Some of the movements referred to in this book are *not nativistic*. One has to be careful not to exaggerate secondary non-Christian features, and to classify the movement accordingly. A thorough analysis of each movement is necessary to determine whether it is a Church or a nativistic movement. Although there are adherents in most of the Churches in Africa who still carry out some non-Christian practice or other, it will be possible to determine whether a movement is a Church or is merely nativistic. It is often most difficult to determine from existing material in which category a movement falls. The recurring theological problems are followed in the book, and we analyse the position of the Trinity; whether God reflects himself so much in the Prophet that *he* is considered to *be* God, or a likeness of God, as the father is reflected in the son; or whether he absorbs the position of Jesus Christ and becomes the Black Christ; or whether the Holy Spirit receives the functions of the ancestor spirits. The Spirit becomes for them the source of vital force and numinous power, which the ancestors had and conveyed, and his work of glorifying Jesus Christ in the hearts of men is not mentioned. The relationship between the Word and the Spirit has broken down in the nativistic movements, and the prophet lives through his own visions and revelations. For others, the Bible has merely become a fetish. It is then no more merely a case of heresy, but of a *new religion*. Magic plays a new role: one has only to see Shembe sitting with a holy stick ('holy' here means magically loaded; if not, it falls into the profane and thus the ordinary, and has no value) resting on the head of the patient at his healing services. The magical personality creates his own world, in which he reigns, and this is precisely what many of these prophets and messiahs do. Is it strange then that Holy Communion is not in the centre of the nativistic movement? Or that adult baptism is used as a purification rite or is merely a rite of admission, or a way of getting 'the Spirit'? Magic here has very little to do with faith in Jesus Christ, and the moralism and legalism of the nativistic movements do not help the adherent to see clearly the sufficient work of Jesus Christ – neither does much of the ritual, the function of which is the continuation of primordial events. In spite of the fact that some movements have laid out their new Jerusalem with white stones, that they have their Paradise, their Bethlehem – a sign of mythical, cyclical and ritualistic thinking – these often refer not to the Jesus Christ of the Bible, but to the holy place of their own Saviour. His representation becomes identification. All nativistic groups are ethno-centric communities, which came into existence very much in the same way as a clan or tribe. Being ethno-centric, they are not Churches, because the Church can only be defined as the body of Christ. There are, of course, issues which are misinterpreted in the Churches also, such as the problem of sin and the doctrine of resurrection of the dead interpreted as the continuation of the Spirit after death. Here we have also to do with the most complex issue, that of the soul, where a person can have different souls, such as the bodily soul which remains in the grave, the free spirit, which becomes the ancestor spirit, as well as the shadow soul.

But the Churches, however, remain true to the basic creed of the Christian faith, and in the final analysis one will discover that many of the independent movements are Churches, where the Word is rightly preached and the Sacraments rightly administered. However, there are many which are nativistic and which constitute a new religion in spite of their outward appearance. The Good News in Christ is the content of Christian communication, and it remains the same. If it changes, it is no more the Good News, and becomes post-Christian. What is needed is a Church that takes note of the situation in which it finds itself, instead of being merely a carbon copy of something else. This is why the problem of communication and theological education have received attention in the book: it is necessary to look at these in the context of separatism. The indigenisation or relevance of the Church in Africa is most important, but this is a dangerous task, which should be based on sound theological judgment. The Church in Africa, however, often floats on the surface, and communication in depth has hardly begun. One could be accused of not giving the Holy Spirit his due, but this type of piety does not solve the problem. The repetition of recurring phenomena amongst the groups in Africa enables us to see more clearly the major difficulties faced throughout the whole continent.

REFERENCES

1. *Practical Anthropology*, Jan.–Feb. 1961, 1–15.
2. *The Church and Cultures: an Applied Anthropology for the Religious Worker*. Techny., Illinois, Divine Word Publications, 1963, 239–48.

1

THE CHURCH IN THE AFRICAN CONTEXT

In the early part of the fourth century Christianity was firmly rooted in North Africa. By the middle of the fifth century Egypt was a Christian country. But the Church in North Africa had an inherent weakness – it was not a truly African Church; its members were from the Roman and Greek middle classes, the colonists, who lived apart from the indigenous peoples.[1] As a result of a latinised Christianity the Punic and Berber populations were only partially or superficially Christianised – they 'became Christian only to the degree that they became latinised and that the Latin language was the sole vehicle of Christian preaching'.[2] The Nubians were the first people of Negro descent to adopt Christianity. Nubia, also known as Ethiopia in those days, came in contact with Christianity very early. Origen (AD 185–253), in his commentary on Matthew xxiv.14, maintains that 'it is now claimed the Gospel has been preached to all the Ethiopians'.[3] The first missionary enterprises of which there is specific knowledge were during the sixth century. This North African Church failed to be a missionary church and to penetrate the life of the indigenous peoples.

Prophecy took an important place in the Early Church and persisted for a few generations, especially in the Montanist movement.[4] Montanus experienced certain 'convulsions', fell into trances, spoke with tongues, was carried away by inspiration and believed that he was the new Paraclete.[5] This movement thought that it received the Holy Spirit in a special way, and a fresh outburst of the early prophetic enthusiasm took place; there was also emphasis on the rapid approach of the *Parousia*.[6] The movement also reacted against secularism in the Church. It is believed that Montanus was in contact with the Phrygian fanaticism or ecstatic type of religion.[7] Different sects started later in North Africa. There was Donatism which had broken up into various factions, to which Augustine refers: 'There is Primianus at Carthage, he has one stall; Maximian, he has another; Rogatus in Mauretania another; there is another in Numidia, sect after sect, now past our powers even to name.'[8] The story of

Donatism begins with the Great Persecution of AD 303–05[9] under Diocletian; it claimed to be the only true Church with a clergy free from 'deadly sins' and thus exercising the only valid sacraments.[10]

These movements give an indication of the inner strife experienced by the Church in North Africa with its emphasis on the Latin language to the detriment of the vernacular of the Punics and Berbers.[11] It was a latinised Christianity, and it disappeared from North Africa during the eighth century,[12] a Church limited to the static moulds of a static language,[13] failing in its missionary task. Its internal strife on questions of dogma; its over-emphasis on ceremonial and cult forms instead of on a devoted Christian witness; insufficient instruction in the Bible; isolation from the rest of the fold of Christendom; suppression by and attraction to Islam – all these factors contributed to its deterioration.[14]

In tropical Africa the Portuguese discovered the mouth of the Congo River in 1482, and established the Roman Catholic faith in 1490 with a missionary expedition.[15] Bartholomew Diaz rounded the Cape in 1486. This gave the Portuguese an impression of both the political and the missionary possibilities of Africa; state and Church worked hand in hand, and wherever the Portuguese flag went the Jesuits were on its trail and established missions.

Protestantism had its strongest foothold in Africa before 1800 at the Cape, where the Dutch formed a settlement and in 1685 the Huguenots started to enter the colony. Quite a number of the slaves were baptised (1,121 between 1665 and 1731), and in 1683 a regulation was passed which declared that all baptised slaves should be free.[16] Organised modern missionary activity is thus over two and a quarter centuries old in sub-Saharan Africa. In 1737 Georg Schmidt of the Moravian Brethren came to South Africa, and the latter half of the eighteenth century witnessed the beginning of British missions in Africa.[17] Europe's chief contact with sub-Saharan Africa before the nineteenth century was through the slave traffic, which Latourette rightly describes as 'the most extensive selfish exploitation of one set of races by another which history has seen'.[18] The campaign against the slave trade, which William Wilberforce and Thomas Fowell Buxton untiringly pursued, brought many missions to Africa in the nineteenth century;[19] in the middle of the century Livingstone began his travels.[20] Internal strife amongst the tribes was also responsible for providing slaves to the Arab and European traders. Missionary reaction against another social evil that was frequently encountered is exemplified in the 'Society for the Suppression of Human Sacrifices', formed in Calabar.[21] Then

2

followed the Scramble for Africa,[22] and at Berlin in 1878 the continent was divided amongst the European Powers.

It was soon clear that missionary work was more than preaching
the Gospel, and that it included education, arts, crafts and medical
work. The transplantation of Western civilisation also became an
important issue to the mission.[23] John and Rena Karefa-Smart write
of this development as follows: 'Mission stations grew up around
these church–school–dispensary units . . . and reflected very little of
the African life of surrounding villages. African Christians living in
the mission were almost in effect, therefore, living in a foreign land
and acquiring a foreign culture and religion.'[24] European names were
given to African Christians on the mission stations. The complaint
of foreignness in approach, in worship, in life and way of living –
'the persistent attachment to non-African patterns and institutions
that mark Christianity as a foreign faith'[25] – has been heard all
over Africa.

This fallacy in the Western approach has been due to the development of Western Christianity itself. Hemmed in by Islam, the Gospel
had been accommodated to the social and personal life of the
European peoples to such a degree that the false idea developed that
a nation can be conceived of as *corpus Christianum*.[26] This fallacy is
alive in the concept of Western Christian civilisation. The synthesis
that has taken place between Gospel and culture in the West has
not only affected the expansion of Christianity but distorted its very
depth and vitality. Henry Venn's three-self formula of self-support,
self-government and self-expansion was changed by others into 'to
make the African civilised in his ways, Christian in his beliefs and
English in his language'.

Outstanding men in Africa have deeply pondered this problem,
men such as Westermann, Willoughby, Tucker, Shropshire, Gutmann
and Edwin Smith. They tried to stem the tide of the Church's prevalent attitude to the cultural heritage of the inhabitants of Africa.
Gutmann, a missionary amongst the Chagga in Tanganyika, repeatedly spoke about the *Selbstbewegung der Gemeinde* (the spontaneous
expansion of the Church). The tribal culture of the Chagga, as indeed
that of any other people, is actually the manifestation of an inner
spirit (*Volksseele*) ordained by God. Gutmann maintained that the
more fortunate pattern for Church and schools is that of the household, the kinship village and the wider kinship group.[27] His approach
to the important question of indigenisation cannot be accepted,
because it leads to an ethnic concept of the Church in which the
process of accommodation will end up in syncretism. Sociologically
the Church must take hold of the main aspects of the African

3

cultural pattern, otherwise it will remain foreign and without roots.[28] This does not mean adaptation or accommodation, or seeking points of contact, but rather taking possession of what can be utilised in the indigenous culture to the advantage of the proclamation of the Christian message.[29] This should be done with the greatest care and humility; there are so many pitfalls of which we learn in the history of missions.

How can the Church belong to African society while so evidently giving the impression that it is part of the Western way of life? The Church has a great opportunity in this era of rapid social change, and of social disintegration, to work for a recovery of psychological strength in the African community. The organic relationships in which every individual is involved have their origins far back in history, in anthropological, physical, psychological and sociological values. In Africa the Church has generally only taken note of this in antithesis and negatively. These factors have never been taken seriously in order to make the Church more efficient in its expression, but have been frowned upon, thereby inculcating in the African an inferiority complex regarding his own culture. Of the five classic examples of Christian experiments in the contact between the Gospel of Jesus Christ and culture,[30] the viewpoint of Tertullian the Montanist has been accepted with regard to the indigenous culture, while with regard to the Western culture that of Abelard and the early European approach has been accepted. This explains why Christianity in Africa is not only foreign but why it is being violently rejected by those who have discovered themselves and seek to salvage the African personality.

The question is often asked: 'Why does the African, in times of crisis, revert back to non-Christian practices?' The question itself reveals quite a bit of ignorance. The answer lies in what has been said above, and it shows that in Africa a new synthesis should be found between a saving Gospel and a total, unbreakable unity in the Christian fellowship.[31] In Africa the evangelical method of 'one soul conversion'[32] has been applied. This method suited Western individualism very well, but in Africa it obscured the group processes;[33] it created the impression that people were 'urged to leave their own and join the Christian "tribe" '.[34] Because the African's past has been ignored and no attempt has been made to penetrate it with the regenerative power of the Gospel message, the converted African lives on two levels and, says Lediga, the 'young people are now saying again that we worship the white man's God. They are alienated by social and political disturbances; they feel Christianity does not belong to them. The fact is that they never had a real

4

connection with Christianity itself.'[35] Many of the established Churches serve as convenient bridges to the Nativistic, Prophetic and Messianic movements because their attitude towards human values is not that of the Gospel.

These movements often come into existence as a result of the lukewarm spiritual life in the established Churches and, says Taylor, 'it is good that we should see in the sects the expression of a demand for the Church to be more African, but it may be more important to recognise in them the demand for the Church to become more Christian'.[36] Prof. G. C. Baëta, Chairman of the Division of World Mission and Evangelism of the World Council of Churches, says: 'The task of the mission is to help build a real African Christendom.'[37] Prof. K. A. Busia points out quite rightly that the Church can only overcome its artificiality and superficiality in Africa 'if it comes to grips with traditional practices, and with the world view that these beliefs and practices imply.'[38] Many Christians have left the Church because the Bible, as they say, stops them from taking part in the affairs of the world, and has brought them into a strange world where the concern is only for souls. Paternalism has been evident in the missions' attitude to the new African ruling powers. The Church should not take part in the party politics, but it has a costly task to put fearlessly in a prophetic way the principles of Scripture right at the centre of the political arena. Alan Booth rightly accuses the Church of 'remoteness', which leads to 'estrangement of awakened Africans' who go in search of new possibilities in indigenous spiritual societies.[39]

At the International Missionary Conference, Whitby, Ontario, in 1947, a strong emphasis was placed on the supra-nationality of the mission and the Church.[40] This was a timely warning in our era of nationalism, which sometimes flourishes in its most extreme form on the African continent.[41] The role of the Church is to be independent from the world, but at the same time responsible for it. In Africa, more than anywhere else, the Church could have an important part to play in assisting the State to maintain and even to recognise the supra-temporal foundations on which the good society is founded. Africa needs today the ecumenical Church, not the isolated nationalistic 'ethnic Churches'; not the conforming but the transforming Church, to conserve those supratemporal foundations. The question to be asked is: are nationalism and Christianity reconcilable? The Reformation accepted nationalism 'almost as a sacred principle of the life of the Churches'.[42] Christianity, a foreign religion in a certain sense, must become nationalised with the people, but without losing its contact with wider fellowships in which mutual loyalty in

5

Christ receives more pertinent emphasis because 'Christianity can never be anything but an international religion. A Christian, in so far as he is sunk in local and national preoccupations, ceases to be a Christian, which is why in the end all totalitarian systems must make war to the death on the Churches'.[43] In many ways nationalism in Africa has developed an anti-Christian attitude,[44] but here the Churches are called to do a thorough self-searching because of their past aloofness from the national aspirations of the people. However, in Africa there is the myth of past greatness – you cannot have a nation without ancestors and the personality cult.[45] African nationalism has been a reaction against colonialism, and has positively contributed to the independent national life. In its essence colonial nationalism is different from absolute nationalism;[46] it can be compared in many ways with the 'class struggle' of socialism.[47] African nationalism is also to no small extent a revolt against inferior economic status. The missionary is seen in colonial nationalism as a colonial type, because the missions never clearly said 'No' to the colonial status. Missions, ironically, played an important but involuntary part in stimulating national consciousness.

The rise of nationalism has also led to the resurgence of the old pre-Christian religion: the old gods are not yet dead. The old forms, including ancestor worship, have received greater significance since the rise of nationalism, so that festivals associated with the original pre-Christian religion draw thousands. The ancestor cult receives a new emphasis even from Christian leaders.[48] The separatist movements, discussed later, encouraged nationalist enterprises.[49] Any political movement which has set out to arouse the mass of Africans to a new conception of their rights and duties has used religious symbolism for this purpose.[50] The Church itself in Africa lived on imperial and political favour, and the Christian missionary was at times a pioneer of the white man's penetration. Livingstone blazed the trail for 'Christianity and commerce'. If Christianity can utilise politics in its service, why can't the peoples of Africa utilise Christianity for their political ends? The Nkrumahs and Bandas were not the first at this game. Nkrumah and his Convention People's Party succeeded in using religious symbolism for political ends with great effect, and accepted a creed in which Nkrumah took the place of Christ and Sir Charles Arden-Clark that of Pontius Pilate.[51] In Malawi the rules for the discipline of the Malawi Congress Party stated: 'The rules and regulations are based on the view that the Malawi Congress Party is supreme and no member, high or low, is above the Party. Further, the Life President, Ngwazi Kamuzu Banda, as the supreme symbol of the Party, is the supreme leader and Father

6

of the Nation.'[52] The titles of Messiah and Saviour are amongst others that have to be used in honour of the Life President;[53] Jomo Kenyatta was also the object of such a messianising process.

It is a mistake to see the independent movements, especially the Ethiopian movements, as nationalistic enterprises with political aspirations. The Church cannot associate itself unconditionally with the freedom movements and some of these movements have realised this very well. But Ethiopianism has been a reaction against what Willoughby calls negrophobia,[54] and the inborn Western assumption of superiority, which led to financial domination of the Church by the missions.[55] Although the deepest motive of many of the independent movements has been religious, one of their essential points is the transferring to the spiritual and ecclesiastical plane of opposition to white authority, which could be made effective only by reconstructing the African communities under African leadership. Religion was the only field within which emancipation was possible. It may seem ironical that 'ecclesiastical colonialism' still prevails in many of the independent African countries, not to mention the Church in South Africa and its seminaries. In many parts of Africa the building up of a new community is paramount, and in this process there may be an 'emancipation' away from religion, and still further away from the Church, as has been the case with the prophetic, messianic and nativistic movements. These movements need to be studied and are the concern of both the Protestants and the Roman Catholics.[56] Attention to the foreignness of the Church will lead to a better understanding of what an indigenous church in Africa should be. The indigenous nativistic movements, with their emphasis on healing and the 'local' prophet, and the Ethiopian movement, with its 'chief' structure, stress the indigenous media – hymns – and absorb Bible truths in the indigenous religious context.[57] In all parts of Africa there was a strong desire for new patterns of worship, but very little opportunity was given by the established Churches to new converts to express their religion in familiar ways. John and Rena Karefa-Smart say that 'the songs and hymns and choruses were plainly transliterated almost word for word and phrase by phrase from the English and other European hymnals . . . even African music was very seldom encouraged as a medium of worship'.[58] Taylor says: 'Clearly the missionaries preached from within the culture of the nineteenth-century Evangelical Protestantism – or nineteenth-century Roman Catholicism – while the Baganda heard from within the culture of the traditional African world view.[59]

The African's view of life and his experience of reality are in many respects different from those of the Westerner.[60] This fact should be accepted, and the African personality should find expression in different fields such as liturgy, theology, architecture, music, hymnology and other spheres.[61] Attention should be seriously given to the development of an indigenous liturgy. There are Churches which transplant what they have received *in toto*, with the result that no spontaneous development can ever take place. Every form of indigenous expression has been discouraged, without ever being studied. The Church in Africa was forced to continue a parasitic mode of existence because no scope was given for its spontaneous development.

Christian thought is not geographically divisible. J. Spencer Trimingham summarises the Church's difficulty in Africa as follows: 'Protestant Christianity has carried with it opposition to the basic elements of African religious expression. Its antipathy to emotionalism; its divorce from art, its lack of true understanding of ritual through which the African apprehends religious truths . . . are only a few of the things which have led to the arrest of the African religious genius. In consequence local Churches are introverted in their life, and deaf to the call of missionary encounter and outreach, hence, too, the birth of pathological forms of African religions. . . .'[62] The impact of 'foreign' Christianity will be still further weakened when socio-religious structures inherited from colonial regimes are broken up at greater speed. The African liturgy, the African Church hymnal, the African theology and the African's unique existential situation are confronting the Church today.

Theological education is perhaps the main focus in the development of the young Churches in Africa. Separatism is partly due to the failure of the Church in its theological task. Theological education should not just be limited to the so-called 'ministry' but should also reach the 'laity'. It is a fact that a relatively uneducated 'ministry' will be ignored by the educated minority,[63] but it is also a fact that the 'laity' have to give constant justification for their faith, and those who are not in a position to do it fall an early prey to all kinds of influences. The Church has been regarded too much from the standpoint of the 'ministry',[64] and this had a negative effect on the Christian situation in Africa, causing many to link up with the independent movements in order to do something positive and exercise the priesthood of all believers. The Church is undoubtedly a divine society but it is a society immersed in history;[65] it must live perpetually in action and reaction with the society in which it finds itself – this is the function of the laity. The Church-centredness and mission-station-centredness have seriously weakened the force of the apostolate,[66] as has been realised by the Roman Catholics.[67] The revival

8

movement, which started in 1929 and swept through many parts of Central and East Africa, has been a lay movement, keeping within the Church. Not only was it a lay movement, emphasising the priesthood of all believers, but the Churches became conscious of their unity.[68] In revival, the sense of belonging, of community, so much emphasised in the independent movements, receives its Christian emphasis so that 'the revival represents a remarkable recovery of the indigenous structure of the Church which . . . consisted primarily of living Christian community groups, or clusters, around some natural head of a household . . . the local leader . . . who gathers around him, in his home or in nearby houses, a considerable community of brethren'.[69] The Methodist Church's 'class' system has been most effective in the work in Africa, both in villages and towns.

Theological education and the indigenous 'ministry' should be the great concern of the Church in Africa today. Many Christians in Africa who broke away from the Church saw in it no opportunity to exercise their desire for Christian service, and if there were any such opportunity, they were subjected to missionary management. The 'slogan' of the IMC Conference at Whitby (1947)[70] – 'Partnership in Obedience' – was essential, although belated. The consecration of Samuel Crowther as Bishop in West Africa was considered to be a portent of the temporary nature of the missionary in the Church in Africa until an African ministry under African bishops should be fully established.[71] The name of Crowther was the symbol not only of African leadership but also of its supposed failure, which influenced indigenous leadership for more than half a century. Sundkler shows through statistics how slowly the indigenous ordained ministry developed – from 408 with a Christian community of 560,000 in 1900 to 5,760 with a Christian community of 10,950,000 in 1957.[72] In South Africa 8,300 lay workers or 20% were Methodists, and in West Africa 25%. This, together with the 'class' system, gave the Methodist Church a tremendous impact, to such an extent that 'the Methodists appear as the characteristically Protestant Church in Africa in the first half of the twentieth century'. Sundkler further calls attention to the fact that of the 11 million Christians in 1957 nearly one million, or about 9% of the total Christian population, belonged to the Seventh Day Adventists and Pentecostal groups, whereas 1,141 out of the 5,760 or one-fifth of the total number of ordained Africans belonged to them.[73] Thus in the established Churches African leadership has been accepted only with great reluctance.[74] The Methodists compensated, however, with their unordained forces. Missions in Africa or ecclesiastical colonisation, with white missionary settlers managing mission stations, have

9

failed to provide a channel for spontaneous development, and it is only a miracle that so many Africans remain true to the Church in spite of it all; this augurs well for the future of Christianity in Africa.

An indigenous ministry calls for an indigenous theology, and in particular indigenous confessions of faith. Each of the independent movements has its own confession of faith, whether published or unpublished. There are three main approaches in Africa to the question of confessions: the non-confessional policy, the traditional confessional policy, and the indigenous confessional policy. Many Churches of the non-confessional group have accepted confessions. The report of the Commission on 'Faith and Confession' of the historic Lutheran conference held at Marangu (Nov. 12–22, 1955) tried to answer the question as to what form and content a confession of the Church in Africa should take in order to be faithful to the purely African and historic heritage. It maintained that the Christian truth should be expressed in the African context, and that a *Confessio Africana* should be drawn up in which the existential situation of the Church is taken into consideration.[75] The confessions of the Churches from the West, although significant (many of the Church members have no idea for what they stand!), are especially Western and have a specifiic historical background. Confessions that take the environment, the Church's existential situation, into consideration, that speak to the concrete situation, are not only necessary but essential, especially in this process of indigenisation of the Church. The Church in Africa needs, apart from its confessional inheritance, its own related interpretation of Scripture. In an interesting symposium[76] Arne Sovik maintains that Lutheran theology, for example, cannot be divorced from its environment as it conflicts with local culture, with the result that it has 'to get its cue for its application from the African environment and not from the West'.[77] It is necessary to guard against approaching a confession as 'crystallised truth', a museum piece, instead of being the living truth.

Church union movements have been very few and far between in Africa. A few schemes have been drawn up in Nigeria, Ghana and East Africa, and discussions have taken place in Central and South Africa and the Congo. Denominationalism has been Africa's main source of division and a principal cause of separatism. Church union has tended to be on denominational lines in different parts of Africa; for example, in February 1956 the new Presbyterian Church of East Africa was inaugurated by the unification of the Overseas Presbytery of Kenya of the Church of Scotland with the Presbyterian Church of East Africa;[78] the United Church of Central Africa in Rhodesia in 1958 was the outcome of the 'United Missions in the Copperbelt'.

Dr. J. P. Bolink has written a doctoral thesis on Church union in Zambia. In South Africa the five Provincial Synods of the Dutch Reformed Churches (NGK) came together in a national body and a similar union has taken place in the African daughter churches.[79] There have been union discussions in Nigeria for many years, and a Nigeria Church Union Committee was established in 1947, representing the Anglican, Presbyterian and Methodist Churches in Nigeria and the Cameroons. Use was made of a scheme of union prepared by the East Nigerian Church Union Committee, which was already formed in 1933.[80] In 1957 the 'Proposed Scheme of Church Union in Nigeria' was published and in 1963 the Church Union Committee received the third edition of the Scheme, a revision of the 1960 Scheme of Church Union in Nigeria. It was formally decided that December 1965 should be the provisional date for the union of the Anglican, Methodist and Presbyterian Churches in Nigeria.[81] The Anglicans approved the Scheme in 1964 and the other two Churches in January 1965. This union was not promulgated mainly due to a clash of personalities – not between missionaries and Nigerians but between Nigerians themselves.

In East Africa, serious discussions on Church union started in 1961 and an *Interim Basis of Union* has been published in the name of three of the five Churches in the consultations, namely Anglicans, Methodists and Presbyterians. The greatest stumbling-block is Chapter IX (8) entitled 'Succession in the ordained ministry and the historic episcopate'. The Lutherans shared the same problem in their discussion with the Church of South India. The Moravians have no difficulty with the historic episcopate unless it is considered a *sine qua non* for the continuity of the Gospel. This was the only unification scheme in which Lutherans took part in Africa.[82] They have, however, withdrawn from active participation in the discussions.

In September 1964 the delegates of the Presbyterian Church of West Cameroon, the Evangelical Church of Cameroon and the Presbyterian Church of Cameroon met at Kumba and decided to appoint a unity committee which would commit participants to collaborate with a view to organic union. The third meeting was held at Douala (Cameroons) in October 1965.[83] No merger has taken place.

In the Congo different Protestant Churches and interested persons met since October 1964 in order to discuss the possibility of a united Church of Christ in the Congo. These discussions are still continued although at the 1965 meeting hope was expressed that the United Church would be inaugurated in November or December 1966.

In Ghana a revised edition of the proposed Basis of Union was published in 1965. The negotiating Churches are: The Diocese of Accra; The Church of the Province of West Africa; The Evangelical Presbyterian Church; The Methodist Church, Ghana; The Presbyterian Church of Ghana.

In South Africa conversations between Anglicans and Presbyterians take place as well as between Anglicans and Methodists. Union discussions between the Congregational Union of South Africa, the London Missionary Society and the Bantu Congregational Church are in progress and negotiations for union are at an advanced stage for amalgamation of the Presbyterian Church of Southern Africa (a mainly European body), the Bantu Presbyterian Church (formerly Church of Scotland Mission), and the Tsonga Presbyterian Church (formerly Swiss Mission).

Protestant missions have co-operated in Africa for a long time. The main medium has been the National Christian Council and also the United Theological Seminaries, such as St. Paul's United College, established in 1955 at Limuru, where Anglicans, Methodists and Presbyterians engage together in theological training. In South Africa the Federal Theological Seminary of Southern Africa has been established near Alice, in the Eastern Cape Province, where the Anglicans, Methodists, Presbyterians and Congregationalists co-operate. This type of united theological training has great advantages both in the ecumenical field and as a pointer to the dividedness of separatism, although in the case of the Federal Seminary near Alice the existence of separate hostels for each denomination is a step backward, as the students of the several denominations had previously stayed together in the Lovedale Bible School (also near Alice).

The divisions in the Church are a tragic reality to Christians. This is felt even in the Roman Catholic camp. Oscar Niederberger says it is tragic that Christendom has no united front against paganism, Islam, secularism, materialism and communism.[84] In his report T. A. Beetham writes: 'The visitor to the Copperbelt can never forget the line of churches alongside one African township, eleven of them side by side: African Methodist Episcopal, Seventh Day Adventist, Anglican, Roman Catholic, Church of Central Africa (Rhodesia), Dutch Reformed, Pentecostal, Salvation Army, Watch Tower and two others. We must never allow ourselves to get accustomed to this.'[85] This is, however, a feature of most African townships. Non-theological factors – psychological, historical, sociological, economical and political – have been the most powerful factors in causing and maintaining this diversity in spite of the fact that only the theological issues have been treated in ecumenical discussions.[86]

12

We come now to a very important part of the concern of the Church in modern Africa, *urbanisation*. The upheaval and the dehumanisation that has resulted from it have bred pathological forms of Christianity. This largest frontier of African mission activity is bound to become more and more significant. Christianity is faced here with almost the greatest spiritual encounter of its history. Industrialisation affects not only urban but also rural Africa, but in the urban areas new types of social personalities are already formed. In those areas, tribal loyalties are maintained, but they are often extraordinarily emphasised in a new context. Ministers and congregations have in the past been so absorbed in Biblical material that they have lost contact with the real situation, and Biblical words, especially those pertaining to man's daily life, have become dead letters in many Churches; communism has often been a stronger moral force than 'empirical' Christianity. The Church has to listen to the confused voices of the peoples of the world and make her message relevant to their need.

Many Africans are locked out of their 'old' houses and find themselves in the barren desert of individualism. The common enemy drives these spiritual 'refugees' into a common camp which forms a marching column and they often powerfully reject the Church and even burn its buildings, as well as the schools, the symbols of association with those in power and thus of oppression. Africans look to the Church for guidance, but are often disillusioned because the Church has usually appeared self-satisfied, and identified with the social *status quo*. This identification is perilous both for the Church and for society. W. A. Visser 't Hooft rightly maintains[87] that the mission of the Church does not belong to a greater extent to its *esse* (well-being) than to its *diakonia* (service), and when the latter is accepted in its real and true sense it becomes *kerygma* (proclamation). The Church has limited itself mainly to the task of charity to the individual victims of social circumstances, to the blind, the leper, the orphan, with a strong emphasis on primary education for the sake of evangelisation. But the root of the institutional development and problems of society have been untouched, and here the destinies of millions are at stake. The Church also fails in its task by identifying God's purposes with the aims of the nation and vice versa – a phenomenon not uncommon in Africa from North to South. Under all circumstances the Church has to fight for justice.

It has already been said that urbanisation is the necessary concomitant of industrial development. In South Africa the urban African population was in 1911 just over half a million; in 1946 1,794,122; in 1951 2,011,337, and in 1957 over 3 million. Between

13

1932 and 1949 there was an increase of 247% in the total employ-
ment of all races in industries other than agriculture and mining in
South Africa, and an increase of 356% in Africans employed.[88]
Over 4 million Africans live in urban areas today. In Rhodesia the
number of Africans in secondary industry increased between 1941
and 1953 by 100%.[89] Ibadan's population has grown from 335,000
in 1952[90] to over 1 million fifteen years later. Kinshasa, Congo,
grew from 26,622 in 1935 to 344,000 in 1955;[91] in the late 1960s its
population is also over 1 million. In Africa south of the Sahara 6%
of the population is in the cities with more than 20,000 inhabitants.
In South Africa, where the breaking up of the socio-economic
structure has developed the furthest in Africa the figure is 30%. In
Ethiopia, Liberia and all West Africa the average is only 1–3%. In
Zambia 77% of the population are in agriculture; in Malawi 92%.[92]
Professor Fritz Baade maintains that over 70% of the world's
population has to be urbanised (only 8% of the population of the
USA practise agriculture). If this is the case, and if South Africa's
independent movements proliferate further as a result of urbanisation, the future holds many problems for the Church, not only with
regard to effective spontaneous indigenisation, but also with regard to
communication.[93] It has to face the moral implications of the break-up
of the socio-economic structures, the development of a 'new' humanity, and such problems as masses seeking a new community, migratory
labour, race relations and polygyny. George Carpenter says that,
of eighty-five households investigated, only five consisted of husband,
wife and children; eight had no permanent male, the head of each
being a woman who housed a succession of male 'boarders'. Many
of these people regard themselves and are considered to be earnest
Christians.[94] In maternity wards the majority of those accepted are
girls of thirteen and even younger. This is one of the results of
migratory labour[95] and the break-up of the original tribal structure
and the distortion of African custom in the new context. Family life
received special attention in the All-Africa Church Conference at
Ibadan in 1958.

God's patience excuses all kinds of indulgences. Taylor came to the
conclusion that the majority of those baptised in Buganda seem to
think of God in the same way practically as they used to think of
their hero gods, which had no concern for practical morality but
only the observance of rites and the offering of sacrifices. Natural
human fear is all concentrated on the present life. Syncretism easily
prevails under such circumstances, and often leads back to paganism.
The standards of Jesus are considered to be too high.[96] A strictly
legalistic, pietistic Church in such circumstances seems to be quite

14

explicable as in the case of the Bhengu Church in East London, South Africa;[97] when Church discipline is strictly observed, many leave the established Churches to join the independent movements. Apart from the fact that there is a tremendous gulf between the Church and the place of work of the people, and that the Church is only superficially influencing the new civilization represented by the place of work, the Church itself has done very little to build together a new community in towns, where people can find refuge and a 'home'. The Churches have to join hands, and a body of thought, theological and social, must be provided by them for lay Christians in modern industry, which can be of assistance to them in the society where they have to form judgments and make decisions.

Ernst Troeltsch[98] has attempted to give an analysis of the social teaching of Churches on a broad, as distinct from a merely local, basis; and in Africa particularly, the Church is indebted to Merle Davis's analysis of the social and economic problems of missions and the younger Churches[99] – problems which require thinking and rethinking. To take an example, the Church finds it difficult to give positive direction to the working-class movement in the cities.[100] Because of its dividedness it cannot assist meaningfully in establishing a new society which is already in the process of revolutionary transformation in the political, social, economic and cultural spheres. Here we have in mind not the Church as an institution but the Church as an organism. A letter written to Diognetus in the second century refers to the Church as the soul of society; this gnostic dichotomy between soul and body had already influenced the Church very early. Where the Church has succeeded in forming a new society, it takes a corporate form, which is absolutely different from what the African is used to: it is the mission station or compound, made up of individuals, a community within a community, having a superficial existence within an organic structure. It is not therefore surprising that many in Africa judge Christianity only by its material results.[101] Mission meant civilization, education, hospitalisation – in short, national welfare. It was even a symbol of prosperity! With these attitudes predominating, Christianity could be expanded without taking the whole of society into consideration. Roland Allen,[102] although he maintained that the social condition is no direct concern of the mission, left open the question of the social involvement of Christians. Christianity is closely linked with social change. The Church has initiated it, but the irony is that it does not understand it, and many young people in the factories and mines learn to get on without the Churches; to them, instead, magic has a renewed appeal as a protection against social forces.[103] The towns

15

have today a positive function in providing new points of human contact and interest. Sociologists use the term New Society for an industrialised, urbanised society; and the Church needs to renew its structure in order to meet this development adequately. The scientific and social revolutions must be looked at in a prophetic way and, says Wickham, 'they must state a profound religious significance despite the confusion they seem to spell for traditional theological thinking'.[104] In this new development secularisation has evoked a more positive attitude in theological thinking, because of the Church's renewed consciousness of its responsibility to the world, and of the need for its concern for its fellow-men to be this-worldly rather than other-worldly.[105]

The discipline of the Church has received differing emphases in the African context and its effects have been various. Persons under discipline either joined another Church or sect, or formed their own movement in which discipline was lax. These ethnic movements have no special concern for discipline, other than in the moralistic, legalistic pentecostal sects in which it has a kind of magical effect. In the original religion of the African, the community is a cult community which embraces the whole of life. Here we find the special temptation of having the whole tribe within the Church, which is in line with the communalistic philosophy. During the revival movement in East Africa, the Church expanded in many instances at the circumference, while in the centre it became superficial. Many would make a formal act of 'joining' the Church, the psychological background being the magical unification with the totality of the dead and the living. This 'people's' or ethnic Church is always a mass Church, with all the accompanying dangers of superficiality.[106] For many baptism has nothing to do with an *act of faith* of the parents – it is the inclusion of the child in the safe stronghold of the congregation, with the *name* as 'sign and seal'. Blood relationship gives the child the right to enter the tribe, with the result that it is the right of the child to be baptised. Emphasis on the Church as institution satisfies the innermost desires of the communalistic mind and, when Christ is bound to that institution, we get a pope [107] – in the independent movements the prophet takes this place in the tribe. The ethnic Church is something made by man: any Church based on race has ceased to be one in the true sense of the word, but has the characteristics of isolation which are prevalent in some movements. This tendency of 'the Church of the whole nation or tribe' affects its discipline and its whole doctrine.

Many of the *financial problems* within the Churches in Africa are due to the fact of their members not being educated adequately

16

with regard to their stewardship. In South Korea, Nevius introduced a method whereby each believer tithes (however little it may be); nothing is bought or built for which the members cannot afford to pay, and each believer teaches a non-Christian the basic principles of Scripture.[108] For this reason their first 'buildings' were poor, but they *belonged* to them; so did their Church. The idea of tithing has taken root in the work of the Sudan United Mission in the Mandara Mountains of the Cameroons, and in that of the American Methodists in Katanga. The fixing of certain amounts as so-called Church Tax has had a negative effect on the Church in Africa. In the Presbyterian Church of Ghana, for example, the Church contributions were fixed at one pound sterling in 1922, and in spite of the economic developments in that cocoa area, this amount remained the same for years. This mechanical approach to stewardship has its effect also on the Holy Communion. When a member is excluded from Holy Communion because the Church dues have not been paid, it is logical to think that one must pay in order to take part in the Holy Communion – some even speak about buying Holy Communion. Issues of this nature, rather than book-keeping, should receive attention at theological seminaries.

Communism in its messianic and prophetic form may yet exert still greater influence on the African continent, especially if Africa fails to achieve economic stability. For the Churches, communism is a judgment on their lack of social concern; it 'rightly criticised the Church and the missionary movement for their entanglement with Western cultural, political and economic domination'.[109] There is today a religiously understood nationalism and a politically understood religion, which satisfy the ideological needs of many; this state of affairs, however, will not last long. In Africa a future generation will surely discover the weaknesses of this ideology, and see an alternative in communism.[110] The messianism of Western civilisation has failed to satisfy Africa's need for security. Different approaches with regard to communism are made by the theologians.[111] Emil Brunner rejects it, and is in agreement with the majority of Western theologians in this respect. Hromadka and his friends want us to see it in the organic whole of the development of history, in which God is mightily at work.[112] Whatever its precise attitude may be to the inhabitants of communist countries, the Church has learned that, in this situation, *diakonia* (service) is of vital importance in the world.[113] It cannot easily refute the communist accusation that it has become a middle class, bourgeois institution. Why did the communist part of the world start to work out its own salvation and create its own hope?

17

Colonialism has left a vacuum in Africa into which communism tries to enter. It has a messianic conviction about destiny which is attractive for some leaders; and which will give it great force in industrialised Africa.[114] Communism *forces* the Gospel to be demonstrated. George Padmore's contention that the African is immune to communism is only true as far as rural Africa is concerned.[115] Several African states have shown strong leanings towards the socialist camp, in spite of the set-backs which students and others from Africa have experienced in communist countries. Communist influence comes in the pragmatic guise of the 'Africa Research Institute' in Moscow, trade unions, universities, technical projects, trade specialists in different fields, medical help, etc.[116] Hence Christians in Africa, as elsewhere, make a distinction between the communist ideology, about which they may have reservations, and what it has achieved for social justice.[117] They have learned to understand Christianity in terms that are 'largely utilitarian and materialistic',[118] and on this level Christianity fails to impress.[119] Many Christians are forced to give a limited support to communist parties in the hope of better days; for many Christians this has been a serious dilemma, as communism has offered the only hope of transforming an agricultural society into an industrial nation. There is little danger of the challenge that this messianic movement holds out to the Church in Africa today being belittled.

A brief reference to Islam is relevant here. The 1958 statistics[120] of the religions of Africa show that Islam is in a very strong position, having grown in the last thirty years to such an extent that it doubled itself without the positive missionary action or financial backing experienced by Christianity. Today the El-Azhar University in Cairo and the instruments of political propaganda contribute to the extension of this religion, which has become missionary in the sense of positively organising missionary activities. Islam is a layman's religion and to this much of its success should be ascribed. Only in Ethiopia is Christianity more indigenous to the exclusion of Islam, but the Church there accommodated the Gospel with the Hamitic culture to such an extent that it lost its prophetic task.[121] Because Islam is animistic it adapts easily to the African culture, with which it was in contact for centuries. It has made its great impact without attention being given to the magic word of Africa: education. Besides being the predominant religion in the north and Horn of Africa, there are 31 million Muslims (the same as the number of Christians) in Africa south of the Sahara, where more than 140 million people live. More than a thousand years elapsed on the East coast of Africa before Africans accepted Islam. The slave trade had brought a deep revulsion against it, but today a different atmosphere has begun to prevail. Islam has the advantage over Christianity, which has been in sub-Saharan Africa for only 150 years, that it lived with animism as a neighbour for many centuries. With its pilgrim rites, its doctrine of jinns and magic, of amulets and charms, it finds much easier acceptance in Africa than Christianity. The African finds here the counterpart of his own animism 'and finds no difficulty in moving his whole world of spirits right into the new religion'.[122] He scarcely needs to leave a thing behind when he enters the fold of Islam, and Islamic polygyny, its superstitions, and its ritual character and purification ceremonies satisfy the traditional African mind. Zwemer says, 'Islam and Animism live in very neighbourly fashion on the same street and in the same soul'.[123] Islam is a world brotherhood, whereas on this score Christianity makes a poor impression. Its main aim is to establish the theocracy of Allah to fit people into the *corpus Islamicum*.[124] Politics and religion are one, and the aim is a Muslim Africa. Its brotherhood in the cities succeeds in establishing a sense of community. The brother orders, Tijania, Quadiria and Senussia, are very much alive in West Africa. It spreads easily among people in urban areas; in fact 'it is a civilisation, and cannot establish itself solidly without a strong foundation of urban life'.[125] It has influence amongst nomads, but its appeal to the farmer, 'the rural mind' with its 'centripetal outlook', is weak.[126]

For many tribes in Africa, Christianity is a civilisation, while Islam is a religion. It is maintained that Islam has no colour of its own but, like a river, it accepts the colour of the rock or sand over which it flows. Trimingham mentions three stages of assimilation in non-Christian societies: (i) superficial adoption; (ii) assimilation of Islamic religious elements; (iii) in the third stage, which has an infinite number of gradations, a genuine belief in the efficacy of Islamic sanctions develops, and a change in custom and habitual conduct takes place.[127] Here the cultural patterns that develop are at the same time African and Islamic, whereas in Christianity a conscious opposition to the African cultural background develops. The most important facts are that Islam is spread by Africans, it becomes indigenous, it emphasises the task of the laity and it develops without an expensive organisation.[128]

The unorthodox Ahmadiyya sect is making a great impact. Its founder, Mirza Ghulam Ahmad, born in the Punjab in 1839, proclaimed himself after certain visions as the Messiah of the Christians, and Mahdi of the Muslims, the Krishna of the Hindus and the Redeemer of the Buddhists. This movement, which has already over

40 million followers, was rejected by the orthodox Muslims, but has been gradually tolerated. They are zealots nevertheless, and at Fez in Morocco African missionaries are trained, while others are imported from Asia.[129]

Prophetism has also been a phenomenon of Islam in Africa. As a result of different political and economic factors a situation developed in the Sudan that was 'set for an outburst of fanaticism'.[130] A certain Muhammad Ahmad proclaimed himself to be the expected Mahdi or Messiah in 1881, and had a great influence among the suppressed section of the population.[131] His reaction was against Turco-Egyptian rule in the Eastern Sudan. In Somaliland, a movement was started by Muhammad ibn 'Abd Alláh Hasan against Abyssinian and British imperialism, 'an aspect of the anti-Western ferment which was running through African Islam during the last quarter of the nineteenth century'.[132] In his aim to drive out all Westernism, he emphasised that which was common to all Somalis, Islam, in an effort to overcome narrow tribalism which was a disuniting factor.[133]

Mahdism in the Sudan emphasised the messianic aspect of Muslim teaching,[134] mainly because of the difficulties it encountered. The eschatology of Judaism and Christianity entered Muslim thought through converts to Islam. In the Last Day, confusion will be experienced and oppression terminated; and Mahdi will appear. His chiliastic kingdom will be destroyed by the Dajjāl; thereafter Dajjāl will be killed by the Prophet 'Isa who will return 'and fill the earth with justice by ruling according to the Law of Islam'.[135] Trimingham maintains that, wherever people have been oppressed by their rulers, Mahdis come to the rescue as deliverers. Such a religious reformer uses political means, because Islam does not make the distinction between the religious organisation (or Church) and the State. According to the author, 'in Africa, where the Arab-negroid and Arab-Hamite peoples form material very susceptible to mass suggestion, their innate anthropolatry saving the would-be Mahdi the laborious work of gaining adherents, Mahdis have been especially frequent, and have almost always been reformers and deliverers, and whenever successful have inevitably founded states'.[136] The above-mentioned Muhammad Ahmad played a very significant role in the Sudan. He was absolutely certain about his call as the Mahdi of Allah; he had a strong personality, and he proclaimed the millennium after the expulsion of the British. The most severely oppressed were the most susceptible to his call for the dissolution of tribal and religious allegiances, which would enforce a community between rich and poor.[137] Muhammad Ahmad believed himself

20

to have had direct revelations, and the central point of his teaching was eschatological. He changed the 'Pillars of Faith' in order to add that he is 'the Mahdi of Allah and the representative of His Prophet'.[138] Doubt on this point could be punished by death. In the movement, religious instruction disappeared, and learning was discouraged, only the Koran and the *Rātib* of the Mahdi being allowed; all else was burned. He tried to reform morals and revolutionise Sudanese customs by forbidding 'intoxicants, tobacco, amulets, magic, music, processions, marriage and circumcision feasts, mourning (*bikā*), and visiting saints' tombs. . . .'[139] All had to live as if they were living in the Last Days; war against the Turks was essential, and those who defended their religion against them would enter heaven, where they would enjoy the greatest happiness and prosperity.[140]

A Mahdi cult developed even though Muhammad Ahmad died before this mission was accomplished. After the overthrow of the Khalifa, Mahdism deteriorated on account of its tyranny, and its adherents returned 'to their old tribal and religious allegiances'.[141] The West Africans, however, maintained their allegiance to Mahdism, and Lord Kitchener was considered to be the Dajjāl, while the son of Mahdi was considered to be the prophet 'Isa. Visits to his grave have been regarded as a substitute for the Pilgrimage to Mecca. Lord Kitchener destroyed his body and tomb, because of the dangers that might develop round his cult. A number of risings took place, and the British Government realised how closely linked were economic and social conditions with outbreaks of fanaticism.[142] Other risings also had economic and religious motives. There was danger of Mahdism spreading rapidly amongst the ignorant and poor negroids of the Western Sudan, who are easily susceptible to fanaticism, and the Government prohibited any Mahdist agents. This movement proves that African Islam, like African Christianity, is subject to the phenomenon of prophetism.

To sum up this chapter, the African personality must be offered positive development in the Church, which means that the Church must discard its foreignness. In the new situation the Churches should work out a *modus vivendi* with regard to the independent states, in the development of which they should be actively interested. The great task of the Church is to be the Church; not an ethnic institution, but the Church of Christ. It is an absolute necessity, as a result of the developing process of urbanisation, for the Churches to plan together, and to keep abreast of new industrial urban planning.[143] The Church should stop planning within the context of the Church; her mission and her obedience should be in the context of society and the world. Finally, the priesthood of all believers should receive a fresh emphasis, and the Church must realise anew what it means to be of one family in Christ.

REFERENCES

1. D. Westermann, *Africa and Christianity*, London, OUP, 1937, 105–07: cf. also C. P. Groves, *The Planting of Christianity in Africa*, Vol. I, London, Lutterworth Press, 1948, 36–38.
2. K. S. Latourette, *The First Five Centuries*, New York and London, Harper, 1937, 93. Islam won the Berbers when it 'assumed the form of national movements'. Cf. J. S. Trimingham, *A History of Islam in West Africa*, OUP, 1962, 18.
3. Groves, op. cit., 49.
4. Latourette, op. cit., 115.
5. R. Knox, *Enthusiasm*, Oxford, Clarendon Press, 1962 ed., 29, 34.
6. W. Walker, *A History of the Church*, T. & T. Clark, 1959 ed., 56.
7. Knox, op. cit., 28.
8. *Homilies on St. John*, No. X, 6. Quoted by R. Knox, 12.
9. Cf. W. H. C. Frend, *The Donatist Church*, OUP, 1952.
10. W. Walker, op. cit., 106.
11. Groves, Vol. I, 65.
12. Ibid., 78–89.
13. Cf. Eugene A. Nida, *Message and Mission*, New York, Harper, 80.
14. Westermann, p. 110.
15. A. Mulders, *Missiegeschiedenis*, Bussum, Paul Brand, 1957, 203. Cf. C. P. Groves, Vol. I, 114–46; K. S. Latourette, Vol. III, op. cit., 1939, 242.
16. Latourette, Vol. III, op. cit., 245.
17. Ibid., 246.
18. Ibid., Vol. V, 1943, 320.
19. Cf. C. P. Groves, Vol. III, 1954, 6.
20. Cf. G. Seaver, *David Livingstone*, Lutterworth, 1957; Cecil Northcott, *Livingstone in Africa*, Lutterworth, 1957.
21. E. G. K. Hewat, *Vision and Achievement (1796–1956)*, Johannesburg, Nelson, 1960, 196.
22. Cf. Roland Oliver, *Sir Harry Johnston and the Scramble for Africa*, London, Chatto and Windus, 1959.
23. Stephen Neill (*Christian Partnership*, SCM, 1952, 22–23) says: 'One of the great nineteenth-century myths was that of "the Christian West", of the idea that the spread of Western civilisation would of itself make easier the coming of the Kingdom of Christ. This mythology is dead. . . .' Cf. Margery Perham (*Lugard – the Years of Adventure, 1858–1898*, Collins, 1956, 112) maintains that 'those who condemn the Missions for this wanting the flag to follow the Bible, should assess the alternatives that faced them in the Africa of the eighties and nineties'. It is interesting to note that in 1957 the Liberian delegate to the United Nations maintained that the reason why his country suffers in comparison with Ghana's progress is that it has not had the advantage of being a colony. Cf. J. E. Lesslie Newbigin, *A Faith for this One World*, SCM, 1961. Colonialism is nevertheless a theological problem which had eventually to be dealt with theologically. Cf. M. A. C. Warren, *Caesar the Beloved Enemy*, London, 1955; J. Hermelink, *Christ im Welthorizont*, Kreuz-Verlag, 1962; H.-W. Gensichen, *Die deutsche Mission und der Kolonialismus in Kerygma und Dogma*, Heft 2, April 1962, 136–49;

W. Holsten, *Kolonialismus als theologisches Problem*, in: G. Hoffman, K. H. Rengstorf (Hrsg.), *Stat crux dum volvitur orbis*. Festschrift für H. Lilje, 1959, 159–70. See especially Stephen Neill, *Colonialism and Christian Missions*, London, Lutterworth, 1966.

24. John and Rena Karefa-Smart, *The Halting Kingdom*, New York, Friendship Press, 1953, 3.

25. Ibid., 75.

26. Lesslie Newbigin, *The Household of God*, New York, Friendship Press, 1953, 3. Thomas Ohm, OSB, in his book: *Asia looks at Western Christianity* (Herder, Freiburg; Nelson, 1959) asserts that Christendom is so embedded in Western civilisation that it finds it very difficult to adapt, but that the Christianisation of Asia must lead to the Asianisation of Christianity; cf. D. T. Niles, *Upon the Earth*, Lutterworth.

27. Bruno Gutmann, *Gemeindeaufbau aus dem Evangelium*, Leipzig, Verlag der Evang Luth. Mission, 1925, 123 ff.

28. John V. Taylor and D. Lehmann, *Christians of the Copperbelt*, London, SCM Press, 1960, 146.

29. Cf. J. H. Bavinck, *An Introduction to the Science of Missions* (transl. D. H. Freeman). The Presbyterian and Reformed Publ. Co., Philadelphia, 1960, 179; Stephen Neill, *The Unfinished Task*, Edinburgh House Press, 1958[2], 90–94.

30. Cf. Richard Niebuhr, *Christ and Culture*, New York, Harper, 1951. These examples are the following, namely, Christ against culture (Tertullian and Kierkegaard); the Christ of culture (Abelard, and the early European and now American presuppositions); Christ above culture or the merging with the Word Incarnate (Aquinas); Christ and culture are paradoxically opposed (Luther); Christ changes culture because He is its Saviour (Calvin and John Wesley).

31. Cf. J. V. Taylor, *The Growth of the Church in the Buganda*, London, SCM Press, 1958.

32. J. C. Hoekendijk, *Kerk en Volk in de Duitse Zendingswetenschap*, Amsterdam, Kampert & Helm, 1949, 43–51.

33 D. A. McGavran, *The Bridges of God*, World Dominion Press, 1957, 8–10.

34. D. A. McGavran, *How Churches Grow*, World Dominion Press, 1959, 23.

35. S. P. Lediga, 'The Disciple of Jesus Christ Facing African Religions', The *SA Outlook*, May 1, 1962, 69.

36. J. V. Taylor, 'Saints and Heretics' in *Basileia*, Stuttgart, Evang. Missionsverlag, 1959, 312. The young Churches themselves live simply by 'carrying on'. Cf. H. Kraemer, 'On Tour through South-East Asia', *Ecumenical Review*, IV (1951), 126.

37. Quoted by Jan Hermelink, 'Rundschau über die deutsche evangelische Missions, Deutsche Evangelische Weltmission, *Jahrbuch* 1954, 65. See also the report on the Marangu All-African Lutheran Conference, Geneva, LWF, 1956; 'The Church in Changing Africa', Report of the All-Africa Church Conference, Ibadan, Jan. 1958.

38. *Christianity and Culture*, publ. by the Christian Council of Ghana, Accra, 1955, p. iii.

39. Alan Booth, *Christians and Power Politics*, SCM, 1961, 114.

40. Report of the IMC Conference, Whitby, Ontario, 1947, Edinburgh House Press, 1947.

41. Cf. Thomas Hodgkin, *Nationalism in Colonial Africa*, London, Frederick Muller, 1960[3], 80–86; A. M. Thunberg, *Kontinente im Aufbruch*, Göttingen, van den-Hoeck & Ruprecht, 1960. For popular reading see G. McLeod Bryan,

Whither Africa? Richmond, John Knox Press, 1961; G. L. Carpenter, *The Way in Africa*, New York, Friendship Press, 1960; Emory and Myrta Ross, *Africa Disturbed*, New York, Friendship Press, 1959.

42. Neill, op. cit., 91.
43. Ibid., 93.
44. Cf. Phillippe Maury, *Politik und Christliche Verkündigung*, Stuttgart, Calwer Verlag, 1959, 20, 42.
45. Cf. Hans Kohn, *The Idea of Nationalism*, New York, The Macmillan Co., 1961; C. J. H. Hayes, *Nationalism: A Religion*, New York, Macmillan Co. 1960.
46. J. A. Verdoorn, *De Zending in het Indonesisch Nasionalisme*, Amsterdam, 1945, 110 ff.; see also Ndabaningi Sithole, *African Nationalism*, OUP, 1959.
47. H. Dür, 'Die Stellung der Mission und des kapitalistischen Bürgertums', *Evang. Miss. Zeitschrift*, Nov. 1947; Rupert Emerson, *From Empire to Nation: The Rise of self-assertion of the Asian and African Peoples*, Harvard University Press, 1960. Cf. J. V. Taylor, *Christianity and Politics in Africa*, African Series, 1957, 94. Both Taylor and Kraemer make the mistake of limiting its origin to colonialism.
48. W. Ringwald, 'Experiment Goldküste', *Evang. Miss. Zeitschrift*, April 1952, 44; Lediga, op. cit., 69–72. Many Christians accept the fear of wtichcraft, of evil spirits and the use of 'magic medicines' as a matter of course. Cf. Taylor & Lehmann, 100.
49. Cf. G. Shepperson and T. Price, *Independent Africa*, Edinburgh University Press, 1958. G. Shepperson, 'The Politics of African Christian Separatist Movements', *African Affairs*, Vol. XXIV, No. 3, July 1954.
50. Cf. G. Balandier, *Sociologie Actuelle de l'Afrique Noire*, Paris, Presses Universitaires de France, 1963; G. Balandier, 'Messianismes et Nationalismes en Afrique Noire' (*Cahiers Internationaux de Sociologie*, XIV, 1953). See also R. Pierce Beaver, 'Missions and the New Nationalism', *Occasional Bulletin*, Vol. XII, No. 1, Jan. 15, 1961. Missionary Research Library, New York.
51. H. Witschi, 'Missionsdienst gestern und heute'. *Evang. Miss. Magazin*, January 1952, 12. See K. Nkrumah, *The Autobiography of Kwame Nkrumah*, Edinburgh, Nelson, 1957.
52. Cf. R. H. W. Shepherd, 'Totalitarianism and the Personality Cult in Nyasaland', *S.A. Outlook*, April 1, 1963, 55.
53. Ibid., 55.
54. W. C. Willoughby, *Race patterns in the New Africa*, OUP, 1923, 237–41; see also J. H. Oldham, *Christiantity and the Race Problem*, SCM, 1925.
55. Cf. Michael Hollis, *Paternalism and the Church*, OUP, 1962, 58–65. What applies here to India is true of Africa.
56. Cf. *Deutsches Pfarrerblatt*, Sept. 15, 1960, under heading 'Wenn die Bekehrten wieder Heiden werden?' It refers to the Bishop of Luluaburg as saying that the faith is not rooted in the daily life of Christians, that the Africanisation of the Church must be speeded up and that the white missionary is in many parts the greatest obstacle to autonomy. See also encyclicals of 1919 and 1926 which indicate a new tactic of the Vatican in preparing Catholic clergy and missionaries from among local populations 'with the aim of adapting propaganda to local customs and mores'. (Cf. *Occasional Bulletin*, Aug. 15, 1959.) See also encyclicals of April 12 and May 16, 1957, *Ecclesia Docens, Encyclia Fidei Donum*, especially. Publ. Hilversum, Gooi and Sticht, 1957. See also A. Morant, *Die philosophisch-theologische Bildung in den Priesterseminarien Schwarz-Afrikas*, Schöneck-Beckenried, 1959; Ed. J. Beckmann, *Der einheimische Klerus in Geschichte und Gegenwart*, Schöneck-Beckenried, 1950. Johannes Hofinger,

Liturgy and Missions, P. J. Kenedy and Sons, NY, 1960; A. Mulders, *Inleiding tot de Missiewetenschap*, Bussum, Paul Brand, 1960.

57. Eugene A. Nida, *Message and Mission*, New York, Harper, 1960, 139.

58. Karefa-Smart, op. cit., 19, 20.

59. Taylor, *Buganda*, op. cit., 253.

60. Cf. Placide Tempels, *Bantu Philosophy*, Paris, Présence, 1959; John V. Taylor, *The Primal Vision*, SCM, 1963.

61. Sundkler says: 'Our analysis of the activities and ideology of Independent Zulu Churches has *inter alia* revealed an *emphasis on ritual* as characteristic of these organisations, which is an important intimation of the true *interpretatio Africana*, of the Christian message.' (B. G. M. Sundkler, *Bantu Prophets in South Africa*, OUP, 1961², 296.)

62. J. Spencer Trimingham, *The Christian Church and Islam in West Africa*, IMC Research Pamphlet No. 3, SCM, 1956, 36.

63. Roland Oliver, *The Missionary Factor in East Africa*, Longmans, 1952, 292.

64. Cf. Hans-Ruedi Weber, 'The Marks of an Evangelising Church' in *The Missionary Church in East and West*, ed. by Charles C. West and David M. Paton, SCM, 1959, 101–03.

65. J. Blauw, 'The Mission of the People of God', in West & Paton, 91–100.

66. Cf. A. A. Van Ruler, *Theologie van het Apostolaat*, Nijkerk Callenbach; J. C. Hoekendijk, 'The Church in Missionary Thinking', IRM, July 1952, 324–36; J. C. Hoekendijk, 'Mission und Oekumene', EMZ, Sept. 1951, 146–56.

67. Ed. J. Specker and W. Buehlmann, *Das Laienapostolat in den Missionen*, Schöneck-Beckenried, 1961.

68. Cf. F. B. Welbourn, *Rebels in East Africa*, SCM, 1961, 9. Also Max Warren, *Revival: an Enquiry*, SCM, 1954; Gerhard Günther, *Erweckung in Afrika*, Stuttgart, Evang. Miss. Verlag, 1959.

69. Taylor, *The Growth of the Church in Buganda*, 103.

70. Cf. Whitby Report; also Stephen Neill, *Christian Partnership*, SCM, 1952; Stephen Neill, *Creative Tension*, Edinburgh House Press, 54–80.

71. Peter Beyerhaus, *Die Selbständigkeit der jungen Kirchen als missionarisches Problem*, Wupperthal-Barmen, Rheinische Missions-Gesellschaft, 1956, 124.

72. B. G. Sundkler, *The Christian Ministry in Africa*, SCM, 1960, 62. In 1961 there were 22,048,376 Roman Catholics in Africa including Madagascar, Mauritius, Réunion and Seychelles. Cf. W. Bühlmann, *Die Kirche unter den Völkern*, Mainz, Matthias-Grünewald, 1963, 338.

73. B. G. Sundkler, *The Christian Ministry in Africa*, SCM, 1960, 62.

74. John Mott was tireless in prophesying that the rising tide of nationalism in Asia and Africa would destroy Christianity together with Western imperialism unless it could be early established under indigenous leadership. (Cf. *The Decisive Hour of Christian Missions*, New York, 1912, 29–31.) Roland Oliver in an article entitled 'Data and Distribution of the Missionary Enterprise' (International Missionary Council, London, 1943) indicates that it was partly due to negative reasons, e.g. the limitation of missionaries, that missions of the most modern period were so successful in establishing the Oriental and African Churches on an indigenous basis.

75. Paul D. Fueter, 'Marangu', IRM, July 1956, 290. Cf. *Marangu, A Record of the All-African Lutheran Conference*, Geneva, 1956, 37–45. Cf. Heinrich Meyer, *Bekenntnisbindung und Bekenntnisbildung in jungen Kirchen*, Bertelsmann, 1953.

76. Cf. Ed. Arne Sovik, 'Confessions and Churches – an Afro-Asian Symposium', *Lutheran World*, March 1959, 366–67.

77. Ibid., p. 366. The Batak Church has set an example. Cf. *Das Bekenntnis der*

Huria Kristen Batak Protestant, transl. and Ed. H. F. de Kleine, Verlag der Rheinischen Missions-Gesellschaft, 1952. See also L. Schreiner, *Das Bekenntnis der Batak-Kirche*, Munich, Kaiser, 1966.

78. Keith Cole, *Kenya: Hanging in the Middle Way*, London, The Highway Press, 1959, 63.

79. Cf. DRC Newsletter, June–July 1963. In a booklet entitled *Die Sendingbepalinge van die Ned. Gereformeerde Kerk van Transvaal*, Dr. W. D. Jonker has indicated that the separate Synods and Assemblies for white and non-whites is in principle untenable.

80. Proposed Scheme of Union including draft basis of Union and Constitution of the United Church prepared by the Nigeria Union Committee, April 1957.

81. Cf. T. S. Garrett & R. M. C. Jeffrey, *Unity in Nigeria*, London, Edinburgh House Press, 1965.

82. Cf. The Dodoma Conference Report (1965) signed by R. Macpherson; N. P. Moritzen, *Wegen zur Kircheneinigung in Östafrika*, Una Sancta, 1964.

83. Cf. *Bulletin Évangélique d'Information et de Presse*, Nov. 1965, mimeographed; Flambeau, Kinshasa, Nov. 1965.

84. Cf. *Kirche, Mission, Rasse*, Schöneck-Beckenried, 1958.

85. Cf. IRM, January 1957, 28.

86. Cf. Elmer T. Clark, 'Non-Theological Factors in Religious Diversity', *The Ecumenical Review*, July 1951, 348. See also: Richard Niebuhr, *The Social Sources of Denominationalism*, NY, Meridan Books, 1958.

87. Cf. *The Church and the Disorder of Society*, WCC, Amsterdam, 1948, New York, Harper and Bros., 1948.

88. J. D. R. Jones, 'The Effects of Urbanisation in South and Central Africa', *African Affairs*, Jan. 1953, 37.

89. H. F. Oppenheimer, 'Industrial Relations in a Multi-racial Society', *African Affairs*, Oct. 1956, 318.

90. Cf. S. Herbert Frankel, 'Some Reflections on Civilisation in Africa', S. Africa Institute of Race Relations, 1952, 21–23.

91. Hodgkin, op. cit., 67.

92. J. B. Wyon, 'Christian Responsibility in the Population Problem', IRM, July 1958, 292.

93. T. M. Aluko, *One Man, One Wife*, Nigerian Printing and Publ. Co., 1959, states that the white man with his religion 'has won our brothers, and our clan can no longer act like one. He has put a knife on the things that held us together and we have fallen apart.' These developments may have been unavoidable, but the closing words are nevertheless 'rich in tragedy'. (Cf. Max Warren, CMS *News-letter*, March 1960.)

94. Carpenter, *The Way in Africa*, 58–59.

95. Helpful studies in this connection, apart from those already referred to, have been published recently: Ed. A. Southall, *Social Change in Modern Africa*, OUP, 1961. Michael Banton, *West African City*, OUP, 1960². B. A. Pauw, *Xhosa in Town: The Second Generation*, OUP, 1963. See also Egbert de Vries, *Man in Rapid Social Change*, SCM, 1961.

96. Taylor, *Buganda*, 139.

97. Philip Mayer, *Xhosa in Town: Townsman and Tribesman*, OUP, 1962², 192–205.

98. Cf. *The Social Teaching of the Christian Churches*, Vols. I & II, Allen & Unwin, 1949 (first published in German in 1931).

99. J. Merle Davis, *Modern Industry and the African*, Macmillan, 1933; ibid., *The Economic and Social Environment of the Younger Churches*, Edinburgh House

Press, 1939. See especially Paul Abrecht, *The Churches and Rapid Social Change*, SCM, 1961. Also *The Mission of the Church in Urban Africa*, Report, All-Africa Church Conference, March 1961; *Industrial and Urban Development in Nigeria*, Report, CMS, 1959; K. A. Busia, *Africa in Transition*, Project papers, Geneva, 1957; Report of Inter-Church Study Group, S. Africa, 1958.

100. Cf. E. R. Wickham; *Church and People in an Industrial City*, Lutterworth, 1960[3]. Richard Taylor, *Christians in an Industrial City*, SCM, 1961.

101. Cf. J. V. Taylor & D. Lehmann, *Christians of the Copperbelt*, SCM, 1961, 272–78.

102. Roland Allen, *Missionary Methods, St. Pauls or Ours?* World Dominion Press, 1927; ibid., *The Spontaneous Expansion of the Church*, World Dominion Press, 1927. Donald McGavran, in his book entitled *How the Churches Grow*, World Dominion Press, 1959, ignores the social and political situation in which the young Churches exist.

103. E. de Vries, 'African Travelogue', *Ecumenical Review*, Jan. 1959, 170.

104. E. R. Wickham, 'The Encounter of the Christian Faith and Modern Technological Society', *Ecumenical Review*, April 1959, 265.

105. Cf. D. Bonhoeffer, *Communio Sanctorum*, Kaiser, 1960.

106. Cf. G. F. Vicedom, *Das Dilemma der Volkskirche*, Claudius, 1961, 89–93.

107. Cf. F. C. Kamma, 'De ethnologische "Kerk" en de Kerk van Christus', *De Heerbaan*, May 1949.

108. C. A. Clark, *The Korean Church and the Nevius Methods*, Fleming H. Revell Co., 1930, 33, 34. See also V. S. Azariah, *Christian Giving*, Lutterworth, 1954; Tambaram Madras Series Vol. V, OUP, 1939.

109. Paul Abrecht, 126. See also Jan Hermelink, *Christ im 'Welthorizont'*, Kreuz-Verlag, 1962.

110. Cf. J. Kitagawa, 'Christianity, Communism and the Asian Revolution', *World Dominion Press*, July-Aug., 1955, Vol. XXXIII, 199–206.

111. Cf. C. C. West, *Communism and the Theologians*, SCM, 1958; J. C. Bennet, *Christianity and Communism Today*, Association Press, 1961; F. W. Price, *Marx Meets Christ*, Harper, 1958.

112. Joseph Hromadka, *Student World*, Nos. 1–2, 1961, 170.

113. Cf. Dietrich Ritschl, 'The Challenge from the East', *The Christian Century*, March 29, 1961, 389–92. See also booklet of United Evangelical Lutheran Churches in Germany entitled *Der Atheismus als Frage an die Kirche*, Lutherisches Verlagshaus, 1962.

114. See J. Verkuyl, *Evangelie en Communisme in Azië en Afrika*, Kampen, J. H. Kok, 1966; W. Bühlmann, *Afrika*, Mainz, Matthias-Grüneweld Verlag, 1963, 273–88.

115. Cf. G. Padmore, *Pan-Africanism or Communism?* Dennis Dobson, 1956.

116. Cf. Stanley David, 'Communist Penetration into Africa', *Christian Century*, Aug. 1, 1960, 122. George W. Carpenter, 'Congo, Communism and Church', *Christian Century*, Oct. 12, 1960, 1176. Harold John Ockenga, 'The Communist Issue Today', *Christianity Today*, May 22, 1961.

117. Paul Abrecht, op. cit., 126.

118. Taylor & Lehmann, op. cit., 272.

119. Cf. William Temple, *Christianity and the Social Order*, Pelican Books, 1956, 23. Banners used in earlier unemployed or socialist processions were 'Damn your charity; we want justice'. He further adds: 'It is . . . evident that it is part of the common Christian tradition from primitive times to the fullest development of medieval thought that Christian faith should find expression in relation to economic questions' (ibid., 42).

27

120. Cf. *Karte der Religionen und Missionen der Erde*, Ed. M. Schlunk and H. Quiring, London, International Missionary Council and Missionary Research Library. Protestants, 12,625,000; Roman Catholics, 18,193,000; Orthodox Churches, 4,870,000; Muslims, 80 million; Jews, 600,800; Hindus, 0·5 million. Total population = 223 million. Today, the population is 290 million; Protestants number about 16,000,000 and Roman Catholics about 28,000,000.

121. Cf. J. S. Trimingham, *The Christian Church and Mission in Ethiopia*, World Dominion Press, 1950; also his *Islam in Ethiopia*, OUP, 1952.

122. G. Bernander, *The Rising Tide*, translated by H. D. Friberg, Augustana Press, 1957, 50.

123. Samuel U. Zwemer, *Across the World of Islam*, Fleming H. Revell Co., 1929, 198.

124. G. F. Vicedom, *Die Mission der Weltreligionen*, Kaiser, 1959, 13.

125. J. S. Trimingham, *Islam in West Africa*, OUP; 1959, 25. See also J. S. Trimingham, *A History of Islam in West Africa*, OUP, 1962, 226. With European control, there were few Muslims in coastal towns of West Africa. Today the position has changed. Lagos is 50% Muslim, Dakar ±85%. Even in 'freed-slave' settlements, Muslims are on the increase. In Sierra Leone Colony in 1891, they comprised 10%; 1911 14%; 1921 19·5% and in 1931 26·2% of the population. See also W. A. Bijlefeld, 'Islam-Studium und Islam-Apostolat', *Evangelisches Missions Magazin*, 1/1965, 40–51; by same author, 'Anmerkungen zur Begegnung zwischen Christentum und Islam in Westafrika', *Evangelisches Missions-Zeitschrift*, May 1965, 49–57; I. M. Lewis (ed.), *Islam in tropical Africa*, OUP, 1966.

126. Ibid., 25.

127. Trimingham, *Islam in Ethiopia*, 271–2.

128. Cf. also E. Kellerhals, *Der Islam*, Basel, Missionsbuchhandlung, 1956. Lyndon P. Harries, Islam in East Africa, UMCA, 1954. S. A. Morrison, *Religious Liberty in the Near East*, World Dominion Press, 1948. Kenneth Cragg, *The Call of the Minaret*, OUP, 1956. H. Kraemer, *De Islam*, The Hague, Boekencentrum, 1938. J. N. D. Anderson, *Islamic Law in Africa*, Stevens, 1954.

129. J. S. Trimingham, *A History of Islam in West Africa*, 226.

130. J. S. Trimingham, *Islam in Ethiopia*, OUP, 1952, 123.

131. Ibid., 123–25.

132. Ibid., 133.

133. Ibid., 134.

134. J. S. Trimingham, *Islam in the Sudan*, OUP, 1949 (148–63); 148. Cf. Saburi Biobaku and Muhammad Al-Hajj, *The Sudanese Mahdiyya and the Niger-Chad region in Islam in Tropical Africa*, ed. by I. M. Lewis, 425–41. A. B. Theobald, *The Mahdiya*, Longmans, Green, 1951. On the Ahmadiyya movement in Africa, see H. Fisher, *Ahmadiyya*, OUP, 1964.

135. Trimingham, *Islam in the Sudan*, 148.

136. Ibid., 149–50.

137. Ibid., 153, 154.

138. Ibid., 155.

139. Ibid., 156.

140. Cf. ibid., 157.

141. Ibid., 158.

142. Ibid., 158.

143. Cf. Henry D. Jones, 'Urban and Industrial Missions', New York, *Occasional Bulletin*, MRL, June 15, 1959. Chukwoneka, Nwanko, *Industrialisation of Nigeria*, William Frederick Press, 1952. International African Institute, *Social Implications of Industrialisation and Urbanisation in Africa South of the Sahara*, Paris, Unesco, 1956. International Labour Office, *African Labour Survey*, Geneva,

1958. United Nations Dept. of Economics and Social Affairs, *Processes and Problems of Industrialisation in Underdeveloped Countries*, NY, United Nations, 1958. Christian Institute for the Study of Religion and Society, Bangalore, India. Excellent bulletin, surveys, etc. *The Mission of the Church in Urban Africa*, Report distributed by Commission of World Mission and Evangelism, Industrial and Urban development in Nigeria, CMS, 1959.

2

THE INDEPENDENT MOVEMENTS
IN AFRICA: AN INTRODUCTION

THE Report of the International Ecumenical Study Conference held
at Salonika, July 25–August 2, 1959, states that 'rapid social change
throws man back upon the traditional "world view", which the
churches have often failed to understand. Meanwhile the old African
and the "prophet" religions are adapting their teachings to meet
modern situations and to attract the Christian, while fundamentally
they continue to rely upon traditional culture.'[1] The intensity of the
pressures experienced by people leads to frustration, and eventually
to their finding their own solutions.[2] Katesa Schlosser maintains
that the appearance of prophets is due mainly to economic and
political reasons, and very seldom exclusively to religious reasons.[3]
But, if one scratches away the crust of outward appearances and
reasons, one will more often find renascent Africa, and discover the
undercurrent of traditional religion and culture. David B. Barrett,
in a mimeographed paper entitled *Two Hundred Independent Church
Movements in East Africa*, read at a social science conference at
Makerere, Uganda, in January 1967, claims that 'the basic cause
common to the entire movement of independency' is 'the clash of three
impinging cultures, the traditional, the colonial and the missionary.
Where this culture clash has been strongest – for example, among
the Kikuyu – independency is strongest; where a tribe has been
studiously protected from the shock of culture clash – as among the
Masai – independency is absent.' The tribe was a family writ large.
Its members shared the same mythological past, and received security
within the community. Here, the great questions of human existence
found an answer even before they were asked. The answers were
given in the traditional religion. Harvey Cox, who does not claim
to be an anthropologist, has nevertheless seen the issues at stake
very well: the individual 'does not so much live in a tribe; the tribe
lives in him. He is the tribe's subjective expression.'[4] Many of these

30

movements look again for the old securities in the face of the bewildering destruction of their society by the new threatening forces. This is done through the prophet, who may later develop into a messianic figure on his own convictions, or is elevated into one by his followers. But no messianic movement came directly out of the Church, as is often wrongly stated;[5] this only takes place after a certain process of development.

When missionaries first appeared, active steps were taken by the tribes to discourage its members from accepting the Christian faith, as it meant deserting their families, forgetting their traditional life[6] and allying themselves with organised political opposition to the chief (the mission stations).[7] Christianity was not only a political and social threat, but destructive and dangerous. This assessment of one specific denomination in South Africa illustrates the tribal attitude to all missionary activity in Africa, in its initial stages and thereafter.

It was Karl Graul who directed missionary thinking to the idea of the indigenous ethnic 'Church' (*bodenständige Volkskirche*).[8] Henry Venn (1796–1873) propounded the three-self formula: self-support, self-government and self-extension, which was changed by the American Congregationalist Rufus Anderson (1796–1880), because of his belief in progress, 'to make them English in their language, civilised in their habits and Christian in their religion',[9] to the direct detriment of the indigenisation of Church forms. Against this foreignness and the association of missions with Western political ideals, a reaction from those under the influence of missions was bound to come.

The reactionary movements which came into existence emphasise healing by magical means and witchcraft, the indigenous aspect of worship and leadership, and millenarian-messianic expectations.[10] Political self-expression,[11] indigenisation in organisation, the paternalism of missionaries, and theological expression are some of the major motives behind the establishment of these reactionary movements. The race issue, of course, is implied in much of the political reaction, and has played its part in these secessions.[12] Discrepancies between Christian practice and teaching, and the actual standards of governments which professed to uphold Christianity, led in Europe to atheistic ideologies,[13] and in Africa, where people also suffered economically and socially, to rival religious movements. They serve as a means of expressing 'internal solidarity and differentiation from other social groups' – a means full of emotional appeal.[14] As soon as primitive man passed from the mythological and ontological stages to the functional stage, and realised that he is in history and has a destiny, he immediately discovered the obstacles to its attain-

31

ment. Belief that social problems can be solved by supernatural forces is replaced by the belief in political forces from which, as already stated, a nationalistic religion or religious nationalism develops. Much of the political frustration found its outlet in the formation of separatism, which was less distrusted by the authorities than outright political movements. While Christianity brought involuntary emancipation, and monotheism brought a principle of unification, their own messiah, although in some cases subjected to rough handling by the authorities, was finally triumphant, and served as an example to others. All the revolutionary power, which was so manifest in Christianity at the time of its origin, was introduced, as well as the eschatological hope of Jewish messianism, interpreted by people in an underprivileged situation, or in a position of frustration or danger.[15] Historically, separatism in Africa has been associated with radicalism, but it also has links with quietism, especially where it becomes pietistic and isolated from the world. Generally speaking the movements have been psychological safety valves,[16] but repression has always strengthened the nationalistic aspects of the prophet movements.[17] Mwana Lesa, who introduced *Kitawala* (Watch Tower) in the Congo, was hanged in Southern Rhodesia in 1926; Mulomozi wa Yezu and Alleluia, *Kitawala* leaders, were hanged in 1944 for their share in the Bakuma revolt in Stanleyville district. In 1921 Simon Kimbangu, the Ngunzist leader, was sentenced to death; his sentence was commuted to life imprisonment, and he died in 1950 in the Elisabethville prison. The same happened with Matswa André, leader of the Matswanist movement; after being deported to Chad in 1930 from the Middle Congo, he died in prison in 1942.[18] Simon Mpadi, who was 'the representative of a powerful prophet rising',[19] escaped four times from prison. Ideas of martyrdom and resurrection are prominent in these movements.[20] The growing nationalism in southern Africa during the last two decades of the nineteenth century was called by the unsatisfactory term 'Ethiopianism'.[21]

In this chapter we shall group our description of significant movements geographically. In the analysis of characteristics in following chapters, geography will be referred to only in so far as it is relevant to those characteristics.

(i) SOUTH AFRICA

The history of separatism in South Africa starts with the founding of a tribal Church by Nehemiah Tile, a Wesleyan Tembu minister, in 1884, and in 1892 a general 'Ethiopian' Church was founded. After the abolition of slavery the American Negroes felt a messianic calling to assist the peoples of Africa in their struggle against white

32

rule. First had to come ecclesiastical independence which the American Negroes had already experienced. In 1898 the American Negro bishop Henry M. Turner, of the African Methodist Episcopal Church, encouraged by James M. Dwane, who left the Wesleyans, came to South Africa and established affiliation with the South Africa (African) independent churches.[22] During his visit Turner ordained sixty-five African ministers,[23] which had an immediate negative effect on educational standards as a qualifying factor for the ministry. Dwane's discussions with the Anglicans led in 1900 to the establishment of the Order of Ethiopia as part of the Church of the Province.[24] Many of the 'Ethiopians', however, did not follow Dwane, and continued their membership in the African Methodist Episcopal Church, which today has more than '150,000 adherents led by 2,275 pastors, local preachers and licentiates'.[25]

Mzimba's Church, or the African Presbyterian Church, founded by P. J. Mzimba in 1898, when he seceded from the United Free Church of Scotland, was tribal in the sense that only the Fingos, and not the Xhosas, went with him. The Zulu Congregational secession in 1896 was a result of African denominationalism, when the African leader, Samungu Shibe, reacted against the transfer of the 'Table Mountain' mission station in Natal from the American Board to the (English–South African) Congregational Union of South Africa. Membership of the Zulu Congregational Church increased during the Zulu Rebellion in 1906.[26]

Ethiopianism was at this stage mainly a movement of ministers,[27] who were the closest in contact with the needs of their own people. Ethiopianism is not only 'a mark of radical adolescence', according to Willoughby, but also 'a reaction against negrophobia', 'facilitated by our denominational cleavage' and 'in harmony with Bantu character and tradition'.[28] The reaction resulted from the desire to implement the principles set by Venn and Anderson in missionary activity which was facilitated by the demand for political self-expression with the result that it was both political and religious. The aim was 'to plant a self-supporting, self-governing, self-propagating Native Church, which would produce a truly African type of Christianity suited to the genius and needs of the race, and not be merely a black copy of any European Church'.[29]

South Africa, with its separatist 'Churches' approaching 3,000, has all the conditions congenial for the formation of such movements. Its breaking up of tribal life as a result of urbanisation, together with what has been mentioned above, have contributed to the movement's formation and expansion. Lea also mentions as a contributory factor the African custom of branching away from the family when it becomes too big.[30] Labour centres have been an important source of such movements,[31] and Sundkler overstates the land issue: 'the increase in the number of Bantu independent Churches could be shown on a diagram as a parallel to the tightening squeeze of the Natives through land legislation'.[32] One of the worst grievances of the African in South Africa was the Natives Land Act of 1913,[33] whereby the African was seriously restricted in the purchase of land; after this followed the Native Trust and Land Act of 1936. The African National Congress was born as a reaction to the Land Act of 1913, and some 'Ethiopian' leaders played a part in it. As a result of the 1913 Act many Africans moved to the cities, and the Urban Areas Act of 1923, amended in 1930, again emphasised the policy of segregation. Then followed the Amendment Act of 1926 ('Colour Bar Act') which limited skilled jobs in the mining industry to the whites only, resulting in 'loss in earning power and opportunity for the Native, the growth of anti-white prejudice, and the general embitterment of race relations throughout the Union'.[34] Unemployment amongst Africans was the result, and, says Sundkler, 'many of the outbursts of the Independent Church movement occurred during this period of bitterness caused by African unemployment', and he adds that a considerable number of Independent Church leaders were artisans and craftsmen prior to the enforcement of the 'Colour Bar Act'.[35] African trade unions are not recognised by the law, and, as a result of the Native Labour Regulation Act of 1911, the African is unable to strike.[36] Sundkler's analysis has unfortunately minimised the problems of the acculturation process, and the grave social disturbances created by urbanisation to a traditionalistic African society.

Behind the independent movements in South Africa stands also an American Independent Movement, namely, the Christian Catholic Apostolic Church in Zion founded in 1896.[37] Black Zionism among American Negroes was inspired by the Universal Negro-Improvement Association and African Communities Imperial League, founded by the Jamaican Marcus Aurelius Garvey, 'the greatest black prophet and visionary since Negro emancipation'.[38] He thought of himself as the Moses of the Negro race and his fanatical racialism brought him into conflict with Dr. W. E. B. DuBois, 'the "father" of Pan-Africanism, the rival political ideology to Garvey's Black Zionism'.[39] Garvey adopted the Black Christ and Black Madonna as symbols of his African Orthodox Church.

The prophetic messianic type of independent movements in South Africa thus have their roots in Zion City, Illinois, but claim to emanate ideologically from Mount Zion, Jerusalem. Their main

34

object is to establish a theocracy. It is theologically a new syncretistic African movement, concentrating on divine healing, triune immersion, purification rites, ritual prohibition, speaking with tongues, and witch-finding, and its indigenous approach to religious activities gives the right emotional atmosphere, e.g. in hymns and rhythmic movements. Some proclaim with great zeal the imminence of the Second Coming of Christ.[40] In the nativistic movements, African myth has been revitalised and modernised, due mainly to visions and supernatural contacts of the prophet or messiah, whose interpretation of scripture in the light of these revelations is final. These movements are associated with the personality of a particular prophet who takes the central place and who may have 'direct telephonic communication with the Holy Spirit'.[41] Much of their force and appeal comes from the inspiration of the 'apocalyptic hopes of a total reconstruction of society'[42] which the prophet holds before them with his usually forceful personality, just as in the original religion this community is a cult community which embraces the whole of life to such an extent that the whole family and tribe march into the 'Church'.

(ii) SHEMBE, LEKGANYANE AND MGIJIMA

Isaiah Shembe was a minister of the African Native Baptist Church who practised faith healing until several visions compelled him to preach, heal, and drive out demons. In 1911 he started the Nazareth Baptist Church (called Nazarites or *ama-Nazaretha*), in whose hymn no. 73 (also 154) is found their confession of faith:

> (i) *I believe in the Father*
> *of the Nazarites,*
> *who is Almighty;*
> *in the creator of heaven and earth,*
> *and in the holy spirit.*
> (ii) *And in the holy congregation*
> *of the Nazarites,*
> *and in the communion of saints*
> *at Nazareth.*[43]

In the Old Testament a group of charismatics who differed from the seers (cf. Balaam, Num. xxiv. 3) and were predominantly ascetic in character, observing the priestly rule of abstinence, were called Nazarites. The Nazarite was distinguished outwardly by his long locks. He served Yahweh by struggling against the nation's enemies and his warlike feats are described as effects of the spirit of Yahweh (Judg. xiii. 25; xiv. 6; xix. 14, 15). He was actually a lonely person, to be distinguished from the prophetic 'men of the spirit'.[44] The Nazarites did not form a religious group. Ecstatic effects of the spirit in Israel never led to 'a mystical withdrawal, but were seen to be the means whereby mighty works might be done for the nation's God'.[45] These men operated during the conquest of Canaan, and also on occasions when the country had no organised force to defend itself. They were men *born out of a political situation*. It is interesting to note that even the most violent ecstatic experiences of those days were kept within the ancient religion of Yahweh; God maintained His position. The significance of the Nazarites lay in their 'contribution to the strengthening of the sense of nationhood and of the religious basis on which it was built'.[46] They emphasised Israel's sense of its distinctiveness, its uniqueness, and the election of the nation separated from what is Canaanite.

At times when ideas of African racial purity, White domination and African emancipation have swept through this continent, these aspects have been uppermost, with the Old Testament taking a prominent place.[47] Shembe himself developed into a Zulu messiah who became the God of the Blacks in their hunger for realised revelation.[48] He is in a real sense their Moses, their real personification of the Zulu kingship. The priority of Jesus is excluded from this movement: the 'Black Christ dogma' has developed here further than in any other indigenous movement because of the demand of the Zulu social system for a living mediator acting on the inspiration of the spirits of the chiefs and the royal ancestors.[49] In traditional African thinking, representation means identification, and Shembe I represented Jesus Christ, as the king or chief represents the royal ancestry. In their unhistorical cyclical mode of thinking, such a revelation is possible.

The movement of Shembe – the outcome of the meeting of two cultures and two religions[50] – has developed doctrinally[51] into a syncretistic post-Christian movement, in which certain external elements of the old Zulu religion find a new emphasis, e.g. 'dancing before the Lord', which echoes the Old Testament. Certain days are set aside for dancing, and at the 'July festival' the Nazarites dance in a dignified and quiet manner as was the case at the Feast of the First-fruits in the Old Testament. These periods of special festivals are not chosen arbitrarily: they are special periods loaded with numinous power, vital force, in which the Nazarite covenant is renewed. Their raiment is white, which is the symbolic colour of priesthood in Africa. (Shembe employed a black veil at his healing ceremonies.) From the exegesis of 2 Chronicles xxiii. 11 we learn that the royal garments were for a Semite not just something supplementary. Somebody's *kabōd* (majesty) comes from his clothing because his soul's content penetrates his whole physical body and also his clothing,[52] which is why the priestly garments are so meticulously described. The Nazarite Zion is at Ekuphakameni, meaning 'the exalted place', the visible token of the promised land. The legalism of this movement with its pentecostal background is based on a misinterpretation of the Old Testament and an acceptance of the ritual prohibition of the animistic religion. Summing up, this movement emphasises: baptism by immersion; sanctification of the Sabbath; fasting before Holy Communion, which takes place at night; glorification of God through dances; participation in the main feasts during January and July, and sexual abstention during this period; taking off of shoes at the holy place and sometimes in prayer; using first fruits not before December 25 nor without giving first to Shembe; outward signs of identification, such as that women are not allowed to have their hair cut nor men their beard; both sexes have to make a hole in the ear lobe; they discard medicine, pork, beer and tobacco; cattle are slaughtered; the dead are placed in a sitting position; ritual purification of all those who come into contact with the dead is practised; pastors are limited to one wife, but polygyny is allowed to the believers, even though there may be theoretical limitations; and reconciliation to God is made by way of sacrifice and initiation. Sin, however, is seen more as anti-social than as guilt.[53]

The *Zion Christian Church* of Lekganyane also calls for attention.[54] The Church's centre is about 25 miles from Pietersburg in the Transvaal, and is called the Zion City Moria, the 'chosen city of God'. Edward Lekganyane, son of Ignatius Lekganyane, the founder of the Zion Christian Church, is hailed as King of Zion, the mediator between God and the people, the embodiment of the messiah. The whole dogma of the Church centres round the person of Edward Lekganyane.[55] Here Jesus is also pushed into the background, although in one of the two main texts in its constitution, Eph. ii. 20 (the other is Hebrews xii. 20, 23), Jesus Christ is referred to as the corner-stone. Faith healing, baptism by immersion and the speedy return of Christ, are the major emphases, as with Shembe. Lekganyane lays on hands during his healing ceremonies, water is the only medicine, he proscribes witchcraft, tobacco, pork and alcohol, and observes the Jewish law with regard to the slaughtering of animals. The Bible has lost its significance, the Old Testament only being read occasionally. Symbols and symbolic colours are very popular with the movement. A star of David is worn on a green and black ribbon. A brass band and soldiers follow Lekganyane wherever he goes in the country. A revival of ritual dancing is also found here. Stewardship is meticulously and liberally observed.[56] Lekganyane does not only concern himself with the so-called spiritual aspects of life but also with the material ones – he confronts unemployment and 'makes rain'.

Limba, the late Zionist leader of Port Elizabeth, was also considered to be Christ and, like Lekganyane, took a serious interest in the material welfare of his followers.[57] These movements have taken the concrete situation seriously, and the Old Testament with its theocratic way of life appeals to them; the *malkuth Yahweh*, the Kingdom of God, has to do with the here and now. In the tribal 'Church' of Lekganyane, the detribalised feel the ties of a common bond, in which they find a sense of belonging and security.[58] For this reason they contribute in the way they do. However, adherents know very little about the Christian side of the dogma.

Church of God and Saints of Christ. In 1910, when Halley's comet appeared, an African lay preacher, Enoch Mgijima, at Bulhoek, Ntabelanga, near Queenstown, interpreted this event as of special significance, and declared that it was Yahweh's warning that they should return to the ancient religion of Israel. Hymn-singing, prayer and preaching marked the nocturnal assemblies which he initiated.[59] He also had a vision that the Africans would crush the Whites. The New Testament is considered a white man's book, a fiction. He soon had a following, being a forceful personality, and founded the 'Israelite' colony of the Church of the *Ama-Sirayeli*, with himself as 'Bishop, Prophet and Watchman'.[60] They were asked in 1920 to leave the common land at Bulhoek, but refused and, when eventually in May 1921 an armed police force of 800 came, with orders not to fire, the Israelites charged fanatically, with the idea that the bullets of the white men would turn to water.[61] In this most tragic event 117 of the Israelites were fatally wounded. This clash between the authorities and a religious sect made a deep scar on the African memory, especially with regard to land, to which the African is mystically connected; and the European saw a grave danger in the indigenous 'Churches'. A Government Commission made recommendations in order to counteract the fissiparation among these movements, when there were already between 120 and 140 in South Africa; in 1932 they totalled nearly 350, and in the 1960s about 3,000.

The chief tenets of this movement are the following 'seven keys' which unlock heaven, namely: (i) membership of the Church of God and Saints of Christ; (ii) the avoidance of wine; (iii) communion in the form of unleavened bread and water; (iv) observance of the command of feet-washing, John xiii. 1–23; (v) the disciples' prayer;

38

(vi) acceptance in membership by way of breathing a prayer over the person and by the holy kiss; (vii) the Ten Commandments. They baptise by immersion; alcohol and pork are ritually prohibited; they have their own specific dress and black frocks, and the men's hair is shaved.[62] Polygyny only came in after the battle of 1921.[63]

It is interesting that in 1849 a group of Afrikaners, under Johan Adam Enslin, known as the *Jerusalem Gangers* (Jerusalem pilgrims), who were religious and political fanatics, were met by the Rev. A. Murray in Marico. Enslin was known as 'the prophet'. They aimed to reach Jerusalem, and reacted against anybody who was in contact with the British Government, which they considered to be the Anti-Christ, the beast with the horn (cf. Daniel vii). They also refused to acknowledge the jurisdiction of the magistrate at Potchefstroom. Enslin opposed Andries Pretorius and, after a court case which he lost, he refused to submit and was gaoled.[64]

The other independent Churches mentioned by Schlosser will be referred to later, namely the Bhengu Church, the 'Independent Lutheran Mission Church of South Africa' and the African Methodist Episcopal Church.[65]

In the *Matita* or Moshoeshoe Church (*Kereke ea Moshoeshoe*) in Lesotho,[66] the Old Testament is also important. The Nazarite laws (Num. vi) are observed. Tobacco, alcohol and hair cutting are prohibited. The symbol of the Cross on the floor of their Church takes a prominent place. The sick kneel on the Cross, their bodies are pressed against it while the 'believers sing and speak with tongues';[67] these are commonly known as 'healers'. Walter Matita, the founder of this movement, claims to have received his mandate from the Lord after being 'resurrected' in about 1921. He was able, although illiterate, miraculously to read and write.

(iii) THE CONGO

The Congolese *Simon Kimbangu*, like so many of the independent leaders, was a Baptist, a good preacher and a natural mystic who, from the beginning, practised faith healing. Kimbanguism, as the movement is called which he founded in the Congo, is undergoing a 'great period of growth and organisation'[68] at the moment. Kimbamgu received his education from the schools of the Baptist Missionary Society. In the 1920s he experienced a series of calls to Christian service by way of visions and dreams. He was no *nganga*, or witch-doctor, but could rightly be called a prophet, 'an inspired man, a religious leader, a zealous and indefatigable man whose mission is his lodestar, and who tries to fulfil his appointed task'.[69] People had implicit faith in his healings, and also in him as preacher, and it seemed as if he was organising a Protestant movement. Missionaries even welcomed it as a peoples' movement, which brought men to Christ; however, 'the faith healing, ecstatic expression, and native elements in the ritual repelled many missionaries'.[70] *Nkamba*, Kimbangu's home village, became the centre of all the activities, with many leaving their jobs, the Catholics losing their members,[71] and even the dead being carried there. The reaction of both the Government and the missionaries was the major factor in the development of the movement into one with anti-White and revolutionary features. Because this movement was identified with national aspirations, many non-Christians joined, and animistic elements quickly found their way into it. The prophet himself established the 'New Jerusalem' at Nkamba. He was subject to violent shakings, like the heathen medicine man, which was a sign that he was seized by the Holy Spirit. After persecution he became not only the prophet, the messenger of God, but also the messiah. In this atmosphere of anti-European feeling, his adherents proclaimed that they had found the God of the Blacks.[72]

In the religion of Israel, there are particular places where God reveals himself, as in all other religions, which have such sacred places. In Israel there are places like Sinai, the sacred spring of Kadesh, Shiloh and Mizpah. All these were ultimately superseded by the Temple of Zion, which became after the exile the major centre of the Jewish religion. The more such a place becomes the centre of worship, the greater is the danger that God becomes localised.[73] As in Israel, Kimbangu's holy place also became the means of emphasising the concrete historicity of the revelation.

In 1921 Kimbangu was arrested and, after a quick trial, he was condemned to death, but the sentence was commuted eventually to life imprisonment. This made the people so hostile that evangelical congregations in some places almost completely disappeared. The movement was declared illegal. A multitude of prophets now came forward in the Ngunzist movement, and many Ngunzists reverted to heathenism; Kimbanguism itself formed this bridge. As soon as the doctrine of the Spirit became more popular, Christ and the Bible became less significant. Ecstasy, quaking, speaking in tongues, ritual prohibitions, uniform apparel and, with many groups, ancestor worship and *ndoki* or 'witchcraft hunting', came to the forefront.

The *Matswa Movement*, founded by André Matswa (born in Brazzaville in 1899) in the Middle Congo, also had political tendencies. In Paris, Matswa came in contact with communist and Pan-Africanist circles.[74] He founded the Association Amicale des Originaires de l'Afrique Equatoriale Française in order to give financial assistance to Africans in France, and money was collected also in the Congo, leaving the impression with the contributors that they would become the equals of the Whites if they contributed towards its funds.[75] The collectors were eventually arrested, tried and sentenced. At the trial anti-White feeling ran very high.[76] After the death of Matswa the movement continued under several names, and was strongly influenced by ancestor worship. A number of myths have been built up around Matswa's ability to escape unharmed. Like Kimbangu, he is the messiah, especially of the educated class, and both are referred to as kings and saviours of the Congo, in a country where the Divine Kingship was very prominent. For both, the Kingdom of God is from this world; both had to struggle against the colonial situation of the time, with its suppression and race discrimination, which was overtly practised in the social, economic and political fields. Thousands of the leaders were deported. Both movements had to do with missionary problems – many of the followers of Simon Kimbangu were betrayed to the authorities by missionaries. Balandier states that when the adherents enter the chapel, the sign of the Cross is made 'in the name of the Father and Matswa André and Simon Kimbangu'.[76]

CENTRAL AFRICA

The *Lumpa* '*Church*' of Zambia (the explanation of the name varies: 'the church which goes far', 'excels all', 'hastens to salvation') founded by Alice Lenshina Mulenga, an illiterate peasant woman, is remarkable in that it has been successfully counteracting magic and charms.[78] Lenshina's status is that of a woman chief, with tremendous influence. She does not reject witchcraft as nonsense, but claims to have the power to neutralise it. Magic objects are voluntarily brought to her for destruction, and people flock to her to confess their sins. Baptism itself is an act of purification.[79] Before baptism the neophytes confess their use of white and black magic and hand over their medicine horns and charms, as well as rosaries and crucifixes. Her success in this field, where the missions often failed, is due to 'the eschatological message and the promise of redemption for those who surrender their magic objects'.[80] The strict rules of the Church of Scotland Mission find practical application here. Those who undertake the pilgrimage to Kasomo, which is the stronghold of the 'New Zion', the 'Temple', return cleansed. The Bible and Holy Communion are neglected: the Bible because Alice is illiterate, and the Holy Communion because she maintains that they are not led the same way as the other Churches, and the movement is still developing.

41

The laws of this movement indicate that Alice Lenshina gave special attention to the heathen practices such as primitive dances, witchcraft and polygamy. Special reference is also given to the race issue: 'In this organisation there shall be no racial discrimination, white and black, men and women, shall be in Brotherhood and love each other.'[81] This millenarian religious body was described during the emergency of 1957 as being more like an Ethiopian political group. So-called radical African politicians found the movement sympathetic towards their cause, and it was maintained that the African National Congress had declared that the Lumpa Church was the only real African Church suitable for their members.[82] Taylor and Lehmann maintain that the movement has not, in spite of what has been said, been used by the politicians.[83] The bloody struggle in 1965 between the followers of Lenshina and Government forces in Zambia took place after the followers of Lenshina had felt themselves to be politically intimidated.

In the Lumpa movement, preachers and teachers have to earn their own living. The sung word is the most important medium of communicating the message and their singing processions make a great impression. Discipline serves as a strong unifying force amongst people from a variety of spiritual backgrounds. Ritual prohibitions and dreams 'were the front doors through which Christians went back into the African past'.[84] 'Right' behaviour and 'purification', in which the Holy Eternal Water is used,[85] received renewed emphasis in the animistic sense. This moralism also has magical power to assist in obtaining salvation and freedom from fear, sickness and death. The strongest moralistic groups are usually amongst the underprivileged, where the emphasis is often on man's own efforts. The doctrine of synergism suits the labourer. The influence of Adventism and Pentecostalism is due to the fact that, apart from emphasis on indigenous leadership, they have made Africans familiar with 'more fundamentalist, egalitarian interpretations of Scripture'.[86]

The *Watch Tower Movement* has made a great impact in Zambia. In the social break-up of the traditional African way of life resulting from the development of the copper mines, where 'the latest mechanical appliances and amenities of Western civilisation' entered in a short space of time,[87] this movement found congenial soil for development, although in the beginning it was stronger in rural areas. In these circumstances it has managed to increase its membership, and at some mines it has shown greater advances than any of the established Churches.[88] This movement seems to have appeared in Nyasaland in 1906–07, where it was introduced by Joseph Booth, a

Baptist missionary from Melbourne.[89] It has been at times strongly anti-European. The main places of influence of the movement have been Malawi, Zambia and Katanga, where it is known as *Kitawala* or *Bacitawala*. In Zambia, where the movement has a very strong position (it was banned in Katanga), the cultural contact has reached a breaking point.[90] Hodgkin says that the argument in contemporary Africa that 'we are living in a time of unparalleled woes' has encouraged the central Watch Tower doctrines, such as the millenarian outlook and that '(i) the Kingdom is at hand in this generation; (ii) only Witnesses will be accepted into the Kingdom; (iii) life in the Kingdom is earthly and not spiritual; (iv) in the Kingdom there will be a complete absence of all the ills of this world . . . and all women will have children'.[91]

Social, political and economic factors thus had a definite bearing on the success of this movement. The apocalyptic element received special emphasis; the coming of Christ is imminent, governments will be overthrown, Churches and ministers will be brought before God's judgment seat and millions living will never die.[92] Speaking in tongues is practised. Missions are vehemently attacked, not only because of their doctrinal bases, but because of their European origin, their association with the Government, and their disciplinary measures – large numbers of people being disciplined, especially in matters of adultery and divorce. Segregation, unemployment, exploitation in the economic field and the breaking up of social ties have all contributed to the growth of the movement. Quick indicates that 'the economic depression of 1932–3 and the return of large numbers of disgruntled workers from mining areas resulted in renewed Watch Tower activity'.[93] Many came from the Congo, when indigenous organisations were prohibited there in 1934. They later formed villages of their own. The movement is 'entirely self-supporting, self-propagating and free from foreign control'.[94] 'Native tax' was regarded as an injustice. Work is organised on a rural economy; by contrast, Christianity has in Africa so often given the impression that it is a 'luxury religion'. The literature produced by this movement made a great impact, because 'it satisfies community tastes and interests and is read in groups'.[95] Both this and the Lumpa movement attract educated men, although the standard of education of the Watch Tower members is often low. House congregations, the New Testament idea of the *Oikos*, have found expression here.[96] Cunnison ascribed the impact of this movement, however, to the fact that it has ready answers for everything, and here one agrees with Taylor and Lehmann that this appeals at a fundamental level to semi-literate and even educated

43

people in Africa. It is a substitute for the old authority, and it is something to hang on to.[97] The members have a strong sense of belonging to the chosen people, and there is a radical break with the old customs. From the outside, it looks all-African, because of the small number of Whites in it. There is an absence of master–servant relationship within the movement.

Many Africans have developed critical attitudes towards the established orthodox Churches sponsored by missions, because of their failure to make the prophetic voice heard on political issues. Fear of the dispossession of land and the industrial colour bar have here also loomed over their minds.[98] In later years their reaction was strong against the Central African Federation, and they have developed the sense of being responsible also for the political and economic development in the country.

The *Bamulonda* ('the Watchmen') is a relic from the early enthusiastic days of Jehovah's Witnesses. Their 'Church' is in a village known as one of the main centres of the Bangulu spirit possession movement.[99] A certain Elliot Kamwana from Malawi was their leader, and his sons inherited the leadership. The movement started before 1947 in the Luda country. On the walls of their houses and on men's jackets and women's head scarves are written: *Ndi wa Yehova na Mikaeli* (I am of Jehovah and Michael). Drumming, dancing (based on Ps. cxlix. 3) and singing play an important part in the service. A white and red flag is planted next to a tree in the centre of villages where services are held. In an address one said: 'There are no Europeans in our church at all. We don't tell lies.' Michael is to them Jesus, 'our Christ'. A hymn has the following words:

> *I am the Lord in Zion,*
> *I, Michael, am the Lord.*

Another says, *God sent Michael. His wife is the Church. The white clothes are the work of the saints. New Jerusalem is coming, but first there must be war. Armageddon must be in* 1984.'[100] (To others it will take place in 1995–97.) The preacher was eventually led into a dance shouting a sentence, and a refrain followed. This is the typical dialogue in African fashion. Converts from the London Missionary Society and from Roman Catholicism are rebaptised, but not those who have already been baptised by way of total immersion, e.g. Seventh Day Adventists, Pentecostalists and Baptists.[101] Old Testament ritual prohibitions on food are observed, polygyny is allowed, also with the authority of the Old Testament. Most of the members Taylor and Lehmann met 'belonged to the lowest income

44

group'.[102] There is general lack of interest in them because they have no schools and reject hospitals and medicine. One old man said, 'If a child has a headache they strike it on the head with a Bible'.[103] Many of their doctrines are reminiscent not only of the Watch Tower Movement, but also of the Zulu Zionist movements, with which Elliot Kamwana was in contact.[104]

EAST AFRICA

In East Africa the independent movements were often, as elsewhere, closely related to political aspirations and frustrations, as well as to an anti-medicine attitude. Only a few separatist movements started in Buganda, and most of them very soon returned to established Churches. Taylor ascribes it to the unified structure of Kiganda society, the small number of Christian missions in the field and the Roman Catholic and Anglican Churches with their disposition to accept authority from above, an important aspect in African society. The Roman Catholic and Anglican Churches furthermore satisfied the ritualistic approach of the African, and there was freedom of interpretation within limits. The Anglican Church has in Buganda also an evangelistic tradition, expressed in its special 'missions', 'and continually in the preaching of individual decision in conversion and sanctification'.[105] The Roman Catholic Church maintains a pastoral ministry, and so satisfies the needs of the people. The Revival movement in East Africa, with its more than two decades of Christian witness, and its emphasis on the laity, never developed into a separate sect, which has so often been the case within Protestantism when there is dissatisfaction with a lukewarm church.

The first anti-medicine sect of Uganda we shall mention here is that of the 'Malakites', founded by an African teacher, Malaki Musajakawa, in 1914. Together with an ex-Chief, Yosuwa Mugema, who had already held the same view for years, he based his protest on Deuteronomy xviii. 9–11 ('charmer' in xviii. 11 translated as 'doctor'), also on Jer. xlvi. 11 and James v. 8 ff. Mugema was a forceful and influential personality, who was aware of the social and religious revolution taking place in the country. No tests, other than subscription to the 'no-medicine' formula and acceptance that God is Almighty, are demanded from the members. Thousands were baptised – mention is made of over 2,000 in one day – and polygyny is allowed, monogamy being rejected as un-Biblical, which added to the popularity of the movement.[106] Resistance to vaccination and inoculation (the anti-syphilis drug 606 was confused with 666 the number of the Beast) affected the health of the community, and

45

after a murderous attack on a European sanitary officer in 1929 the movement declined in numbers.[107]

This movement was called by its adherents 'The Church which does not drink medicine', but today holds the name of 'The Society of the One Almighty God', *Ekiba Kya Katonda Omu Ayinza Byona* (abbrev. KOAB). Welbourn says about this movement that 'in the story of Christians against medicine, which must one day be written, the KOAB must stand alone in its total rejection of any attempt to heal by whatever means'.[108] The KOAB is governed by local church councils, county councils, tribal councils and the Great All Churches Council which meets at least twice yearly at Lugala; it ordains its clergy, and has a 'prayer book' which consists of the following: (i) the 'grace' from Num. vi. 24 ff.; (ii) the Lord's Prayer, Matth. vi. 9–14; (iii) authority for baptism of infants, Mark x. 13–16; (iv) authority for the baptism of adults, Mark xvi. 15 ff.; (v) questions to be asked of those desiring baptism, Acts viii. 37; (vi) the Song of Moses: Deuteronomy xxxii, divided into seven parts. This, sung between prayers, lessons and sermons, forms the basis of the weekly sabbath service.[109] This movement, like others, has its political context. Welbourn maintains that 'his act of schism was a gesture not only of deep religious conviction but of rejection of the new politico-ecclesiastical order in Buganda'.[110]

In the Eastern Province of Uganda a certain Kakungulu, who was discontented with both Church and Government, reverted to a polygynous life, and became a Mumalaki, after having been baptised, together with his first wife, as an Anglican.[111] He came under the influence of an Abyssinian Jew after which Zech. 8. xxiii became imbued with special meaning for him, so that he and his followers started to appear in Jewish robes and head-gear, introduced circumcision, and passed as *Bayudaya* (Jews). Sulemani Mutaisa took over the leadership of the Bamalaki, and styled himself *Omulevi Omukulu* ('Chief Levite'). In a Muslim area, it was said of this religion that 'it never required people to go to Church to read before they were given names', and there was no need for one who wanted a new name either to be circumcised or to fast, as the Muslims demanded. 'There was no need to look for godparents (for whom you had to do a lot of work before they would stand for you) as the Protestants expected'.[112] The Bamalaki were very influential in some parts because of their baptisms, but had no schools and gradually deteriorated. This movement held no messianic expectations, not even after the deaths of Kakungulu (1928) and Malaki (1929), and the deportation of Mugema.[113] Although the Bamalaki reacted against every sanitary and health measure taken by the Government for man and beast, their reaction was not just against European medicine. Change and adaptation to a new social and political situation certainly had their effect on the people who were led by Mugema in Buganda and Kakungulu in the Eastern Province.

The KOAB observes only the Passover (13th *Abibu*), Christmas being considered a pagan festival. It has split up into a number of groups of which one, the *Endagano Empya* (New Testament) sect, with headquarters at Nabataka, 'is no longer ruled by the slavish Mosaic laws of the Old Testament but by the liberal teaching of the New'.[114] In the 1930s the Bamalaki were influential in Buganda, and the KOAB remained limited mainly to this province. More men than women belonged to this movement in 1931 (in 1921 there were more women than men), whereas in the major Churches (Anglican and Roman Catholic) and in the Muslim religion, there were more women. Welbourn thinks this may be explained by women more quickly realising the disadvantages of not using medicine.[115]

Mabel Ensor, a White woman, started a schism on October 10, 1928, by establishing the Mengo Gospel Church. She tried to identify herself with the African people, but managed all the Church's affairs to such an extent that it left the indigenous people very little spiritual independence. She tried her best, but failed to understand Africans, who did not expect a White to lower his standards in order to make contact with them. In spite of trying to identify herself with Africans, she felt that 'Christian schools must remove children altogether from the influence of African Society'.[116] But the Africans opposed this unconscious manifestation of Western superiority. The aversion to schism of Baganda society checked her schismatic tendencies.[117]

Another Church movement, which however kept contact with ecclesiastical catholicity, is the *African Greek Orthodox Church*; this movement also has a political background, and is also a reaction against paternalism. Marcus Garvey, who had been a Catholic, established his own African Orthodox Church under a black Patriarch, and successfully spread the idea of independent African Churches as an instrument of African liberation.[118] His idea spread into what were then British and French West Africa, East Africa, the Cameroons and South Africa. Padmore says of Garvey that his 'nationalistic psychosis knew no limits in his efforts to instil racial pride and self-respect in his followers'.[119] The African Orthodox Church in America was a reaction against the subduing of Negroes in the American Protestant Episcopal Church. Reuben Sebbanja Ssedimba Mukasa came under the influence of the African Orthodox Church in South Africa, which 'combined a delight in the worship forms of the eastern churches with Marcus Garvey's mystique of a world-wide black nationalism'.[120] On January 6, 1929, Spartas, as Mukasa was later called, publicly announced that he had broken away from the Anglican Church and formed a new Church called 'The African Orthodox Church'. He does not deny the nationalistic, or rather Pan-African, background of this Church which, according to him, was 'for all right thinking Africans, men who wish to be free in their own house, not always being thought of as boys'.[121] Spartas himself later became active in politics, and in 1949 he was gaoled for alleged co-responsibility for the riots of that year[122] and, says Taylor, 'this Church arose out of a protest against European domination rather than against spiritual lukewarmness in the more established Churches'.[123] In Kiganda society (East Africa), the early missionary was seen as a new kind of chief, with both spiritual and temporal power and with the backing of the colonial powers.[124] The missions became not only a spiritual power in the country, and the reaction naturally was 'Africa for the Africans'.

This movement also included Orthodox-oriented Churches in the Kikuyu and Nyanza provinces of Kenya, and it had the enormous advantage that, while drawing on the liturgical and doctrinal riches of Orthodoxy, and enjoying the prestige of recognition by Alexandria, it was in effect entirely independent in its government'.[125] In the constitution it is emphasised that this Church shall be controlled by Africans, and be absolutely independent under the 'protection of the Holy Patriarchal Sea [sic] of Alexandria, Egypt'.[126] The colour and ritual of the worship service attracted many Africans, and many of those who were under discipline[127] in both the Anglican and Roman Catholic Churches joined the African Greek Orthodox Church.

The Archbishop and Primate of the African Orthodox Church in America became also the Patriarch Alexander of the African Orthodox Church 'of the World', and agreed in September 1929 to visit Uganda. He wrote: 'You will also want to get the vestments for your ordination, tunicle, alb, chasuble, chalice, paten. I will bring the Bible with me. I hope that the Day will be a great Day for Africa, when an African in the heart of Africa will be ordained to the Priesthood by an African Archbishop'.[128] In February 1934 the Church became 'The African Greek Orthodox Church'. This schismatic Church created a double problem for the Anglican Church, not only because of the secession but also because the Anglican Church was on friendly terms with the Orthodox Patriarchate of Alexandria.[129]

This Church exists as part of world Orthodoxy, and although in some instances it allows polygamy and administers baptism after very superficial instruction, it nevertheless maintains this association. A secession from this Church has already taken place because of leadership inefficiency, and they would like to have the word 'Greek' omitted.[130] The AGOC church buildings are mostly of mud, but they insist on the *ikonostasis*, 'a screen with three doors bearing ikons, set between the altar and the congregation'.[131] The liturgy, vestments and ritual are Orthodox in character; the instruction of clergy and laity in ritual and music is done most carefully, and, Welbourn adds, 'not the least impressive element in the service on July 19, 1959, was the fitting together of Greek solo with Luganda chorus'.[132] This service took place when Reuben Spartas vowed obedience to the Greek Metropolitan for East Africa, appointed by the Patriarch of Alexandria. Welbourn says: 'It is ironic that, just as the Anglican Church in Uganda is on the point of becoming autonomous, with the right if it wishes to appoint an African Archbishop, a church which started with the cry "Africa for the Africans" should come under the immediate authority of a Greek'.[133]

Amongst the Kikuyu there is a saying, 'There is no difference between a missionary and a settler'.[134] Even though it was 'less and less assumed that Christianity must be presented to non-Europeans in the political, social and economic context of European culture',[135] the anti-White feeling was already deep-seated within the African. Even though 'the numerical growth of Christianity between 1914 and 1944 was phenomenal',[136] and the ecclesiastical organisations, with their largely African personnel and emphasis on self-support, have set an example in indigenous development, there was reaction against established missions.

In Kenya the European farming interests had much influence on public policy, the European farmers being primarily concerned to safeguard their ownership in the Highlands area. There was little conflict between European and African interests in the industrial sphere.[137] Writing in 1927, W. M. Ross took up a position critical of the White minority, who he thought were struggling to maintain their selfish interests.[138] Gradually, anti-White reaction was built up. In June 1921 the 'Young Kikuyu Association' was formed, with Harry Thuku as leader. It is no wonder that Kikuyu reaction was strong on account of the continual pressure by the white settlers to alienate their land, and to force them to work for the settlers while the reserves were overcrowded. The actual revolt against missions, the deep frustration of Africans showed itself, culminating in the tragic murder of Miss Hilda Stumpf of the African Inland Mission at Kijabe on March 3, 1930. In 1922 the Kikuyu Central Association, which had Jomo Kenyatta as its President for some time, came into

49

existence. Two separatist Churches, which had close associations with this political organisation, were then founded, namely the 'Kikuyu African Orthodox Church' and the 'Kikuyu Independent Pentecostal Church'. Anti-European religious fervour was fostered in these Churches. The Kikuyu *Karing'a* Schools Association (*karing'a* means 'pure') supported the former, while the Kikuyu Independent Schools Association supported the latter, both being supplied with teachers from the Kenya Teachers' College at Githunguri of which Jomo Kenyatta was principal.[139]   The Kikuyu Independent Schools Association was loyal to the Government, whereas the Kikuyu *Karing'a* Schools Association was 'potentially anti-Christian and politically subversive'.[140]

The basis for this separation must be found in their disagreement on educational policy; and in the controversy on female circumcision, a practice among the Masai and the Kikuyu, which led to the defection of many members from those Churches which took a strong stand against it. Throughout the Kikuyu, female circumcision became a live issue from 1928 in education, in which area they desired self-determination. The Kenya Independent Schools Association differed in nothing from the mission Churches except that they held that Christian girls should be circumcised if they so wished. Membership of the Association was open to all who subscribed to the principles of the 'African Independent Pentecostal Church'. The Bishop of Mombasa was approached in 1933 by a group of this movement for permission to send two men to the Theological College to learn how to baptise in their schools; they also asked him to send 'a good African' to baptise those who were ready for it – an indication of the importance attached to the name-giving rite. The Bishop naturally refused to be used to create independent clergy. Archbishop Alexander, however, eventually consented, and ordained men as priests, who preach and baptise. Two of these priests declared their loyalty to the Archbishop, and adopted the name African Orthodox Church. The two, Arthur Gatung'u and Philip Kiande, split, the latter being accused of organising 'baptism by post' for those too far away. Kiande's chief lieutenant broke away from him. Gatung'u and the *Karing'a* movement combined tribal custom, included support for polygamy, with Western education, in which baptism played an important part. Gatung'u developed his movement, which was recognised by Alexandria in 1946. Morals were lax, and the Church centres round Gatung'u's individualism.

In the African Greek Orthodox Church, the Anglican Book of Common Prayer and the mission hymn-books (all translated) were used on the advice of the Archbishop. 'Those ordained by him adopted the use of cassock, surplice, stole and biretta; considerable emphasis was laid on the seven sacraments, which seem to have exercised some fascination; and the use of candles . . . appealed to the traditional Kikuyu use of fire during circumcision, sacrifice and burial.'[141] These independent Churches tended to be isolationist or tribal, but they maintained the ideal to be Christian which brought them in contact with a wider community.

Mau Mau, which had been 'a cruel and murderous reversion to barbarism',[142] had crystallised within itself the anti-White hatred, which could already be discerned from a speech by Thuku on February 22, 1922, which was not only nationalistic and anti-European, but also anti-missionary.[143] Mau Mau arose as a result of a deep-seated reaction, also the clash of two different cultures, and the failure to integrate them successfully, which resulted in 'the enslavement of the tribe through exploitation of their inherent fear of magic and oathing ceremonies, and of secret societies.'[144] Land hunger and racial discrimination and tension stimulated the Kikuyu political movements. Mau Mau developed into a religion – to which it owed its success.[145] Hymns were changed by substituting the name of Jomo Kenyatta for that of Jesus Christ, and Mau Mauism was further spread and propagated by perverted hymn tunes. Many Christians lapsed into heathendom and polygamy. Much of the superficiality of these lapsed Christians is laid by Dr. Leakey at the door of twentieth-century Western Christianity, but one cannot agree with him that the moral code should be made easier, or that this code of the Christian Church is inappropriate, because it does not permit in Africa the practice of polygamy, female initiation rites and observance of levirate obligations.[146] The foreignness of Christianity was a stimulus to Mau Mau, not the Christian moral code. It was those Christians influenced by the Revival Movement, who formed the Revival Fellowship and who stood by their convictions 'while the merely nominal Christians slipped away like a landslide'.[147] Warren says: 'When the real days of testing came, with blood and flame and sword, it was the men and women of the Revival Fellowship who saved the Church.'[148] This Revival Fellowship came about due to the work of African Christians. Welbourn rightly says: 'The psychological strains involved are even greater than those which led to the formation of independent churches in 1929.'[149] He sees in Mau Mau and the Revival 'two poles of the social tension of contemporary Africa – the one, based on a synthetic paganism . . . the other a retreat into an esoteric piety which rejects social and economic action as irrelevant apart from conversion'.[150] The political loyalty of Christianity to the West was shaken during this period, and the reaction was syncretistic paganism, a pathological phenomenon, such as can only be counteracted by an intelligent approach to the problems of people where two cultures meet, and where injustice prevails.

Independentism in Nigeria could not be ascribed to colour, as Parrinder indicates,[151] but rather to a desire for independence and revival, and, it may be added, for building up a new community in the city. There has nevertheless been a reaction against white missionary paternalism. It has already been indicated that the Islamic brotherhoods have gained ground, especially in Ibadan, the city which Parrinder described from the separatism point of view. He divides these movements into (i) the 'Orthodox' separatists; (ii) Prayer Healing Churches, and (iii) syncretistic Churches.

The first of these sections includes the United Native African Church, the African Church (Incorporated), the United African Methodist Church and the Unity African Christ Church.

The *United Native African Church* seceded in 1891 from the British Church Missionary Society as a reaction against missionary control and against Samuel Crowther, the first African Bishop on this continent, who was thought to be too friendly with the Whites. From this a small group seceded in Lagos in 1903, becoming the *Unity African Christ Church*. In its constitution it was stated that 'a purely Native African Church be founded for the evangelisation and amelioration of our race, to be governed by Africans'.[152] American Negro influence was present. This movement is strictly Anglican in most of its doctrines, but baptism is by immersion, and polygyny is permitted to all the Church members and ministers, and this has isolated it from other separatist movements. They follow the Anglican Prayer Book, but have their own hymn-book, and adhere to the ecclesiastical hierarchy of bishops, priests and deacons, as well as to surplices and cassocks, and even the chasuble.[153]

The African Church (Incorporated) was the first mass secession (1901), because of the transfer of a priest, James Johnson, after his consecration in England, from Lagos to the north. It affected other Churches as well, and a split came in 1905, the two sections being called Bethel and Salem, or Zion, respectively. Reunion was established in 1916 in what is called the African Church of Bethel. It was decided at a conference that there is no Biblical evidence for monogamy, but that, according to 1 Tim. iii. 2, 12, all clergy are obliged to be monogamous;[154] hence they refuse to be in communion with the United Native African Church, which allows polygyny for the

52

clergy also. They follow the Anglican Prayer Book. In this autonomous unit of the Anglican Church in the Niger Delta Pastorate, there appeared a self-styled prophet, Garrick Sokari Baird, who called himself the Second Elijah (cf. Malachi iv. 5). He had visions, healed the sick by prayer, and many followed him. He was anti-medical and anti-alcohol, and denounced all idol worship to such an extent that the civil authority had to step in, when private premises were invaded in order to destroy idols.[155]

The *United African Methodist Church*, whose origin was due to polygyny and a desire for independence, follow the doctrine and discipline of the Methodist Church, but consider monogamy an invention for Africans which they reject. Chairmen have been substituted for bishops, 'probably because they have learnt that Liberian and American Methodists are episcopalian'.[156]

Of the *Prayer Healing Churches*, or anti-medicine churches, described also as 'owners of prayer', there are several kinds. The *Christ Apostolic Church*, the largest group of its kind, has a puritan, anti-magical, anti-medical outlook, and condemns infant baptism; it split away from the Anglican Church on these issues. It is the nearest to the Orthodox outlook, and sometimes uses the Anglican Prayer Book, but it has its own hymn book. 'Hallelujah', 'Amen' and 'Holy' are heard in its services: baptism is by immersion, and it adheres to the Bible literally – only oil may be used for anointing. Polygamy is rejected.

The *Christ Apostolic Gospel Church* and the *Saviour Apostolic Church* are two other Churches of this type.[157] The *Prayer Church*, and a secession from this, the *Apostolic Prayer Church*, permit polygamy, because many people are kept away from the Church because of monogamy. Intoxicants are forbidden, and 'speaking with tongues' is practised.[158]

The *Sacred Cherubim and Seraphim Society*[159] was founded mainly by Moses Tunolashe, who had several visions based on Biblical ideas. It was revealed to him that the Society should be called Seraf, and, as a result of another vision, Kerub was added. The robes worn are white, the colour of priesthood in animism, and coloured sashes in red, blue and purple, and sometimes also hoods are added. Holy water is brought from a little white house in the compound, with a large white cross standing nearby; this is the centre of faith healing. The Bible is repeatedly referred to; Holy Communion is observed; wall pictures are of the Catholic type; candles and incense are means of sanctifying churches and rooms; nearly the whole congregation wear white and cross themselves on entering the church; the hymns are of the Orthodox type; alcohol, tobacco and pork are prohibited;

a metal cross called a 'spiritual sword' is used to drive out evil; shoes are removed on entering the church, 'speaking with tongues' is practised, and interpreted by others; and drums and bells have a place in the service, with much hand-clapping, although musical instruments are forbidden during Lent. Menstruating women may not enter the Church. The water cult has here a prominent place, and periodically they visit the hills outside Ibadan, which they call the Seraphim *Mount Tabor*, to which they were directed as the result of a vision. This is considered holy ground. They make much of dreams and visions, and are Adventist in outlook. These factors lead them away from the main Christian doctrines. They are influenced by and get their members from among Roman Catholics, Muslims, Protestants, and Animists.[160]

The *Holy Flock of Christ* exercise no ritual prohibitions on alcohol or pork, but they oppose magical remedies. Dreams and visions have a place in their system. *The Church of the Lord's People*, a secession from a Prayer Church, calls its leader by all kinds of venerable names. He holds an 'Honorary Degree of Psychic Doctorate', conferred on him by the Spiritualists' National Union. They use 'seal' words, 'undecipherable inventions', which are 'given in ecstasy, when speaking in tongues'.[161] The usual prohibitions are observed, holy water is used, the cross is placed flat or diagonally on the table, on which seven candles are placed.[162] *The Church of Christ's People* also have bottles of holy water, in which are wooden crosses. They have an open-air praying place, which they call 'the Hill of Salvation', where a deaconess is in charge. *The Church of the Spirit* split away from the *Church of the Lord*, and they have two meeting places with a prophet and a prophetess in charge of each respectively. Water plays a part also in this sect, and taboos are observed.

Outright syncretistic movements have also had their influence in Ibadan – although those mentioned above have already syncretistic tendencies. In 1943 a book was published in Lagos entitled *Orunmlaism, the Basis of Jesuism* by A. F. Beyioku, which tried to show that Christianity originated from the Ifa oracle called Orunmla. 'Imported' religions have to be discarded in the same way as imported governments, says Beyioku, and the Bible should be rewritten 'with Yoruba philosophic and theosophic terminologies therein' and God painted as an African, as well as the Angels, and the Devil in any other colour. Christ is the Ifa priest, who is consulted in fortune telling, and the Order of Melchizedec is the Order of Paganism, which was in existence before Christianity and 'Jesuism'. The followers call themselves 'the Holy Ethiopian Community Church'. The leader is

54

called 'Chief Spirit Commander Prophet, Primate African, Doctor of Divinity'. The Bible is not used in the service, and prayer rods and a crucifix are placed in the sanctuary.[163]

The Zikist political movement in Lagos, under Dr. Nnamdi Azikiwe,[164] sponsored an African Church called the 'National Church of Nigeria and the Cameroons', which preaches an 'indigenous' God and denounces foreign religions such as those from Rome, Canterbury and Mecca. The Ethiopian 'Church' is affiliated to it, from which a secession came in 1947, namely the *Ethiopian Communion Church*, which uses the Bible in its services. The Divine Spirit is found in Ifa, the Bible and the Quran. Muhammad has a place, but Jesus' name is not found except as Mesaya and Imanueli. Dreams and visions have a place in it.

The *Spiritualism Science Fellowship* is, according to Parrinder, a 'Herbalists' Research Institute' holding a mixture of all kinds of religion and magic. Its name is written on the door of a house with 'a clay snake carrying an egg in its mouth under the lettering'.[165] The house has an inner room, over which is written 'Home of Free Thought and Elysium'. The semi-literate leader is called by the name 'Doctor'.[166]

Baëta maintains that the *Bensu* sect is the nearest movement to what is generally known as a messianic prophetic movement.[167] Here, however, the main aim was not to oppose British rule, but to set prisoners free. Baëta terms as 'Spiritual Churches' the independent Churches which he describes, but would prefer the term 'Spiritist'. The word 'Spiritual' in this connotation means that 'in their worship, the groups concerned engage in various activities, which (by their own assertion) are either meant to invoke the Holy Spirit of God, or are to be interpreted as signs of his descent upon the worshippers'.[168] These movements in Ghana satisfy the emotional needs of people who have to adapt themselves to a new world where change in the economic and social sphere breaks up the traditional way of life. According to Baëta, the adherents and leaders of these Churches are psychologically normal and 'relaxed' persons, confidently facing ordinary human problems.

The Church of the Twelve Apostles traces its origin to the Grebo (Kru) prophet William Wade Harris, who visited the then colony of the Gold Coast. He hailed from Cape Palmas in Liberia, and had been a teacher in a school of the American Protestant Episcopal Mission, but had been gaoled because of his share in a revolt against the Liberian Government.[169] He eventually went in about 1913 to the French Ivory Coast to preach the Gospel after several visions from the angel Gabriel, and there started a mass movement, which

55

the colonial Government at first took to be political. He had a simple message and simple equipment. He wore a long white gown, a large cross, and carried with him a small Bible, a staff and a bowl of water which was used for baptism.[170] He admonished his prospective followers to burn their fetishes, to keep the Sabbath and to reject alcohol, to be faithful in marriage (polygamy included), and to believe in one God and his Redeemer, Jesus Christ.[171] He rejected all syncretistic tendencies. His bamboo cross was often mistaken for a fetish, and when this happened he broke it up and made another one. Baptism took place in the following way: the convert knelt on the ground, grasped with both hands the staff of the bamboo cross and Harris put the Bible on his head saying, 'This is God's Book, you must obey it'. He then sprinkled water from the calabash on the head, 'in the name of the Father, Son and Holy Spirit'.[172] He lived in poverty and distributed to the poor whatever gifts he received. He was quietly removed to the Liberian frontier during the war, as the Governor thought it a risk to have such an influential African in the country at such a time. During this period he visited the Appollonia and Axim districts in the then Gold Coast. His followers in the Ivory Coast were then estimated at between 60,000 and 100,000. They built small, simple churches, and secured a Bible for each, although they could not read, in the hope that a missionary might come some day who would explain it further to them.[173] This movement remained on friendly terms with the missions. Other independent movements, however, 'grew by drawing off the less mature of mission adherents'.[174] Harris, long regarded as the John the Baptist of Africa, was later deified as the Christ, and millenarian eschatological trends predominated in the movement.[175]

Harris appointed twelve apostles in each village to take care of his adherents, but this practice has been discontinued. His converts, in particular Grace Tani, carried on the work in Ghana. The movement's educational standards are, however, the lowest among all non-animistic religious bodies in that country, and most of the prophets and healers are completely illiterate. All training is done by practice – 'learning by doing'[176] – the only adequate method for illiterates, to whom the Church has given very little attention. They themselves consider their illiteracy as their main difficulty. On the other hand, a literate member, an evangelist, maintained that the mission-related Churches miss much as a result of the neglect of the 'spirit'.[177]

The letterhead of another prominent leader reads: 'The Twelve Apostles Orthodox Church of Ghana, Divine Faith Healing Church, Rt. Rev. Prophet Michael George, Presiding Bishop . . .'[178] Healing is indeed their main concern. The English Bible, although not always read, is at all their meetings, and 'held over the head of a candidate at baptism, and of each patient, preparatory to the healing exercises, sometimes again when the exercises are in progress'.[179] The other sacred object is the 'African dancing gourd-rattle', a calabash with white bead strings on the neck, which is 'rattled rhythmically to accompany singing and dancing'.[180] These rattles 'chase away' evil spirits; they are used by the prophets and prophetesses, who wear long white robes. Here also, as elsewhere, certain food prohibitions are observed, e.g. pork, stinkfish, shark's meat and snails. Great importance is attached to fasts. Polygamy is accepted. Baptism 'consists in signing the neophyte with the mark of the Cross in the name of the Triune God, after he or she has been thoroughly bathed and scrubbed in all parts several times over with sponge and soap.'[181] A Love Feast once a year, at which bread is eaten together, signifies brotherhood and unity in Christ and in the work of the Church. The centre of the activities takes place in what is known as 'the Garden', where prospective prophets and prophetesses receive their training. The symbol of the Cross plays an important part; a tall wooden cross, usually painted white, stands in the centre of the compound, and a basin of water is raised towards it with a fervent prayer for its blessing by the Holy Spirit, and this 'consecrated' water is used for healing, which takes place mainly on Fridays; since Christ died on this day His blood is more effective then. Prayers at the services of worship, where 'there is little or no teaching or exposition, . . . are accompanied by sharp shrieks, deep groans and all sorts of other ejaculated interruptions, often ending in ecstatic song'.[182] They believe that the intensity of the shaking by the 'Spirit' indicates the effectiveness of the treatment; music is played to bring patients into a state of ecstasy. The Bible is used to counteract barrenness by rubbing it on the stomach of the woman. Although this movement rejects idolatry and fetishes, Baëta rightly concludes that they are 'in fact using the Bible as a sort of ju-ju or fetish'.[183]

The Musama Disco Christo Church[184] (or 'Army of the Cross of Christ Church') was founded on October 19, 1922, by Joseph W. E. Appiah, who was later known as Prophet Jemisemihan Jehu-Appiah, Akaboha I. He had three 'baptisms' and somebody saw 'a liquid poured down straight from heaven on to Appiah's head, wetting his clothes'.[185] The 'Holy Spirit' came upon him, and he could 'speak in tongues'. After this first baptism he received a second, through which he received power over evil spirits and, at the third, the 'Holy Spirit' came upon the whole group. They met regularly on

Thursdays for seeking 'the Holy Spirit as the Apostles did', to the accompaniment of drumming, dancing and singing. The sermons are full of announcements of the coming judgment. Names announced by the Holy Spirit are given to the new converts. The movement has a 'rich and complicated angelology and demonology'.[186] 'Holy' water is used in healing, baptisms and ceremonial ablutions, and is obtained from the 'House of the Holy Well'. Baptism has become a purification rite, and this emphasis has made this movement ana-baptist, as they consider their baptism to be the only effective baptism. In the other 'Holy Place' are found the Ark, the Book of the Holy Covenants and the 'Holy See', and the final rites for the consecration of prophets and ordination of ministers are carried out there. The *Akaboha* alone enters the 'Holy of Holies', and there he intercedes for the people. The most sacred object is the Ark, a box which contains the Ten Commandments, and during times of national crisis, epidemics and earthquakes it may be carried round Mazano, the 'holy' city, in a 'holy' procession.[187] They use a fifteen-bead rosary. Men and women sit separately at chapel, though both sexes exercise the prophetic ministry. Certain food prohibitions are observed, and several fasts are held. Healing is the most important activity. The movement rectifies some African customs such as 'son inheritance' and traditional burial and funeral practices at which no alcohol is served. It administers extreme unction, but the burial is according to Methodist rites. Holy Communion is administered every three months. The movement has its own version of the Apostles' Creed.

This Church has drawn not only from the Methodists and Anglo-Catholics, e.g. 'High Mass', candles and vestments, but also from the African heritage. The priesthood of each head of a household recalls an important feature in African religion. The head of the Church is referred to as *Omanhane* or 'Paramount Chief', also King.[188] This Church has great political importance in Ghana, as well as pointing to a whole range of customary practices. The founder himself was 'a typical ardent Gold Coast nationalist of a generation ago'.[189]

The Memeneda Gyidifo (Saviour Church), was founded in 1924 by a staunch Methodist, after he had received messages from God through dreams. Saturday is the Sabbath, and the Ten Command-ments have to be strictly observed, the seventh Commandment – as well as prohibition of intoxicants – being enforced by fetish priests and ju-ju medicine. Baptism takes place by immersion three times, and in Church men wear long red gowns and women white – pictures are supposed to indicate that Jesus dressed this way – and footwear is not worn. In general, Methodist practices still play an important part.[190]

Apostolowo Fe Dedefia Habobo (the Apostolic Revelation Society) came as a result of the prophetic witness of C. K. N. Wovenu in 1939. He received several revelations, visions and dreams. He holds that his movement adheres to the same doctrine as the Ewe (now Evangelical) Presbyterian Church, and the food prohibitions of the Old Testament. Polygyny is allowed, they assert, 'according to the Scriptures'; however there is restraint in sexual matters. Baptism of adults and confirmation take place after one year's instruction, except in cases of emergency when the instruction period lasts two weeks.[191] The movement claims more than 50,000 members, and Groves says that it is an efficient, purely African organisation which runs a hospital, a chain of primary schools, a middle school and a training centre for pastors at Tadwezu, the main centre.[192] This movement has a very strong 'emphasis on "progress", i.e. the advance towards modern Western civilisation, combined with good works'.[193] Baëta maintains that in general it follows the example of the African Methodist Episcopal Zion Mission, which is represented in the area, rather than the spiritual churches which have been referred to in this Chapter.[194]

The Prayer and Healing Group of the Evangelical Presbyterian Church at Etodome[195] was founded by F. K. Do, who, after receiving several visions, started healing activities. Prayer is with 'tongues', and confessions and the 'expelling of evil spirits' are both important. It remains within the Church as a revivalist group, and the Church authorities are very careful in their handling of it.

The African Faith Tabernacle Congregation is found only at Anyinam and at 'New Bethlehem'. Healing activities are carried on by Prophet Nkansah, and many come to receive power, both for themselves personally and for their businesses and farms. The prophet himself is wealthy, mainly through numerous gifts from the farmers and others; he himself is also a farmer. Admission is by baptism through total immersion in a running stream. Polygynists may join but may add no wives after joining. At all important occasions there is much drumming, singing and dancing, while the prophet exorcises evil spirits and diseases or pronounces blessings.[196]

Here also is found the sect of the Cherubim and Seraphim, which consists of two groups founded by Moses Orimolade.[197] Both groups are small, and one claims its prophet to have had a miraculous birth. This group, at Kaneshie, Accra (from which a further group split away), receives members by laying-on of hands and by baptism. A third group, named the Sacred Order of Cherubim and Seraphim

Society, is composed mainly of those with a secondary and higher education, and is a strictly secret society.[198]

The Church of the Lord (*Aladura*, meaning 'owners of prayer')[199] has spread all over West Africa with many groups. They accept the Bible, the hymn-book of the organisation, and other hymn-books. They have all the offices in the ecclesiastical hierarchy down to 'male cross holders'. Friday is the healing day; marriage contracted according to African custom is recognised. The leader in Accra joined in order to be free from misfortunes 'through the Church's power of prayer'.[200] An offspring, 'The Redeemed Church of Christ' (*Aladura*), under Prophet Asaja, is also found in Accra.[201]

I have attempted in the following paragraphs to summarise the factors which have led to the existence of these movements:[202]

I. Disappointment with White civilisation, with which official Christianity is associated; acculturation through a process of selection and reinterpretation; tension between old and new ways within African society itself; race consciousness among the African races – i.e. tribalism; social and economic upheaval, with an accompanying feeling of injustice; illiteracy; the struggle against disease, which seeks in vain for an answer from Christianity; chiliastic expectations due to social and political pressures but also to lack of a sense of history; little knowledge of the historical background to Christianity, and lack of an established Church tradition; the desire for symbolism – in which the mind takes refuge when two realities meet; visions and dreams – the African's predilection for the emotional rather than the rational approach; suppression of witchcraft and witch doctors by the state; the African's attachment to a trusted leader.

II. Reaction against missionary paternalism; the foreignness of Christianity and the need for an integrated religion; unfulfilled emotional needs in a Western-oriented Church and the longing for a religion, which means something in all situations and which gives scope for the laity in a 'priesthood of all believers'; lack of pastoral care in mission and Church activities; unnecessary delay in establishing autonomous African Churches; the need for more ritual and a richer liturgy than that offered by Protestants (very few prophetic movements have grown out of the Roman Catholic as compared with the Protestant Church, although many individual Roman Catholics have joined prophetic movements); resentment of the strict demands of Church discipline, especially with regard to polygamy and the ancestor cult, which flourish in many independent movements.

III. Injunction of 'the Spirit'; a world view in which the ancestors play a prominent part; the destruction by established Christianity of the African's tribal customs, which weakens him in the sight of the ancestors, resulting in renewed emphasis on ritual prohibitions and hence a legalistic kind of religion; the desire for dependence on their own leaders and a restoration of their authority, which was forfeited in the mission – hence some of the resounding titles, such as Archbishop, Very Reverend, etc., adopted by independentist leaders: these leaders understand their people's situation both in this world and in the context of their supernatural world; the need to exercise their own initiative in organisational procedures, and to use the vernacular in services (cf. many hymns are composed within the movements); literalism and subjectivism in Biblical interpretation.

Basically, it is this: the misunderstanding by White-dominated non-indigenous Churches of the psychology, philosophy, languages, culture and traditions of the African, resulting in very little communication in depth and leading, via frustration, to fanaticism.

REFERENCES

1. 'Dilemmas and Opportunities, Christian action in rapid social change', WCC, 1959, 20.

2. Cf. H. J. Margull, *Aufbruch zur Zukunft*, Gütersloh, Gerd Mohn, p. 10.

3. Katesa Schlosser, *Propheten in Afrika*, Limbach, Braunschweig, 1949, 401.

4. Harvey Cox, *The Secular City*, London, 1965, 10.

5. Cf. P. Beyerhaus, 'Kann es eine Zusammenarbeit zwischen den prophetisch – messianischen Bewegungen Afrikas geben?' (Part II), *Evangelisches Missions Magazin*, Vol. 2, 1967, 83.

6. Cf. *Methodist Missionary Society Notices*, Vol. 6, 1829–31, 371.

7. *Methodist Missionary Society Notices*, Vol. 8, 1835, 187–88.

8. Respect for and appreciation of *Volkstum* is one of the main emphases in his thinking. Cf. K. Graul, *Die Evangelische-Lutherische Mission zu Dresden an die evangelische Kirche aller Lande* (1845), 3 f., 8 ff., 19 ff.

9. Cf. P. Beyerhaus, *Die Selbständigkeit der jungen Kirchen als missionarisches Problem*, Verlag der Rheinischen Missions-Gesellschaft, 1956, 53.

10. Taylor & Lehmann, 248. 'They reveal . . . also persisting elements of *pre*-Christian thinking and the real spiritual needs of the people. . . .'

11. Cf. G. Shepperson & T. Price, *Independent African*, Edinburgh University Press, 1958. They maintain that the West African separatist Churches have a strong spirit of political independence. 'The so-called National Church of Nigeria and the Cameroons is overtly political' (ibid., 502). The Lord's Prayer and Apostles Creed have been adapted to nationalistic circumstances. Cf. Bankole Timothy, *Kwame Nkrumah*, London, 1955, 80–1, 101–02; H. Witschi, 'Missionsdienst gestern und heute', EMZ, Jan. 1952, 11, 12; Cecil Northcott, 'New Gods in Ghana', *The Christian Century*, Nov. 23, 1960, 1367. Hodgkin says that after ratification of the Uganda Protectorate by the British Government, much 'subsequent political unrest among the Baganda has expressed itself in Christian formulae', Hodgkin, 97.

12. Cf. Sundkler, *Prophets*.

13. L. P. Mair, 'Independent Religious Movements', in *Comparative Studies in Society and History*, Vol. I, No. 2, Jan. 2, 1959, 134.

14. Ibid.

15. Cf. G. Balandier, *Afrique Ambigue*, Paris, Plon, 1957, 273.

16. Shepperson & Price, 74. 'That the African separatist movement often acted as a safety-valve for the discontents of leading African elements . . . the growth of numerous little black churches, often made combinations amongst their members for common aims of revolt more difficult.' The slogan of Ethiopianism was 'Africa for the Africans' – the forerunner of Pan-Africanism.

17. Baëta's contention that prophetism is 'a perennial phenomenon of African life', 'that the basic operative element in it seems to be personal in character', can easily be refuted when the whole African situation is taken into account (C. G. Baëta, *Prophetism in Ghana*, scm, 1962, 6).

18. Hodgkin, 111.

19. Harold W. Rehderau, 'Kimbanguism: Prophetic Christianity in the Congo', *Practical Anthropology*, Vol. 9, No. 4, July-Aug. 1962, 169.

20. Hodgkin, 112.

21. Cf. Shepperson & Price, op. cit., 72. Cf. Psalm 68, xxxi. The Abyssinian defeat of the Italians at Adowa in 1896 may have evoked the dormant nationalistic tendencies, as occurred in the East when Japan defeated Russia.

22. Ibid., 73. Cf. B. G. M. Sundkler, *Bantu Prophets*, op. cit., 41–43; W. C. Willoughby, *Race Problems in the New Africa*, oup, 1923, 235–49. C. P. Groves, *The Planting of Christianity in Africa*, Vol. IV, Lutterworth, 1958, 127–29; C. T. Loram, 'The Separatist Church Movement' in irm, XV (1926), 476–82.

23. Sundkler, *Prophets*, 65.

24. P. B. Hinchliff, *The Anglican Church in South Africa*, Darton, Longman & Todd, 1963.

25. A. W. Jordan, *The Methodist Episcopal Church in Africa*, New York, Missionary Headquarters, No date (1961 ?), 61.

26. Sundkler, *Prophets*, 42–43; cf. James Wells, *Stewart of Lovedale*, Hodder & Stoughton, 1908, 287–99.

27. Wells, 288.

28. Cf. Willoughby, 239, 241, 238, 237 respectively.

29. Wells, 289.

30. A. Lea, *The Native Separatist Church Movement in South Africa*, Johannesburg, Juta, 1926.

31. Cf. Willoughby, 242.

32. Sundkler, *Prophets*, 33.

33. Cf. I. Schapera, *Western Civilisation and the Natives of South Africa*, 1934, 287. The discussion at the International Missionary Conference at Le Zoute is in this respect important: 'Missionary experience is unanimous in emphasising that the question of land holds a central place in the consciousness of the African peoples, and that consequently guarantees to the Native peoples that the tenure of their land is absolutely secure are essential to secure peace and goodwill among all Native communities, and must be the basis of all endeavour to promote Native welfare.' Cf. E. W. Smith, *The Christian Mission in Africa*, 121.

34. Sundkler, *Prophets*, 34.

35. Ibid.

36. Ibid., 34. It is not necessary to indicate for our purpose the further development of Ethiopianism in South Africa. Central African Ethiopianism (1892–1915) was more than a replica of Ethiopianism in South Africa. During the time of John Chilembwe, who actually led a revolt in 1915, white rule was brought

under suspicion as a result of Joseph Booth's activities. From the Cape to Nyasa-land, Ethiopianism had a network of centres, 'a unity shaped by the general conditions in British-ruled territory, both restrictive and permissive' (Shepperson & Price, 425). Chilembwe is significant in that he worked for the economic and intellectual development of the African by way of industrial mission: he became the synonym for a 'pro-African and anti-European' African, working through a Church organisation to achieve political ends for his people (ibid.). In the Cameroons, a Native Baptist Church seceded from the Basler Mission during the time of Chilembwe, and became the major centre of agitation against German rule. During this time the whole of Douala sang anti-European hymns (ibid., 426). In Kenya, Harry Thuku was responsible for the grievances of Africans about Europeans finding some expression (1921–32), by which the leaders of his movement made a religious as well as a political appeal. Ibid., 4262–27.

The African National Church, an independent movement in the Nyakyusa–Ngonde area along the northern part of Lake Malawi, maintains in its statement of beliefs, *inter alia*, that 'We believe in the fatherhood of God and the brother-hood of man regardless of colour and creed, and that the African religion with its traditions, laws and customs was instituted by Him so that the Africans may realise Him by their own observance' (Monica Wilson, *Communal Rituals of the Nyakyusa*, OUP, 1959, 191).

37. Sundkler, *Prophets*, 48.

38. George Padmore, *Pan-Africanism or Communism?* Dennis Dobson, 1956, 87.

39. Ibid., 89.

40. K. Schlosser, *Eingeborenen-Kirchen in Süd- und Südwest-Afrika*, Mühlau, 1958, 196. Not all nativistic movements (Schlosser speaks of Zionist Churches following Sundkler's typology) expect the return of Christ soon. For some, He is personified in the person of their messiah; others expect their culture hero to return as messiah.

41. Hodgkin, 99.

42. Ibid., 100.

43. Cf. G. C. Oosthuizen, *The Theology of a South African Messiah*, Leiden/Cologne, Brill, 1967, 23.

44. Walther Eichrodt, *Theology of the Old Testament*, Vol. I, transl. J. A. Barker, SCM, 1961, 304–05.

45. Ibid., 305.

46. Ibid., 306.

47. Cf. Schlosser, *Eingeborenen*, 244. Isl. 214 Shembe is the Liberator of Dingaan's people.

48. Oosthuizen, *The Theology of a South African Messiah*, 145–56. Sundkler, *Prophets*, 278–79; Schlosser, 242; Bengt Sundkler, Bantu Messiah and White Christ, *Practical Anthropology*, Vol. 7, No. 4, July-Aug. 1960, 170–76.

49. Oosthuizen, *The Theology of a South African Messiah*, 35–37. Cf. P. Tempels, *Bantu Philosophy*, Paris, Presence Africaine, 42, 'The true chief . . . following the original conception and political set up of clan peoples, is the father, the master, the king; he is the source of all zestful living; he is as God himself. This explains what the Bantu mean when they protest against the nomination of a Chief, by Government intervention, who is not able, by reason of his vital work or vital force, to be the link binding dead and living.'

50. On Acculturation see also B. Barber, 'Acculturation and Messianic Movements', *American Sociological Review*, Vol. VI, No. 5, 1941, 663–69; R. Linton, *Acculturation in Seven Indian Tribes*, New York, 1940; R. Bastide,

'La causalité externe et la causalité interne dans l'explication sociologique', *Cahiers internationaux de Sociologie*, Paris, Vol. XXI, 1956, 77–99; ed. W. R. Bascom & M. J. Herskovits, *Continuity and Change in African Cultures*, Univ. of Chicago Press, 1959.

51. Ancestors become prominent. Cf. *Isihlabelelo zama Nazaretha*, hymn 148[4] (referred to in this book as Isl (singular), Izl (plural):

> *They have been called out of the graves*
> *they are already out, we have seen them,*
> *they have entered the city that is holy. . . .*

The superscription to Isl. 220 states that it was written after his (Shembe's) rising from the dead. Shembe II, Isaiah Shembe's son, a university graduate, has collected and published his hymnal.

52. Tempels, 43. 'A Chief in the class of humans shows his royal rank by wearing the skin of a royal animal.'

53. Schlosser, *Eingeborenen*, 246.

54. Ibid., 181–218.

55. Ibid., 'His followers honour Ignatius not "like" a God, but as God, as they honour Edward now as God' (ibid., 187). 'The King of Zion is Edward and not merely a human being. All others are only servants of the Lord.' This was said in a sermon at Zion City Moria, his holy city (ibid., 193). For his members he is the 'light of the world' (ibid., 200).

56. Ibid., 200, 'Much money is collected at the great feasts at Zion City Moria.'

57. Ibid., 200.

58. Bishop Limba, of the Church of Christ, built up a community where a puritan ethic is practised, and the worth of its leader is considered to be 'the key to salvation from the oppressive laws imposed by the white man, and from exploitation. This is made clear by the fact that a great deal of emphasis is laid upon material strength; and business enterprise, as a means to independence, is encouraged.' L. Mqotsi and N. MKele, 'A Separatist Church: *Ibandla lika-Christu*', *African Studies*, V.2, June 1946, 124–25.

59. Groves, Vol. IV, 128.

60. Sundkler, *Prophets*, 72.

61. Groves, 128. In the revolt in German East Africa of 1905, the so-called 'Maji-Maji rising', it was also alleged that the bullets of the Europeans would turn into water, if the rifles did not themselves spurt water (cf. Groves, Vol. III, 253). This is the same type of thought as that of Poqo, where carvings were made on the forehead in which a black powder was put in order to make them invisible. For a record of the Government deliberations with Enoch and his 'Church', see Schlosser, *Eingeborenen*, 133–50.

62. Schlosser, *Eingeborenen*, 155.

63. Ibid., 157.

64. *Almanak*, Ned. Herv. Kerk, 1949, 120–24.

65. Ibid., 12–58; 59–70; 71–124.

66. Cf. M-L. Martin, 'The Church facing Prophetic and Messianic Movements', *Ministry*, Jan, 1963, 49.

67. Ibid.

68. Harold W. Fehderau, 'Kimbanguism: Prophetic Christianity in the Congo', *Practical Anthropology*, Vol. 9, No. 4, July-Aug. 1962, 157.

69. Efraim Anderson, *Messianic Popular Movements in the Lower Congo*, Uppsala, Almqvist and Wiksell, 1958, 1; Schlosser, *Propheten*, 297–311.

70. Fehderau, 159.

71. Roman Catholic authorities emphasised the Protestant background of Kimbanguism, that evangelical pastors were its apostles and that the practice of individual interpretation of the Scriptures, which leads to nothing else but subjectivism, as a result of subjectivistic reliance on the inspiration of the Holy Spirit, was the main cause of this movement. (Cf. J. van Wing, 'Le Kibanguisme vu par un témoin', *Belgian African Review*, Vol. XII–6, 1958, 262.)

72. Anderson, 63.

73. Eichrodt, 103.

74. Anderson, 117–18.

75. Ibid., 119. Cf. G. Balandier, *Sociologie Actuelle de L'Afrique Noire*, Paris, Presses Universitaires de France, 1963, 398–416.

76. Andersson, 121.

77. Cf. G. Balandier, *Afrique Ambigue*, 217–49. Ibid., 232.

78. Richards maintains that it is 'a modern movement of witch-finders', a repetition of the old witch-finding movements; A. I. Richards, 'A Modern Movement of Witchfinders', IRM, Oct. 1958. In this connection the activities of Tomo Nyirenda, who appeared in the backward Mkushi district in 1925, should be mentioned. Calling himself *Mwanalesa* (God's Child) he claimed himself to be a prophet and witch-finder. The 'rite of baptismal immersion was adapted by him to the ancient craft of witch-finding'. Baptism disclosed the witches in the sense that they could not go deep into the water. He held some 'Watchtower' doctrines and was anti-European and anti-mission (Taylor & Lehmann, 26). In Angola the Kyoka movement also had as its aim the destruction of fetishes. Cf. Balandier, 1953, 43. F. van Wing, *Études Bakongo II*, 'Réligion et Magie', Bruxelles, 1938. In this connection the Kausapala movement, which is also anti-White, should also be mentioned.

79. J. V. Taylor & D. Lehmann, 251. See also *Basileia*: J. V. Taylor, 'Saints and Heretics', 305–12.

80. Cf. ibid., 252–53.

81. Ibid., 253.

82. Ibid., 254.

83. Cf. J. V. Taylor, 'Saints and Heretics' in *Basileia*, 308.

84. Ibid., 266. Emilio Mulolani, who did not succeed in being ordained in the RC Church, had several visions of the Virgin and of the Sacred Heart. He broke with the Church because of the separate seating of men and women, since it is not applied in the White congregations. After being forbidden to attend the RC Church in Lusaka, his followers met as separatist congregations. They met in the houses of the members, and 'encourage one another in mortification, fasting and prayer'. Some have dedicated themselves to complete poverty in order to preach. The sacrament means to them a love feast, because when Christ said 'This is my body' He meant that He gave food to others in need. Everything must be shared. In the mine towns they share all they possess with the poorest, irrespective of what tribe they may belong to. Husbands assist wives in domestic service. Taylor says: 'An indigenous group which so deeply understands the meaning of asceticism and charity, and values them so highly, is an almost unknown phenomenon in Africa today.' Taylor concludes that the demand for the Church is not only to be more African but also more Christian. J. V. Taylor, 'Saints and Heretics', in *Basileia*, 320–22.

85. Ibid., 267.

86. Cf. Hodgkin, 102.

87. Cf. J. Merlé Davis, *The Economic and Social Environment of the Younger*

Churches, Edinburgh House Press, 1939; Report by same author: *Modern Industry and the African*.

88. Taylor & Lehmann, 60.

89. G. Shepperson, 'The Politics of African Church Separatist Movements in British Central Africa', *Africa*, XXIV, 3; July 1954; Shepperson & Price, *Independent African*, 147 ff., 230 ff.

90. Cf. O. Quick, 'Some Aspects of the African Watch Tower Movement in Northern Rhodesia', IRM, April 1940, 216–26. See also R. L. Buell, *The Native Problem in Africa*, New York, 1928², G. Balandier, 'Messianisme et Nationalisme en Afrique noire', *Cahiers Internationaux de Sociologie*, Paris, Vol. XIV, 1953, 41–65.

91. Hodgkin, 109.

92. Quick, 217.

93. Ibid., 219. For details on social, political and economic developments see A. L. Epstein, *Politics in an Urban African City*, Manchester University Press, 1958.

94. Quick, 221.

95. Ibid., 226. Cf. Janheinz Jahn, *Through African Doors*, Faber & Faber, 1962, 225. Dancing, rhythmic music, hand-clapping, convulsions are typical of the Jehovah's Witnesses in Benin, Nigeria.

96. I. Cunnison, 'A Watchtower Assembly in Central Africa', IRM, Oct. 1951, 456–69 (459).

97. Taylor & Lehmann, 233.

98. Ibid., 122.

99. Ibid., 238.

100. Taylor & Lehmann, 242, 243.

101. Ibid., 243.

102. Ibid., 245.

103. Ibid., 246.

104. Ibid., 246.

105. Taylor, *Buganda*, 99.

106. Groves, Vol. IV, 124–25; Schlosser, *Propheten*, 368.

107. Roland Oliver, *The Missionary Factor in East Africa*, Longmans, 1952, 281.

108. F. B. Welbourn, *East African Rebels*, SCM, 1961, 34. For the Church of Christ in Africa and The African Israel Church Nineveh, see F. B. Welbourn and B. A. Ogot, *A place to feel at Home*, OUP, 1966.

109. Ibid., 50, 51.

110. Ibid., 25.

111. Ibid., 44.

112. Ibid., 46.

113. Ibid., 48.

114. Ibid., 51.

115. Ibid., 57, 58.

116. Ibid., 71.

117. Taylor, *Buganda*, 99.

118. Hodgkin, 102.

119. Padmore, 96.

120. Taylor, *Buganda*, 98.

121. Welbourn, 81.

122. Cf. *Report of the Commission of Inquiry into the disturbances in Uganda during April 1949*, Uganda Government Printer, 1950.

123. Taylor, *Buganda*, 98; cf. Welbourn, 27.
124. Oliver, 50.
125. Welbourn, 83.
126. Ibid., 83.
127. Already at the end of the last century, missions gave special attention to matters of discipline 'and set them to probe solutions preventive rather than punitive' (Oliver, 210).
128. Ibid., 86.
129. Ibid., 101.
130. Ibid., 232.
131. Ibid., 232.
132. Ibid., 232.
133. Ibid., 93.
134. Ibid., 111.
135. Oliver, 232.
136. Ibid., 234.
137. Cf. Lord Hailey, *An African Survey*, OUP, 1938, 382–93.
138. Cf. W. M. Ross, *Kenya from Within*, Allen & Unwin, 1927.
139. Keith Cole, *Kenya Hanging in the Middleway*, The Highway Press, 1959, 48. See also L. S. B. Leakey, *Defeating Mau Mau*, Methuen, 1954, 131.
140. Welbourn, 151.
141. Welbourn, 144–61 (157).
142. Groves, Vol. IV, 266.
143. Welbourn, 129.
144. Cole, 47.
145. Cf. Leakey, 153. 'Two years ago I stressed that Mau Mau was nothing more than a new expression of the old Kikuyu Central Association; a political body that was banned in 1941 because it had become wholly subversive. . . . What I did not realise then was that Mau Mau, while to some extent synonymous with these political organisations, *was in fact a religion, and that it owed its success to this fact more than to anything else at all.*'
146. Ibid.
147. Groves, Vol. IV, 312.
148. M. A. C. Warren, *Revival, An Enquiry*, 57; cf. E. M. Wiseman, *Kikuyu Martyrs*, The Highway Press, 1958.
149. Welbourn, 133. Cole mentions also the Johera sect, known as 'The Church of Christ in Africa', which broke away from the Anglican Church in the Nyanza area, to which it is thought about 20,000 Anglicans lapsed (Cole, 81).
150. Ibid., 133.
151. Parrinder, G., *Religion in an African City*, OUP, 1954, 107.
152. G. McLeod Bryan, 'Revelation and Religion in Africa', *Christian Century*, Jan. 4, 1961, 13.
153. Parrinder, 109, 110.
154. Ibid., 112.
155. Groves, Vol. IV, 126.
156. Ibid., 113.
157. Ibid., 115–18.
158. Ibid., 118–19.
159. Cf. J. V. Taylor, 'Saints and Heretics', in *Basileia*, op. cit., 305–06. The author relates here that he preached in the Anglican Cathedral at Lagos in the morning to an upper and middle class congregation, and during the evening he went into the slums and came across a Cherubim and Seraphim service, and one

of those present remarked, 'We preach in the poorer parts of the town where the other Churches do not go. But we think that is where Jesus Christ wants us to be' (306). Jahn, *Through African Doors*, 227, says, after referring to the rhythmic movements, music, and songs which lead to ecstatic singing and dancing in movements like the Jehovah's Witnesses, the so-called Holy Chapel of Wisdom, the Assemblies of God, the Cherubim and Seraphim, that they draw the biggest audiences, and that here is a 'process of re-Africanisation . . taking place in the form of religious expression'.

160. Ibid., 119–22; Groves, Vol. IV, 353; C. G. Baëta, *Prophetism in Ghana*, SCM, 1962, 129, 168–69.

161. Ibid., 123.

162. Ibid., 123.

163. Ibid., 126–28.

164. The movement pledged itself to defend Dr. Azikiwe against his enemies, cf. G. O. Olusanya, 'The Zikist Movement – a Study in Political Radicalism', *Modern African Studies*, Vol. 4, No. 3, 223–333.

165. Ibid., 129.

166. Ibid., 130.

167. Baëta, p. 4.

168. Ibid., 1. Cf. Point No. 5 of the Ghana Apostolic Church, 'The baptism of the Holy Ghost for believers, with signs following', ibid., 1. Point No. 7 of the Summary of Beliefs of what The Musama Disco Christo Church believes: 'We believe that the Holy Spirit can declare its presence emotionally or solemnly', ibid., 153. The Catechism of the Apostolic Revelation Society gives the first of the seven essentials of the anointment as follows: 'That I should completely surrender myself to the Holy Spirit and inherit the Holy Spirit as my only real wealth', ibid., 158.

169. Groves, Vol. IV, 45; B. H. M. Sundkler, *Propheten*, RGG, Vol. V, Mohr, 1961, 611; see R. L. Buell, *The Native Problem in Africa*, New York, 1928; Guariglia, 219.

170. Ibid., p. 45.

171. H. A. Wiersinga, *Geschiedenis van de Zending*, Kampen, J. H. Kok, 1959, 168–69; see also F. D. Walker, *The Story of the Ivory Coast*, 1930; W. J. Platt, *An African Prophet*, London, 1934; W. Ringwald, 'Westafrikanische Propheten', EMZ, 1/1940, 118–22, 145–55; R. T. Parsons, *The Churches and Ghana Society*, E. J. Brill, 1963, 5. See also B. Holas, *Le Séparatisme réligieux en Afrique Noire*, Paris, Presses Universitaires de France 1965, 237– 285. His study centres mainly on the movement of the prophet Boto Adaï and the Harris movement as it developed in the Ivory Coast.

172. F. D. Walker, 14–16.

173. Groves, IV, 46.

174. Ibid., IV, 124.

175. Guariglia, 19.

176. Baëta, 12.

177. Ibid., 14.

178. Ibid., 13.

179. Ibid., 15.

180. Ibid.

181. Ibid., 18.

182. Ibid., 19.

183. Ibid., 25.

184. Cf. W. Ringwald, *Experiment Goldküste*, EMZ, June 1955, Heft 3. 'Dieses

rein afrikanische, seltsam synkretistische Gewächs mischt Heidnisches, Methodistisches und amerikanische Sekteneinflüsse mit einem rohen Biblizismus' (ibid., 82).

185. Baëta, op. cit., 32, 33.
186. Ibid., 44.
187. Ibid., 48, 49.
188. Cf. ibid., 49–61 (61).
189. Ibid., 62.
190. Ibid., 68–75.
191. Ibid., 82–83. The Ghana Presbyterian Church had all kinds of regulations with regard to the indigenous customs and *mores*, hoping to isolate in this way the converts from their 'heathen' environment. All of these customs were rejected as works of darkness (Parsons, *The Churches and Ghana Society*, 79). Polygyny in this Church was rejected on the basis of Gen. ii. 20–25; Matt. xix. 4–6; Eph. v. 28–33, ibid., 76. The first stand taken by this Church against polygyny was in 1919 (ibid., 98). It was also admitted that the traditional custom kept women pure, whereas when the Church stopped this, immorality increased (ibid., 104).
192. Groves, IV, 252–53.
193. Baëta, 90.
194. Ibid., 93.
195. Ibid., 94–112.
196. Ibid., 113–15.
197. Ibid., 116–18. See Groves, IV, 353. Moses Orimolade Tunolase is given as founder. Cf. Parrinder, 119.
198. Ibid., 118.
199. See Parrinder, *Religion in an African City*, 115; Groves, Vol. IV, 353. L. Proudfoot ('Toward Muslim Solidarity in Freetown', *Africa*, Vol. 31, 1961, 154) refers to this movement as being in Freetown also, although its priesthood is mainly Yoruba, and its secret society robes are still imported from Lagos. Cf. also H. W. Turner, *African Independent Church*, 2 vols., Oxford, Clarendon Press 1967. In Vol. 1 the history of the Church of the Lord (Aladura), and in Vol. 2 its life and faith are discussed. One misses in this excellent study the traditional religious setting which here also, as in the rest of Africa, exerts definite influence.
200. Ibid., 119–26.
201. Ibid., 126.
202. See also Guariglia, 256 ff. Louis J. Luzbetak in his book entitled *The Church and Cultures* (Techny, Illinois, Divine World Publications, 1963) rejects the identification of what is called *Christo-paganism* in Latin America with Roman Catholicism. He states it is 'a theologically untenable amalgam'. He suggests that the problem of syncretism should be studied with the following main points in mind: (i) an exact historical analysis must take place. Syncretism, due to a subtle interplay of different factors, demands a study of such factors. Syncretism depends on the traditional religion, which differs from one part to the other, and on the type of Christianity preached; (ii) Christo-paganism is largely due to undirected selection; the tendency to select those innovations which fit into the culture, which often leads to the distortion of the Christian message; (iii) Christo-paganism is largely also due to undirected reinterpretation; (iv) Christo-paganism is also due to the fact that an innovation fails to satisfy all the functions of the traditional counterpart as in the case of polygyny, which has to do with prestige and with labour, and provides social security for widows, etc; (v) uneven social acceptance of Christian ways and values leads to syncretism

and distortion of the Christian message. Strong non-Christian views neutralise the power of the missionary's teaching; (vi) unsound catechetical approaches which encourage the likes and dislikes of a community to prevail rather than sound theology. Ibid., 239–48, 273–75, 297–301.

3

CLASSIFICATION OF THE INDEPENDENT MOVEMENTS AND THEIR ESCHATOLOGY AND CHRISTOLOGY

(i) CLASSIFICATION

Before attempting a theological analysis of what have so far been called 'independent movements', a classification of these movements is necessary. The terms *separatist* or *independent* really say nothing because what are today accepted as established Churches have also been described in the West by such terms. Neither is it helpful to call the movements without further qualification *Churches*. One could also easily be led into generalisations. One should actually analyse each and every one of these movements thoroughly, and then determine under which category it falls. This, however, is impossible with, literally, thousands of them mushrooming today in Africa; one therefore has to limit oneself to a few.

There are three main classes amongst these so-called separatist or independent movements, and much of the confusion in the analysis of these movements is due to the fact that they are all simply bundled together, although there are vast theological differences amongst them. One can neither classify them into two groups, as Sundkler did in the first edition of *Bantu Prophets*, namely, the *Ethiopian* type, which seceded from White Mission Churches chiefly on racial grounds, and other Bantu Churches which seceded from Bantu leaders in White Mission Churches, and the *Zionist* type, which is a syncretistic movement.[1] In spite of the fact that Sundkler discussed the messianic movements, he only adds this as a type in his second edition of this book.[2] H. W. Turner has given a comprehensive classification of these movements.[3] Apart from his ambiguous use of the word 'Church', although he also speaks of movements, his classification is the more penetrating.[4]

For practical purposes, the following classification is proposed, namely:

71

(a) Churches

Some of the groups which are described as separatist are Churches, such as the African Methodist Episcopal Church, the Bantu Methodist Church of Africa and the Presbyterian Church of Africa. Here the Word, the Sacraments and Church discipline have the same position as in the Churches from which they seceded. These Churches Sundkler would describe as Ethiopian, but their secessions are not mainly due to racial issues but to the indigenisation of the Church in leadership and methods of communication. Important in these Churches is to discern the place of Jesus Christ, His person and work. Some of these Churches are less interested in confronting the ancestor cult than are some legalistic Christian sects.

(b) Christian Sects

Under a 'sect' is here understood Jesus Christ *plus* something else, especially adult baptism or the Sabbath. This group, mainly Christian revival movements, could be subdivided into two main sections, namely:

(i) the *Pentecostal* type with its emphasis on the Holy Spirit, such as 'The Church of the Lord – Aladura',[5] the Africa Assembly of God in East London.[6] These groups are of a revivalistic nature; defensive and apologetic, but at the same time positive in proclaiming the Christian message. They could be very legalistic, a characteristic of many African Churches, either because ritual prohibitions sanctioned by the ancestors played a major role in the traditional religion, or because they have received the message in this strain from pietistic missionaries. The leaders of this group cannot be described merely as prophets or chief types; however, Bhengu has a strong position as mediator, and is the very life and soul of his movement, to which many illiterates and semi-illiterates belong. Faith-healing and public confession of sin play a prominent role in many of these groups. As in the case of the traditional Xhosa, which form the bulk of the African Assembly of God membership, many tribes in their traditional state emphasised public confession in crisis situations.[7] In most of these groups, adult baptism is a *sine qua non* for salvation. These groups are usually perfectionistic in outlook, and often react strongly against traditional customs which are considered to be to the detriment of the Christian faith.

(ii) the *Adventist* type, such as the Seventh Day Adventists, which is a strong movement in southern Africa. This group is very legalistic, and thus relies on the magic of moralism, i.e.

through their acts they consciously and unconsciously try to influence the supernatural, which is the very basis of magic. When these sects take a nativistic form, Jesus Christ is pushed into the background, and the Sabbath becomes the key to salvation, as is evident in the *Izihlabelelo zaManazareth*, in which Isaiah Shembe states:

> *The Sabbath is the key*
> *the gates may be opened.*   (Isl. ccxii. 2)

(c) *Nativistic Movements*

While most of the Christian sects are literalistic and fundamentalistic in their interpretation of Scripture, the nativistic movements again are also fundamentalistic, i.e. they wish to restore aspects (at least) of the traditional African religion. The difference between them in this respect is that the one accepts Scripture as basic, while the other regards the traditional religion in this light. A further difference between them is that the Christian sect often isolates itself from the world and its secular value systems, while the nativistic movements are interested in secular matters, as was the case in the traditional religion. The Christian sect concentrates mainly on the world beyond, while the nativistic movement keeps itself busy with this world, and often takes the form of a welfare society. The sect emphasises individual conversion, while the whole group, all the relatives and next-of-kin, can enter into the nativistic movement. The sense of community, also with those in the supernatural world, is still strong in the nativistic movements.[8] These movements, which are revivalistic and revitalistic, are defined by Linton as 'any conscious, organised attempt on the part of a Society's members to revive or perpetuate selected aspects of its culture'.[9] Here one finds:[10]

(i) *Revival Movements.* The emphasis falls on the old in the light of the new, and not on the new. As all great religious revivals call back to the glorious past, so also do these nativistic revival movements.

(ii) *Reformation Movements.* It could also be that new life could be blown into the new, where the impetus comes from outside and a reformation of the old takes place. Here something new is emphasised in the background of the old, and the new element belongs essentially to the old. One could see reformation in the concept of mediatorship, namely, that of the chief, as revealed in the prophet or messiah, but this does not give the full story. The nativistic movements could hardly be called reformation movements.

73

(iii) *Vitalistic Movements*. These are due to forces from without and within. A reinterpretation of the fundamental truths of the traditional religion takes place so that it acquires a new vitality. It is not merely a question of reviving the past culture and religion or perpetuating the existential situation, but certain aspects of the contact religion are of such appeal that they are naturalised and given symbolic value in the light of the old, or vice versa. Only in closer and continuous contact does this process develop, especially when the old sees its own limitations in the light of the new and feels threatened. A double reaction takes place, namely, what Linton calls *revivalistic* nativism, which attempts to revive extinct or moribund elements of culture, and *perpetuative* nativism, which perpetuates current elements.[11] The cult form in the nativistic movements gives religious meaning to the defence of the indigenous culture as a whole. Those aspects of the contact religion which find acceptance are never the same after they have been integrated in the new creative centre, but receive their final meaning from here. Not before this is understood will effective contact be made by the 'established' Churches, and communication of the Gospel message take place.

Linton's further distinction between magical nativism and rational nativism, the first attaching magical value to symbols of the past, while the latter attaches only psychological value to it, postulates only a theoretical possibility in Africa, namely in that a nativistic movement attaches merely psychological value to the past in a rational way. One could safely say that all the nativistic movements attach magical value to the symbols of the past, because magic in its many forms, whether as legalism, moralism, in ritual prohibitions, in symbols, or in ritual and liturgy, attaches magical value to the things of the past and to those aspects of the contact culture which are accepted.

Magical nativistic movements which react against the contact culture through an individual who considers himself to be totally dependent on supernatural forces, in and through whom *numinous* power or vital force is conveyed, assumes the role of a prophet or even a messiah. The nativistic components of such a movement may be very low at the beginning, but due to reactionary outside forces it becomes stronger, as in the case of Isaiah Shembe and Simon Kimbangu. The magical element is continuously a problem, even within the established Churches: for example, with regard to the baptismal water and the Sacrament of baptism itself, and the elements in Holy Communion. The magical structure of the old is

74

often being used in the nativistic movements to manipulate the supernatural forces in order to restore the golden era or to create it. Symbolic displacement takes place; Shembe becomes the messiah and his dwelling place the new Jerusalem. Shembe states in Isl. 1. 8:

> *Leave ye the earth*
> *Come ye to Ekuphakameni*

(this is the centre of the Shembeites). He not only displaces the Zulu King and diviner, but also the Christian Messiah. Kimbangu, on his return (*parousia*), will occupy the royal chair of the Congo. Nkamba, the centre of this movement, has become the holy city.

Two groups coming in contact may both reject assimilation, and much of nativism in Africa is due to this development. Where culture contact was not so strong in other parts of Africa as in the Republic of South Africa, the reaction has often been against missionary-dominated Christian activity, and the fear of total destruction of what was held dear in the old culture. These movements cannot merely be ascribed to racialism and denominationalism, because there are societies which had very little racial experience, but where numerous new religions, sects and syncretistic nativistic movements have developed. The cultural break-up has much to do with these developments. There are relatively few independent movements amongst the Coloured population (people of mixed race) in South Africa, because these people have practically originated out of Western culture.

These nativistic movements can either be prophetic or messianic.

(i) In the *prophetic* movements the prophet is the leader who has special healing powers; he is the middleman, and the soul of the movement. Jesus Christ still plays a role in the movement, but He is more a magical personality, a wonder-worker. Basic, however, is the traditional religious world view with its ancestors, ritual prohibitions, and so on.

(ii) In the *messianic* movements, the prophet has developed into a messiah, and usurps the place of Jesus Christ, to become himself the Black Christ. Here the emphasis is usually on realised eschatology. The messiah is the sum and substance of the movement, the person in whose hands its future lies. There are three types in the typology of the messianic phenomenon:

1. The messianic figure is historically present, as in the case of Isaiah Shembe and Ignatius Lekgenyane;
2. There are the cases where the messianic figure is not present – he will establish his Kingdom when he returns;

3. Between these two extremes one finds many variations, such as forerunners, substitutes, and so on.

A feature of messianism in Africa is that it does not isolate itself from the world, although there is some sense of isolation. Followers tend to become a third race. Political nativism, of course, is the extreme form of accepting the world. Much of Africa's nativism is not merely socio-economic, as is the case with Western revolutions and their messianic character, although this does play an important role.

Messianic nativism introduces ritual prohibitions, regulates clothing, has magical places, and uses magical elements such as holy water. The causal chain between nature and history is broken for some prophets and messiahs, so that for Enoch Mgijima, for example, the bullets of the soldiers will turn into water. The intervention has a divine origin, and for the Kimbanguists it would take place on his return.

This brings one to another aspect of these nativistic movements:

(iii) They could also be *millenarian* in the sense that they emphasise an apocalyptic transformation of the world as a result of the intervention of supernatural forces. In the enthusiastic period a number of the nativistic movements, such as that of Enoch Mgijima, and the later developments of the so-called Lumpa Church of Alice Lenshina, belonged to this category. These movements find a peculiar dynamism in their social aspirations, bitterness and fear, and can also develop into apocalyptic messianism, as in the case of some of the political messianisms.

The nativistic movements may include most of the characteristics mentioned above. Out of a magically oriented Christian sect could develop, through a specific individual, a magically oriented nativistic movement, which again could become messianic. Characteristic of such revitalisation movements is what Wallace calls the 'personality transformation dreams or visions',[12] or destiny dreams. The reaction to specific events (such as earthquakes) all over the world displays a uniform pattern, although covered by local cultural differences. These so-called 'behavioural units' are also to be discerned in cultural and socio-economic change, as seen in Japan's social disruption as a result of industrial and technological developments. There are deeper issues at work than colour and protestant denominationalism.[13] Igor Kopytoff, in his manuscript entitled *African Religious Movements: Indigenous versus acculturative Factors* (1963) maintains that the Holy Water movement in the south-western Congo is a re-examination of religious and magical technology, and an effort to substitute for it more vigorous forms, where it has become fatigued and outmoded. Kopytoff clearly reacts against a superficial analysis which sees the Holy Water movement as a specific response to colonialism, while there were other disasters and frustrations the people had to face earlier in their history. Sundkler's reference to the Land Act of 1913 as one of the major reasons for so-called separatism in Africa, and to the disregard for many African needs evident in the Report of the Native Economic Commission (1930–32) and the White Paper of 1936, overlooks the fact that the climate for independent religious developments was created long before these events. Amongst the Coloureds, the process of acculturation was more smooth, while with the African, especially because of his involvement in the mines and industries, it came as a rude shock. Malinowski states: 'The conception of culture change as the impact of Western civilisation and the reaction thereto of indigenous cultures is the only fruitful approach.'[14] Michael Banton has also warned against a merely social–economic–political bias in assessing these movements.[15]

The impact of technology and industrialisation and the resulting social disturbance will stimulate these movements in Africa even further. The different stages in the revitalisation process as discerned by Wallace[16] will be helpful to those interested in this phenomenon.

(i) The first stage, when two cultures meet, is a steady period, but there is severe stress in the minds of those who consider their way of life threatened.

(ii) In the second stage, conflict arises and individual stress increases as a result of interference with the culture; the pressure becomes abnormally severe, so that the old stress-reduction techniques are unable to solve these problems.

(ii) Conflict multiplies because the culture feels that it is being distorted. The contact culture is now blamed for breaking up what is considered to be a meaningful way of life, and this disillusionment leads to reaction against adaptation.

(iv) Different revitalisation movements come into existence in the fourth stage, in which a reformulation takes place in the light of the new, or in reaction to the new. The prophet or leader becomes the personification of the process as a result of visions or dreams, which are received through a supernatural being. Neglect and violation of the old ways of the ancestors are given as reasons for the present plight. The prophet's dreams reveal a keen desire for a satisfying relationship with the supernatural. The visionary enters into an intense relationship with the supernatural world, and the same intense relationship that exists between the prophet and that world exists between him (or her) and their followers. The prophet himself has undergone a radical change in his personality as a result of 'personality transformation dreams'. These destiny dreams are different from those born out of neurotic conflicts. They give him a sense of destiny and insight into the future – he becomes a person creating the future; eventually himself being the future, the basis of realised eschatology, as in Shembe's case. In his *Isihlabelelo* lxxxiv. 6 one reads:

Beautiful are you leopard of us
Beautiful are you our Christ,
Stand up you iNkosi of us
That you may crush our enemies.

The sudden and radical changes in the personality are a familiar phenomenon in African society in which the diviner first goes through an initiation period, when his/her personality becomes transformed. Some schizophrenics in periods of severe stress consider themselves to be supernatural beings; however, the prophet-to-be's visionary experiences are not psycho-pathological, but rather a synthesis is born in his innermost being, which meets the stress demands of the situation, of which he becomes the Saviour. The deification of the leader is not merely a reaction against a so-called pale white Christ of the white man, but it is an effort to have through him powerful contact with a world they fear they may lose. In him their hopes and aspirations are crystallised. The myth of the Black Christ is an effort to remain in intimate contact with the supernatural. His preaching emphasises subjection to the old supernatural forces, as well as to the new explained in the light of the old. Indigenous methods of communication are employed, which contribute tremendously to the expansion of the movement. Many of the converts themselves undergo a revitalising personality transformation, with a sense of destiny carved into their very being. Many of these movements are later used by politically minded individuals and give them the impression of political reactionary movements. One does not minimise the social, economic and political issues in the development. The Kimbangu movement started as a revival movement, but the handling it received from the civil authorities forced it into a political situation and nativism increased. The movement develops as a group apart and, although it modifies its doctrine and political attitudes, it remains basically the same, and the performance of ritual becomes more or less routine. After the process of adaptation

78

has been completed, a new and steady stage exists which is different from the early period of upheaval and stress, that of a society sick as a result of abnormal pressures, which often results in apocalyptic irrational fantasies. The steady development of many of the secessions from established Churches into nativistic syncretistic movements is a great problem in Africa.

Although some of the movements referred to in the analysis are *not* nativistic, they have nevertheless non-Christian elements in their bosom, as in the case of many Churches in Africa, which are easy bridges to nativism. All this shows how dangerous an emphasis on indigenisation or relevance for its own sake is for the Church, because it is easily misunderstood.

It is difficult to analyse some of the nativistic movements because, like the traditional religion, they have no creed or systematised statement of faith. What they believe has to be detected from what they do and what they sing and pray, their ceremonies and sacrifices. Such religion is expressed in ritual rather than in dogma, and some of these rituals are elaborate.

The analysis begins with the eschatology of these movements, because from here one sees them in a clearer perspective. One has here to do with a later stage of development, the only stage actually described in the work on these movements. The early stage of reaction against the breaking-up of what they hold dear has mostly been ignored or neglected. One should thus not get the impression that these movements are merely the result of political, economic and social issues.

(ii) ESCHATOLOGY AND CHRISTOLOGY

In the messianic movements, the first and basic expectation is of freedom from need, whether that need be in the material, social, political or moral sphere. 'Salvation', of a kind which has nothing to do with sanctification, is sought for the whole tribe.[17] The second component of the messianic idea is a better future, and the third is that of mediatorship between God and man. From this naturally follows eschatological and chiliastic expectations embedded in nativistic and revivalistic concepts.[18] Messianism is preached by prophets, and there can be no question of messianism without a prophet. Prophetism could be a wider concept than messianism, as it could include more, in the 'here and now' as well as the 'then and there', and is not limited to the well-being of the individual, but includes the tribe, the nation.[19] The prophet can be either male or female. Again, there is no prophet without the 'spirit'. He or she is the mediator between the living and the dead, and must, if of the shamanistic type, have an ecstatic nature.[20] The prophet receives an official calling and has tremendous authority. He may use magic, but rather tends to consider his power to be derived from supernatural inspiration. Schlosser makes a sharp distinction between the prophet and the magician,[21] but this cannot be accepted *per se*, as we will indicate later in discussing the use made of water that has been 'prayed for', amulets, charms, etc. In most cases the prophet has a close relationship with the medicine man. He is of a shamanistic nature, and is primarily religious in disposition, his magical attributes taking second place, the priestly acts on behalf of the people conforming to a fixed religious system. The contact of traditional religion with the Christian mission brings forth a new religious mentality, by which the new concepts are used to revitalise the old, as the new is seen to be part and parcel of the White civilisation.

The initial stimulation of the political consciousness of the African came from the United States independent Negro Churches, where it acquired a messianic-chiliastic character as a result of political, social and economic tension. 'Ethiopianism' has been used not only in South Africa, but in many parts of Africa, as a general term for African nationalism.[22] Even the most pietistic isolationist missions in East Africa considered entry into politics the only real antidote against the slave trade.[23] The preachers became the natural leaders of the people during those years of emergence, and had much political influence. The disturbances in Jamaica during 1831 were spoken of as 'the Baptist war', and the Baptist name was associated also with the 1865 Jamaican Rebellion.[24] This Negro Protestant tradition, which 'elaborated along a Baptist stem with roots that went back to the revolutionary Anabaptists of the European Reformation',[25] had a tremendous influence in Africa, especially after the emancipation of the slaves in the United States. After the emancipation, two alliances of independent Negro Churches came into existence, the African Methodist Episcopal Church and the National Baptist Convention, through which Ethiopianism emerged on the African continent, and these were often the source of revolt. In some countries, like Ghana, political motivation has played a minor role in the formation of indigenous movements, but religious nationalism has taken its place and developed into a movement with its own myths, ancestors and prophets.[26] The nationalistic element has received so great a religious significance that the leader becomes the messiah, and all futuristic expectations are derived from him.[27]

The above factors, as well as historical influences, religious conditions and psychological reactions, played a part in the formation and development of the indigenous movements. Many white mis-

80

sionaries, intentionally or unintentionally, gave the impression that the Church belonged to them, to be established when they so decided after the mission had developed to maturity. Even the Revival movement in East Africa, which remained within the Church, arose in a time of ferment in East Africa – 'in Ruanda a famine, in Uganda a devastating scourge of locusts, in Kenya unrest as new ideas surged in to overthrow the ordered round of an older world'.[28] The Revival answered a special need, when personal contacts in the Church had been diminished to the minimum. The Church grew in the circumference, but in the centre it lost much, in the sense that real fellowship had been neglected. In the Revival, 'effective sub-groups' emerged, 'in which intense corporate participation was made possible'.[29] The new form of leadership, with its charismatic leaders and fellowship groups, which exercised real *koinonia*, had strong ties between leaders and followers. However, the Revival in the Congo, with its inadequate spiritual instruction, formed the necessary background from which the first Prophet movement emerged.[30] Superficial motives came into the mass movements. Education was considered to be a new kind of magic and its emphasis was on the winning of souls.[31]

Cultural contacts and cultural encroachments call also for solid leadership, in order to guard the traditional ways, when these are seen to be in danger of extermination. The insecurity which cultural contact has brought in its train in Africa has been congenial soil for the messianic-prophetic movements with their materialistic, futuristic approach. The breaking up of the tribal structure as a result of Western impact in its many forms, not least as a result of Christianity, and intensified industrial and technological development, have underlined the real insecurity of the African. He often lives both in the mythical *and* functional stages of man's development.[32] In South Africa and other countries settled by Europeans, he became very conscious of the present and all the suffering brought by way of social upheaval, restriction to the reserves, forced labour, alienated land, racial segregation in Church and society, lack of information about legislation, restrictions on his movements; all this caused a deep sense of frustration. Exaggeratedly severe control, often entailing injustice, has given impetus to the African form of religious reaction with an emphasis on magic. Economic depression breeds emotionalism, a fruitful ground for pathological forms of religious development, and the prophets are, with exceptions, 'commonly men with labile psyche and with a tendency to ecstatic states and trances, men with a definite shamanistic disposition'.[33] Under these circumstances they find a ready response.

81

Among an animistic society in New Guinea, the Western impact led to what the Dutch missionaries called 'Revivalling Paganism' or 'Papuan Adventism'. The futuristic outlook, the eschatological expectations, as well as the re-enactment of tribal myths, are typical.[34] Kamma says, 'Christianity came to them as an isolated religious appeal, leaving the economic and social aspects out of account'.[35] Christianity, as far as they experienced it, failed at this vital point and 'has led to many a tragic reaction because all primitive religion, in its essentials . . . aimed at helping in all kinds of material distress'.[36] Education itself has often not opened new avenues for personal self-expression, but only opened the eyes to new possibilities for self-discovery. Christianity attached itself, furthermore, to the victims of society, without trying to change society and its individualistic tendencies. Christianity is thus regarded as the ultimate danger to tribal culture, and also as the main instrument of White domination. 'White domination' is often used as a bogy for their frustrations and inability to meet the onslaughts of the contact culture.

Among these movements there is also an 'easily discernible *common tendency to create new communities*, which should function like kinship groups'.[37] This is indeed a 'common tendency' in Africa. It is the basis out of which one-party states, centred round a 'personality', develop; the position of the leader in the African congregation is often heavily emphasised, which also contributes to this tendency. Max Warren says that 'our generation has seen the disintegration of so many traditional patterns of human life, has seen so many ancient unities destroyed, that it is to be expected that a search for a new unity should be one of the marked characteristics of our time'.[38] The Revival movement in East Africa emphasised the most important fact that the unity of reconciliation is profoundly social, as it included others.[39] Missionary activity had split up the original unity, but in the Revival the idea of including the fellow-man in the meaning of the unity of reconciliation was recaptured in a Christian way. Bonhoeffer has emphasised this aspect well in stating that Christ exists as community and the community exists for the sake of Christ in the world, a *sanctorum communio*, bound to nothing else but the Word.[40]

The collapse of the old system seriously affected the power of the chiefs, because administration was now mainly in the hands of foreigners. The chiefs considered even the prophet movements a threat to their position. When efforts to uphold the religious prestige and authority of the chief failed and resulted in political frustration, the idea of the Divine Kingship was transferred to the new religious leader.[41] In this way a Church-tribe was formed, 'the leader of which borrows his traits from the Kingship pattern of old'.[42] Western infiltration by way of administration helped to undermine the influence of the chief, and the social pattern generally, and it was now the new leader who had to find the remedy for this political, social and material distress. The true chief was the father, the king, 'the source of all zestful living; he is as God Himself.'[43] A tremendous responsibility now fell on the prophets wherever they took over the responsibility of the chief; wherever the role of the latter dwindled in Africa, the Church was called upon to compensate by taking up and channelling the political consciousness of the people. It was difficult to attempt this in the established Churches because the Christian missionary gave the impression of himself being a pioneer and architect of the white man's penetration.

Another important aspect which has only briefly been referred to is the break-away from the cyclical to the historical approach to life.[44] Here time – the future, the present and even the past – receives a new meaning and is seen in a new perspective. This aspect provides a new 'revelation'. The sense of destiny in Western civilisation has brought to the African the realisation that he is part of the course of history, and actually at its mercy. History inculcates a sense of eschatology because both history and eschatology go hand in hand.[45] The preaching of the Gospel to all nations is itself eschatological. Holy Communion can also only be eschatologically understood – it is an eschatological sacrament: 'until He comes'. In the Jewish eschatology the historical and cosmological points of view are combined and the end is seen as that of the world and its history.[46] The Kingship of Yahweh, which took with Isaiah a universal character, comes to the foreground with the Chronicler (I Chron. xvii. 14, xxiii. 5, xxix. 23, etc.) when he speaks of the *malkuth Yahweh*, the kingdom of Yahweh.[47] This theology has dangerously come to the point of associating the Kingdom of God with the Judaic conception of the naturalistic notion of Israel, which was already opposed by the prophets.[48] In the New Testament, the expression *malkuth Yahweh* is used frequently, but in a universal and eschatological sense.[49] Hope and salvation in the Old Testament comprise the welfare of the people, and 'the responsibility of the individual coincides with the responsibility of the whole people'.[50] Divine judgment is brought about by supranatural forces when a cosmic catastrophe takes place. In the apocalyptic literature, frightening events like war, famine, natural disasters and epidemics are signs of the end.[51]

In the African nativistic religious movements, eschatology has been secularised and interpreted in terms of the African's own existential situation, as was the case also with Israel in times of distress and confrontation. In these movements, it is maintained that the adversaries will be conquered, and the African will live in abundance and happiness in a new earth which has developed out of the old. In some movements, the Kingdom has already been established, with the Messiah in their midst. The messianic element of these movements is a statement of hope and it requires as its ideological basis the myth of the *parousia*, or reappearance of a culture hero, who will lead them, as Moses did, to an earthly Canaan. In some of the nativistic movements, the resurrection of such a hero has already taken place. In the traditional society, such a person's spirit is called back through the slaughtering of a beast as a guardian spirit soon after death.[52] The history of Israel appeals to them because here a goal is promised, although the realisation of this promise is conditional upon the obedience of the people to their past. Through visions and dreams, the ancestors receive a prominent place and animism again forms the basis of the movement; much in the Old Testament influences them to return to their past. This affects also the Church concept – the ecclesiology – because in this new community the idea of a tribal or ethnic community develops: the whole tribe is the Church without any idea of personal decision. Its basis is purely ethnic, i.e. based on blood relationship.[53] What appeals in the Old Testament to these movements is the fact that salvation comprises the welfare of the people, not just of the individual. The idea of a new privileged community, in opposition to the mission station idea, where only a few received special privileges, takes now precedence in their 'theology'. The new order is now seen from a materialistic point of view. Religion is related to the material welfare of the tribe: they had discovered the same in Christianity, but it had been limited to the elevated few.

Andersson maintains that African culture has produced reformers and prophets, and some of these were not without messianic features.[54] He refers especially to the prophets in South Africa. The type of eschatology described above started early in South Africa, e.g. Nxele, Tlapane and Ntsikana, and Umhlakaza and his daughter, Nonquase.[55] Nxele reacted against witchcraft, and preached the resurrection of the ancestors. These prophets tend to be hostile to foreign culture, and emphasise the return to the old customs, and only when they obey 'the Spirit' – the message to return to the old paths – would they experience prosperity or find 'grace with the Great Spirit'.[56] The other way of receiving this Golden Age, which has been most widely propagated, and found in South Africa with Umlanyeni (1850) and Umhlakaza and his daughter Nonquase

(1856), is by killing cattle, which in itself has religious significance, by destroying crops and by not tilling the soil or planting crops. On a specific day, February 18 and 19, 1857, it was believed that the sun would rise in the West, the Whites would be driven into the sea, innumerable herds of cattle would emerge from the earth, and the fields would be covered with maize: the dead would rise from their graves and return to their relatives.[57] Kraals were enlarged, as well as the maize containers. There was great expectation, but also a tragic disillusionment. Why all this killing and destruction? As regards Umhlakaza, there are different explanations. For example, when somebody wishes to become a diviner, all cattle belonging to him are killed; and before a war many cattle are killed in order to prepare the soldiers physically, to make shields, etc.[58] It has also been suggested that this 'Last Day' was planned by Chief Sarili, who had hoped in this way to drive the Xhosa to despair, so that they might then react against England in war.[59] Natural catastrophe will precede the Golden Age of the 'new heaven and the new earth'; the sky will crush the enemies and, according to Umhlakaza, the new aeon will be established by the ancestral factors who will drive out the Whites.[60] Umhlakaza even thought that help would come from *Amaryss* (Russians), as the opponents of the English during the Crimean war, who would arrive in a ship. Here we find messianic eschatological tendencies, as well as myth.

The same features are *inter alia* prevalent in the *Naked Movement* and the *Cargo Cults* – the arrival of the ship which would introduce the new era is the main motif in the latter.[61] Anti-European feeling was strong in a number of these movements, accompanied by wild expectations. An example was the Dinka Freedom Movement in the Anglo-Egyptian Sudan in 1921, which was organised by prophets and chiefs against White rule. They preached the return of the ancestors, and said that the rifles of the soldiers were harmless.[62]

Missionary preaching in Africa has opened up to the African new possibilities. There are two main types of dreams which play an important part in the life of the African in general: the free or ordinary dreams, and those that have a meaning fixed to them by the spcific culture.[63] The latter are really visions,[64] and in these the future comes into existence. This is most clearly seen in the cases of André Matswa and Simon Kimbangu, each of whom will establish the kingdom when he returns with authority and rules over his adherents.[65] The culture hero is a necessity for these futuristic expectations. In the case of Umhlakaza and Nonquase, the spirits of the deceased fathers take this place. As in the 'Cargo Cults', so in the Kimbangu movement a big ship is expected. At the back of these expectations lies the desire to obtain force, vital force, which, to the traditional African mind, is the supreme value.[66] Western civilisation has given to its members this special force which enables them to live strongly, but has kept it away from the African. The prayers of the pre-Christian African to the ancestral spirits continually ask 'Give me power'. The greatest obstacle to true conversion lies in the conviction that the discarding of the traditional customs will lead to destruction because they are then cut off from the source which gives them vital energy, life force, to live strongly.[67] All these futuristic expectations are now built on the return of the prophet, because he has taken the place of the king, the chief, from whom all zestful living was expected. In highly institutionalised Churches, the personality of the leader is not always so important. The missionaries, so the reactionaries maintain, have withheld from them the central aspects of the Christian religion; they have not even permitted them to know the full Bible truth concerning *minkisi* (fetishes) and *makundu* (sorcery), or the secret magic with the help of which they have procured wisdom and power, which they keep jealously to themselves. They even have their own secret communion, which really can 'wash away sins'.[68] The Khakists in the Congo continuously criticise the missionaries for not giving them 'The Spirit'.[69] It is significant in this connection that the greatest mission-sending nations had been the most prosperous ones with the highest standard of living.[70]

As a reaction against this, *their* prayers should now be answered instead of those of the Whites.[71] In prayer, their prophets are put on the same level as the patriarchs; this is not a prayer in which dependence on God is uppermost, but a claim on God, who should be a tribal god. This god is incalculable, yet the prophet prays to draw God's pity on his people. The expectation from God is a future in which they will live unhindered by human limitations. Both Kimbangu and Matswa will break up the old order, in which they are slaves to the Whites, and all will share in the new order. These dreams and visions are perversions of Biblical expectations, to which the material welfare of the Whites, which is seem as a concomitant of Christianity, has contributed.[72] It has given the impression of henotheism, that God has favoured some people only. Now the prophet claims God for himself and his people. A claim is laid on the future, which holds in store for them the African kingdom wherein God can be worshipped not only as their God but also in their own ways.[73] Their future, made up of their religious longings and political expectations, is bound up with Simon Kimbangu and

André Matswa, of whom Kimbangu is the 'original and real messianic figure of the movement'.[74]

Andersson mentons that, in the areas where the Ngunza revivals came, namely the Umsana mission field in Lower Congo during 1921–24, the people were 'bound with extremely strong ties to Kimbangu'.[75] Kimbangu is now seen as the saviour of his people, in the same sense as the prophet is regarded in the nativistic type as the Saviour and Christ.[76] Andersson indicates that the messianic features in Kimbangu gradually increased, and it seems certain that he would have taken the position of a black Christ if he had remained with them. Van Wing, a Roman Catholic, says in an appraisal of Kimbangu that only somebody with dynamic strength could succeed in enticing his people to abandon *minkisi* (fetishes), *ngoma* (drums) used for obscene erotic dances, and polygamy which was the very basis of the traditional culture.[77]

The preaching of missionaries was from the beginning directed against the strong sense of fear that ruled the mind of the African. In the Gospels the main theme is: 'Fear Not!' The power of evil spirits is broken, and this makes an immense impression on the converts from the animistic world. But this relief creates a vacuum which is later filled again in times of crisis either with the old or with all kinds of utopian expectations. Man, who has been bound up with nature, whose whole being had to struggle against its enigmatic powers, finds relief in knowing that everything has a beginning and an end, that he can overcome mythological thinking by supplanting it with an historical outlook. Salvation has to do with history. Jesus Christ will come again, and the end will be a new earth and a new heaven. In the old religion, the power of the dead had tremendous influence, the forces of the elders having vitalising influence on the living. Here the problem arises of witchcraft,[78] a psychologically effective instrument in a superstitious animistic world view. Christianity brings a tremendous psychological relief, above all a realisation that there is a yesterday and a tomorrow, a destiny, and that life is not an endless cyclic event. It means freedom, a new life with new possibilities; when the light of the Gospel shines on superstition and fear, it means a new concept of freedom.[79] The old powers of evil are conquered, and conversion means that one is not subjected to the past, but can reach out for the future with all its glory. Even if the decision to accept the lordship of Jesus Christ has not been genuine, a change has still taken place. A new hope has taken possession of the convert, the powers of evil are overcome, and immediately he has a sense of future.[80] The grace of God has replaced the old sorcery and witchcraft, which means a new day, a definite approach to the future. This can take the form of ecstasy and can develop into ecstatic movements, 'which provides fertile soil for exalted futurist expectations'.[81] This was also the case in the Dervish movement in Islam, with its Mahdist hope.

In this fertile soil grave misunderstandings develop. They enter upon the future instead of God approaching them. The difficulty is that there is a great difference between the word preached and the word heard. What is heard and understood depends on the existential situation of the hearer, who receives the word, but can only interpret it from within his world view and specific experience and expectations.[82] Vital force is with the African the 'key principle'. 'The activating and final aim of all Bantu effort is only the intensification of vital force'.[83] This can be strengthened if there are no obstacles in the way. The 'luxury', from the African point of view, in which the missionaries live is due to their vital force having been strengthened. In other cases, it is projected to the future life. Monica Wilson says that again and again the reason for conversion amongst the Nyakyusa is given as 'There is life' (*ubumi buhlipo*), a futuristic rather than existential life, with emphasis on rewards, punishments and resurrection, themes which often recur in dreams.[84] In Sundkler's Ethiopian Churches and *Mission des Noirs* the hope is in a vague future, whereas the nativistic movements offer immediate results on a personal basis.[85]

In the syncretistic movements the philosophy of vital force does lay the emphasis first on 'these things', which have been very prominent in missionary activity with its privileged few on the mission stations. The soul of the African has for centuries hankered after force and life. Everything has force and because of this it has specific value. For us the definition of being is 'that which is', or 'the thing insofar as it is', while the African definition is 'that which is force', or 'the thing insofar as it is force'.[86] In traditional African philosophy, things (*bintu*) are forces or 'beings', although not endowed with reason and life. When a traditional African maintains that he is becoming stronger, he does not refer in the first instance to his physical nature but to his nature, his personality, his status;[87] in the same way Kimbangu's messianic features gradually increased. Man's being thus increases, and what he has in a material sense is part of his being, part of himself. This naturally leads to a misunderstanding of the Biblical concept of eternal life, and of suffering and mortification with Christ. The idea of eternal life in heaven, and 'there and then', is unacceptable in the face of the 'here and now'. It is for this very reason that Western culture, with its material benefits, has made a greater impression than Christianity. This emphasis on vital force deeply affects the true understanding of the meaning of the death of Christ on the Cross.[88] The call to new life means a call to new vital force, with the result that a true theology of the Cross is unacceptable. Freedom means the unhindered possibility to increase your vital force. If God is 'slow' in this, the hunger for vital force, for revelation, leads to the Black Messiah who will fulfil these demands and understand them better. It is most difficult in such a situation to associate God's love with sickness, poverty and suffering.[89] Shropshire says that 'he has a desire to possess, and be *en rapport* with this abundant life and, indeed, much of his time is given to a cult of health, for he fears famine, plague, pestilence, death and sickness'.[90] Time and again the healing aspect is specially emphasised, in order to prove the truth of the Gospel message. The consequence of salvation is freedom from these things. The Gospel itself is used as a magic agent in procuring this freedom (even though it is not even read in some movements, it is there on the table!). Magic means getting control over another, and in this way upholding or strengthening your vital force.[91] In this way it is possible to get hold of the authority of Jesus, and to monopolise it. Even Christ can be manipulated, and this is self-evident and right.[92]

All the questions about death, sickness, poverty and social conditions indicate how seriously the message is taken in all its aspects. The old religion had to do with the whole life, not just the soul; with the supernatural divine presence in all spheres of life through the presence of the ancestors. The Greek dichotomy between body and soul means nothing to the African. The same is the case with the natural and supernatural because to Africans 'the supernatural is natural; it is strange and unaccountable, but there is no element of otherness about it, for it belongs with everything else to the here and now'.[93] These questions are thus desperately important in Africa. Because the supernatural belongs to the 'here and now', it is difficult to understand the tension between the present and the 'not yet'. Promise, in the traditional sense, thus means immediate action.[94] Suspicion then arises that what is most vital in Christianity is withheld.[95] The Roman Catholic fathers are accused of having kept back something of vital importance in the message.[96] When government officials are seeking wanted men, the following song is sung:

> *Ah, it is only to accuse us. We shall wait.*
> *Ah, it is only to bind us. We shall wait.*
> *Amen, Halleluja! We wait for the promise*
> *that the Father has given.*[97]

This waiting has already an element of fulfilment in it.

The *African Kingdom* has become uppermost in the minds of the followers of Kimbangu. They would like tangible evidence of the future through signs. These could be produced by external means, for example, by the singing of Ngunza songs 'with power and gladness'. Their expectations might not be realised after they exhausted themselves in singing, and they would be accused of having sung too lazily.[98] Singing in the traditional religion not only leads to contact with the supernatural forces, but also influences them. The traditional African acts his religion; what he *does* is important – a sign of the magical approach in which man through his deeds influences the supernatural forces. The African drama has magic power. The liturgy in this religion enacts what must happen afterwards, or at the same time, because of the liturgical drama. There is no differentiation between content and form.[99] Expectation in that religion is much more realistic, and it is much more concerned with the immediate than is the case in empirical Christianity.

The old myths are now partly historicised through the prophet or messiah or a culture hero, who will return as messiah and will create a terrestrial paradise. The coming of Jesus Christ is interpreted as the coming of those heroes and vice versa. In some cases the Black Christ is the outcome of a hunger for revelation in the face of disturbances of old securities. They have visions about Jesus Christ and about their heroes in whom they see their own glory reflected so that not only the old gets a new meaning but also the new. The result is a new religion. In some instances the name of Jesus Christ is pushed completely into the background, and those of the culture heroes take full precedence.[100] Here the impersonal aspects of Christianity as they experience it are made personal by accepting and adhering to their old *oikos* (religious and cultural home) in which they feel at home; this is especially the case in a society with so strong a sense of personal relationships. Jesus Christ and the culture heroes become part of their world view, but at the same time they give the old world view a new dynamism. Shembe, for example, refers continuously in his hymns to the Zulu culture heroes. The mythological world view has been confronted with the functional world view, which has drawn them into the process of history with a sense of destiny. Those with extreme vital force now control things to the advancement of the group; and in their own peculiar way they work out the destiny of the group. This is made available to their followers, and a specific aim is put before them. At a certain stage, some of the movements consider the Whites to be the main obstacles in attaining this goal, which they think is witheld from

90

them. The mixture of the old and the new, by people who stand in the old and select from the new, leads to syncretism pure and simple.[101] Syncretism is basic to all naturalistic religions and becomes a problem when a prophetic religion like Christianity which is 'based on the assumption of God's initiative in the act of self-disclosure, and naturalistic-cosmic (or naturalistic-monistic) religions meet each other'.[102] In such a case Christianity is severely criticised for its intransigence. In the movements we have discussed, it was relatively easy to work out a *syncretistic third* or *post-Christian religion* (a religion neither Christian nor traditional), because of the leaders being influenced by Christianity but also steeped in the traditional religion. Here the chiliastic-messianic element becomes the major emphasis covered in magic nativism, and it comes with great vitality and expectation. On this issue it stands opposed to the teaching of Scripture.[103]

The prophet comes now in the place of the Great Chief or Divine King. The Bible, as well as Jesus Christ, is pushed into the background. Shembe says, 'You, my people, were once told of a God who has neither arms nor legs, who cannot see, who has neither love nor pity. But Isaiah Shembe showed you a God who walks on feet and who heals with his hands, and who can be known by men, a God who loves and who has compassion'.[104] Sundkler explains this as a 'hunger for revelation', but it may also be added that here is a hunger for true understanding of their deepest needs and aspirations which can only be provided by their own kind, and thus people are admonished that 'when dancing before Jehovah they must not wear European clothes, but should as true Zulus appear in *ibeshu* and *isidwaba*'.[105] In the Church of the Nazarites of Shembe, the Black Christ is also identified with the pronounced pre-Christian name for God *uMvelingqangi*, which is not used in the Zulu Bible translations.[106] The cult of *Nzambi ya Minda*, in the Congo, centres round the figure of André Matswa, and the figure of Christ is replaced by his. Prayers are directed to him: '*Tata Matswa Kuula Kongo*' (Father Matswa, deliver the Congo).[107] This is closely related to the African social system, where the chief or king is the mediator. Here the personality of the 'prophet' comes vividly on the scene and becomes the focal point in the tense encounter of these chiliastic-messianic movements with the future. Prophets are at the same time the personification of their followers' idealistic expectations, as the chief is 'the sum and substance of the whole community'.[108]

The African, although he accepted the Christian teaching, which often emphasised the idea of the great God far above and beyond and a heavenly country which is 'somewhere else . . .' has not 'modified the belief that Nature, Man and the Unseen are inseparably involved in one another in a total community of which it might be said that all is here and all is now. . . . When things go well with him he knows he is at peace, and of a piece, with the scheme of things, and there can be no greater good than this.'[109] The privileges of the mission stations enticed many to become Christians but some Christians who found adverse circumstances in their path have left the mission. The opposite is also true in a Church which is not without its martyrs. Many however have a 'deep-seated tendency to equate material well-being with "a state of grace" '.[110]

The deep misunderstanding of the missionary message has been partly due (apart from the misunderstanding of the missionary's preaching) to the magic of education. School children regarded 'the White man's books as a kind of secret *minkisi*', and what is associated with the school has been considered as being 'introducing rites of the European religion',[111] which means receiving the vital force of the Whites. Mission and school went hand in hand in Africa, and all the mistakes made in education had been made by missions, because they were the first and only bringers of education. Growing frustration led many to believe that the real Bible was hidden by them from the Blacks.[112] This suspicion was also evident with regard to the Holy Communion.[113] In this complicated situation the revelation of old securities often led to the rejection of the White Christ, who is too distantly removed from their world view and aspirations. His teaching, as put forward by the missionaries, could not be accepted in a society in which vital force is the main concern and not suffering which is a sign of weakness. Against this background of frustration, these prophets come forward with their own testimony about their election. Shembe's was based on these 'vision-inspired declarations by media and the need of the masses to worship and to believe in a man of Miracles'.[114] Prophetism becomes under these circumstances messianic. The prophet is now not only a Moses, he is also 'Christ'. The 'White' Christ, in their minds, has been the personification of the needs of the Whites; now the Black Christ has become the same for the Blacks as in the case of Kimbangu.[115] Few references in the hymn-book of Shembe are related to *Jesu Krestu*; the same is true of the Kimbangu adherents' songs. In the latter, one finds only sporadic reference to Jesus – Christ is not mentioned. Shembe, who died and was resurrected, is now God in the Zulu sense, the mediator and saviour, and so is Kimbangu. Divine presence through the ancestor spirits is most vital in traditional African religion, which has been affected negatively as a result of the preaching of the missionaries, whose God remained for many obscure, uncertain and uninterested.

92

These prophets know the future. Just as the eldest of the group, the chief or king, was by divine law the sustaining link of life, binding ancestors and their descendants,[116] and was the course of zestful living, so the prophet now holds in his hands the future, of which he is the bearer. These prophets are not only the founders of a new religion but are charismatic leaders, the *mediators* between God and His people, who have a *concrete historical task* in the time of crisis, as had Moses. They are the messengers who proclaim God's will for political, social and cultic life. As we find, in the initial stages of Israel's religion, the charisma, a person specially endowed,[117] so we find these figures in the prophetic movements. Furthermore, the idea of the existence of a nation rooted in the 'will' of God is here also uppermost. The crisis which the prophets create, as a result of their strong personalities and influence, is intensified by them. In the syncretistic movements, the old forms the basis on which the new is being built, indeed the old gets a new dynamic inspiration from the new. In the Orthodox movements, like that of William Wade Harris, the old is strongly rejected, but polygamy is retained on the basis of the Old Testament. There has been no opportunity for messianising the persons of William Harris and Alice Lenshina because of their rejection of the old. Isaiah Shembe has led his people to their ancestry in a unique way, and even reintroduced the rite of circumcision. In the African context a messiah will preserve the old. (Harris was messianised after his death by some of his followers.) Harris and Lenshina have been careful not to take the place of Christ, although both spoke very little about him. Thus in both, the violent rejection of the old has been the main reason for the lack of messianic features being built into their persons by their followers.

Shembe's accommodation with the old led to a different approach. As soon as Shembe takes the place of messiah with the old context, his position has changed from one within Christianity to that of the prophet of a new religion.[118] He stands in the centre of the present, firmly rooted in reality and thus not a revolutionary messiah.[119] With Shembe I, realised eschatology became central. This is not the case with Simon Kimbangu. Here the future is much more in the centre.

Dreams and visions are the experience of these prophets.[120] Through them they are called to be God's representative on earth. Through dreams they receive the Spirit, in the same way as ancestors visit through dreams. Practical proof for the receiving of the 'spirit' was 'symptoms of ecstasy and the shaking of the body', which in the case of Kimbangu was not only violent but reminiscent of 'the heathen *banganga* (diviners).[121] (At his first healing, he was sub-

93

jected to violent convulsions.) To begin with he concentrated on preaching, but gradually healing became the most important activity of the movement.[122] Singing accompanied his work and many experienced ecstatic convulsions. In the beginning he refused to secede from the missionaries, and Protestant missionaries in general did not oppose him.[123] The most important factor in the success of Kimbangu was the 'implicit faith of the people in the prophet's ability to heal the sick', which emptied hospitals and dispensaries.[124] All kinds of rumours about his work and miracles were spread, and thousands went to *Nkamba* to be healed, even corpses were carride there. [125] As a result of missionary and government reaction, Kimbangu's ideological position was strengthened, and Africans maintained that they had 'found the God of the Blacks'.[126] Mass movements are fertile soil for exalted futuristic expectations,[127] as is obvious in this case. Kimbangu was arrested at Nkamba, because of the fears of the colonial administration, and all those who were subsequently imprisoned or transported were considered martyrs. They were so considered because of their belief in the Bible. According to them missionary interference had been the main reason for their arrest. Kimbangu voluntarily submitted to arrest (September 14, 1921) and tried to imitate Jesus' capture by having a long prayer and giving his soul into the hands of God.[128] Gilis, in his controversial book, states that Kimbangu's sacrifice, in order to bring Christianity into an African setting, was worth while.[129] He became now the symbol of opposition to the mission and Government.[130] Kimbangu's death sentence was commuted to life imprisonment, after which he was imprisoned in Elizabethville, Katanga (November 1921), where he died as late as October 10, 1951.[131] William Harris, although also accused of political activity, nevertheless preached submission to secular authority. When the futuristic, millenarian aspects of the doctrine and their implications were to the fore, this produced a clash, because it envisaged an African kingdom against the intentions of European imperialism. In the Congo as elsewhere, the economic and political issues played a significant role in the later development of prophetism.[132] This has been especially the case in South Africa.[133]

Kimbangu, having started as a Christian revivalist, later preached strongly against the Whites, that the white man would be wiped out by fire from heaven. Nonqause had already predicted in 1856 that the sky would fall down on the white man and crush him, but here was a clash from the beginning between the Xhosas (South Africa) and the Whites intruding into their territory. Elijah Masinde's sect rejected European medicines and maternity homes for African women, just as a Kikuyu sect *Watu Wa Mngu* (People of God) burn foreign articles as being ritually unclean.[134] Even Kimbangu followers maintained, like Enoch in South Africa, that the bullets of European rifles would become like water. Here one sees how official repression 'has strengthened the nationalistic aspects of the prophet movements'.[135] Deportation and imprisonment for life were the lot of many during the Colonial era, some even being executed, as has already been said. André Matswa died at Mayama, and the road to Mayama was regarded as his way to the Cross and Mayama as his Calvary.[136] Martyrdom and resurrection are now closely associated. The messiah here carries an ideological cross,[137] not a cross of redemption from sin, but redemption from the human powers of oppression, and he has risen again, eventually to return in power and majesty for the sake of retribution upon the Whites and their Black troops. After such pressures, the prophetic movement is often changed into a messianic movement. The figure of Christ was gradually replaced by that of André Matswa. Many await the second coming of Matswa whom they call 'Jesus Matswa', and in Brazzaville his name even appeared on ballot papers after his death.[138] So strong was the notion of the return of Matswa and Kimbangu, that the *parousia* of Jesus was pushed into the background completely.[139]

Kimbangu has received the position of the priest king or great chief, and, like Shembe, he enjoys absolute power in heaven and earth.[140] Shembe has been called in his mother's womb,[141] and took the place of the diviner-king filled with the spirit. Kimbangu has been considered to be a *ngunza*.[142] He is a messiah, to be equated with the hero-prophets, a semi-eschatological figure.[143] By 1930 a considerable change could be detected in the movement, with its hostility to the foreigner, its subsequent nationalistic and revolutionary aims, with the Bible and Christ becoming less significant and the doctrine of the Holy Spirit more popular.[144] This development is discussed later. To the Africans, Kimbangu was now the 'God of the Blacks',[145] the messiah who would 'deliver the Black race',[146] and, in Ngunza-Khaki congregations, Matswa was thought to be the one chosen by God to liberate the Congo.[147] There were other prophets with messianic features, like Sebuloni Nsonde and Ta Lukaya,[148] but Kimbangu and Matswa took precedence. With the appearance of Simon Kimbangu will coincide the establishment of the kingdom, and all God's promises will be consummated in and through Kimbangu, who will occupy the ancient throne of the Congo.[149] The creed of the Ngunza-Khaki congregation in Pointe Noire, briefly referred to above and probably still in use, gives an indication of the expectations focused upon Kimbangu. Among

95

other things it states the following: 'He is the one in whom lives the Lord God, the gracious father of the Blacks . . . [he] is the priest that the Lord God has exalted to be an eternal priest, like the priesthood of Melchizedek. He is the priest of the Black race . . . he is the cup with the oil of blessing for the black race . . . he is the ruler's rod of the Blacks . . . the mighty sword of government that the Lord has given to the Black race . . . he is the banner of dominion for the Black race . . . the shining lamp that the Lord has given to the Black race . . . the prepared way upon which the Black race may enter heaven . . . the river with the living water for the Black race. . . . He has become the stair on which they reach the heaven of their God. . . . *Mfumu* Simon Kimbangu is the open door that the Lord God has opened among the Black race that they may enter by it. It is the city of the new Jerusalem, the Jerusalem of the Blacks and God's very holiest city. He is the door through which they enter the heaven of their God.'[150]

During the age of the enlightenment, ethics centred round happiness, utility, virtue and reward, which is no more or less than egoism. In these movements it is also material well-being – a utopia of Africanism – that provides the essence of a chiliastic-messianic expectation. As far as the future is concerned, Christ has no meaning.[151] As the Saviour of the Whites he is superfluous. He has been tested and found wanting; he is of another lineage. All hopes are now concentrated on their own Saviours, whether they be Shembe, Matswa, Kimbangu or Lekganyane. The members of the Ngunzist movements pray, 'In the name of the Father and of André Matswa and of Simon Kimbangu'.[152]

In this worship of the new messiahs there is longing for a realised future. The entry of the Salvation Army into the Congo in 1935 'caused a great sensation and aroused considerable unrest among the Africans'.[153] The singing, the music of the drums, the uniforms, 'the free and cheerful proclamation of grace and forgiveness for every sin', this appealed to the African people, and they thought the Millennium had begun. The Ngunzists, who had gone underground during the hostilities between the movement and the Government, now joined the Salvation Army. Their hope that Simon Kimbangu, who was for many years in exile in the Upper Congo, would return by supernatural means, was now fulfilled. The Salvation army *is Simon Kimbangu himself*, who transformed himself into a white person and thus acquired a white man's power; now he cannot be imprisoned again. (An old Congo myth holds that their heroes will return one day as Whites.) This took hold of the African imagination, and people thought that Ngunza's God had arrived. Teachers who had lost their posts because of their belief in Ngunzism now joined the Salvation Army, the 'symbolic letter S on the officers' collars obviously signifying Simon, Simon Kimbangu, whom God had so miraculously restored to them'.[154] It was now believed that the Army had the magical power of exorcising evil spirits and *bandoki* (witchcraft), and thousands came to its meetings in Brazzaville. Eventually, a nativistic movement came into existence, the independent, Ngunzistic Salvation Army, under Simon Mpadi.[155] If the rites of this Salvation Army were observed, it was possible to become immune to witchcraft and gain health and happiness.

The longing for a realised future led these people to believe that the return of Kimbangu had been realised. When this failed, the old practices which stood in the way of the future, witchcraft and witch-doctors, were considered to be checked within the movement. The recovery which takes place after expectations have not materialised, as was the case with Enoch Mgijima, is always interesting. This snatching of the future remains, in spite of disappointments, because for the African, who connects the natural with the supernatural, the eschatological outlook in which there is still a future is superior to the orthodox concept of that future with its emphasis on the 'there and then'. In all their visions this snatching of the future is apparent.[157] There is no idea of the tension between the present and the 'not yet'; the Christian hope plays no part, here is the old natural man, freed from the cyclic concept of his religion, to which he was so inexorably bound; but he has not found his feet in the new freedom. He has no central point on which these expectations are built. Furthermore, in this process of snatching the future, force plays a great role with some movements. Margull indicates how destruction took place in the Congo in an ecstatic state with drums beating, 'The Whites are fleeing, the Whites are fleeing. . . .'[158] Ecstasy due to a similar cause was obvious during the independence day of the Somali Republic (July 1, 1960) in the capital, Mogadishu.[159]

During the early days of Kimbangu, the old beliefs received a hard blow. The detection of fetishes played a great part, and *banganga* or supernatural powers were rejected. Idols and bags used in witchcraft were destroyed, and even aged priests destroyed their collections.[160] The prophet movement of Simon Kimbangu looked in the beginning like a mass movement towards Christianity, and like a religious revival. The same attitude to these aspects of the African religion occurred with Lenshina of the Lumpa Church. Crowds brought their magical objects, including rosaries and crucifixes.[161] Sundkler says, 'It is against different forms of magic that the Zionist prophet, as a diviner, directs his attention'.[162] Witchcraft is one of

97

the main objects of attack, as it affects health and results in death, aspects which are of special concern in the prophetic movements. Sorcery is considered to be 'the most degraded crime, the most cynical prostitution of the sacred laws of nature',[163] here man is the prisoner of his natural surroundings and is under constant threat of death. One of the greatest fears in African society is that of being bewitched. Old physical instruments are used to perform witchcraft; the 'medicine' is secretly planted at a place where the victim will make contact, such as his house or garden, and he has to learn in some indirect way that he is bewitched. This sets off a psychological reaction and the physical instruments used in the process of bewitching have to be discovered and destroyed. Different kinds of protective medicines are used.

In the early years of the missions, the missionaries and those under their influence, were often accused of having learned to read and write, skills otherwise unattainable through the aid of witchcraft. People were even accused of hiding their witchcraft in Christianity.[164] This deeply embedded belief is most difficult to overcome. It still signifies for the African the misery of the past. Putting away witchcraft means the end of the Old; the end of sickness and death, and freedom from total destruction. The missionaries are expected in their preaching to counteract it, but when they fail the prophets take their place and their eschatological promises are more effective than the ways of orthodoxy. Debrunner says, 'Not only do the sects offer protection and healing, they are also thought of as a powerful agency to find out witches and evil spirits and to exorcise them. Witches are said to feel themselves urged to go to the prophets and there to confess their evil doings, and to ask for deliverance from the spirit possessing them.'[165] Economic distress and political and social disturbances are fertile soil for witchcraft.[166] Such witchcraft is directed not against the Whites in the first instance, but against forces in their own midst. Witchcraft signalises both the desire to be free from the past, and the need for security in the future. However, just as witchcraft is psychologically potent, so is the futuristic outlook, which inculcates a vision of a new world into those whom it emancipates from the world of blackmail. Social and economic tension have led to the increase of witchcraft in the urban areas of Africa; but the people of Simon Kimbangu, Shembe, Lekganyane, Matswa and others, maintain that they have the power to overcome it. These 'Christs' can give prosperity, life and health, and have the power of resurrection of the dead, and of overcoming evil spirits. The people's battle was against life destruction, and therefore for the future.[167]

If all fetishes are destroyed, this struggle can be victorious. This is the reason for Lenshina's and Kimbangu's success in bringing about the destruction of the life-destroying objects of witchcraft. In the Salvation Army also the ceremony of clasping the hand of a Salvation Army officer was performed in order that a sign from heaven should proclaim one's guilt or innocence of witchcraft; later the practice of the Salvation Army rites made one immune to witchcraft. Individual handshaking soon became impractical, so then purification could be obtained 'by touching the officer's clothes, or the red cord that encircled the platform, or even by contriving to place oneself beneath the red flag when it was waved over the heads of the repentant sinners, or simply by getting inside the Army building.'[168] Those who observed the Army rites, which guaranteed them eternal bliss, were regarded as holy.[169] Only by being absolutely free from the past can the new 'arrive'; so in initiation, the old is burned and the initiates receive everything new.[170] They reach a completely new status with new possibilities, and 'the light of tribal revelation bursts upon the initiate out of the shadow of fear, privation and bodily pain'.[171] The destruction of the economic system in different chiliastic-messianic movements belongs in the same line of thinking – only by destruction of the old can the new be realised. In this snatching for the future the Whites take the place of the Anti-Christ, the greatest obstacle to the African messianic kingdom. This had already started with the Xhosa prophets, discussed above, and continued in the syncretistic nativistic movements. The future means freedom from all opposition and an eventual Utopia. The messianic impact of communism is of the same order. Asia and Africa cannot respond to 'the promise of a society in which all imperialistic exploitation will be a thing of the past, and in which humiliating discrimination, from which the coloured races suffer, will be done away'.[172]

As a result of the heavy sentences passed on Kimbangu and other leaders of Ngunzism, 'nascent anti-White tendencies blossomed and throve'.[173] After the sentences were pronounced, a chief with twenty followers came to the Government post at Thysville (Congo) and, with Bible in hand, they proceeded to sing 'the new battle-hymn against the Whites'.[174] Thereafter Ngunzists were forbidden by their leaders to visit White mission or trading stations, or to have any contact with them whatever. They had to wear *mbadi*, an African gown, and children were sent to African-governed schools. It was compulsory for leaders, though not for ordinary members, to isolate themselves from Europeans.[175] Mission stations were burned time and again – one got rid of the old by destroying it.

The old witch hunt has been directed against the Whites. A certain Yoane Mvubi (meaning 'John the Baptist') writes, evidently on behalf of Simon Kimbangu, to all 'the pure' in *nsi a Yelusalemi* (tract of Jerusalem), exhorting his people to prepare for the war of the great kings and heroes, and declaring that they should have no dealings with Catholics, Protestants or Government people. The kingdom of the Whites will be overthrown and this will 'be preceded by signs of blood and rain'.[176] Simon Kimbangu is already approaching. This is the Holy War, in which the Whites will be judged because they have loved money and worldly fame instead of serving Jesus Christ. The apostles of Christ will then be released and return to their country in ships, and the meeting of the Covenanters will take place in Kinshasa.[177] They considered the exegisis of Scripture by the Whites as having been done in their own favour – a new régime is foreseen in which the truths of Scripture will be applicable only to the Blacks. The Government and the missions adhered to the old order and the missions, through their interpretation of Scripture, prolonged White superiority and paternalism, and thus were a hindrance to the future Utopia. They not only stand in the way of the future of the oppressed; they act against God's will and prevent the execution of His plans.

The end of White rule is seen in apocalyptic terms. It was so in the cases of the Xhosas mentioned above, of Enoch Mgijima, and with Mau Mau, and the same is discernible in the messianic movements of the Congo. Just as Mgijima considered Ntabelanga to be the Chosen Place, the holy place of the Chosen, and was waiting there on the command of Jehovah,[178] so Yoane Mvubi saw the faithful, the Covenanters, gathering at Kinshasa after the Holy War.[179] In the Ngunzist movement, the Second Coming of Christ was given prominence. Jesus Christ was to have returned to earth, at Kingoyi; the date was set for October 15, 1934, and work stopped for two to three weeks.[180] The influence of Adventism is apparent in the fixing of dates, which always indicates lack of historical sense. They desired a realised revelation, a Utopia, that could be seen and experienced. Basically this is a revolutionary approach, accompanied in most cases by blind fanaticism. Knox says about the philosophy of enthusiasm that 'more generally characteristic of ultra-supernaturalism is a distrust of our human thought-processes. In matters of abstract theology, the discipline of the intellect is replaced by a blind act of faith. In matters of practical deliberation, some sentiment of inner conviction, or some external 'sign' indicative of the Divine will, claims priority over all considerations of common prudence'.[181] It was thus with the

Israelites of Mgijima, who accepted with stoicism the outcome of the 'battle', after which he carried on as leader of the 'Church of God and Saints of Christ'.[182] The people at Kinkenge went 'disconsolately' back to their villages, but there were no after-effects.[183] They went out to meet Jesus Christ for the first time in July 1921, and in September they expected Nzombo, a catechist and an ecstatic, to return 'in the clouds' with great power.[184] Great crowds gathered on September 6 in Haku, even including teachers, to meet the prophet. When he failed to materialise, life carried on and a great spiritual awakening was experienced.[185]

The complicated ontological order can so easily be upset. So many factors influence this order that anything is accepted as an excuse except a miscalculation; for example, either a ritual prohibition has been broken, or witchcraft has been applied. The old plays here a specific role in the explanation of the delay, but the expectation of and faith in the new life have been so deeply embedded in the minds of those freed from the cyclic limitations and its way of thinking, that nothing can shatter them. Limitation in historical knowledge and perspective has been characteristic of all movements with an Adventist strain. The Adventist expectations of 1843 in England, based on the visions of William Miller, a Baptist, were put forward 'without historical knowledge or critical acumen'.[186] Adventists believe that not only will man bring forth his own redemption, but he can also work out the time when this will happen – he has special contact with those who are 'his' and from whom he receives special revelations. This leads to direct confrontation with the existing order, as with the Anabaptists, who confronted the power of secular government. They were the shock troops of the Reformation, but were not interested in the Calvinistic and Lutheran theology of grace, because for them self-assertion, based on anthropocentrism, had taken precedence. The authority and Lordship of Jesus, and what He gives, is not accepted in the nativistic movements – only what man can attain. This is seen in the creed of Kimbangu, used at Pointe-Noire,[187] and these were the expectations of their followers. They are 'Fathers', 'Gods', the sources of all zestful living.

A *henotheism* (tribal god) now develops. God is a god of the Blacks, their own god whom they *possess* and who possesses them, who is the personification of all their needs. They now occupy the heavens, and the future is in their hands. The magically oriented person uses his god as he uses objects to influence the supernatural. This new religion emphasises on the one hand man's own efforts, and on the other their god's assistance. Jesus Christ is now considered to be a prophet for His time, a benefactor, a forerunner, whose work was really limited to His time and for His people. As myth is reproduced in ritual, so the nativist reproduces the Bible story in his own magico-religious context, in which his own prophetic or messianic figure is central. In the post-Christian religion, magic enters with the idea of man's ability to overcome his difficulties by performing certain acts. What they do is more effective than what takes place in the missions. 'In contradistinction to the mission baptism, which is only a John the Baptist affair, the baptism of the Bagunza is a baptism of the Holy Spirit.'[188] In this new religion the 'Spirit' takes Christ's position. The old receives a new vitality, and Christianity is one of the main reasons for the resurgence of the old, even in Asia. 'Christian missions enable non-Christian faiths to re-vivify and re-vitalise themselves. . . .'[189] The resurgence of the old in a new form is a world phenomenon. The basis remains the same. The Cross is not scripturally understood; sin is not seen as guilt, and Christianity itself is valued as a kind of social improvement plan. In times of stress and strain and of birth, marriage and death, many Christians revert to old practices where the dynamism of magic is more effective.

The old has the commanding position in the Prophetic movements where the hero prophet, the mediator, has become the personification of the new dynamic outlook. The prophet or messiah is not only a religious personality but also a magical one, who creates a world in which his will reigns supreme; here is the will for power. He struggles with the forces 'outside', such as spirits and gods, but he also takes these forces within his circle in order to control them. Magic is reaction, an effort to make of the given world *my world*. It is therefore always a question, for the traditional African, of 'Who is the strongest?' Because the New Testament concepts of faith and hope, faith as pointing above man and hope as promise – are not understood, a syncretistic process is put into action with the Old Testament in a significant role. The Old Testament legalism and moralism have magical effects, and immunity to the message of Jesus Christ, especially the Cross, is the consequence. Freytag gives four elements which are typical of a post-Christian religion: (i) human self-assertion, by which the group becomes absolute; (ii) a this-worldly kingdom, in which God recedes into the background; (iii) this post-Christian religion adapts and enriches itself, and (iv) it becomes immune to the Christian message. To be after and beyond Christ is tantamount to being against Him without a consciousness of superiority.[190] Nobody is immune to Christianity but one can build up an inner resistance against its real message. The dynamic of

Christianity, however, has been the main reason for revitalising the old, and the power of anthropocentrism is used against empirical Christianity. It is not faith that has been built up in this process, but resistance to faith. What matters is progress, which is taken from the new and transferred to the old, and this establishes a syncretistic entity in which secular eschatology receives the main emphasis.

The missionaries reacted against the old without interpreting it, and so left a vacuum. Furthermore, their pietistic concentration on souls left all the other spheres in the air. The vacuum left has been filled by the people themselves, and they go time and again to the old fountain to have it filled. They fill it with what they believe to be basic, with the result that they revert to the primary basis of the old.[191] So now Jesus Christ is excluded as the central figure of African futuristic expectations, and the new representative, the hero prophet or the political figure, the bringer of 'salvation', comes to the centre. In animism, there has been no centralised creed, which made the African religion an easy object of missionary endeavour. In this new religion, however, such a central focal point has been established in the creed, that is in their saviour or messiah. The dynamic Western world view forms the background of this development. In the process of cultural change and adaptation to new social, political and economic circumstances, and to new technological and scientific developments new messianic movements have come forward each with its own programme of salvation. These nativistic movements gave a sense of stability in the cities or rural areas wherever the socio-economic structure is being broken up. The old, which included also the political, is now the actualising principle. There is no room here for 'mere' hoping; the prophets themselves are their promises personified. But it is necessary to remember that Christ was also asked to be a political messiah, to reveal Himself to the world (John vii. 3, 4) but when he indicated his true mission the world left Him.

Only in this syncretistic way can they now understand the Gospel, which means *freedom to self-assertion,* and more vital force to attain one's own ends and the ends of one's community. Here is no idea of losing oneself for Christ's sake. It is in a sense a selfish morality, and a type of expectation which is non-Christian. The world is ruled through and through by the ancestors, and God is naturally there. In the traditional religion He was removed far away, but with Christianity He came into the orbit of man's activities, and can be used.[192] There is thus no problem of faith. The Christian message on the other hand, teaches that no man can add anything to the all-sufficient work of Christ. It is God who acts.

To the Christian, God cannot be identified with either man or world. For the natural man, however, these are the main concepts, and in the Scriptures it is God who in Christ Jesus approaches mankind. The world view of the traditional African mind is here of the utmost importance in explaining this approach; in this view, the world is characterised by unity and coherence, i.e. naturalistic monism.[193] The fact that the prophet receives precedence over God is mainly due to the role of the mediator in the African society, and to the fact that, in their concept, the Creator is regarded as 'active' primarily in the cosmic sphere, in the rain and the thunder, but never influencing their lives. They believe that God lives, but what they believe about Him is so radically different from the Christian point of view, that it cannot be maintained that the Christian concept of God is a development of what the traditional African believes.[194]

For the traditional mind, no sharply defined aspects exist by themselves; wish and reality, knowledge and belief, thought and imagination, the realms of secular and religious life are interwoven and fundamentally one.[195] There is no place here for the Biblical concept of hope. Abraham persisted in hope, believing contrary to all human hopes (Rom. iv. 18). The promises of blessing were lodged in Abraham, but all the conditions of this blessing were only fulfilled in Christ, in whose resurrection Christian hope is grounded (1 Pet. i. 3; see also Rom. v. 1–5). In Hebrews the author speaks of hope as the anchor of the soul, (vi. 18 f.) and of 'hope unto the end' (iii. 6, vi. 11; cf. x. 23). Peter exhorts Christians to be ready with a *apologia* for their hope (iii. 15), and the author of John follows the New Testament concept of hope as referring to the *parousia*. Richardson says that 'the New Testament conception of hope has nothing at all to do with any this-worldly prospects; it is as far removed as possible from any notion of an earthly Utopia or any secular optimism. It is through and through eschatological, always bearing reference to the return of the Lord Jesus at the end of the age.'[196] *Future* thus signifies God coming to man – to create, elect, save and recreate.[196] The natural man works out his own future into which he enters, and establishes his own kingdom, over which he himself rules.[198] Calvin has sufficiently indicated how the natural man also has a concept of God, but has lost the true sense of Him and made idols of Him which he worships.[199] This is best described in Romans (i. 18–32) where Paul shows how God is taken up in the empirical reality and is further misunderstood as 'power'. Paul says that the heathen has no hope (cf. Ephesians ii. 12).[200] The emphasis on immediate results leads to the accusation that the mission has not the Holy Spirit, that one cannot receive vital force there, that its Baptism and Holy Communion are not effective.

104

Only when man understands the future as God coming to him does the miracle of faith occur. The words 'faith' and 'belief' denote the criterion of right relationship with God. In the Old Testament it means to hold on to something with firmness, and in relation to God it implies personal conviction and confident reliance. In Paul and John 'faith' refers to the acts of Jesus and 'to believe in the technical Christian sense, is to be related to God in trust and self-abnegation, via those historical events'.[201] Self-abnegation is here of the essence; faith has no expectations, but only hopes.[202] Faith is to live with Christ the Crucified and Resurrected One. To live in hope is to live with Christ in His suffering and resurrection, and here the future of man plays no part. [203] The God of hope is at the centre (Rom. xv. 13). The congregation is called upon to stand in the world, to be concretely involved, keeping before it this eternal hope. The missionary motives of the nineteenth and twentieth centuries have so often centred around the idea of Western civilisation and progress. Competition between missions also created a worldly impression. Implicit in the Western idea of a *corpus Christianum* was a great effort to secularise Christianity – to have a Kingdom on earth; this had far-reaching effects on missionary activities. Margull says the Mission should never preach expectations, but rather present itself as an act of hope, coming in and from hope.[204] The secularised form of Biblical hope is the expectation of an earthly kingdom, which observes the Biblical message. Nevertheless, it is imperative that the Church should always let its prophetic voice be heard in all spheres of human life, as it is called upon to let the principles of Scripture come to fruition in man's daily life. The Church as an organism should be in the world, although not of it. This rejects any 'social Gospel' emphasis, in spite of the necessity of the Church's concern in social issues. Man's expectations have to be freed from this world, because his future is given to him from the Cross of Christ alone. But the Cross stands in the world, not in the Church;[205] this world is blessed through the Cross, and through everyone who takes it up. The aim is the realisation of all things in Christ, and not that all the things of 'here and now' have no importance (cf. Matth. vi. 33, 34). The twentieth century is characterised by the rediscovery of the central place of eschatology in the Biblical message. Famous are the words of Barth that 'Christianity which has not totally and fully and completely to do with eschatology has totally, fully and completely nothing to do with Christ'.[206] Bultmann has given to it an existential meaning. Whatever our view on eschatology, it is a fact that the Christians are 'in Christ' responsible for the world. In Christ, God acted for man, and the Holy Spirit can witness for none but Christ;

as there is no other name in heaven or on earth by which man could be saved. Biblical preaching always means preaching God's judgment on the self-assertion of man, who wants to be like God. This is the deepest motive of all his expectations. The key emphasis of Jesus, however, was on discipleship, a life fully lived in the existential situation, but lived as foreigners and sojourners.

REFERENCES

1. Sundkler, *Bantu Prophets*, 53–55.
2. Cf. 1961 edition, 302. H. W. Turner, strangely enough, states that the syncretistic element and messianic outlook in African independents 'have been much exaggerated', cf. 'Pagan Features in West African Independent Churches', *Practical Anthropology*, July–Aug. 1965, 151.
3. Cf. V. E. W. Hayward, *African Independent Church Movements*, Edinburgh House Press, 1963, 13.
4. See also the outstanding classification of A. F. C. Wallace, 'Revitalisation Movements', *American Anthropologist*, Vol. 58, 1965, 265 ff. R. Linton, 'Nativistic Movements', *American Anthropologist*, Vol. 45, 1943, 230. G. Guariglia, *Prophetismus und Heilserwartungsbewegungen als Völkerkundliches und religionsgeschichtliches Problem*, Horn-Wien, Verlag Ferdinand Berger, 1959. J. W. Fernandez, 'African religious movements, types and dynamics', in *Modern African Studies*, Vol. 2, No. 4, Dec. 1964. K. Symmons-Symonolewicz looked only with political spectacles at these movements. Cf. 'Nationalist Movements' in *Comparative Studies in Society and Religion*, Vol. VII, No. 2, Jan. 1965, 221–30.
5. Cf. H. W. Turner, *African Independent Church*, see page xxn.
6. Cf. K. Schlosser, *Eingeborenenkirchen in Süd und Südwest Afrika*, 12–58. P. Mayer, *Townsmen and Tribesmen*, OUP, 1962², 195 ff. A. B. Dubb, *The African Church in the East Bank Location, East London*, M.A. Thesis, Rhodes University, Dec. 1961.
7. Monica Hunter, *Reaction to Conquest*, OUP, 1936, 148, 283 ff., 325 ff.
8. Cf. G. C. Oosthuizen, *'n Antropologies-Teologiese Ondersoek van die Nativistiese bewegings*. Referaat gelewer op algemene vergadering, S.A. Akademie, 1966, 378–98.
9. R. Linton, 'Nativistic Movements', *American Anthropologist*, Vol. 45, 1943, 230. The analysis of Linton and A. F. C. Wallace, op. cit., have been most helpful.
10. See article by G. C. Oosthuizen entitled 'Isaiah Shembe and the Zulu World View' in *Our Approach to the Independent Church Movement in South Africa*, Mimeographed Lectures given at the Lutheran Theological College, Mapumulo, Sept, 30 to Oct. 6, 1965.
11. Wallace, 231. How naïvely these movements are often discussed could be discerned in the article of Fernandez referred to above, in which he finds Sundkler's two types – Ethiopian and Zionist – 'Appropriate in typing the religious movements there' (i.e. South Africa with nearly three thousand of them) because of the South African history, says he, as this area has been cut off from 'new world revivalism and millenarianism' (Fernandez, 534). No country however has been more influenced by this on the African continent. These movements have been due to South Africa's racial policies, 'a dynamic factor in separatism', but in a footnote he adds 'On the other hand, South African separa-

106

tist Churches, though sensitive to their relationship to the larger society, strongly support apartheid and the *status quo*' (ibid.) (he refers to Sundkler's *Bantu Prophets*, 310–11).

12. Wallace, 267.

13. For J. W. Fernandez, referred to above, the formation of these movements in West Africa is due to an 'urge to create and preserve cultural autonomy'. Cf. 'The idea and symbol of the Saviour in a Gabon syncretistic cult', *International Review of Missions*, July 1964, 289.

14. B. Malinowski, *The Dynamics of Culture Change*, Yale University Press, 1949, 47.

15. M. Banton, 'African Prophets' in *Race*, London, V. 2, 1963.

16. Wallace, 267 ff.

17. A. Brunner, *Die Religion: eine philosphische Untersuchung auf geschichtlicher Grundlage*, Freiburg, 1956, 186.

18. Guariglia, 22 ff.

19. Ibid., 35.

20. Guariglia, 41 ff.

21. Schlosser, *Propheten*, 60.

22. Cf. Shepperson & Price, 224 ff., Hodgkin, 99 ff., Sundkler, *Prophets*, 53–59.

23. Oliver, 163 ff.

24. Shepperson & Price, 423.

25. Ibid., 423. The *Anabaptists*, a third movement during the time of Luther and Zwingli, gained influence between 1520 and 1530. The rebaptisers formed a separate community, especially amongst the underprivileged, and emphasised legalistic sanctification, held revolutionary ideas about the future (they were messianic-chiliastic), had their New Jerusalems, and were believed to be 'enemies of the social-political order'. (See W. Walker, *A History of the Christian Church*, T. T. Clark, 1959, revised ed., 326–32 (332); H. Berkhof, *Geschiedenis der Kerk*, Callenbach, 1941, 176–79; G. R. Elton (Ed.), *The New Cambridge Modern History*, Vol. II, CUP, 1958, 119–33. Luther experienced the Peasants' Revolt, which was due to economic and political tension, which also had religious repercussions because of clerical exactions. He confronted them in his 'Against the Heavenly Prophets' (1524). He had to confront Thomas Münzer, an Anabaptist, who was suspicious of authority, and who played to the gallery of 'the poor common man' and the 'elect friends of God'. Cf. Elton (Ed.) 87. Carlstadt, another leading figure in the movement, emphasized a puritan and Old Testament legalism. Münzer . . . 'in a state of endemic mental intoxication was issuing bloodcurdling orders of the day, signed "The Sword of the Lord and of Gideon" ' (ibid., 87).

26. Prof. Baëta has indicated in his book *Prophetism in Ghana* how sects generally start on the basis of the religious experience of the leader grouping around him and forming a community.

27. Cf. H. Witschi, 'Missionsdienst gestern und heute', EMM, Jan. 1952, 11, 12.

28. Warren, *Revival*, 42.

29. Sundkler, *Ministry*, 72.

30. Anderson, 43, 44.

31. It is interesting to see how the Pentecostal movements concentrate on the other worldly aspect. The Assemblies of God in Liberia faced the problem of losing their ministers who took secular vocations and adapted the curriculum: 'Therefore, in teaching Geography we concentrate on the map of the Holy Land; in History we teach the history of Liberia only, and the maths. course does not take them any further than helping them to count Church money' (Sundkler, *Ministry*, 236–37).

107

32. In a very penetrating article Prof. C. van Peursen, the well-known Dutch philosopher, discerns three stages in man's development: the mythical, onto-logical and functional stages. In the mythical stage, man is still overwhelmed by the forces of the social-mythical world, numinous forces are everywhere. In the ontological stage, man tries to free himself from magic; here are the first traces of history, although still against the background of nature; while the functional stage is our era of secularisation. C. van Peursen, 'Man and Reality – The history of human thought' in *The Student World*, Vol. lvi (1963) No. 1, 13–21.

33. Andersson, 225; cf. Guariglia, 37 ff.

34. Cf. Kamma, *De Messiaanse Koréribewegingen*.

35. F. C. Kamma, 'Messianic Movements in New Guinea', IRM, Apr. 1952, 158.

36. Andersson, 222. Cf. William D. Reyburn ('Africanisation and African Studies', *Practical Anthropology*, Vol. 9, No. 3, May-June 1962, 103) who indi-cates that 'the African concept of the visible demonstration of the blessings of power in a person's or community's life is parallel to that of ancient Semitic life. . . .' Cf. Gen. i. 27–28, Abraham is blessed because he has wealth and power. Gen. xxiv. 34–35.

37. Baëta, 131.

38. Warren, *Revival*, 39.

39. Ibid., 40.

40. D. Bonhoeffer, *Communio Sanctorum*, Kaiser, 1960.

41. Andersson, 234; Reyburn, 'Africanisation', 107–08, rightly concludes that 'Authoritarian religion with its legalistic emphasis throws the African back upon the authorities of his life, his kin group . . . he finds a certain security in this lineage dependence. . . .'

42. Sundkler, *Bantu Prophets*, 297.

43. Tempels, 42.

44. Cf. R. Bultmann, *History and Eschatology*, Edinburgh Univ. Press, 1957; R. Niebuhr, *Faith and History*, Nisbet & Co., 1949.

45. The traditional mentality in Africa considers what is natural to us as his-torical and vice versa. The seasons do not change naturally, but the tribe has to co-operate through certain rites. Man's actions, on the other hand, are actions which have already happened before and are only repeated: all events are mythi-cal, i.e. they must be repeated. Cf. G. van der Leeuw, *De Primitieve Mensch en de Religie*, J. B. Wolters, 1952, 91.

46. Th. C. Vriezen (*An Outline of Old Testament Theology*, Basil Blackwell, 1962) distinguishes four periods in the development of the idea of salvation in the Old Testament, namely the pre-eschatological, proto-eschatological, eschatologi-cal with reference to the near future and transcendental-eschatological. In the last, the world is secularised and the divine transcendentalised (367–69).

47. Cf. J. Vansina, 'A Comparison of African Kingdoms', *Africa*, Vol. 32, No 4, Oct. 1962, 325. The King is of divine origin and rules by divine right, whose royalty is sacred (and not his person) which 'is expressed by the existence of and the ritual paid to the royal regalia'. (The emphasis on regalia is seen in the re-actionary movements.) As symbol of the kingdom the king's prosperity is related to that of his country. He possesses the land, in the sense that he controls it, and all the people belong to him, he commanding their labour at will. He is the supreme judge, having the life and death of each member in his own hands, although his authority is checked by councils and courts. (Cf. E. E. Evans-Pritchard, *The Divine Kingship of the Shilluk*, OUP, 1948; I. S. Schapera, *Govern-ment and Politics in Tribal Societies*, London, 1956.) These aspects are seen in the

reactionary movements, e.g. Limba, Lekganyane and others receive money from their members for whom they in return provide via their social and economic schemes.

48. Vriezen, 350.
49. Ibid., 350.
50. Bultmann, 31.
51. Cf. Lucien Lévy-Bruhl (*Primitives and the Supernatural*, tr. Lilian A. Clare, Allen & Unwin, 1936, 235) speaks about 'the spontaneous, ever-present tendency of primitives to shun what is unfortunate, and to connect themselves with what is successful'.
52. In Isl. 220's superscription that this Isl. was written by '*nKosi* (King) Isaiah Shembe May 1939 after his rising from the dead' (*Emva Koku vuka Kwakhe Kwabafileyo*). Shembe II states with obvious reference to his father's victory over the grave:

> Death today you have been conquered
> You no longer have power.
> And your grave has been overcome
> by him who is above. Isl. 229

53. This was the danger in B. Gutmann's approach (cf. *Gemeinde-Aufbau aus dem Evangelium*, Leipzig, 1925). Civilisation with its emphasis on individualism, has become for him a deadly enemy of the African way of life. He speaks about the 'Spiritual bastardisation' that takes place in Africa. The African ethnic structure becomes the anthropological basic structure, and the European civilisation becomes the universal disintegrating factor. Individualism is for him equal to disintegration, and on this the missionary policy has been built as a result of the pietistic background of the nineteenth and twentieth century missionary revival. Christian Keysser, who worked amongst the Papuan animists, has tried to indicate that the old Testament, which emphasises the national aspect, and the New Testament, which emphasises personal decision, supplement one another (cf. 'Die Papua und das Wort', EMZ, 1944, 218). J. C. Hoekendijk's comment is that personal decision before God is completely suffocated in the massive collectiveness of Keysser's approach (cf. *Kerk en Volk*, 183).
54. Andersson, 259.
55. A. Kropf, *Das Volk des Xosa-Kaffern im östlichen Südafrika*, Berlin, 1889; A. Kropf, *Ntsikana*, Berlin, 1891; A. Kropf, *Die Lügenpropheten des Kaffernlandes*, Neue Missions-schriften, Berlin, 1891. Schlosser, *Propheten*, 24 ff., 29 ff., 328 ff. Cf. also O. F. Raum, 'Von Stammespropheten zu Sektenführern' in *Messianische Kirchen, Sekten und Bewegungen im heutigen Afrika*, ed. by E. Benz, Leiden, Brill, 1965.
56. Andersson, 226.
57. Andersson, 226; Horton Davies and R. H. W. Shepherd, *South African Missions* (*1800–1950*), 1954, 38 ff.; Charles Brownlee, *Reminiscences of Kaffir Life and History*, Lovedale Press, 1896. A. Kropf, *Das Volk de Xosa-Kaffern*, 30; Schlosser, *Propheten*, 32 f., 36 ff.; G. M. Theal, *Compendium of South African History*, Lovedale Press, 1876. Pauw refers to Kgokong, a local prophet in Taung, anti-White, who told his followers to kill their goats as well as to throw away their household utensils, prophesying that they would be able to fly. He exercised baptism by immersion in a stream (Pauw, *Religion*, 49). In Africa ritual actions may be the opposite of what is intended, e.g. when the Zulu bride hurls an assegai aggressively into her husband's cattle kraal, or when the king is insulted. This disposition may also play a part in the idea of destroying everything in order to

receive abundantly. Cf. Max Gluckman, *Custom and Conflict in Africa*, Blackwell, 1963, 121 ff. Gluckmann says: 'This scheme of rejection and hatred of the king is so built into this great national ceremony that we have to ask again, how the affirmation of rebellion can be so strong in a ritual which the people believe unifies and blesses their nation' (ibid., 125). During initiation ceremonies, e.g. circumcision, the old is completely destroyed before the young men become adults.

58. Prof. O. F. Raum, Anthropologist, Fort Hare University College, in an interview, Aug. 8, 1963. See also E. Benz (ed.), *Messianischen Kirchen, Sekten und Bewegungen*, Cologne, E J. Brill, 1965.

59. Schlosser, *Propheten*, 36; G. McCall Theal, *History of South Africa since 1896*, Vol. 3, London, 1908, 191 f.

60. Schlosser, *Propheten*, 54; Theal, Vol. 3, 190 ff.

61. Cf. Peter Worsley, *The Trumpet shall Sound*, London, MacGibbon & Kee, 1957.

62. V. H. Ferguson, 'The Holy Lake of the Dinka', *Sudan Notes and Records*, Vol. 5, Dec. 1922, 163–66; H. Baumann, R. Thurnwald, D. Westermann, *Völkerkunde von Afrika*, Essen, 1940; Schlosser, *Propheten*, 63.

63. Cf. Sundkler, *Bantu Prophets*, 266.

64. Cf. R. H. Lowie, *Primitive Religion*, Routledge, 1925, p. 8.

65. A member of this movement is quoted by Andersson as saying, 'Matswa André will come. He will come to save the people from their misery (*mpasi*), especially from their slavery, for now we are slaves, but on the day when Matswa André comes we shall have part in his power and dominion. . . then the whites must return to their country. . . over us blacks Matswa André shall rule' (Andersson, 193). The older Ngunzists give first place to Kimbangu: 'All God's promises will be consummated in and through Simon Kimbangu' (ibid., 194).

66. Tempels, 30.

67. Tempels, 31–33. Cf. Oosthuizen, *The Theology of a South African Messiah*, 57–62.

68. Andersson, 191.

69. Ibid., 192.

70. Cf. Tambaram Series, Vol. V, 27.

71. Mavonda Ntangu, one of the prophets in the Ngunzi-Khaki movement, prayed: 'God of Abraham, God of Isaac and God of Jacob, God of Simon Kimbangu and God of Matswa André, when shall we receive the blessings and be free? Thou shalt no more hear the prayers of the whites, for Thou hast heard them for a long time and they have received blessing enough. Hear now us. Amen' (Andersson, 193). Their reaction is against the Christian faith, because it made them give up their former customs, so that they no longer know whether they are Bakongos, Basundis or Balaris, and they pray to André Matswa and Simon Kimbangu, as they suffered for the Blacks while Jesus suffered for the Whites only. G. Balandier, *Zwielichtiges Afrika*, Stuttgart, 1959, 233 ff. With regard to the frustrated intelligentisia in South Africa, who 'see civilisation as the overpowering medicine of the white man', see Peter Sulzer, *Schwarze Intelligenz*, Atlantis Verlag, 1955.

72. Men belong to a certain class of people because they share in a certain type of supernatural power. Cf. van der Leeuw, *De Primitieve Mensch*, 45.

73. Andersson, 193

74. Ibid., 193.

75. Cf. ibid., 193.

76. Cf. Sundkler, *Bantu Prophets*, 288. The prophet takes the place of the deified king who was acclaimed as the saviour of his people.

Vital power is the basis of differentiation of beings into species in African ontology. God is the one who increases force. Then come the founders of clans, the first to whom God has communicated his vital force, then follow the dead, following their order of primogeniture; they form a link via the elders to the living who come after the dead. Here is a hierarchy built again on vital power. The chief is the source of 'all zestful living', and is as God himself (Tempels, 41–42). These may easily be identified with God because both are called by the same name, but, says Tempels in a footnote, 'there is, however, no identification, but a simple comparison, a practice analogous to that in which a chief's deputy is treated as the chief himself. . . .' (42) This comes out clearly in a study made of J. N. Limba's church in Port Elizabeth, *Ibandla lika Krestu*. In this church God is referred to as *uThixo ka Tata* (the Father's God). Bishop Limba is the Father and God is Tata's God. The God here referred to is their God in a special way because he is their Tata's (Father's) God. This God has given to their Father (Bishop Limba) his vital force (L. Mqotsi and N. Mkele, 'A Separatist Church, Ibandla lika Krestu', *African Studies*, V, 2, 1946, 124–25). J. Taylor also indicates that the person of the chief or King is 'the sum and substance of the whole community. Many Bantu people speak of a headman as *mwene-muzi*, the very self of the village' (*Primal Vision*, scm, 1963, 135). The Kabaka of Buganda holds this divine office, as was the case with the ancient divine kingship in the Congo. In the Congo, this throne will be occupied by Kimbangu (Andersson, 194). In a kind of creed from the Ngunza-Khaki congregation in Pointe-Noire, Simon Kimbangu is described as follows: 'He is the one in whom lives the Lord God, the gracious father of the blacks' (Andersson, 195). See also B. Bernardi, *The Mungwe*, oup, 1959. Here one sees how representation means identification.

77. Van Wing, 569.

78. Cf. B. Malinowski, *The Dynamics of Culture Change*, oup, 1949[4], 94–99. He calls witchcraft 'one of the most characteristic of African superstitions and symptoms of benightedness' (ibid., 94). In spite of Christianity it is on the increase for the very reason that it is 'primarily rooted in the psychological reactions of those suffering from ill-health, misfortune, inability to control their destiny and fortunes. . . . To free human beings from the belief in sorcery, it would be necessary to endow them with gifts of eternal prosperity, health, and life' (ibid.). 'The belief in witchcraft will always remain a symptom of economic distress, of social tension, of political or social oppression' (ibid., 97).

79. Warneck, *Die Lebenskräfte des Evangeliums*, Berlin, Martin Warneck, 1908, 256.

80. Cg. Margull, *Aufbruch*, 30.

81. Eichrodt, Vol. I, 234.

82. Taylor, Buganda, 253.

83. Tempels, 114; see also Janheinz Jahn, *Muntu* (Eugen Diederichs Verlag, 1958).

84. Wilson, *Nyakyusa*, 187. The idea of better times in the future recurs in all movements in Africa. Cf. Guariglia, 273.

85. Mair, 133.

86. Tempels, 35. J. C. Carothers (*The African Mind in Health and Disease*, Geneva, World Health Organisation; London, hmso, 1953, 108), maintains that 'African adult psychology might be described as monoideic, and the attitude to life as "all or none" . . . logic is also used in the affairs of life, but this technique is never granted an exclusive or even leading role. . . . The monoideic consciousness that results from African culture tends to be highly static through the centuries.' Paul D. Fueter ('Theological Education in Africa', irm, Oct. 1956,

378) maintains that traditional Africans do follow one idea at a time and find synthesis difficult.

87. Tempels, 38. G. Parrinder, *West African Psychology*, Lutterworth, 1956, chp. 2. The basic human aspiration for the increase of 'life-force', vitality and more zestful living is, according to Baëta, due to different reasons, e.g., climate, malnutrition, diseases. Baëta, 134–35.

88. Margull, *Aufbruch*, 34. Cf. M. L. Martin, *The Biblical Concept of Messianism and Messianism in Southern Africa*, Morija-Lesotho, Morija Sesuto Book Depot, 1964.

89. 'Jesus, the white God, seemed so mute and so remote, and all the white people are dying here on earth' (Sundkler, *Bantu Prophets*, 279).

90. Shropshire, xxviii. W. Reyburn, 'Africanization and African Studies', *Practical Anthropology*, Vol. 9, No. 3, May-June 1962, 102. 'The existence of power in the community is made visible through the blessings of fertility, wealth, and control.'

91. G. van der Leeuw, *Inleiding tot de Phaenomenologie van den Godsdienst*, Haarlem, Erven F. Bohn, 1948, 142.

92. Margull, 35.

93. Taylor & Lehmann, 280.

94. This had a strong influence on politics in Africa, for example, in the Nyasaland Rising of 1915. (Cf. Shepperson & Price, *Independent African*; cf. Cunnison (op. cit.) in his Report on a Watch Tower Assembly, held in Central Africa, the following was stated *inter alia* . . . 'the earth will be a paradise' (ibid., 459); 'The Kingdom is at hand in this generation. . . . Life in the Kingdom is earthly and not spiritual. . . . We all come from one ancestor' (ibid., 469). See also F. Sierksma, *Een nieuwe hemel en een nieuw aarde*, Mouton, 1961, especially the chapter on Messianism and Politics, 211 ff.

95. Cf. F. C. Kamma, *Koréri-bewegingen*, 193. Andersson, 192.

96. Balandier, *Afrique Ambigue*, 219.

97. Ibid., 192; Tempels, 43. 'The present human generation living on earth is the centre of all humanity, including the world of the dead.' In this case it is the African.

98. Ibid., 197.

99. Weber, 37, 38. 'The ritual dance has power; it is part of the whole cosmic movement, and without it the cosmic dance, the cycle of the year, would be confused, or even stop.'

100. Cf. The 'creed' of the Ngunza-Khaki congregation in Pointe Noire. Andersson, 194.

101. H. Kraemer, *Religion and the Christian Faith*, Lutterworth, 1958, 399–400. Here a mixture takes place 'on a substratum of primitive religiosity'.

102. Ibid., 403.

103. '. . . many Africans, failing to learn the trick of holding the religious and the secular spirit in separate compartments, have abandoned themselves to a meaningless immediacy – "eat, drink and be merry, for tomorrow we die". Nevertheless, a great deal of African "materialism" is actually accompanied by the most lively sense of a spiritual world.' Taylor & Lehmann, 275.

104. Sundkler, *Bantu Prophets*, 278.

105. Ibid., 286.

106. Cf. Isl. 93[4]; Oosthuizen, *The Theology of a South African Messiah*, 11–12.

107. Andersson, 125. E. Dammann (cf. 'Jesus Christus, das Christus verständnis im Wandel der Zeiten' in *Marburger Theologische Studien*, Marburg, Elwert Verlag, 1963) indicates that there are different approaches to the understanding

of Jesus Christ in the independent movements, namely (i) no difference from that of the historic churches; (ii) Christ accepted but the prophet receives great prominence; (iii) Jesus is in the background; (iv) those who have completely discarded the biblical figure of Jesus; (v) the person of Christ is transferred to that of the political figure.

108. Taylor, *Primal Vision*, 135.

109. Taylor & Lehmann, 276.

110. Ibid., 276; see also G. Balandier, *Afrique Ambigue*, 219; 'They imagine that European religion tends to leave the riches in the hands of these people, and hides a secret that no one wishes to reveal.'

111. Andersson, 44.

112. Sundkler, *Prophets*, 278.

113. Andersson, 190–91. The Ngunza Khaki movement rejects the Holy Communion administered by the missions as false as it has evil medicine in it. It cannot wash away sin. The missionaries have another effective communion which gives secret wisdom and the gift of prophecy. Mavonda Ntangu maintains they should wait until Nzambi 'sends the right communion from heaven'. The practice of taking communion at the mission varies from area to area. For the lowest grade of members it is permitted but to the 'enlightened' it is not only considered to be superfluous but it is forbidden. In the Congo it is reported that it is celebrated with water and bananas, and at other places the bread and wine are replaced with African ingredients. Ibid., 190–91.

114. Ibid., 282.

115. Andersson, 195. '*Mfumu Simon Kimbangu* is the cup with the oil of blessing or the calabash with the oil of blessing that the Lord God has given to the black race that it may be blessed in Him.'

It has already been indicated that the chief's person is the sum and substance of the whole community. In the traditional mentality representation means identification (cf. van der Leeuw, *De Primitieve Mensch*, 42). In this way they develop their own Christology. In the case of Kwame Nkrumah, a confession of faith was worked out on the basis of the Apostolicum (cf. Witschi, 12). Nkrumah's activities and suffering for the sake of freedom have been compared to those of Christ. W. Ringwald even maintains that 'Kwame Nkrumah is the true Christ, (ems, 12, 1955, 15; cf. Cecil Northcott, 'New Gods in Ghana', *Christian Century*' Nov. 23, 1960, 1367). Jomo Kenyatta has also been hailed as a messiah, but his messianic features are gradually being removed. In Nyasaland *The Malawi News*, official organ of the Malawi Congress party, published certain rules and regulations for the discipline of this Party. It states *inter alia* 'that the Malawi Congress Party is supreme and no member, high or low, is above the Party. Further, the Life President, Ngwazi Kamuzu Banda, as the supreme symbol of the Party, is the supreme Leader and Father of the nation', that he shall be addressed, amongst others, with the following titles and slogans, 'Messiah, Saviour' (R. H. W. Shepherd, 'Totalitarianism and the Personality Cult in Nyasaland', *The South African Outlook*, Apr. 1, 1963, 55). The late Albert Luthuli was hailed by many as the messiah of South Africa, and a painting representing him as the crucified, and Dr. Verwoerd and Mr. Vorster as the Roman soldiers, was widely applauded. The traditional masked dance with its magical aim, whereby those who take part identify themselves by way of the mask with the spirits and gods, is very popular. They do not represent these powers, but are themselves these powers who move in the dance, In this way rain. fertility or other material benefits are obtained. (Cf. van der Leeuw, *De Primitieve Mensch*, 42.)

116. Tempels, 42.

117. Eichrodt, Vol. I, 289–309.

118. Shembe I states in Isl. 218.[1]

Come ye Zulus, we have seen our Master,
We come from the world that is to come.

119. Sundkler, *Prophets*, 288; 'Before we did not know that Jehovah was ours. But now we see that Jehovah is ours, our very own.' In these circumstances *apartheid* is even accepted by some. 'Their emotional Utopia thrived in the world apart . . . one should therefore not expect to find radicals or even the politically conscious in these groups' (ibid., 304). Sundkler's description of these movements leads him to maintain in the second edition of *Bantu Prophets* that the anti-*apartheid* prophets now developed into pro-*apartheid* prophets.

120. Van der Leeuw, *De Primitieve Mensch*, 54 ff. In the dream we see the boundlessness of the traditional mentality. There is no real distance between the world of sleep and that of being awake. What happens in the dream is as real as what happens when he is awake: adultery committed in a dream is punishable. Dream consciousness is thus evaluated as being on the same level as day consciousness, although it does not express itself in concepts but in images, figures and symbols. The ancestor may visit somebody through a dream, especially when he warns him of danger, during illness or death, or in times of crisis. Cf. Taylor, Vol. II, 26 ff.; also Sundkler, *Prophets*, 265 ff. Dreams are an important means of revelation, and many are called to the ministry through dreams; others are converted in this way.

121. Andersson, 58.

122. Ibid., 56.

123. Van Wing, 571.

124. Andersson, 56.

125. This became the New Jerusalem, cf. Balandier, *Sociologie*, 430.

126. Andersson, 63.

127. Cf. E. Sellin, *Der A. T. Prophetismus*, Berlin, 15 ff.

128. Balandier, *Sociologie*, 430.

129. Charles-André Gilis, *Kimbangu-Fondateur d'Église*. Bruxelles: La Libraire Encyclopédique, 1960, 34.

130. Balandier, *Sociologie*, 431.

131. Ibid., 430.

132. Cf. Hodgkin, 108; Schlosser, who overlooks the problem of acculturation, concentrates mainly on political and economic reasons (*Propheten*, 401); Baëta relates the words of Charles Kobla Nutonuti Wovenu, founder of the *Apostolowo fe dedefia Habobo* (the Apostolic Revelation Society) as saying: 'There will be bicycles in your gates, and many human beings shall lie round about. There will be an abundance of money in your hand. O, where are now those who insult and mock you?' (*Prophetism*, 80). Political motivation was, however, not important in Ghana. This was concentrated on the figure of Nkrumah. Where the Whites were in a strong minority, political and economic reasons did play a role. Edwin Smith says: 'A smart Native learns by watching his master mix paints and wield the brush; and presently he does a good deal of the work while the master sits by and draws pay at European rates, handing the boy his wages at Native labourers' rates. Is bringing of Jesus Christ in narrow sense an only obligation?' (*The Way of the White Fields in Rhodesia*, World Dominion Press, 1928, 130). Cf. Tambaram Series Vol. V, 32. The mission station as an island of economic activity and security is a familiar sight to the traveller in Africa

133. In South Africa the policy of separate development satisfies the ideological needs of many separatists, and Sundkler says, 'The Separatists go out of their

114

way to state that they take no part in politics' (*Prophets*, 305). This, however, is not true of some established Churches, which react strongly against government policy. Basically the nativistic movements find satisfaction in indigenous development, which enables them to live separately from the 'fountains of old', as Shembe calls his inheritance.

134. Hodgkin, 109.
135. Ibid., 111.
136. Andersson, 124. See also Sundkler (*Prophets*, 287) on Shembe 'the death-resurrection drama'. This same theme is found in a sermon of a certain Rev. J. J. G. Boshoff, after the unsuccessful attempt on Dr. Verwoerd's life, which he compared with Christ's passion, death and resurrection.
137. See also Jules Chome, *La Passion de Simon Kimbangu* (*1921–1951*), second edition, Brussels, Les Amis de Présence Africaine, 1959. He presents the story of Simon Kimbangu and the movement as paralleled with events in the life of Christ. This book is not a good authority on the movement.
138. Hodgkin, 112.
139. Margull, 66.
140. Cf. Sundkler, *Prophets*, 290. Kimbangu was to set himself on the ancient throne of the Congo being the All Powerful One.
141. *Isihlabelelo* 197, 2:

> You called me, Lord, with your voice,
> I was still in my mother's womb.

142. The *ngunza* is 'an emissary from the divine world. He has received a call and has been entrusted with a mission. He cures the sick, and reveals that which was hidden, not with the aid of medicinal herbs, magical rites, or the power of a *nkisi*-god, but as a consequence of the divinity incarnate in him. When he is in a state of ecstasy, his speech and actions are not his own, but those of the spirit of the god which possess him' (Andersson, 3). He has a mission to fulfil, being not private but prophetically inspired, not a negative one as that of the *nganga ngombo* (the divine seer) namely to rid the community of the *bandoki* (witchcraft), but a positive task, namely, to revive the faith of the fathers. His power is due to the divinity incarnate in him (ibid., 3). In later Ngunzism conceptions about Nzambi (God) were those of the pre-Christian era; He is in the background and cannot 'figure in the front rank of the powers to whom man in need must address himself' (Andersson, 108).
143. Cf. Bernardi, 159, 188. The Mugwe represents his people before God, in a way identified with God; he even has political power, although his authority is religious. He is 'Father', 'God', although he is not a divine incarnation. Here the traditional idea of representation which means identification has kept the distance but this is not the case in post-Christian messianism.
144. Fehderau, 161.
145. Anderson, 63.
146. Ibid., 196.
147. Ibid., 197.
148. Ibid., 194. The popularity of Kimbangu's work led to the mushroom growth of prophets. Cf. Fehderau, 160.
149. Andersson, 194.
150. Ibid., 195–96.
151. Margull, 69.
152. Balandier, *Afrique Ambigue*, 232.
153. Andersson, 126.

E   115

154. Cf. ibid., 128.

155. Andersson, 134.

156. Both Van Wing and Jules Chomé are impressed by the impact of Simon Kimbangu on the Bakongo in the destruction of fetishes, *ngoma* dances and polygamy; even the rosaries, scapularies, and other Catholic religious objects. (Van Wing, 105; Chomé, 16). Cf. also Sundkler, *Prophets*, 253. In the African society witchcraft and sorcery were considered to be the main sources of instabilit within the tribe. (Cf. J. H. Soga, *The Ama-Xosa: Life and Customs*, Lovedale Press, 1931, 45.) Witches are blamed for disasters in general (Field, *Security*, 36). The most degraded crime is that effected by sorcery (Tempels, 82). Cf. J. A. Omoyajowo, *Witches?* Ibadan, Daystar Press, 1965. The overcoming of this in Christianity is the greatest joy.

157. Margull, 82.

158. Ibid., 84.

159. Ibid.

160. Andersson, 57.

161. Taylor & Lehmann, 251. They had difficulty in finding out whether this was another witch-finding movement as the one which came from Nyasaland in 1934. (Cf. A. I. Richards, 'A Modern Movement of Witch-finders', *Africa*, Oct. 1958.)

162. Sundkler, *Prophets*, 253.

163. Tempels, 82; Taylor, *Buganda*, 195. The sorcerer deals mainly in destructive medicines or poisons. Andersson, 23. People in the Congo call their sorcerers or witches *bandoki*, i.e. people who "eat" others especially at night time. H. De Brunner, *Witchcraft*, 34. Witchcraft has to do with the eating of souls and nocturnal meetings. Cf. H.-J. Grechat, '"Witchcraft" und kirchlicher Separatismus in Zentral-Afrika', in *Messianische Kirchen*, etc., ed. by E. Benz, 91–104.

164. Wilson, 173.

165. De Brunner, 157.

166. Malinowski, 96, 97. Cf. M. A. Murray, *The Witchcult in Western Europe*, OUP (1921) 1962[2], 11 ff., who classifies witchcraft into the operative and the ritual. The first has to do with charms, amulets, etc., and in the latter, ritualism plays a significant role.

167. Margull, 88.

168. Andersson, 131.

169. Ibid., 135.

170. Margull, 90.

171. Shropshire, 85.

172. J. C. Bennett, *Christianity and Communism Today*, NY, Association Press, 1961[2], 31.

173. Andersson, 69.

174. Ibid.

175. Ibid., 70.

176. Andersson, 98. The command of Dingaan, the Zulu King, to his soldiers was to kill the sorcerers (Whites) when they entered Natal.

177. Ibid., 98, 99.

178. Schlosser, *Propheten*, 158.

179. Ibid., 99.

180. Ibid., 76–77, 108. Margull, 95, 96.

181. R. A. Knox, *Enthusiasm*, OUP, 1st publ. 1950, 585.

182. Schlosser, *Eingeborenen*, 161.

183. Andersson, 77.

184. Speaking about himself, Shembe I states in Isl. 24[1]:

> *Look ye, he comes with the clouds*
> *He comes to call all people.*

185. Ibid., 78, 79. Shembe did appear according to Isihlabehelo 7.
186. Horton Davies, *Christian Deviations*, SCM, 1957[6], 54.
187. Andersson, 194–96.
188. Ibid., 109.
189. E. Asirvatham, *Christianity in the Indian Crucible*, Calcutta, YMCA Publishing House, 1957, 35. Cf. P. D. Devanandan, *The Gospel and Renascent Hinduism*, SCM, 1959. In Nigeria the 'National Church of Nigeria and the Cameroons' preaches an African God 'rejecting the foreign religions from Canterbury, Rome and Mecca' (Parrinder, *Religion in an African City*, 128). These should be ousted because 'we cannot become politically free if our heart and stomach are controlled by aliens . . .' (ibid., 187). Sundkler says, '*The syncretistic sect becomes the bridge over which Africans are brought back to heathenism. . . .*' It can be shown how individuals and groups have passed step by step from a 'Mission Church to an Ethiopian Church, and from the Ethiopians to Zionists, and how at last via the bridge of nativistic Zionism they have returned to the African animism from where they once started' (*Prophets*, 297).
190. W. Freytag, 'Der Islam als Beispiel einer nachchristlicher Religion', EMZ, 1955, 102.
191. K. Aldén, 'The Prophetic Movement in Congo', IRM, July 1936, 352, maintains that the revival was only on the surface and that 'there remains still in the hearts of the people an element from the pagan days'. He stressed, in a personal interview with the writer, the fact that it was a genuine effort for revival in the initial stages, in spite of the methods used.
192. Margull, 114.
193. D. Westermann, *The African Today and Tomorrow*, OUP, 1949, 83.
194. G. C. Oosthuizen, *Theological discussions and confessional developments in the Churches of Asia and Africa*, Franeker, Wever, 1958, 253.
195. Westermann, 83.
196. Ed. Alan Richardson, *A Theological Wordbook of the Bible*, SCM, 1962 ed., 108–09.
197. Margull, 114; Martin, 158.
198. See K. Barth's view of religion as *a parte homini*. *Church Dogmatics*, I[2], T. & T. Clark (transl.), 1956, 280 ff.; J. M. Vlijm, *Het Religiebegrip van Karl Barth*, van Keulen, 1957.
199. Johannes Calvyn, *Institutie*, Part I, Book I, Chapter IV, ed. A. Sizoo, Delft, Meinema, 1956.
200. Margull, 115. 'Heiden haben keine Hoffnung.'
201. W. A. Whitehouse, *On Faith in Alan Richardson*, (ed.), 76.
202. Cf. Paul Tillich, *Dynamics of Faith*, Harper & Bros., 1957. 'Faith is the state of being ultimately concerned' (ibid., 1). Cf. Deut. vi. 5: These words 'state unambiguously the character of genuine faith, the demand of total surrender to the subject of ultimate concern.'
203. Margull, 116.
204. Margull, 118: 'Mission is much more an act of hope, undertaken in and from hope.' Cf. H. J. Margull, *Hope in Action*, Muhlenberg Press, 1962.
205. Cf. D. Bonhoeffer, *The Cost of Discipleship* (transl.) SCM, 1948. Bonhoeffer also accepts the complete break with the word and that we should sever all

natural ties as a *fait accompli*, but he accepts that we are responsible for the world and have to stand in the thick of it (78). See also *Sanctorum Communio*, op. cit. 206. K. Barth, *Römerbrief*, 1921, 71.

4

THE MISUNDERSTANDING OF THE BIBLICAL MEANING OF THE HOLY SPIRIT IN THE INDEPENDENT MOVEMENTS

IT has been clear so far that the main emphasis of many of the nativistic movements is on man's destiny. They are interested not in the creation of the universe, but in divine involvement. The God of the missions is too remote for a system in which men's 'gods' belonged to their lineage, and, although far removed, could be approached through their ancestors. The God in the Christianity with which they came in contact had much to do with their souls, and with certain individuals, but not with them in all spheres of life and as a whole community. It was selective, and Isaiah Shembe often repeats that he is not selective. The African sense of divine involvement finds its expression in these movements where God acts through the prophet as the middle-man, or where the prophet himself becomes a messiah. Here, representation, as is the case in traditional thinking, means identification. For a society in which the ancestors and the super-natural world were ever present, the revelation of Jesus Christ will be interpreted according to their own categories. Their own prophet or messiah will satisfy this need for divine involvement.

The kingship or chieftainship type of leadership is usually combined with the office of the diviner, both in the prophet and messiah. As the king or chief forms an important link with the supernatural world, so do the prophet or messiah, who work under the injunctions of 'the Spirit', as is the case with the diviner. The prophet is often taken possession of by 'the Spirit', like the diviner, but this is not the case with the messiah who, like the king, only receives advice. In this case, Kimbangu was only a prophet – it was his followers who elevated him to the position of a messiah. The psychological and religious disposition for the re-establishment of the traditional kingship through a messianic figure is strong, because of the office of kingship in most tribes of Africa, which in some cases has a specific mystical value with a 'divinity' of its own. The prophetic

119

office of the diviner is stimulated and inspired by the inspiring agency of the ancestors. He derives his power from the ancestors themselves through which he/she guards over the spiritual life of the tribe, confronting the negative and destructive forces of life. His contact with the spirits through dreams and trance situations is a religious-magical contact; this is especially evident in the prophetic movements. Shembe had this contact which he described in Isl. 218. 1, 2 saying *We come from the world that is to come.* Through healing and witch-finding, the diviner opens the way to a brighter future, thus fighting his way through the magical world. The diviner is in this sense a prophet with messianic characteristics, struggling for the welfare of his people. Just as the ancestors are recalled and put into office as guardian spirits after they have passed away, so these prophetic and messianic figures in the nativistic movements continue to exert their influence on these movements after death. In this connection, one finds the most difficult theological problem in Africa, namely, the confusion that exists with regard to the ancestral spirits and the Holy Spirit.

The misunderstanding of the person and work of the Holy Spirit in Africa is not confined to the nativistic movements, many of the Pentecostal Churches revealing the same difficulty. These movements in Africa have been greatly influenced by Negro Baptist and Pentecostal sects from the United States. The misunderstanding of the Holy Spirit, which is the great difficulty the Church faces in Africa, is not due only to the African's strong sense of the supernatural world, but also because of his essentially suprarational and suprahistorical disposition.[1] In many of the independent movements there is no question of ordinary heresy, which is the result of doctrinal disagreement, and ordinary schism, i.e. defection from the general body of Christendom; it is a matter of a new religion. Here the ancestors become prominent again. Referring to the messianic figure, Shembe, Sundkler states: 'In his creed there is no longer a place for the pale White Christ. His place has been usurped by somebody else. In this case as elsewhere, the refusal to accept White Christ leads men back to the ancestors, to the "blood and soil" of the tribe.'[2] Detribalisation has not destroyed the African's sense of community, and hence his tribal values, of which the most important is the reverence and 'worship' of the ancestors.[3] Only a small minority have rejected the traditional ancestor beliefs completely. Even in the established Churches many adhere to these beliefs. Great importance is being attached to the clause in the *apostolicum* which refers to Christ's descent into Sheol. In an extensive survey made in the Ciskei area recently, more than 9 out of 10 from established Churches

120

clearly stated that their non-Christian forefathers are saved. Theological understanding rather than the rejection offered by some missionaries, is the practical approach of the Churches to the independent movements.

What Busia observes is not limited to the Ashanti but is true about the Church in Negro and Bantu Africa, that 'Many Christians still believe that the ancestors send help and blessing, and above all, they share with non-Christians the sentiments of unity and continuity which are given expression at the religious ceremonies centering around the chief'.[4] Pauw maintains that a large number of the Xhosa Christians in all types of denominations still adhere to the beliefs and even rituals relating to ancestors, and that 'the minimum belief that misfortune may result from disregarding the wishes of the ancestors is held by a distinct majority of Xhosa Christians of all shades of denominations'.[5] This has been substantiated by our own research.

Among the many reasons already mentioned for sectarianism, the reaction against spiritual dryness and 'quenching of the Spirit' has been a recurrent one. The Pentecostal movements have given special attention to this aspect with their 'hot Gospel' approach, where services are highly emotional, and where members are expected to 'speak with tongues'. People are attracted to these 'Churches', because those who belong seem ' "to have more of the Holy Ghost" '.[6] Of the 'Spiritual Churches', Baëta says that 'in their worship, the groups concerned engage in various activities which (by their own assertion) are either meant to invoke the Holy Spirit of God, or are to be interpreted as signs of his descent upon the worshippers'.[7] Too often, Sundkler tells us, the absence of sermon preparation 'is compensated for by a deep and deafening volume of sound which is supposed to show the presence of the Holy Spirit'.[8]

The 'uMoya theology'[9] or the theology of 'the Spirit' or Holy Spirit is a fundamental concept in practically all the indigenous and Pentecostal movements in Africa, i.e. in both Christian sects and nativistic movements. The reality of the spiritual world with its ancestors poses many problems to the Church. The Africans, as Baëta maintains, live with their dead, and he indicates that proscription is no solution here but rather pruning, purification and guidance. Whether or not the ancestors are worshipped is, according to him, still an open question.[10]

The Garvey movement and the independent movements amongst the Negroes, which had influence in Africa, were mainly of the Baptist, Pentecostal, Apostolic Faith and nativistic types, where the Holy Spirit is the central theme; whereas the African animists' main

121

object is 'to acquire life strength or vital force, to live strongly'[11] for themselves and for the tribe.[12] The texts pertaining to this will have special significance, such as 'you will receive power when the Holy Spirit comes upon you' (Acts i. 8) and 'they were filled with the Holy Spirit and began to talk in other tongues, as the Spirit gave them power of utterance' (Acts ii. 4). It is said that when Nicholas Bhengu preached at King William's Town a smoke screen surrounded him, which is a manifestation of the Holy Spirit.[13] In this movement, however, the concept of the Holy Spirit is still orthodox, because the Word is still norm, but wherever the relationship between the Word and the Spirit is lost all kinds of queer ideas come into the picture. Sundkler says that 'this same spirit, by the Zionists interpreted as the Holy Spirit, can be cited as the authority for any subjective fancy or predilection which the particular prophet may have'.[14]

In these movements the Holy Spirit receives the same uncertain position as is the case with their Christology and with the deity in general, although the uncertainty with regard to the Holy Spirit is more acute. Pauw maintains that 'the belief in the Spirit . . . does not completely displace the belief in ancestors in Zulu Zionist Churches, and in spite of substituting it in some instances, it is nevertheless used to uphold and sanction it in others'.[15] Sundkler indicates how indiscriminately Spirit and Angel are used in what he calls Zionist Churches although uMoya may be described as the 'general state of being divinely possessed', and the Angel is the channel of revelation by uMoya. The Spirit is 'the latent to-be-possessed-feeling', whereas the Angel, which appears chiefly in dreams, is ever active denouncing misbehaviour and 'showing the way out of an impasse'.[16] The main reproach of the Angel in these nativistic movements is that ancestor spirits have been neglected. Their main work is to guard the gates at Ekuphakameni and to expel sinners.[17] The cult of the ancestors is less marked among the Tlhaping than the Zulu.[18] There is a definite line in the independent movements between the 'Holy Spirit' and the ancestors.[19] 'Instruction from the Spirit', for example, can lead to the acquisition of two or three wives.[20] The number of wives in African society is associated with status, and polygamy in itself is a morally accepted custom. The Spirits' activity is not related to moral guidance but rather to vital force. The Spirit can be obtained before baptism while one is still a non-Christian, and a man may leave a wife of whom he is tired for another, younger one on the injuction of the Spirit.[21] People may 'have' the Holy Spirit in these circumstances even though they readily accept that it has no Biblical support.[22] According to them, the Spirit does not manifest itself so freely in the mission

Churches as in the movements, because in the former it is being suppressed. The mission Churches react adversely against emotion- alism, making a clear distinction between man and Holy Spirit, whereas in the indigenous movements there is room for emotional expression, and a unity between subject and object, man and Spirit, the primal identity, which is the background of all mysticism. Sundkler's definition of *uMoya* as the general state of divine posses- sion[24] should be seen in relation to the African concept of authority. The Supreme Being is the one who possesses 'Force in himself' and who is 'also the source of the Force of each creature'[25] This autho- rity is being given to the tribe in hierarchical order through the ancestors. One receives authority in the family, clan or tribe through one's ancestors, whose authority when they were alive determines the authority they can impart after death.

In the Kimbangu movement, the most important section in their set of beliefs is that relating to the Spirit. One can lose the Spirit. which is understood as a great misfortune.[26] The baptism of this movement is considered to be a baptism of the Holy Spirit, a true baptism which should be distinguished from the 'ineffective' baptism of the missions 'which is only a John the Baptist affair'.[27] Syncretism between the African concept of God and the Scriptural doctrine also takes place. God can be more lenient in the new context and one is not always certain whether he is on one's side.

Andersson states 'the doctrine of the Spirit is the wide gate through which a number of pre-Christian conceptions have entered'.[28] 'The Spirit' is the channel through which ancestral ideas enter Christian concepts, with the result that something different is produced. Genea- logy is popular with the nativistic movements, because 'the further one can go in one's prayers to the spirits, the more certain one is of being answered, for the nearer one gets to God'.[29] God is thus far away not spatially, but rather in a hierarchical sense so that the Spirit becomes prominent. This calling upon the ancestral spirits accounts for the renewed emphasis on tribal forces in the nativistic movements.

Amongst the African communities 'dreams are regarded as common channels of divine communication' and 'all dreams are construed into visits from spirits of deceased friends'.[30] Most serious attention is paid to the cautions and warnings which come through this channel. It is easy to see that these spirits must have one upper spirit. In African ontology, beings are differentiated according to their vital power, so that above all will be God, Spirit and Creator, who has power in himself.[31] The patriarchs of the clan exercise their influence on all posterity. Shembe, for example, continuously refers in his hymns to Dingaan, and Shaka. Sundkler observes that 'the ancestor cult and its corollary, sacrifice, form the pattern on which Zionist Spirit-religion, and its cult of angels and sacrifices, is built'.[32] This is true of the nativistic movements in Africa, because in the traditional religion spirits are believed to exist, and act freely in the world and even become 'incorporate for more or less time in solid bodies'.[33] As there are two types of spirit possession, people will say that they are no longer troubled by 'the Spirit',[34] as the spirits of the dead continuously seek to enter into contact with the living.[35]

When Scripture as norm has been isolated from the worship service, nativistic ideas enter the very core of the creed. The African universe is 'not a chaotic tangle of unordered forces blindly struggling with one another'.[36] The interaction of forces and the impact of vital influences take place according to determined laws, in spite of the unforeseeable working of certain influences. What happens as a result in the nativistic movements can be best explained from the African background. In the Ngunza-Khaki movement, founded by Simon Mpadi, certain rings are worn by each member which enable him to 'hear in the Spirit';[37] here the old fetishism receives a new emphasis.[38] One of the main tasks of the prophets in this movement is to 'give the Spirit to members' which he 'whips' into the sinner 'with a whisk'.[39] Baëta relates that in the Musama 'Churches' in Ghana one finds 'a revivalist tradition and a sort of baptised African spirit possession'.[40] Those who leave the Church cannot get back the Holy Spirit, according to Mavonda Ntangu, the leader of the Ngunza-Khaki 'Church', who claims that he has brought the Holy Spirit to the world and who has founded 'the Church of the Spirit'.[41] The Spirit has here become the monopoly of the leader;[42] it is actually at his disposal, as in the case of the ancestors, who could even be ceremonially scolded if they do not react favourably after sacrifices have been offered to them. A niece of Zakayo Kivuli, the founder of the African Israel Church Niniveh, believed that she was pregnant after receiving the Spirit.[43]

Most of the leaders of the Ngunza-Khaki movement were from the missions. Their hostility against the missions was summed up in the accusation that they had no spirit in the congregations, and they maintained that, with rare exceptions, none of the missionary evangelists had it either. The Whites who built up the missions do not fall into line with the ancestral cult, whereas Mavonda Ntangu not only has 'the Spirit', but he also gives it to his people. Ntangu has now the special role of revealer of divine truth in his role as Mediator. In point 17 of their catechism, these aspects are emphasised, and it is specifically stated that the spirit will not return again.[44] In this confusion of the ancestral spirits, spirit-possession, the Angel

124

and the Holy Spirit, the last-named is distinguished from God, but both allow the return to pre-Christian notions such as polygamy. A distinction is made between God and the Holy Spirit in the sense that they are not co-equal and co-eternal, as confessed in the Athanasian creed.

The visions and dreams based on the subjectivism of 'the Spirit' working in a person have led to many divisions. The power to discern between good and evil spirits comes from 'the Spirit', which reveals hidden sin, as it gives the prophet power to see through a person. It even prophesies about general calamities, and gives direction to the liturgy. Healing takes place through 'the Spirit', and so does baptism. Even the ancestor spirits are baptised. The majority in the established Churches believe that the pre-Christian ancestors are redeemed, although not on the basis of baptism, but through Christ's presence in their world.

Spirits are 'seen' in dreams and visions.[45] Kimbangu was called 'in a sequence of dreams and visions of a dynamic and compelling character'.[46] Possession by the Spirit subjects a person to 'violent convulsions', which is a necessary precondition in many movements in cases of healing. There is much confusion in this respect because 'being religious' means 'being possessed'. The man who represents most distinctly this spirit possession is the prophet.[47] In Shembe's case, the Black Christ becomes the personification of the Holy Spirit. Shembe, by his own testimony in his hymns, is the Promised One. He refers very seldom to the Holy Spirit in his hymnal, and thinks of himself rather as the messiah who has 'the Spirit' as a counsellor at his disposal. Shembe II states in Isl. 223[1]: *I am your follower and that of the holy spirit.* He also excludes Jesus Christ; 'your follower' in this Isl. refers to his own father.

The person who forms the link with the ancestral spirits receives a prominent place. Tolonyane, for example, was looked upon amongst the Tlhaping as a 'prophet', as a 'man of the ancestral spirits'.[48] Andersson makes a distinction between private and prophetic inspiration – the first having to do with the individual's own consciousness, and the latter being concerned with a mission to reveal, and to act as an intermediary between one's people and the supernatural powers.[49] *Nganga* is the title most used in the Bantu languages for such a person; the term is etymologically derived from *ngangu* meaning 'supernatural intelligence'.[50] The different types of *banganga* receive their 'knowlege' after a series of dances and playing on friction drums, which induce a state of ecstasy. The diviner, the shamanistic seer – who points out the guilty one, who cures diseases by way of medicine is a general African phenomenon.[51] At the initiation of a diviner, an ancestral spirit reveals himself most spectacularly. The *ngunza*, a diviner of a superior nature, has a mission to fulfil, and 'when he is in the state of ecstasy, his speech and actions are not his own, but those of the spirit of the god which possesses him'.[52] While others unmask witches in a state of ecstasy, the *ngunza* serves 'as a channel of communication for the injuctions of a divine or human master'.[53] In the Zulu culture the diviner (*isangoma*) goes through purification rites in order to permit of a clear vision 'and to cause her to become totally possessed by the spirit'.[54] Rhythmical dancing also plays an important part, as does singing to please the Spirit in whose honour it is done. Once the Spirit has made known its desire to enter a person, all obstacles in its way should be removed.[55] The Congo *ngunza* who speaks on behalf of a chief, and who is preacher, prophet, herald, is bound to take precedence in a syncretistic post-Christian religion, when he is possessed or guided by 'the Spirit'. Those who followed Kimbangu maintained 'We have found the God of the Blacks'.[56] A new christology develops to satisfy the desire for concrete revelation. When the relationship between the Spirit and Scripture is lost,[57] the word of the prophet or messiah takes precedence. The word is for the traditional African an act, a deed, loaded with vital force. A blessing is power to the good, and a curse not just an unfriendly expression but a definite danger. From every word of the prophet or messiah power comes forth. This is why their word often takes precedence over Scripture. These prophets are emissaries from the supernatural world with specific tasks entrusted to them, working under the guidance of 'the Spirit' of the one which possesses or guides them. The condition of ecstasy, in speaking with tongues and convulsions, is the outward sign of possession. The *ngunza*'s state is uninfluenced by medicines, herbs and magic; he is divinely possessed, with 'the divinity incarnate in him'.[58] In the Congo, the *nganga ngombo* is the divine seer, while the *ngunza* is the prophet – the first adhering to the magical *nkisi* cult, while the second opposes it violently. The diviner in Zulu religion receives her power as a result of having been taken possession of by one of her ancestors. The prophet in Zulu society is the result of a combination between kingship pattern and the diviner or witch-finder.[59] Isaiah Shembe never claimed to be possessed by a spirit, but rather considered 'the Spirit' as a counsellor.

The mystic state of inspiration, in some movements called 'spirit possession', has often been interpreted as a form of hysteria, and as epileptic fits. Taylor and Lehmann maintain that, to the African, 'God is still unpredictable, so religious experience is arbitrary and tends toward the ecstatic and visionary. If it comes upon a man it is irresistible and all-demanding.[60] The emphasis on spiritual experience in African society is evident in the Pentecostal and Adventist sects and this, apart from other factors, explains the influence of these sects in Africa. Not less than 9% of the Protestant Christian population belongs to these movements. In the ordained ministry the emphasis is on experience rather than adequate training, yet this has been effective in building up membership statistics.[61] In the old religion the diviner as well as the prophet resorts to ecstasy. The prophet's own inspiration is his only authority, and no argument is used; his pronouncements are categorical. This has made the prophet 'effective' in many African risings against the Whites, not only because of his special gifts, but because his claim of supernatural authority for his message is based on 'contact' with the world of spirits. These prophets are expected to return after death. The prophet Makana, for example, who led the Xhosas in 1817 against the British forces at Grahamstown, South Africa, was banished to Robben Island, whence he attempted to escape but was drowned in a boat. The Xhosas expected his return until 1870, when they abandoned hope, and his mats and ornaments were buried.[62] The same strong impression has been left by the Ngunzist prophets.

Field maintains that there is a similarity between 'the technique and tradition' of spirit possession in Ashanti and that of the Hebrew prophets. Acording to her analysis, there were three kinds of Hebrew prophets: (a) those who simply had dreams (Jer. xxiii. 28); (b) those who were hallucinated either visually like Gideon, or auditorily like Samuel and others; and (c) those who were intermittently possessed by 'the Spirit'.[63] Fison holds that the earliest Old Testament writers use the word *ruach*, spirit, to describe the abnormal.[64] In the Old Testament, men meet the living God and not a spirit from God; e.g. Moses met God and not a spirit in the bush; the primitive Hebrews never spoke of Spirit in connection with material things.[65] The relation between the prophet and the word is here of major importance. The prophets are to bring the Word of God, on His authority, and 'in so doing they are reforming the previous primitive ideas of inspiration through *ruach*, by attributing their messages to the word and not to the spirit of Jaweh'.[66] The prophets' message is not derived from *ruach*, nor is *ruach* the criterion of its authenticity; it is rather 'the explanation of his strange psychological condition and experiences'.[67] Neither is ecstasy considered fundamental in Old Testament prophecy, as it is in most of the movements. Some scholars discern in the Old Testament a development from the abnormal concept of *ruach* to the more normal, as is evident in the later Isaiah. In a comparison between Elijah's experience on Mount Sinai and that of

Moses, Martin Buber says that the 'still small voice' heard by Elijah is a reaction against the 'optical and acoustical pomp and circumstance' which accompanied the Mosaic revelation in an earlier era.[68] Here is no question of outbursts of energy, nothing 'rude and rough and boisterous',[69] but the quiet working of God through His Spirit (Zechariah iv. 6).

Field's explanation of the so-called spirit-possessed prophets in the Old Testament is merely psychological. There is the case of the Nazarite Samson who, through the Spirit, could perform incredible feats of strength, but this is not an overall characteristic of those termed as prophets. The message of the prophet was not derived from 'the Spirit', even when we read that the spirit 'took him', 'rested upon him', 'entered into him', 'fell upon him', or 'moved him' – the word *spirit* merely explains his strange psychological experiences and his condition. The Old Testament prophets were never literally and physically moved by the possessing spirit as the source of their message, nor did a predisposition to ecstasy, visions and dreams prove the transcendental authority of their message. Their message was not derived from their psychological condition. Amongst the so-called animists the production of ecstasy figures large; swooning is induced by bodily exercise, chanting and screaming, which has been accepted as an evidence of demonic possession,[70] as well as evidence of the prophets' contact with the spiritual world. The false prophets in the Old Testament were another type who were considered to be prophesying out of their own heart. Among the Hebrews the ecstatic state was a fact, although not fundamental: the oracles of Balaam were delivered in a state of ecstasy, those of Gideon (Judg. vi. 34), Jephthah (Judg. xi. 29) and Samson (Judg. xiv. 6, 19, xv. 14) also. The Baal prophets revealed similar features (1 Kings xviii. 20-28); prophets as a class were considered to be made (2 Kings ix. 11). The greater prophets also saw visions, but this is not an overruling characteristic. Christianity itself came into existence in an environment 'surcharged with such phenomena'.[71] Early Christianity had much to do with enthusiasm: signs and wonders accompanied the work of Jesus Christ and, for the onlooker, gave meaning to what He did. This, however, did not last very long as Paul declared that there were 'greater gifts' and pointed to a more excellent way.

Ecstasy is a phenomenon in both the nativistic movements and the orthodox spiritual or Pentecostal sects. According to Sundkler, the prophet movements in South Africa (and in other parts of Africa, as indicated earlier) received their initial inspiration and impetus from the 'radical Protestant sects of the "hot Gospel" type',[72] and further that 'via the syncretistic bridge of Zulu Zionism, radical spiritualised Christianity from the west was changed into African spiritism'.[73] Baëta states that the spiritist Churches emphasise a kind of baptised spirit possession, together with their revivalistic trends.[74]

The overruling position of the ancestor spirits is clearly stated by the Rev. S. P. Lediga, who maintains that 'in Africa we worship either fetishes or generally spirits. We worship the spirits of our ancestors . . . we feel and see their existence. African religions have laws, formulae, cultures, ways of life, but the essential thing is that your life should always be identified with the will of the spirit, at work and play, at worship, at a wedding perhaps, at meal times, in the harvesting and preparation of your food. Everything you do is governed completely by the will of the spirits, which behave according to the laws of the community'.[75] The functions of the ancestor spirits have been transferred to the Holy Spirit, or simply 'the Spirit', so that in the independent post-Christian movements their 'holy spirit' is no longer the Holy Spirit of whom we learn in Scripture. The sense of community is so strong with the traditional African, the interchange between the natural and supernatural world so vivid that it is most difficult to be freed from the 'blood and soil' relationship, and Christianity will always be in danger from these syncretistic moods. Lediga even wishes to see that the African religion 'should have been the basis of our Christian belief. But this is not allowed by the soapbox, narrow-minded type of Christian. In my own primitive religion I get the mysticism that I miss in the Christian religion.'[76] He reverts to his own African religion, because it seems as if 'the whole world does not walk with the Lord'.[77] This is a careless statement that needs to be treated with reserve, but it is necessary to give meticulous attention to all the implications involved when two religions, 'two different spiritual worlds',[78] happen to meet. Every religion has a creed, a cult and a culture. The last two can change but the creed remains basically the same: it is interrelated with the whole life-structure of a person. We cannot borrow a leg here an an eye there. What is essential, however, is that the creed be interpreted in relation to the cult and culture of a people, and here the norm is nothing less than Scripture.

The Church in Africa has, as a result of the antipathy of missionaries to emotionalism, gone to the other extreme and 'carried with it opposition to the basic elements of African religious expression'.[79] Andersson whole-heartedly agrees to this, and adds: 'The constantly repeated accusations against the mission and its lack of Spirit bear eloquent testimony to the African's need for an enthusiastic

Christianity'.[80] The identification of ecstasy with the effects of the Spirit has put the missionaries on their guard, but their fears have often been exaggerated. Andersson indicates that the Swedish Pentecostal Revivalists have practised the enthusiastic type of Christianity, but 'against fears, this preaching of the Gospel has not, either in Liberia or in Ruanda-Urundi, led to syncretism or separatist formations'.[81] When the African can vent his strong religious feelings, in spite of the inherent dangers, there is not the precondition for a slide into 'pathological forms of African religion, morbid excrescences which constitute a menace to society'.[82] It is, however, the antipathy to emotionalism, 'its divorce from art, its lack of true understanding of ritual through which the African apprehends religious truths . . .'[83] that gives birth to such pathological forms of African religion or to an introvertedness in the Church's life. The basic problem in West Africa, to which these excerpts refer, is thus not race or denominationalism, which are considered major factors in South Africa.

Dreams, convulsions, visions, trances – these states to which prophets are subject have generally been described as hysterical phenomena. They give the impression of epileptic fits, in the same way as demonic possessions in the old religion.[84] They can also be a sign of inspiration, of a spirit taking hold.[85] The Zulu diviners get into such a state because of possession by *amatongo*, or ancestral spirits.[86] Andersson's observation is that the pathological conditions associated with shamanism are only experienced during the call of the prophet, and during the initial stages of his prophetic activities which, he says, should not be correlated with abnormality whether incipient or latent. The *banganga* in the Congo were actually specialists in treating epileptic cases. There is a clear distinction made amongst Africans between those who are 'spirit possessed' and those who suffer from mental disturbances.[87] Simon Kimbangu, for example, displayed certain nervous automotions when he acted in his capacity as a prophet, such as 'quakings, head-shaking, rolling of the eyes, jumpings, muscular spasms and attacks of cramp'.[88] Later on, however, when the prophets entered upon the task of healing and casting out evil spirits, they produced ecstasy by using music, song and dancing, in order 'to attain the state required of them'.[89] Sundkler relates this statement: 'I now often get *uMoya* when singing, always when praying for the sick.'[90] In the case of the Shembe movement 'certain hymns, especially those about the heavenly Jerusalem or about Ekuphakameni and Zion . . ., will stir up [such] feelings that *uMoya* appears. . . . During prayer, and especially prayer for the sick, the Spirit wakes up with irresistible power.'[91] At most of

130

the meetings of Simon Kimbangu, new initiates began to quake as a result of receiving the Spirit, and the symptoms of ecstasy and shaking of the body were practical proof of the authenticity of the experience. Kimbangu said that 'the hymns must be sung loudly and enthusiastically for then he would be given the power of healing. The louder the song, the stronger became the Spirit.'[92] Ecstasy is considered by many to be an essential accompaniment to healing, with the result that the traditional artificial methods mentioned above are used to reach such a state. In the case of Kimbangu, the bodies of the people started to shake, and kept on for up to three days; some howled like animals, and others leapt high up in the air. It is however agreed that not all shaking is a sign of the Spirit, but that there may also be visits of 'evil spirits' the possible presence of which should be carefully investigated.

Kimbangu and his co-prophets busied themselves in the early stages of his career driving out evil spirits in the name of Jesus. Baëta mentions striking cases of the expelling of evil spirits. For example, a girl had the experience that the spirit of one of her ancestors, an outstanding fetish priest, wanted to enter into her. Several persons formed a ring round her and started to sing, to the rhythm of a tambourine: 'Let the evil spirit depart from the land, may the light reign.' She danced and jumped and raved for over two hours, and then lay prostrate and exhausted on the ground.[93] Another way of getting rid of a bad spirit is by ritual vomiting, while 'the faithful' sing and shout and speak with tongues. This is preceded by confession of hidden sins.[94]

Evil spirits are also driven out by individuals. Shembe went out preaching and driving out demons – guided by the 'Holy Spirit'.[95] Appiah, the founder of the Musama Disco Christo Church, had three baptisms: the first when God's spirit descended upon him and he could speak with tongues; the second, when he received power over evil spirits, and thirdly when the Holy Spirit came upon the whole group.[96] The Salvation Army won great influence in the Congo because of the conviction that it had 'the magical power of exorcising evil spirits and withhcraft'.[97] The independent Ngunzistic Salvation Army became popular because it was believed that, in observing the rites of this movement, one became immune to witchcraft.[98] Here the magic of legalism is fully accepted. In the Ngunza-Khaki movement of Simon Mpandi they use copper wire, a protective amulet, which is placed on the threshold of the hut or hung over the door in order to catch *bandoki* (witches).[99]

In this movement the sick are sprinkled with consecrated water to expel evil spirits and *bandoki*.[100] Evil spirits can be transferred by

131

physical contact, and the members of the Khaki movement are not allowed to shake hands with outsiders, as they may receive their evil spirits.[101] In the Munkukusa movement the aim was to stop the ravages of disease and death. To obtain this, they had to have peace with the spirits of the dead and be freed from *ndoki*.[102] The Church of the Twelve Apostles or *Nackabah*, which claimed to be the first of the 'spiritual Churches' in Ghana (Grace Tani, baptised by William Wade Harris, was its driving force) and subscribed to the main articles of faith of the Methodist Church, use the African dancing gourd rattle to drive away evil spirits.[103] The Bible itself has been used to drive out evil spirits, so that contact between it and the magical world view is established.

The reaction to the Church's failure to satisfy the needs of the indigenous peoples has been a partial or total reversion to the basic doctrines of the indigenous religion. In this situation, men seek their salvation again in the 'glorious' past and the religion of their ancestors. In the Ngunzist movement, as in others, 'the Spirit' became the sole authority. What Andersson says about this movement is applicable to all others in like position, namely that when 'Spirit visions' took the place of the Bible, 'there was no longer any restraining influence to prevent the development of Ngunzism in new directions'.[104] The spirit of Kimbangu, for example, could enter the mbemba bird (a 'sacred' bird in the Congo).[105] During cultic acts, such as the anointing of sick persons with palm oil, the formula 'In the name of the Father, the Son and the Holy Ghost' is found, but God's name was pushed more and more into the background, and names of angels and apostles together with supernatural powers, or ancestral spirits, took precedence. Animism always puts something else between the person and God which is also a heresy of established Churches. The most important article of the Ngunzist creed, like that of the 'Faith Society', which gathered every Thursday in order 'to seek the Holy Spirit as the apostles did',[106] is that of the Spirit, the loss of which is the greatest conceivable misfortune. The Holy Communion in the Christian sense has disappeared, and baptism is considered to be baptism of the 'Holy Spirit'.

The ancestor cult takes precedence in the nativistic and even in Christian movements. In the Musama Disco Christo Church, people not only received a heavenly name when they moved to Mazano, their new Jerusalem, 'but devoted themselves to prayer and invocation of spirits'.[107] When Matopoly Moses, the son of the prophet Jehu, took over, his father invoked 'the Spirit', showing the followers how to 'keep strong in spiritual matters'.[108] The main task – apart from speaking in tongues, foreseeing the future, especially misfortunes, detecting witches and evil persons, exorcising the devil and evil spirits, interpreting their dreams and those of others, discerning the 'spiritual' causes of evil – was to invoke spirits which give vital force. Pauw refers to a prophetess Botlhale, at first a member of the London Missionary Society, but who became an Anglican through marriage; according to his informants, she was given extraordinary powers by the ancestors who always have at their disposal the all-pervading mystic power or vital force. Her son maintained, however, that these powers had to be ascribed to the Spirit of God. The Spirit entered her and 'took her out of the Church', in order that she might preach to the people by whom she was enabled to predict events, and prescribe the necessary medicine for the sick, 'making special use of prayer and water that had been "prayed for" '.[109] In the Ngunza-khaki movement water out of graves is used in their cultic practices, which take place on the graves especially of old, influential and great chiefs. During the proceedings, which begin with prayer and song 'the dead rise up out of their graves and place themselves behind the living, to whom they reveal themselves to give them the Spirit. It is in the Spirit, moreover, that the visitors see the dead and *sakama mungalo* (shake violently).'[110] Here the ancestor cult is reborn, and the old magic reigns again. This 'divine' water from graves is used in connection with healing and the restoring of the spirit, and as a medicine against *bandoki*; it is kept in the hut as protection against this evil. In procuring this water, long sticks and tubes are used which are poked down into the graves as near down to the body as possible in order to get hold of the so-called 'corpse juice'.[111] Shembe simply states: 'pour into me the spirit of power'.[112] The human body and anything associated with it is considered to have the strongest magic. This accounts for many ritual murders in African society, even today.

In the Ngunza-khaki movement, the followers wear rings whereby they are enabled to hear in the Spirit the revelations which come and go; the prophet especially is enabled with these rings to hear what God says.[113] Here is fetishism plain and simple. One of the main tasks of the prophets in this movement is to 'give' the Spirit to its members. Just as in animism, the spirit is invoked by those entrusted with this task; the spirit is 'given', by man's initiative and not by God's. The central doctrine of the Holy Spirit is obscured and distorted here beyond recognition.[114] The position of the doctrine of the Holy Spirit in a Church indicates whether that Church is standing or falling.[115] In a utilistic religion, such as that of the nativistic movements, 'the Spirit' is at man's disposal.

In the Ngunza-khaki movement several methods are used to find out whether or not a person is possessed by 'the Spirit'; for example, when he does not shake after he has been given holy water or water from graves. During this process of testing the congregation sings continuously, and great excitement is created.[116] A method of discerning the righteous from the unrighteous is walking on fire. Here fire and the Spirit are used together; those not affected by the fire are pure. In the fire the followers also receive their baptism. 'The congregation of the Spirit must be baptised in fire',[117] a literal interpretation of the Biblical words in Acts ii.

The *theme of deception*, i.e. of having been misled with regard to the means of commanding supernatural forces, is heard in connection with 'the Spirit'. In the Khakist movement it is believed that the missionaries kept back the Spirit. 'The mission deceives us; it has, certainly, given us much that is good and we thank it for this, but it will not give us the Spirit.'[118] The adherents complain that the missionaries kept back 'central points in the Christian doctrine from their Black pupils', for example, the full Biblical truths were not revealed, especially those concerning fetishes, sorcery and 'the secret of magic, with the help of which they themselves have procured wisdom and power'.[119] According to Sundkler, the African maintains there is 'another Bible, hidden away from the Bantu by the Whites, a book containing the real truth, whilst the "old Bible" . . . was written only to cheat the Black man'.[120] In this way the Bible becomes a 'new opponent',[121] and itself one of the reasons for establishing their own kingdom with their own divine authority, which in this case is the spirit-filled prophet. Many nativists claim they have their own Scriptures. Among accusations against a missionary at a village parish were: 'When we received the Gospel we also received teachers, but when latterly we have begun to receive the Holy Spirit, you report us to the state so that we are bound and put in prison.'[122] In the Munkukusa movement, the reaction against the Whites was so strong that help was eventually sought from the deceased ancestors who 'have died before the Whites came to the country'.[123] They then go to the graves not only of the rich and the powerful, but also of those who have not heard the Scriptural message for the significant reason that 'the Christian spirits' have been so 'tamed' by the Whites that they are 'inefficient with regard to the tasks expected of them, as only the cruel, violent and the hard can bind *bandoki* and not those softened by God's word'.[124] In this the old proves to them to be more effective than the new.

The stage has now been reached in which it can safely be said that in the African nativistic movements spirit possession, the general feature in African religion, has found a new emphasis. Baëta remarks that, in the Twelve Apostles and the Musama Churches, their divine healing 'spiritual' techniques are actually based on the revivalist tradition and 'a sort of baptised African spirit possession'.[125]

Any intense emotionalism in the sectarian movements and in the Churches has easily led to schisms in Africa. In the above-named movements ectasy is looked upon 'as the climax of religious experience; in both it is believed that, in this state, contact and communication with the spiritual world is achieved and values received. The practice of exorcism is connected with both; they employ practically identical methods of inducing the desired state, i.e. rhythmic and repetitious music with special forms of dancing, the presence of a sympathetic and expectant crowd (naturally of very moderate educational attainment) and the encouragement, in various ways, of emotional abandon.'[126] This is a clear summary of what happens in the nativistic movements. Whoever has ecstatic experiences is 'being filled with the Holy Ghost', 'lost in the spirit', 'speaking in tongues' and 'rolling'.[127] In Point 7 of the summary of what the Musana Disco Christo Church believes, it is stated: 'We believe that the Holy Spirit can declare its presence emotionally or solemnly.'[128] In the catechism of the Apostolic Revelation Society, seven essentials for anointing are mentioned, the first of which is 'that I should completely surrender myself to the Holy Spirit and inherit the Holy Spirit as my only real wealth'.[129] It is sometimes difficult to distinguish between the African form of spirit possession and Christian Pentecostalism, with its emphasis on 'having' and 'getting' the Spirit. Taylor and Lehmann distinguish between three kinds of possession: first, that kind which is regarded as a malevolent attack, from which the victim can only be saved by the use of supernatural means of exorcism; secondly, the possession of the spirit of a dead king, which means life-long service at the royal shrine; and thirdly, the supernatural possession of a medium for purposes of divining.[130]

'Emotionalism' is one of the characteristic features of the services. In the nativistic ritual, participants work themselves up to a state in which they can take possession of the Spirit. Here, as reported by Baëta, certain acts have to be performed in order to get the right effect: dancing, singing, night-time services, immersion in a pool, praying for the sick, and, says Sundkler, 'on these occasions the hidden depths of repressed African possession come to the surface in the form of speaking with tongues and shouting in the spirit. . . . .'[131] That the establishment of these movements owes much to the Western antipathy towards emotionalism becomes even clearer.[132] Taylor and Lehmann rightly emphasise that 'generally speaking, communal worship is supremely the means, and the expression, of the realisation of the presence and benediction of God. But it is primarily an emotional experience. . . . To say that emotionalism is paramount would be entirely misleading, yet the fundamental emphasis of their worship is emotive rather than rational.'[133] This approach is governed by the fact that 'action predominates over thinking, and religion is for [the worshipper] rather something that he does'.[134]

The emphasis on the spiritual aspect, or rather on spiritism, is due to the traditional African background. Shropshire says that the African 'is not so much illogical as mystical, having a circumconsciousness of mysterious forces'.[135] He continues: 'He is part of his environment, and is at one with it, which is largely that of spiritual and natural forces.'[136] In the traditional African world everything is controlled by the spiritual world 'which determines and awards weal or woe, abundance or want, illness or health, continuing life or death'.[137] In Buganda, for example, at the naming of a child, the names of the child's ancestors are recited until the baby laughs, which is a sign that it was 'the ancestor just named whose spirit should be the child's guardian and whose name was said to be revived and restored in this way'.[138] In 1913 the Native Anglican Church had to forbid the Okwalula custom relating to the invocation of an ancestor to name a child.[139] The sense of spiritism is so strong that even 'medicines' have what may be called 'attached spirits'.[140] Evil dreams can even take away one's Spirit, but more powerful fetishes can be used to recover it, with the result that prayer as understood in Scripture is superfluous. Fetishes are used in the case of oracles, when songs associated with witchcraft are sung and the gourd rattle is used for its rhythmic effect, as in West Africa. At these oracles, people believe that they can hear even their own disembodied spirits speak. The 'omnipotence of spirits' can even be detected from a sudden gust of wind or the rustling of banana trees.[141]

The founder of the Lumpa Church, Alice Lenshina, is accused of having connection with ngulu-possession – *ngulu* being secondary divinities. A person possessed with these divinities is designated as 'Chief of Spirits', with the power of prophecy and healing, and ability to detect the original of the Spirit related to a specific sick person. Alice signs her name as Mulenga Lubusha, 'the names of two powerful "spirits", one of the new and one of the old religion of her country'.[142] In Zulu society, as has been indicated, the diviner receives supernatural powers 'by being entered into by the spirit of one of her ancestors'.[143] The same aspect – 'being entered' by 'the Spirit' – plays an important role in the Tlhaping Pentecostal Churches.[144] African spiritism thus finds congenial soil in the pentecostal approach to the doctrine of the Holy Spirit, and its emphasis is strongest of all in a situation where the old structure faces the danger of being broken up. In the African world, the spirits of the departed become the guardian spirits of their dependants, helping and punishing the living, depending on the living for sacrifices, desiring that 'the ancient and laudable customs of the tribe and family should be observed.'[145]

Pauw has indicated the points of similarity between Tolonyane, a prophet who followed the traditional lines, and the nativistic prophets and apostles. He emphasises especially the question of 'revelations through direct inspiration by the ancestor spirits, as separatists claim to receive from the Spirit of God' and he continues: 'The ancestor spirits stand in an intercessory position between the living and God, the Supreme Being', and he adds this does not seem a modern innovation.[146] Some even believe that Tolonyane received his revelations not from the spirits but from God. The ancestral spirits occupy a position of mediatorship between the living and the Supreme Being. People subjected to rapid social change, when the social structure is rapidly breaking up, push the ancestral cult slowly into the background. In the movements described by Pauw, magic finds a new emphasis as an antidote to the psychological disturbance of this break-up which partially accounts at the same time for the moralistic, legalistic emphasis in African Churches, sects and nativistic movements. This in a certain sense fills the vacuum.[147] Pauw says: 'As far as a ritual object or act is believed to have a certain direct efficacy it bears a *magical* character. Therefore the moralistic teaching attributing a certain direct efficacy to correct behaviour is akin to magic.'[148]

There is a parallel between the traditional role of the ancestor spirits and that of the Pentecostal enthusiastic concept of the Holy Spirit.[149] Pauw finds it somewhat vague amongst the Tswana, whereas with the Zulu it is more obvious. Spirit-possession has here been transferred to the idea of being 'filled with' the Holy Spirit. The ecstatic forms of Western Pentecostalism find congenial points of contact in African spiritism, which is also characterised by singing, dancing, shaking of the body and even in some cases speaking with tongues. In the nativistic movements this 'Spirit possession' or 'filling with' the Holy Spirit becomes associated with baptism, mostly in running water over which the prophet has prayed. Such baptism could be repeated on the same person every Saturday or Sunday, that is, if he/she feels unclean. It is a purification rite. In many nativistic movements the person baptised stands in the water which has been prayed over, the magical word spoken. While the water is being drunk prayers are offered that the Spirit may descend on the participant, and the congregation indulge in much singing and dancing. In healing sessions this same procedure is followed. Western spiritualism has become African spiritism.

Water and the Spirit are generally speaking closely related in the independent movements. Prophet Elliot Butelezi of the Sabbath Zionist Church blesses the water, brings the sick patient into it and acts in the name of the Trinity, assuming that the water will take away the illness, and that the patient, while drinking, will receive 'the Spirit'. Butelezi, who was haunted by the spirits of the dead, had to appease them by way of sacrifices. The 'Holy Spirit' showed him in a vision the beast appointed for such sacrifice, in which he received the assistance of his pagan father. His father is the mediator, 'who prays to the angels in the cattle kraal. He uses our prayer of old (i.e., of our Zulu) religion and concludes with "Our Father" '.[150] The interpretation of Christianity thus takes place in terms known to him in the Zulu religion, and to which he reverts in times of stress. There is a whole range of similarities between the traditional African diviner and the prophet of the nativistic movements. Even amongst many Christians, the diviner is still important. Taylor states that of sixty-four Christians he questioned in Buganda, all but four or five consulted the spirit-diviner, and the diviner herself was an Anglican, who however never attended church.[151]

Convulsions and Psychological reactions. The diviner is the man in greatest demand in Africa. When he prepares for his work, he 'shudders and yawns' and comes out sometimes 'shouting and laughing hysterically'.[152] External signs have been the main evidence of 'spirit' presence. But 'failing more spectacular demonstrations . . . a Zionist prophet must at least produce the typical Zionist snort during a service to show that the Spirit is very near'.[153] In the Ngunzist movement, 'the Spirit should express itself in external phenomena, in ecstasy and above all in body-shaking'.[145] Before the entering of the spirits, the 'victim' experiences some 'acute psychological tension or frustration'.[155]

The laying on of hands has also found an indigenous interpretation. Characteristically it starts unusual movements which are ascribed to the work of the Holy Spirit.[156] This is a type of religion which wants to see results. In the Pentecostal separatist sects among the Tswana, as in the nativistic movements elsewhere, 'the Spirit' is the main source of revelation and numinous power. While the first still reveal strong Christian characteristics, it nevertheless tends toward the confusion that exists with regard to the Spirit in the latter. Here also dreams, visions and the speaking of a voice are forms of

138

revelation, and here also bodily movements and those utterances known as 'speaking with tongues' are signs of 'the Spirit', revealing his presence which is explained as the entrance of 'the Spirit into the person'.[157] Ecstasy leads actually to depersonalisation. Here the person's own life moves into the background so that another, in these cases the powerful life of 'the Spirit', comes in. Ecstasy could, however, also be a sign of the entrance of an evil spirit.

Action is basic to the African religion, and like ritualism and emotionalism, it may be described as 'a desire for a religion which is vividly experienced'.[158] It provides for strong sensory experience, and these convulsions must also be seen in this light. Spinning around is connected with revelation and often the groups run in circles during the service in houses, usually accompanied by singing or a drum. Those places where the services take place in the open air have circles deeply trodden out – they run round barefooted. The singing and running in circles usually take place *after* confession of sins. When one becomes filled with the Spirit, a repetitive '*zzzzzzzzz . . .*' sound is made through the teeth. Different sounds, however, are made in different areas. All this has to do with the senses and action, which appeals especially to people in poorer material circumstances. Loud 'Amens' and 'Hallelujahs' are interjected during sermons. All this contributes to an intensely emotional service.

Speaking with Tongues. In discussing language perversions in East Africa, Prof. Otto Raum explains the phenomenon as arising from the desire to transmit information in code: in this way communicator and receiver are more closely united than in normal speech.[159] The same idea lies behind the language of the diviner. This language takes different forms. In the primitive society souls or ghosts have voices, and the familiar spirits of the Zulu diviners talk in a low whistling tone; sneezing is a sign of the presence of the ancestral spirit.[160] Callaway maintains that the spirits make the diviner in training cry '*Hai, hai, hai*' in continual repetition. [161] The spirit song starts with '*Ehhe – ehhe – ehhe – ehhe ee ee*' and ends with these syllables.[162] Such apparently meaningless syllables are also found in the Zulu tribal songs, and are sung only on ritual occasions.[163] Ventriloquism is used by most diviners and can be interpreted only by them.[164] Some diviners even claim to understand the language of birds and animals. Prof. Raum has evidence that the diviners in the Middledrift area near Alice, South Africa, produce sounds made by ritually prohibited animals.[165] Many archaisms and obscurities of language are used in African poems and praise songs;[166] thus, understandably, songs composed by apprentice diviners are often claimed to have been

139

received through dreams via the Spirits.[167] 'Speaking with tongues' is well documented as a trait in divination as practised by 'possessed' persons.[168]

Both in animism and in the Pentecostal Christian sects, 'speaking with tongues' has a significant role. It is no problem for the African to understand this. Many African tribes had already various forms of speaking with tongues long before the introduction of Christianity. Sundkler says: 'At least it would show that when the Zulu prophet follows his Corinthian colleague, rather against St. Paul's advice, he does so because it is an old heathen pattern.'[169] In European and American Churches, speaking with tongues has persisted, alone of all related phenomena, and Clark maintains that it owes its survival to its place in Scripture.[170] There is even a Presbyterian Church in New York State where the phenomenon has occurred.[171] It recalls also the Huguenot *Camisards* of Cevennes.[172] In Africa the convulsions and shakings persist, but, as a movement becomes stabilised, these particular phenomena become less. Not all enthusiastic movements have given rise to glossolaly, but we may confidently say that most of them have. There is no evidence of glossolaly amongst the Montanists, the Schismatical Franciscans, the Anabaptists or the early Quakers. It is also absent in early Methodism, but was a phenomenon amongst the Jansenists and, going underground for 100 years, it re-emerged in 1830 near Port Glasgow in Edward Irving's congregation. [173]

Speaking with tongues is 'part of a definite type of spirituality, one which cannot be happy unless it is seeing results'.[174] Its fuller appearance takes place with singing, praying – especially for the sick, during purification in water – and in ecstatic states after much dancing accompanied by singing. For Kimbangu it was 'the language of those who dwell in Heaven' and, after receiving 'the gift of tongues', persons may be fit 'to officiate as prophets'.[175]

Monica Wilson, in discussing the Pentecostal Holiness Church amongst the Nyakyusa, which holds 'highly emotional services' at which members are expected to 'speak with tongues', tells how during prayers the whole congregation turns into a jabbering unit, using unintelligible utterances, although words from foreign languages can be distinguished. Monica Wilson says 'Our informants maintained that the attraction of the church was that its members seem "to have more of the Holy Ghost", as demonstrated by the "speaking with tongues". . . .'[176] The three baptisms of Appiah, the prophet of the Musama Disco Christo Church, have already been mentioned; at the first of these baptisms, the Holy Spirit came upon him and he spoke with tongues.[177] Acts ii. 4 features prominently among their

140

set of beliefs. This Faith Society (*Egyidifu Kuw*) had five prophets in the beginning, whose activities included prayer, healing and speaking with tongues.[178] Pauw refers to the same phenomenon, when meaningless sounds and whole phrases are interjected during praying and preaching, which is usually accompanied by bodily movements, and explained as the 'entrance of the Spirit into the person'.[179] Tolonyane acted on traditional lines and received inspiration from the ancestral spirits: someone who accompanied him to his cave heard a confusion of unusual sounds, believed to be the voices of ancestral spirits. Pauw adds that this is comparable to the Separatists speaking with tongues when they are 'entered' by the Spirit.[180] The traditional religion has here also found a point of contact with enthusiastic Christianity.

'Speaking with tongues' was for Paul quite a normal phenomenon, and the gifts of healing and speaking with tongues are mentioned in the same breath. In translating 1 Cor. xiv. 2, the New English Bible uses the phrase 'language of ecstasy'; the RSV 'Speaks in a tongue', and 'unknown tongue' is used in the New Chain Reference Bible. Glossolaly is considered to be charisma; it is not of man but of God (1 Cor. xiv. 2). In the Hellenistic religions these mystical ecstatic forms were found, and Paul observes their external relationship with phenomena in Christianity; however, he indicates the difference in religious content. Higher than the gift of glossolaly is the gift of prophecy based on God's love (cf. 1 Cor. xiii, xiv. 3).[181] Paul maintains that, under the compulsion of the Holy Spirit, the glossolalist speaks mysteries in the Spirit. He who spoke in a tongue usually did not understand it, but had to 'pray for the power to interpret' (1 Cor. xiv. 13). Thus Paul valued glossolaly, and says 'Now I want you all to speak in tongues' (1 Cor. xiv. 5), i.e. they would then have the sign that they received the Holy Spirit.[182] He himself used it (1 Cor. xiv. 18). Only when interpreted does glossolaly stand on the same level as prophecy (1 Cor. xiv. 5).[183]

Paul makes the accusation against the Corinthians that their desire was directed towards the spirits (he would accuse the independent movements of the same today), and that every gift was ascribed to a specific spirit sent by the Holy Spirit. According to the Christians the Holy Spirit is the source and the spirits the mediators; to this also some independent movements will agree. Paul states in 1 Cor. xiv. 26: 'When you come together, each one has a hymn, a lesson, a revelation, a tongue, or an interpretation.' This, too, could be said of much African independentism. The meetings at Corinth must have been very unruly and chaotic, with enormous enthusiasm, but little sense made out of it all. The speaking in tongues simply for some outward theatrical effect is childishness (1 Cor. xiv. 20);

the congregation has to sit in judgment on the prophetic utterances (1 Cor. xiv. 29–35). Knox says 'Evidently it is the curb, not the spur, that is needed in first-century Corinth'.[184]

The first form of revival in modern Africa is that found in these independent movements whether they are Churches, sects or nativistic movements. This is not merely enthusiasm, in which the individual is primarily occupied with himself, but in the indigenous movements the sense of community is very strong; here the ethnic interpretation overuled the theological interpretation of the Church. Thus the nativistic movements are 'blood and soil' entities which have basically nothing to do with revival in the theological sense. This is in contrast with the revival in East Africa.[185] Spirit-possession opens up to the possessed the whole ethnic natural and supernatural world, through which Christian concepts find a 'new' meaning. Christian sects have often developed into Churches, but where nativism is basic this will not happen because contact has been lost with the World and with Christ's work on the Cross.[186] The Church must face the traditional African spirit world and magic – especially where the action of a Spirit explains every event – it is not too difficult to transfer the function of 'the Spirit' to that of the Holy Spirit.

REFERENCES

1. Smith, *Knowing the African*, 73.
2. Sundkler, *Prophets*, 289.
3. Cf. B. A. Pauw, 'African Christians and their Ancestors', *Ned. Geref. Teol. Tydskrif*, Sept. 1963, 202 ff. In many parts of Africa, South America and the West Indies, African ancestors have been identified with Catholic saints. Cf. M. J. Herskovits, 'African Gods and Catholic Saints in New World Religious Belief', *American Anthropologist*, Vol. 39 (1937), 635–43; *The Myth of the Negro Past*, New York, Harper and Bros., 1941.
4. K. A. Busia, *Position of the Chief in Ashanti*, 1950, 197.
5. Pauw, 207.
6. Wilson, *Nyakyusa*, 189.
7. Baëta, 1. Point 5 of the Ghana Apostolic Church Almanac of 1958 reads 'The baptism of the Holy Spirit for believers, with signs following'. Ibid., 1.
8. Sundkler, *Prophets*, 191.
9. Ibid., 242 ff.
10. C. G. Baëta, *Christianity and African culture*, (ed.) Christian Council, Gold Coast, 1955, 51–61.
11. Tempels, 30.
12. Cf. Sundkler, *Ministry*, 287–88: 'In the system of the clan, the fundamental facts of life are all represented: the vitality and fertility of the individual and the family, marriage, procreation, birth and death – all linked up with the continuing existence of the clan. The demands of the clan consequently present the church with its most persistent challenge.'
13. Schlosser, *Eingeborenen*, 52.

14. Sundkler, *Prophets*, 252; W. C. Willoughby, *The Soul of the African*, SCM, 1928, 104. 'Great ancestor-spirits are thought to enter into individuals occasionally and use them as mediums of communication. They talk with spirits. The spirit which possesses them is that of an important chief or medicine-man.' The difference between a person who is merely possessed and a prophet is that the former delivers a message of local importance while the prophet delivers a message of national concern and appeals for his authority only to the spirit which inspires him. Ibid., 115 ff.

15. Pauw, *Religion*, 207.

16. Sundkler, *Bantu Prophets*, 249.

17. Cf. Oosthuizen, *The Theology of a South African Messiah*, 82–87.

18. Pauw, *Religion*, 207.

19. William D. Reyburn, 'Africanisation and African Studies', *Practical Anthropology*, Vol. 9, No. 3, May-June 1962, rightly maintains that 'Catholic ritual and belief is to many in Africa quite meaningful because it provides a framework for the Christian to maintain his mystical communion with the spirit world. The Christian does not as a rule change his attitude toward the assumed realities of spiritual existence. . . . It is to be observed that the ancestors (Christian and pagan) continue to play an exceedingly important role in the lives of the living.

20. Sundkler, *Prophets*, 252.

21. *UMoya* could mean breath, physical strength, wind, Spirit or free soul.

22. Sundkler, 244.

23. G. van der Leeuw, *De primitieve mensch en de religie*, Wolters, 1952, 171.

24. Sundkler, *Prophets*, 249.

25. Tempels, 31. The Prophet's strength depends on the number of his followers, and such a prophet can strengthen more effectively the force of his followers.

26. Andersson, 109. Andersson relates that when the Administrator came to Kimbangu he was interrupted by the prophet 'who turned away from him and addressed the Holy Ghost'. Andersson, 62. He refers to a certain Ntwalani 'who had been possessed by a Spirit and had been assured by Kimbangu that it was the Spirit of God. . . .' Andersson, 66.

27. Ibid., 109.

28. Ibid.

29. P. D. Fueter, 'Theological Education in Africa', IRM, Oct. 1956, 388.

30. Shropshire, 189.

31. Tempels, 41.

32. Sundkler, *Prophets*, 260.

33. E. B. Tylor, *Religion in Primitive Culture*, Harper, Vol. II, 1958, 209.

34. Sundkler, *Prophets*, 260.

35. Tempels, 44.

36. Tempels, 45. About the individualistic interpretation of Scripture as a result of the role played by the spirit as agent of revelation, see Pauw, *Religion*, 225. Oscar Cullmann rightly says '*God speaks to the Church today through the witness of the Apostles*. As long as there shall be a Church, the witness of the Apostles will be a sufficient norm . . . in all inspiration there is the risk of other spirits putting themselves in the place of the Holy Spirit' ('Scripture and Tradition' in *Christianity Divided*, Ed. Callahan, Obermann and O'Hanlon, Sheed & Ward, 1961, 15).

37. Andersson, 155.

38. Tylor, Vol. II, 230. Fetishism '. . . the doctrine of spirits embodied in, or attached to, or conveying influence through certain material objects'.

39. Andersson, 156.

40. Baëta, 140.

41. Andersson, 189.

42. Shembe also gives the impression that he has 'the Spirit' at his disposal. He received Isl. 144 from 'the Spirit of Jehovah while he himself 'quietened' his own spirit. See also superscription to Isl. 162.

43. Welbourn & Ogot, 81.

44. Andersson, 186. The limitation of 'the Spirit' to a certain person, in this case the prophet, is in accordance with African philosophy. Tempels, 31. Shropshire, 27: 'The chief . . . is not only king but priest; not only ruler and arbitrator but also prayer, intercessor and sacrificer. This fact must never be lost sight of, for it is of the very essence of Bantu government: it is divine, and the person of the chief is sacred. He is the intermediary between the ancestral spirits of the tribe and its subject group and he must perform the ceremonies of worship.'

45. Cf. Tylor, Vol. I, 306, Vol. II, 24, 241, 276, 281, 498. Weber says about the illiterates that 'the art of seeing is highly developed – direct seeing as well as imaginary seeing. It is a well-known fact that members of "primitive" communities often really see the spirits of the departed, or demons, or gods.' Weber, *Communication*, 53.

46. Andersson, 50. Most Africans are called to the ordained ministry by way of dreams. Cf. Sundkler, *Ministry*, 25 ff.

47. In Isihlabhelelo 58[3]: the reference may be to himself where he states:
Let your spirit come, Nkosi,
that it may heal your people.

48. Pauw, *Religion*, 206.

49. Andersson, 2.

50. Ibid., 2.

51. Ibid., 3.

52. Andersson, 3. Ecstasy is a familiar phenomenon amongst African tribes. The diviner works himself or herself up into a state of ecstasy when making rain. The prophet, who comes back from the spirit world with an important message, finds a predisposition to ecstasy, visions and dreams in order to indicate his transcendent authority. His only authority is his own inspiration and thus he uses no argument. Shropshire, 205. In the state of ecstasy the prophet enters the supernatural and then returns to tell what he has seen and heard. Shropshire, 202; vide RGG II, 410–11. The African identifies ecstasy with the effects of the spirit. Andersson, 268.

53. Ibid.

54. Sundkler, *Prophets*, 22.

55. Ibid., 22.

56. Andersson, 63.

57. L. S. Senghor indicates that the word of the prophet now takes precedence (cf. J. Jahn, *Schwarze Ballade*, Düsseldorf 1957, 222). The Prophet who pretends to speak God's word does not need Scripture; through the imperative of the word he rules over the things.

58. Andersson, 3. Shropshire, 205: 'These prophets generally become aware of their vocation after a crisis in which, perhaps, they saw a divine person or were transported to the spirit world, coming back with an important message.'

59. Sundkler, *Prophets*, 109.

60. Taylor & Lehmann, 280.

61. Out of the total of 5,760 ordained African ministers, 1,141 or 20% belong to the Pentecostal and Seventh Day Adventists. Sundkler, *Ministry*, 63.

144

62. Shropshire, 205
63. M. J. Field, *Search for Security*, Northwestern University Press, 1960, 78.
64. J. F. Fison, *The Blessing of the Holy Spirit*, Longmans, 1961, 61.
65. Ibid., 65.
66. Ibid., 66.
67. Ibid.
68. M. Buber, *Moses*, East and West Library, 1946, 110.
69. Fison, 68.
70. Tylor, Vol. II, 505. Tylor tries to show that 'the practice of bringing on swoons or fits by religious exercises, in reality or pretence, is one belonging originally to savagery, whence it has been continued into higher grades of civilisation.' Vol., II, 505. This is, however, refuted later in this chapter: Emotionalism is a characteristic of many Church movements in the West as well as in Africa. The possession of the Holy Spirit either presupposes or, in some cases, leads to a state of violent emotionalism. A. Dubb, in his thesis entitled: *The African Church in the East Bank Location, East London*, 26, divided the Churches into four categories with regard to emotionalism, namely (*i*) emotional display discouraged, (*ii*) as above but extempore prayers and prayer meetings, (*iii*) free emotional expression as a result of Holy Spirit possession, (*iv*) extreme emotionalism.
71. E. J. Clark, *The Small Sects in America*, Abingdon, rev. ed., no date, 86.
72. Sundkler, *Prophets*, 299.
73. Ibid., 299.
74. Baëta, 140.
75. S. P. Lediga, 'The disciple of Jesus Christ facing African religions', SA *Outlook*, May 1, 1962, 69.
76. Lediga, 70.
77. Ibid., 70.
78. H. Kraemer, *Religion and the Christian Faith*, Lutterworth, 1958², 388.
79. J. S. Trimingham, *The Christian Church and Islam in West Africa*, IMC Pamphlet No. 3, SCM, 1956², 36.
80. Andersson, 268.
81. Ibid.
82. Trimingham, *The Christian Church and Islam in West Africa*, 36.
83. Ibid., 36.
84. Tylor, Vol. II, 217, 224, 516.
85. Tylor, Vol. II, 217.
86. Callaway, *Religion of Amazulu*, 183 ff., 259 ff.
87. Andersson, 6. In Kimbanguism 'dreams and visions, speaking in tongues, body shakings and other ecstatic manifestations are proof of the presence of the spirit ... the absence of such phenomena as well as all sickness and weakness are signs that the Spirit has left the person in question. All sorts of external aids are then resorted to get once more into the state of ecstasy' (Andersson, 110).
88. Ibid., 6.
89. Andersson, 7.
90. Sundkler, *Prophets*, 246.
91. Ibid., 246–7.
92. Andersson, 58.
93. Baëta, 109.
94. Cf. Oosthuizen, *The Theology of a South African Messiah*, 122.
95. Ibid., 110.
96. Baëta, 31.
97. Andersson, 129.

98. Ibid., 135.
99. Ibid., 155.
100. Ibid., 156.
101. Ibid., 178.
102. Ibid., 203.
103. Baëta, 15.
104. Andersson, 80.
105. Ibid., 107.
106. Baëta, 33. Animals that behaved at the time in a peculiar way were thought to be possessed by Kimbangu's spirit, although he was still alive. Most African tribes accept at least two souls. The *bodily soul* is associated with life, and the *free spirit* with a person's authority and vital force. Man's free spirit can wander about: it could become bewitched when outside the body, which spells danger to the life of a person. There are also among certain peoples in Africa the shadow and dream soul.
107. Baëta, 39.
108. Ibid., 41.
109. Pauw, 48–49.
110. Andersson, 174.
111. Ibid., 175.
112. Isihlabhelelo 135: 3.
113. Andersson, 155.
114. Cf. H. Wheeler Robinson, *The Christian Experience of the Holy Spirit*, Nisbet, 1952, 40. 'The inclusive name in the New Testament for this new factor is "the Holy Spirit", by which name we denote the whole activity of the divine in relation to the human personality, as mediated through Christ.'
115. Ibid., 42.
116. Andersson, 171.
117. Ibid., 172.
118. Ibid., 192.
119. Ibid., 191.
120. Sundkler, *Prophets*, 278.
121. Cf. ibid., 278.
122. Andersson, 114.
123. Ibid., 205.
124. Ibid.
125. Baëta, 140.
126. Baëta, 140. Andersson, 178. In the Khaki movement a song is sung with the following words: '*And when God's apostle has sinned, he shall not fall into ecstasy. . . . Ah! when the prophet has sinned, he shall not fall into ecstasy*, etc'. Ecstasy and trance are the conditions in which one receives revelations. Cf. Willoughby, *The Soul of the Bantu*, 98 ff.
127. Cf. Baëta, 141.
128. Ibid., 153.
129. Ibid., 159.
130. Taylor & Lehmann, 208.
131. Sundkler, *Prophets*, 200.
132. Cf. Trimingham, *The Church in West Africa*, 36; Andersson, 268.
133. Taylor & Lehmann, 293, 294.
134. Shropshire, xxvii.
135. Ibid., xxviii.
136. Ibid., xxviii.

137. Baëta, 139.
138. Taylor, *Buganda*, 143.
139. Ibid., 144.
140. Ibid., 196.
141. Taylor & Lehmann, 198.
142. Ibid., 267.
143. Sundkler, *Prophets*, 23.
144. Pauw, *Religion*, 203.
145. Shropshire, 166.
146. Pauw, *Religion*, 205–06.
147. Pauw, *Religion*, 212. Cf. Radcliffe-Brown, *Structure and function in primitive society*, London, Cohen & West, 1952.
148. Pauw, *Religion*, 219.
149. Ibid., 207.
150. Sundkler, 'Response and Resistance to the Gospel in a Zulu Congregation', in *Basileia*, 144.
151. Taylor, *Buganda*, 125.
152. E. J. Krige, *The Social System of the Zulus*, Longmans, Green, 1936, 300. It is said about Kimbangu that 'when the sermon found its way into the prophet's heart, it awakened his power . . . and he began to shake in the manner of the Bangunza'.
153. Sundkler, *Prophets*, 248.
154. Andersson, 109. On Kimbangu's convulsions, ibid., 51, 54, 58. Quakings were regarded as practical proof in this movement that they had the Spirit. 'The prophet . . . raised his eyes toward Heaven and, while his body began to quake, put his hands on the patient's head and said: "In the name of Jesus I will cure you, be whole again".' Ibid., 44. Kimbangu's symptoms, according to eye-witnesses, were 'somewhat violent, and greatly resembling those of the heathen banganga'. Ibid., 58.
155. Taylor & Lehmann, 208; cf. Ringwald, *Akanstämme*, 43.
156. Pauw, *Religion*, 198, 200.
157. Ibid., 200.
158. Ibid., 220.
159. Cf. Otto Raum, 'Language perversions in East Africa', *Africa*, Vol. 10, 1937, 225.
160. Cf. Tylor, Vol. I, 98; cf. also Callaway, *Religion of Amazulu*, 64, 222–25, 263.
161. Callaway, 273.
162. Sundkler, *Prophets*, 238.
163. Callaway, 59, 92, 409.
164. Krige, 300.
165. Interview, 6 August, 1963.
166. Cf. Lestrade, in Schapera, I., *The Bantu-speaking Tribes of South Africa*, 296.
167. Krige, 306.
168. Prof. Otto Raum has kindly provided the author with such evidence, e.g., amongst the Tongo, Zulu, Lovedu, Shona, Pondo, Shangaan, Ashanti, etc.
169. Sundkler, *Prophets*, 248.
170. E. T. Clark, *The Small Sects in America*, Abingdon Press, 1949, 93.
171. K. J. Foreman, Romans, Corinthians, in *Longman's Bible Commentaries*, SCM, 1961, 103.
172. Cf. R. Knox, *Enthusiasm*, 551.

F 147

173. Knox, 551.
174. Ibid., 558.
175. Andersson, 59.
176. M. Wilson, *Communal Rituals of the Nyakyusa*, 189.
177. Baëta, 33.
178. Ibid., 36.
179. Pauw, 200.
180. Ibid., 206.
181. Cf. K. Kittel, *Theologisches Wörterbuch zum Neuen Testament*, Kohlhammer, 1957, 723.
182. Cf. F. W. Grosheide, '1 Korinthe', in *Korte Verklärung der Heilige Schrift*, Kampen, J. H. Kok, 1933, 170.
183. Foreman, 103.
184. Knox, 22.
185. Cf. Warren, *Revival*, 27 ff.
186. N. Longford-Smith ('Revival in East Africa', IRM, Jan. 1954, 80) states: 'At the very heart of revival is the Atonement. . . .'

5

REVIVAL IN THE EARLY CHURCH IN NORTH AFRICA AND IN THE WESTERN WORLD

DANCING, shakings, hand-clapping, speaking in tongues, visions, dreams, prophesyings, falling into trances, confessions, convulsions – in other words, the many forms of ecstasy – are not limited to Africa, but have been part of the history of the Church through the centuries. It may be profitable to refer briefly to this as these phenomena eventually arrived with great spiritual zeal in Africa through the Pentecostal sects.

North Africa witnessed, already in the second century, an increasing emphasis on the Holy Spirit as the agent of revelation in reaction to the gradual fading away, going on at that time, of the consciousness of the true work of the Holy Spirit. Montanism exerted great influence during this time in North Africa. Montanus fell into trances, spoke in tongues, prophesied and considered himself to be the personification of the Holy Spirit.[1] Amongst the Montanists, the ecstatic features of some of the mystery cults of Asia Minor are found. Tertullian, a pre-Montanist who, however, joined the Montanists at Carthage in 207, challenged Marcion to explain what he termed an obscure kind of speech which made its way among Christians.[2] Montanus believed that the age of the Spirit, foretold in John's Gospel, had come, and that Christ's Second Coming was at hand. The emphasis was on *continuing* prophecy, and their prophets were held in higher esteem than the clergy. To the Montanist the Holy Spirit had been specially revealed in Montanus, who said: 'I am the Father, the Word, and the Holy Ghost'.[3] In the second century, Orthodoxy distinguished sharply between prophecy and the alienation of the senses.[4] Tertullian, who joined the Montanists in 207 in Carthage, maintained that the unconscious state is the very condition of prophecy. Montanus became the centre of their doctrine, as in the case of Kimbangu, Matswa and Shembe. Maximilla, one of his prophetesses, said, 'I am the Word and the Spirit, and the power'.[5] Here in North Africa the identification was rather with the Holy Spirit, whereas in modern Africa the representation is more with Jesus Christ, while they have 'the Spirit' at their disposal.

According to Tertullian, 'Hardness of heart reigned till Christ came, weakness of the flesh reigned till the Paraclete came', and Knox rightly interprets it as an identification of 'the coming of the Paraclete, not with Pentecost but with the appearance of Montanus.'[6] Montanus was now the highest and last form of Christian revelation. In the case of Kimbangu, Matswa, Shembe and others, the 'Paraclete' speaks through them. Knox maintains that St. Jerome is probably justified in stating that, according to Montanist doctrine, 'God, having failed to save the world by the two first degrees (of his revelation) came down through the Holy Spirit into Montanus, Priscilla and Maximilla'.[7] The above-mentioned prophets of Africa would agree to this description being applied to them. Tertullian considered the Apostles as those who 'have the Spirit wholly in the works of prophecy and the efficacy of [healing] virtues and the evidences of tongues, not partially as all others have'.[8] It is interesting that Tertullian speaks about 'having' the Holy Spirit, which has since been a heresy in Africa. He regarded the Church as a community of saints, awaiting the rapidly approaching end of the world,[9] and in *De Baptismo* defined what later became the Donatist view of baptism. The Holy Spirit was actually present in the waters,[10] and since no heretic by definition could be 'in possession of the Spirit', a baptism administered by a heretic or a person in mortal sin could not be valid.[11] Pepuza was the new Jerusalem, a place of refuge, where the millenium was awaited. They had a rigoristic code of ethics.

During the patristic period, it became a new dogma that a prophet must be conscious and in full command of his senses. Many maintain that prophecy flourished up to the time of Montanus, but fell into discredit as a result of Montanism itself. Even Tertullian gives the impression that he had monopolised the Holy Spirit, e.g. 'Let us leave the Holy Spirit out of the discussion, because after all he is a witness on our side.'[12] The prophet movements in Africa reveal the same notion.

Donatism, a complement to Montanism, 'was no less native, it may be thought, to the burning suns of North Africa . . . [which] has always been an unaccommodating country'.[13] While the Montanists re-emphasised prophecy, which had been neglected in the Church, the Donatists paid special attention to martyrdom. Neither can be induced, hence 'synthetic prophecy is found in Phrygia, and synthetic martyrdom in North Africa'.[14] The early 'Israelites' of the Enoch movement in South Africa, and members of the Ngunzist movement in the Congo took their suffering in a genuine and Stoic manner. The Circumcellions committed suicide in order to be honoured as martyrs. There is a suggestion that the Donatist movement, into which the Circumcellions, also described as political agitators, were absorbed, 'only provided an ecclesiastical façade for some social or nationalist agitation'.[15] It is certain that Donatism found ready acceptance among the village people, who were little affected by classical culture.[16] Africa at the time of Donatus had many who were dispossessed, the rich oppressing the poor, and it had its colonialism, which produced social discontent, desperation and revolt'[17] Thus a large movement of the disinherited, based on the religion of the spirit, swept through North Africa. Anyone who overlooks the traditionalism of these people, which was basic in their reactions to Rome, will overlook the deep-seated cultural issues involved in such reactionary movements.

The Anabaptists, the forerunners of the later Pentecostal movements, themselves had forerunners: Waldenses, Wycliffites and Hussites, who proposed a community of true and real saints. The Anabaptists lived out what they proclaimed and gave their teaching 'embodiment in actual groups living in history'.[18] The general characteristics of that movement are adult baptism, rejection of the authority of the state, a revolutionary eschatology, individualistic mysticism and a moralistic approach to Christianity.[19] Their eccentricities in behaviour were identified with the action of the Holy Spirit. They had visions, dreamt dreams and received divine revelations. The same convulsions as those experienced by the Ngunzists and other prophetic movements, were characteristic of the Anabaptists.[20] In general, these convulsions had always at first to do with miraculous healing, convulsions and spiritualism going together. An apocalyptic atmosphere is congenial to the creation of convulsions.

After the arrival of Jan Leyden at Münster in 1534, that city was proclaimed the New Jerusalem, where communism and polygamy were introduced. Communism was here more a religious conviction than anything else – a combination of 'admiration for the Early Church and a radical interpretation of the Love Feast'[21] – and the practice of polygamy was based here on two arguments: divorce was forbidden in the New Testament, but not polygamy, and God had permitted polygamy to the patriarchs by special revelation.[22] Such revelations were frequent amongst the prophets of Africa. The old Anabaptist movement produced four separate branches:

the Mennonite Baptists, the Familiars, the Seekers and Ranters, and all these – like Quakerism, which absorbed some of them – were to be 'sharply distinguished from the Christianites which surrounded them, because they remained religious of the Spirit, on the pre-Luther model, not religious of the scripture'.[23]

When the Edict of Nantes was revoked in France in 1685, 'the Huguenot world was in a mood propitious to fanaticism.'[24] A certain M. du Serre collected fifteen children from both sexes, and trained them in the art of prophecy; he 'breathed into their mouths to convey the gift of Pentecost'.[25] Mass hysteria was produced in his scholars – someone estimated the number of these child prophets or Camisards between June 1688 and February 1689 as between five and six hundred. The following unusual method of preaching was practised: 'The prophet beat his head with his hands for some time, then he fell down on his back; his stomach and throat swelled up and he remained speechless for some minutes, after which he broke out into utterance.'[26] Some drove knives through their bodies without leaving a mark, walked on fire which did not burn them and fell from rocks without being hurt. Here we are reminded of those at Pendele (Congo) in the Khakist movement who walked on fire without any physical effects.

The Quakers or Shakers have their counterpart in many of the prophetic movements in Africa, as far as the shaking phenomenon is concerned. They resembled the Anabaptists in their enthusiasm and exorcisms, and their miraculous healings. Fox, the founder, believed that 'he had power both to work miracles and to discern spirits. . . . the discerning of spirits was a gift claimed by many of the Anabaptists'.[27] The prophets in the Ngunzistic Salvation Army in the Congo claimed the same ability. The social milieu of the early Quakers was congenial for such strange spiritual phenomena as falling to the ground, foaming at the mouth, roaring, belly swelling and vomiting as a result of the working of the Holy Spirit; a woman even claimed to be the Son of God, in spite of her sex.[28] Quakerism, the Anglo-Saxon parallel of Anabaptism, came into existence to provide a Church for the poor in order of seventeenth-century England, 'to meet the needs an official and middle-class Reformation seemed incapable of supplying'.[29] The emphasis is here on the Divine Light, which leads to God unaided by Scripture or the Sacraments or any ordinances. Its own reception of revelations is primary, with the result that Scripture is completely neglected. One Quaker said: 'Have not I the Spirit, and why may not I write the Scripture as well as Paul, and what I write be as binding and infallible as that which Paul writ?'[30] They laid down their own norms, by which their revelations were judged. Knox adds: 'The prophet may come to think that he (or she) is Jesus Christ, nor should we pronounce, without further consideration, a verdict of blasphemy. For, after all, it is the experience of some mystics that their own personality seems more and more to disappear, more and more to be replaced by the divine presence dwelling in them, identifying themselves with it.'[31] Margaret Fell writes to Fox, whom she later married, 'O thou bread of life . . . O thou father of eternal felicity'. James Nayler claimed that he miraculously resurrected Dorcas Erbury, and was addressed as 'dear and precious Son of Zion, whose mother is a Virgin and whose birth is immortal'.[32] Nayler was worshipped, because they claimed to worship the God who was in him. This is actually a form of Apollinarianism. Resurrection and a visible 'God' are also two main emphases in the nativistic movements in Africa.

The convulsionaries of St.-Médard started their extraordinary dance in the cemetery, which became the scene of men and women falling down like epileptics, swallowing glass and live coals, dancing (some on the tomb), somersaulting, groaning, singing, whistling, prophesying and declaring. All this was described as God's work, by which He showed his 'sensible presence' in the cemetery.[33] in the Munkukusa movement in the Congo, the cemetery was also the scene of religious ritual, where the spirits of the dead are considered to be present, and where the members shout and dance.

The Moravian movement emphasised spirituality in a time of deism, and here eccentricities are also found. Wherever the 'spiritual world' becomes more real than God Himself, spiritualism, which is closely associated with emotionalism, prevails. The inner strength of this movement was based on its central theme, of the suffering of Christ and 'the less enthusiastic practices of religion are spoken of with startling contempt'.[34] John Wesley, a level-headed man, still sympathised 'with enthusiasm in its most violent forms'.[35] He revolted against the mystics of his day because of their isolation from this world and calmness even in the throes of revival fever. He was unsuperstitious, and opposed to the idea of bodily jerks. During a preaching assignment at Bristol, Wesley found people shouting in agony, falling to the ground and foaming at the mouth.[36] He mentions convulsive motions of the body, although not often like those of St.-Médard.[37] These manifestations of the earlier Wesleyan meetings he dismissed either as lunacy or hysteria. The devil also entered the picture. One person cried: 'I am the devil's now . . . I will be his . . . I must, I will, I will be damned.'[38] In such cases, Wesley emphasised the beneficial power of prayer and hymn-

153

singing.[39] He frequently mentions people's cries, groaning, weeping and even shaking. The outward phenomena that accompanied conversion were considered to be evidence of the supernatural. 'Great indeed was the shaking among them; lamentation and great mourning were heard.'[40] Southey's judgment on Wesley is severe: 'Like Mesmer and his disciples [Wesley] had produced a new disease, and he accounted for it by a theological theory instead of a physical one.'[41] A lay preacher in the Wesleyan connection, Cennick, had people lying before him with swollen tongues and necks, held down sometimes, and with difficulty, by as many as seven men.[42] At Whitefield's meetings in America, also, convulsions of the same kind were seen.[43]

Wesley considered these 'Demonstrations of the work of the Spirit' to be 'common at the dawn of a work but afterwards very uncommon'.[44] Here again, the 'disinherited classes which furnished the material for the Methodist revival'.[45] Although the primary leadership was supplied by the upper classes, the other came from the 'lower economic and cultural orders of society. The weavers of Bristol, the miners of Kingswood, the colliers and keelmen of Cornwall, Staffordshire and Wales – these were the groups whence Methodism drew most of its converts.[46] Wesley's own views on the phenomena were summed up as follows: '(i) God began by suddenly convincing people of sin; this naturally resulted in outcries and strong convulsions; (ii) to encourage the believers, He favoured several people with divine dreams, trances and visions; (iii) in some of these instances, after a time, nature was mixed with grace; (iv) Satan likewise mimicked this work of God, in order to discredit the whole work.'[47] Wesley was later quite relieved that there were no visions, as these gave a handle to Satan, but much later he mentions the return of these outward phenomena. For him, it was heart religion. All through the *Journal*, dreams, warnings, convulsions or bodily experiences are mentioned as experiences encountered by those who underwent conversion, or by the faithful, but he admits that men may be mistaken in visions and dreams.

'Speaking in tongues' and shakerism continued to be phenomena in religious movements, when these came to flourish in the favourable climate of the United States of America where it was only a question of trekking further if you had trouble . . . 'build there your New Jerusalem, and wait quietly for the Second Coming'.[48] The Negroes, the religiously neglected poor in America, gave rise to many sectarian movements, which suited their social and psychological needs. They had been kept within White Churches before the Civil War, not so much as a demonstration of the Christian principle of brotherhood

154

and equality, as because the Church relationship sanctified the civil relationship between masters and slaves.[49] The Revolution, with its emphasis on the rights of man, especially influenced Negroes in the direction of self-assertion, and in Philadelphia in 1787 Richard Allen seceded from the St. George Methodist Episcopal Church, and founded the Free African Society. Out of it two independent Negro Churches developed: Bethel Church (Methodist) and the African Protestant Episcopal Church of St. Thomas;[50] and thereafter one independent Church after another came into existence. The Civil War gave strong impetus to this movement and, says Niebuhr, 'Negro preachers showed themselves to be both more zealous and more effective evangelists of their own people than the White missionaries had been, and Negro Churches were organised rapidly under their leadership'.[51] Of 208,000 Negroes in the Southern Methodist Church in 1860, only 49,000 stayed when, in 1866, the General Conference gave permission to the Negro members to organise a separate ecclesiastical body. In 1870 the Coloured Methodist Episcopal Church came into existence, the third greatest Negro Church after the African Methodist Episcopal Church and the AME Zion Churches.[52] This was largely a movement of self-assertion on the part of the oppressed, and 'the Negroes, like the disinherited, required an emotional, empirical religion'.[53] Ecstasy and exhilaration, i. e. emotionalism in religion, were 'not only a reaction against the monotony and misery of laborious days on the plantation or in the factory; [but] also the natural result of America's failure to provide the Negro with those educational opportunities, which have brought about great changes in the religion of the disinherited and of the frontier.'[54] Emotional naïveté was only overcome as the educational standards increased, and today, according to Clark, 'speaking with tongues' alone is discernible as one of the external forms of enthusiasm. One may add interjections such as 'Hallelujah' and 'Amen'.

To summarise, strong economic and political influences are in the background of many revivalistic movements, although in Africa the religious and cultural issues should not be overlooked. In the West it was mostly due to issues other than religious contact. People found themselves ill at ease in the bourgeois Churches, where they were unable to give expression to their emotional natures, where their economic problems were disregarded, and there was no place for their naïve faith. A racial class may also be an economic class, and Churches which were originally racial in character maintain their solidarity because of the economic situation.[55] The economic influence on religion has been extensively discussed.[56] Lutheranism

and Calvinism could not satisfy the emotional fervour of the Anabaptists, neither would it satisfy their need for a social reconstruction. Quakerism developed because of the same social, economic and
religious situation. When the Reformation in England failed to
Christianise society, and instead became dominated by middle class
intellectualist formalism, the poor reacted. Presbyterianism, which
did much for higher education in Asia and Africa, could no more
satisfy the religious and ethical needs of the poor, and 'like Calvinism
everywhere, it was suspicious of the common man'.[57] In England,
Congregationalism stepped in and checked the exodus to the
Anabaptists, Millenarians and Quakers. Later, however, Congregationalism also become institutionalised, and a Christianity of the
disinherited was again necessary, with the result that 'Anabaptists,
Millenarians, or Fifth Monarchy Men, Antinomians, Seekers,
Ranters, Diggers, Levellers and, last of all, the Quakers began to
flourish'.[58] Quakerism had a programme of social reformation and
'its expectation of the coming of the kingdom of Christ had its solid
foundation in the physical needs of the poor.'[59] The Quakers looked
either quietly or in a revolutionary way at the manifestation of the
apocalyptic kingdom.[60] Methodism, which had a middle class
leadership and was nurtured in the ideals of Old Testament prophecy,
tried to accomplish the involvement of the Church in Rapid Social
Change. This change has been one of the causes of the prophetic
movements under discussion; truly church-forming religious movements have come from the lower social strata.[61] The Roman Catholic
Church in the United States, drawing strongly from the lower strata,
has experienced more divisions than any other denomination in
that country.[62] An abstract formal religion will not satisfy the
psychological needs of uneducated people. The ritual of Roman
Catholicism appeals to the African, as does its emphasis on centralised
authority, so that it has experienced very few secessions in Africa.
The African's reverence for ancestry finds satisfaction in the attitude
to saints as mediators.

Traditional Christianity, however, had held its own against the
onslaught of the sects, because it 'is a balance of doctrines, and not
merely of doctrines but of emphases. You must not exaggerate in
either direction, or the balance is distorted.'[63] Troeltsch says: 'Every
kind of reaction to a mere "freedom of the Spirit" in the hope that
it will grow and thrive without organisation, is a Utopian ideal
which is out of touch with the actual conditions of life, and its only
effect is to weaken the whole.'[64]

There is a difference between the 'mystical' and the 'Evangelical'
types of enthusiasm and revivalism. The former departs from the

156

Incarnation and the leader himself becomes the incarnated – in Africa, the Black Christ – while the latter emphasises redemption, as in the Bhengu Church. The former is led by an inner light, or by the Holy Spirit – names given to an individual person's psychological urge. The mystic 'is likely enough, therefore, to be a Nestorian without knowing it; he thinks of our Lord not as God-Man but as man somehow made deiform. A second incarnation on the same lines is not unthinkable.'[65] The evangelical enthusiast emphasises the uniqueness of Christ's revelation; 'mystic' type leads to antinomianism, whereas the 'Evangelical' type leads to a legalistic interpretation of Christian morality. The mystic rejects theology as he rejects Scripture.

As far as the political issues in these movements are concerned, it is held that legal rights belong only to the in-group, as was the case with Huss, the Anabaptists, the Nazarites, Ngunzists and others. All of them have their New Jerusalem, but, says Knox 'the American continent with its vast underdeveloped spaces, gave more opportunity for Jerusalem building. . . .'[66] This applies also to Africa. Here the intellectual is subordinated to the emotional and visionary. External 'signs' as indication of the divine will such as the comet seen by Enoch, claim priority; inner conviction takes precedence over practical insight. The evangelical has regard for Scripture, but the mystical type, as in the case of men like Shembe and Kimbangu, rejects it for the inner light. Knox maintains that the odd physical manifestations of inward revelation may rather be ascribed to the evangelical than to the mystic. This may be the case in Europe, but it is not so in Africa. It is true that convulsions were found among the Camisards, the early Methodists, the Irvingites,[67] but they were also among the Quakers, with mystics like Kimbangu, Matswa and others.

Enthusiasm is not a wrong tendency but, with its eccentricities and exaggerations, it is a false emphasis. All Christianity becomes institutional after a time – even leaders of independent movements (mainly the Church and Christian sect type) today seek better theological training. In Europe, sects become Churches, and in Africa the same process has developed amongst Pentecostals. It will also happen in the case of the Pentecostal and Adventist movements in Africa, which embrace more than 9% of Protestant Christianity in the continent; but it will not happen to the independent movements which are post-Christian, and have lost contact with the Word and the work completed by Christ on the Cross. Revival in East Africa has remained in the Church because it has not lost this contact.[68] Throughout the centuries the prophetic movements have had much to do with the future – always in matters of a political or cosmic nature.[69] These movements are efforts to indigenise Christianity,[70] and furthermore to form new communities in the face of the destructive forces of modern society. They revert to their old customs because of the 'reality' of the spirit world, the world of the ancestor which removes them from the bewildering power which threatens to destroy what they cherish. They ascribe their misfortune to the fact that they abandoned these customs appointed by their ancestors.[71] Taylor accuses the 'mission' Churches of not having honestly come to terms with the spirit world and magic, because of their attitude that spirit possession does not exist. This attitude has led the great majority of Church members to make use of protective charms, and in times of stress, to revert to animism and even witchcraft because that way greater power, immunity and protection are promised.[72] In animism, it is always the action of a spirit that explains every event, with the result that a clear distinction should be made between the meaning of this and of the Person and work of the Holy Spirit, who had an essential place in the earliest proclamation of the *Kerygma*, but who, in spite of the prominence the Holy Spirit receives in the trinitarian formula in the Great Commission (Matth. xxviii. 19), has been neglected in the established Churches and their missionary activities.

REFERENCES

1. Eusebius, *Ecclesiastical History*, Book V, 16.
2. *Contra Marcion*, III, 445–46.
3. Didymus, *De Trinitate*, iii, xli.
4. Knox, 35.
5. Eusebius, v, 16.
6. Cf. Knox, 37.
7. E.p. xxvii *Ad Marcellam*, quoted Knox, 37.
8. *De Exhortatione Castitatis*, 4. Cf. W. H. C. Frend, *The Donatist Church*, Oxford, 1952, 122.
9. Frend, 119.
10. *De Baptismo*, viii, xv.
11. *De Baptismo*, v, xv.
12. *De Monogamia*, iv.
13. Knox, 50–51.
14. Knox, 51.
15. Knox, 62.
16. Frend, 59.
17. Ibid, 72.
18. F. H. Littell, *The Anabaptist View of the Church*, Beacon Hill, Starr King Press, 1952, 46.
19. H. Berkhof, *Geschiedenis der Kerk*, Callenbach, 1941, 176–79.

20. Cf. Knox, 124. Quoting Bullinger: 'When under the influence of the Spirit, their countenances were contorted, they made deprecatory gestures, fell to the ground as if in a fit, and finally lay outstretched as if they were dead'.

21. Littell, 31; H. von Schubert 'Der Kommunismus der Wiedertäufer in Münster und seine Quellen', *Sitzungsberichte der Heidelberger Akademie der Wissenschaften*. Phil.-Hist. Klasse (1919) 11: 3–7; cf. H. R. Niebuhr, *The Social Sources of Denominationalism*, Meridian Books, 1958², 34. 'The Zwichau prophets and Melchior Hoffmann represented the political and economic as well as the religious interests of the poor . . . [they] . . . gave assurance of deliverance from political and social oppressions through the establishment of Christ's perfect brotherhood.' The Peasant Revolt in Germany was in its earliest phases under the influence of the Anabaptist movement. The violent stages which came later were under the influence of the Hussites and Taborites (ibid., 285). See also the significant book of N. Cohn, *The Pursuit of the Millenium*, Mercury Books, 1962², 282 ff.

22. Littell, 32.

23. Knox, 174.

24. Ibid., 357.

25. Ibid., 358.

26. Ibid., 360; Clark, 88. Expectation of Christ's return, millennial views, trances, convulsions and visions were most characteristic phenomena. V. Lanternari, *Les mouvements réligieux des peuples opprimés*, Paris, 1962. N. Cohn (*The Pursuit of the Millenium*, Mercury Books, 1962) analyses revolutionary messianism of the Middle Ages, and indicates how it influenced modern totalitarian movements.

27. Ibid., 149.

28. Ibid., 150.

29. Niebuhr, 39.

30. Knox, 173.

31. Ibid., 159.

32. Ibid., 162.

33. Ibid., 377.

34. Ibid., 416.

35. Ibid., 451.

36. Cf. *Journal*, 17/4/1739.

37. Cf. *Journal*, 15/6/39, 28/10/39.

38. *Journal*, 23/10/39.

39. *Journal*, 12/10/39, 20/5/49, 7/9/55, 1/7/59.

40. *Journal*, 11/6/42.

41. *Life of Wesley*, London, 154.

42. J. E. Hutton, *History of the Moravian Church*, 1895, 319.

43. Knox, 526.

44. *Journal*, 4/6/72.

45. Niebuhr, 59, 60.

46. Knox, 535; *Journal*, 25/11/59.

47. *Journal*, 4/6/72.

48. Knox, 558.

49. Niebuhr, 252–53.

50. Ibid., 255.

51. Ibid., 257.

52. Niebuhr, 257–58.

53. Ibid., 262.

54. Ibid., 262; Clark, 20: ' . . . the advance of education modifies doctrinal

159

emphasis, modes of religious expression, and methods of propaganda within the Churches.' This has still to be proved as far as the nativistic movements are concerned. Some changes, however, do take place.

55. Niebuhr, 26. Barth says: 'The religion of man is always conditioned absolutely by the way in which the starry heaven above and the moral law within have spoken to the individual. It is, therefore, conditioned by nature and climate, by blood and soil, by the economic, cultural, political, in short, the historical circumstances in which he lives.' *Church Dogmatics I²* (*transl.*) T. & T. Clark, 1956, 312.

56. Cf. E. Troeltsch, *The Social Gospel of the Christian Churches*, Vols. I & II, Allen & Unwin, 1931; R. H. Tawney, *Religion and the Rise of Capitalism*, Mentor Book, 1958; Max Weber, *The Protestant Ethic and the Spirit of Capitalism*, Allen & Unwin, 1962, and others.

57. Niebuhr, 41.

58. Niebuhr, 46. See also Cohn, *The Pursuit of a Millenium*, 321 ff.

59. Ibid., 50.

60. Ibid., 52.

61. E. Troeltsch, *Soziallehren der Christlichen Kirchen und Gruppen*, 1911 362 ff.

62. Clark, 17.

63. Knox, 580.

64. E. Troeltsch, Vol. II, 1007.

65. Knox, 583.

66. Ibid., 585.

67. Janheinz Jahn (*Through African Doors*, Faber, 1962, 218) refers to the Irvingites in Nigeria, who baptise their new converts at the river, with women wearing colourful robes and men either white shirts or colourful materials. The priest in his white robes performs the baptism while the others sing and dance.

68. N. Longford-Smith ('Revival in East Africa', IRM, Jan. 1954, 80), states: 'At the very heart of revival is the Atonement, the message of reconciliation of man to God and man to man through Christ crucified . . .'

69. G. Mensching, 'Propheten', RGG, Vol. V, 1961, 610.

70. Cf. B. Sundkler, 'Propheten', RGG, Vol. V, 611. Even Sundkler subscribes to this in spite of the fact that he has laid all the emphasis on racialism and denominationalism as reasons for the existence of these movements in South Africa. He states in this later article: 'To summarize, one could say that the modern African Prophetic Movements are an acute Africanisation of Christendom over against the gradual Africanisation in the Ethiopian Churches and the often very slow adaptation processes in the Mission Churches.'

71. Tempels, 33.

72. Taylor, 'Saints and Heretics', *Basileia*, 309–10.

6

THE OLD TESTAMENT IN THE CHURCH IN AFRICA

A WIDESPREAD revival of Marcionism was experienced in Asia, especially immediately before and after the Jerusalem Conference of the International Missionary Council in 1928. This has not been the case in Africa, where the Old Testament is rather misinterpreted than rejected. One of the great functions of the Old Testament, rightly interpreted, has always been that it encountered paganism, because Israel's religion, as a prophetic religion, was absolutely different from the surrounding natural and cultural religions. At every significant point in the faith of Israel, a radical difference is found from the non-Christian religions; God had chosen by grace, and not by merit, one people as the instrument for his universal and redemptive purpose.[1] There was also the difference in worship from the surrounding religions, in which all festivals were 'cultic re-enactments of myths, based upon elements of sympathetic magic. They aim at preserving and continuing the harmony of the social and natural order. In fact, all means tend towards coercing the gods to act in accordance with human wishes.'[2] The Old Testament can indeed be a norm whereby the nativistic movements may be judged.

The God of Israel is in the *centre*. Even the mythological elements that were borrowed from the other religions were remythologised so that they 'become elements in the acts of the all-transcending God'.[3] The Old Testament clearly shows an encounter with magic and divination (cf. Lev. xx. 6, 23, 27; Deut. xviii. 9–15) – 'the whole pagan world of magic and divination is simply incompatible with the worship of Yahweh'.[4] Israel also had the idea of clean and unclean, of dreams as sources of revelation (Gen. 40–41; Num. xii. 6, etc.), and believed in curses and in true prophecy versus pagan divination (cf. 1 Kings xxii; Jer. xxiii. 9 ff.; Ezek. xiii). Clear references to demons are rare (cf. Is. xiii. 21; Lev. xvii. 7; 2 Chron. xi. 15; Lev. xvi. 8, 10, 26); these passages stand almost alone. Sickness, however, is not ascribed to an evil spirit but to God himself (cf. Ps. xxxviii).

161

Nature itself was emptied of all divinity, since it was believed to have been created by the will of God. 'Magic and divination, so prolific in naturalistic religions, were in principle, ruled out.'[5] The Old Testament clearly shows Israel's struggle against magic, divination and demons, and polytheistic religious festivals.[6] All pagan worship is based on the conception of the efficacy of the individual's work, whether in magic, sacrifices, giving of alms, or any other related activity. The Scriptural basis of faith versus works is always a difficulty to this type of thinking. In the Israelite religion, it is the inner attitude to God that counts; God provides the sacrifice. Legalism is a grave danger in Africa, and salvation is often based on the fact that one must not disobey the commandments of the decalogue.[7]

The problem of religious experience, which was one of the main points of emphasis in nineteenth-century revivalism, has affected the missionary activity. The difficulty arises when, as is often the case, 'spiritual' and 'experience' are coupled together as 'spiritual experience', meaning the sum total of religion.[8] This is acutely felt in both Asia and Africa. That 'experience', coupled in Africa with the spiritual, is often the experience of the old religion. It is here that the Old Testament's message is important: God's transcendent holiness and objectivity can never be contained in 'experience'; nor can the Biblical conception of the eternal, objective, historical acts of God. God cannot make His word and His revelation dependent on psychological factors such as human subjectivism.[9] Furthermore, the polytheisms of the Biblical world died with the civilisation of which they were the buttress, because they had no means of interpreting historical facts. The historical acts of God were not only interpreted in the Old Testament, but the people of Israel saw themselves as part of those acts. The Old Testament, proclaiming that *God acts in history*, is a bulwark against spiritualisation. In the natural religions, nature, society and the supernatural are not sharply distinguished, but the Israelites used only categories of personality and society to depict the divine.[10]

The difficulties encountered in the relation of Christianity to the non-Christian religions, especially to the indigenous independent movements, could find some relief in the Old Testament. So often in the young Churches the New Testament has taken precedence over the Old, and the authority of the OT has suffered, because of the relatively wide distribution of copies of the NT. In many cases only the New Testament has appeared in the vernacular.[11] The Old Testament, however, gives perspective to the New Testament, and to people's religious experience, which should have a historical grounding in election, promise and fulfilment: any religion based simply on religious experience, as proposed by those who see in the Old Testament only relative value, would either disappear or end up in gross syncretism. It is the Old Testament which broke with pagan religion, in so radical a way that it forms the basis on which the New Testament rests.[12]

The young Churches in Africa do not discard the Old Testament or give it a secondary place – not this but its misinterpretation is the problem of Africa.[13] The African's relation to the Old Testament is somewhat different from the Westerner's. Sundkler says: 'The great primordial images of the Old Testament for a time seemed to be desiccated by Western scepticism and rationalism, but in the African Christian's encounter with the Bible message, Living Waters begin to flow again over dry river beds.'[14] Their interest in the beginning – in creation, Adam, Paradise, the Fall, Satan, Sin and Death, in starting a sermon at the beginning and ending with the consummation – all this shows how central the Old Testament is to African theological conceptions.[15] The Old Testament does not receive its rightful place in the seminaries; some Western theological teachers in their ignorance even tried to destroy the interest of students in the Old Testament. For various reasons it demands a thorough study in the African context: Hebrew also should take a prominent place in the curriculum. The contrast between 'Hebrew thought' and 'Greek thought' has become of great importance in modern theology. Hebrew thought, however, is not limited to the Old Testament, but is also found in the New Testament which has a Hebraic content in Greek words,[16] and, while subject to Greek influence, is rooted in Hebraic tradition. It is interesting to see that the IMC Reports on theological education in Africa have nothing to say about Hebrew, except the report on 'Latin' Africa, where reference is made to the teacher who should be acquainted with at least the major Hebrew and Greek terms.[17] Hebrew is considered to be essential for an understanding of the basic thought forms in Scripture.[18] Barr maintains that a Hebrew language study is dogmatically necessary, because without it we should be cut off from the 'Hebrew mind'.[19] Not only should the most fundamental Biblical words be studied[20] but the whole language; only thus can a critical judgment in handling Biblical data be created.[21]

The Old Testament, furthermore, puts the prophetic idea in correct perspective. 'Prophetic faith is faith in a singular, transcendent holy, absolutely righteous God';[22] and there is no *Blut und Boden* in the Old Testament, the whole faith militating against such a corruption.[23] The true basis of the Christian message, namely redemption and resurrection, is essentially Israelite; it is the fulfilment of the Old Testament hope, and fits into Israel's hope of salvation.[24]

In Africa interest in the Old Testament, due to Israel's struggle for identity and freedom, has been extraordinary. Moses is seen as greater than Abraham, the father of the believers, because of his political significance. (The Old Testament here becomes *a political source book*, instead of the basis for the New Testament). The historical emphasis of the Old Testament could rectify the mytho-logical thinking of animism. The God of Israel has no mythology, 'since history rather than nature was the primary sphere of his revelation. Israel's effort was to tell the story of her past in terms of God's activity.'[25] Here the acting and living God transcends nature and history, but acts in both and stands over against monistic naturalism, which is identified with nature and is outside history.[26] In spite of the historical-critical school, which endeavours to put all religions on the same basis, one can safely say that what the authors of the Old Testament borrowed they radically changed, because of their concern with history rather than with nature.

Order, harmony and integration are the watchwords of natural-istic monism. This has been so through the centuries, and Christianity has come as the great disturber. The Biblical tension between God and creation has become in the independent movements a tension between God and the existing religious and social order. In their religion the Exodus assumes the central place, as was the case in the history and faith of Israel. The prophetic protest in the Old Testament against social injustice is unparalleled in the ancient world. Nowhere is there any sign of man's achievement, neither is there any hint in official Yahwism that the primary purpose of any Israelite festival was the re-enactment of a drama, as if by sympathetic magic, by the identification of man with divine power, the harmonious integration of nature and society could be achieved.[27] The prophets reacted strongly against the institutions of cult and of kingship, but if a polytheist of the time had done this, 'he would have been cutting away the very ground on which he stood, leaving himself isolated from the divine world, alone and with no means of help'.[28] Israel had the Covenant 'in which the divine–human encounter was central and possible, apart from cultus and kingship'.[29] Although the Old Testament is incomplete – for example, with regard to the central issues of righteousness and grace, of sin and righteousness and of faith and works – it indicates in what a 'dynamic and revolutionary way' Israel held its own amongst all the nationalistic religions, which indicates 'that it is and will remain the theological basis upon which the Christian faith is established. Without it the church . . . will

164

have little protection against the subtle perversion of the Gospel by naturalism. The New Testament, no more than the Old, can stand alone.'[30] The unity of the Old and New Testaments is an organic spiritual unity.

It is very unfortunate for Africa that the Old Testament has not been given a prominent place in Western theology, and that in Africa its thorough study was considered futile. This led to a distortion of the Old Testament and the Gospel message. The old 'religious-historical' school and its theory of 'mere historicism', a theory of interpretation which secularised and humanised the Old Testament religion, had anyway affected the status of the Old Testament. Karl Barth sees God's revelation as the annulment of religion,[31] religion being unbelief, and an affair of godless man. The only true criterion is Jesus Christ. The Old Testament strongly condemns the surrounding religions (cf. Deut. vii. 2, 5), which are seen in the light of idolatry (*zenut* = adultery, fornication) and ignorance (*chosék* = darkness, ignorance).[32] Just as idols are rejected in strong terms by the Old Testament prophets (Is. xliv. 9, 16, 19), so are exclusive nationalism, externalism and formalism. The faith of Israel was thus unique, perhaps in one sense most plainly of all: viz. that Israel had been chosen not *because it was obedient*, as the independent movements would like to maintain, but *to be obedient* (Deut. vii. 7–11). Furthermore, sin in the surrounding religions was 'not primarily a violation of a gracious and righteous Divine will, a rebellion which destroyed personal communication, as in the Bible. It was rather more of an aberration which destroyed the harmony of affairs in the cosmic state.[33]

The Bible contains no doctrine of God's spirituality but has much to say about God's Spirit or Holy Spirit. Metaphors used in connection with God are definite and concrete; ones derived from breath or mind are not used as descriptive of His being. The Spirit seems superficially important as an instrument of revelation but, particularly before the Exile (as a protest against the outlook of the syncretistic and spiritualistic *nebi'im*), the revelation in the Old Testament is practically always given by the word of God, i.e. directly and personally.[34] The idea of 'Spirit' is something concrete, an activity of God's power. The word '*ruach*' (wind, breath) carries the idea of power; it is of God, and it is also the medium through which God exerts His controlling power. The *Ruach-Adonai* is the power which enters into and controls the prophets. *Ruach-Adonai*, being more than human, cannot be hindered. It came mightily upon Samson (Hebrew = *leapt*, Judges xiii. 25; xiv. 6, 19; xv. 14) and enabled him to perform extraordinary feats of strength. This ecstatic state into which Samson entered was considered to be the safe test of spirit possession in the early days of Israel (1 Sam. x. 6, 10; xi. 6). Some Old Testament scholars discern a long process of developments between this crude stage and prophecy in Nehemiah ix. 30 and Micah iii. 8.

The word *ruach* is also used for man's spirit, that which quickens his inner being.[35] The Spirit of God is a power proceeding from God, an inspiration by God, strengthening and quickening. It can inspire prophets, and man is passive (1 Kings xviii. 12; 2 Kings ii. 16; Ezek. ix. 1, iii. 12, viii. 3, xxxvii. 1): it makes a man capable of bringing about deliverance (1 Sam. xi. 6; Judges iii. 10, vi. 34, xi. 29); it is a life-giving force, moves man to ecstasy, inspires him.[36] Only in Is. xxxi. 3 is God himself used as a parallel conception. Vriezen maintains that the major prophets never connect revelation with the operation of the Spirit, except for Ezekiel (once) and Isaiah. Jeremiah says nothing about the Spirit of God, and this could be seen as an inward opposition to the spiritualism of the false prophets, as is also the case with Paul.[37]

The prophet (*nabi*) is the *typical* and most important figure in the Old Testament. Ecstasy was known in the Canaanite, Phoenician, North Syrian and Mesopotamian world; in the period of the early kings, and still in Ezekiel, ecstatic elements are found in Israel. However, this element is not essential to the Scriptural prophets. There is a fundamental difference between the ecstatic figures of the ancient Eastern world and the classical prophets.[38] The prophet of the Old Testament speaks the word of God, enunciating it as his own. The religion of Israel is fundamentally prophetic, and the Old Testament revelation came to the people of Israel as a result of the mediation of prophets (cf. Hebr. i. 1), who 'appear to be the representatives of God'.[39] There is a close communion between God and the prophet. Moses is neither a king, commander of an army, tribal chieftain, priest or inspired seer and medicine man, but 'the messenger, who should proclaim God's will for social, political and cultic life'.[40] Prophets are martyrs for their people (cf. Amos vii. 10; Micah iii. 8; Isaiah viii. 11 ff.; Jeremiah xxvi). The prophets as servants of God are the image of Jesus Christ – thus Is. xlii, xlix, 1, lii, liii. These classical prophets were political figures, or they were accepted as such.[41] According to Vriezen, 'their intervention went no further than proclaiming to the people and the kings the word of God, also with respect to politics'.[42] The prophets continuously emphasised renewal, purification and sanctification, and in this light God's judgments were interpreted.

Nabism declined mainly because it consisted essentially '*in an*

166

assimilation of prophetism to the forms of social culture, with which it ought to have been in conflict'.[43] With the development of temple prophecy, a sense of office and power developed, which thought itself capable of manipulating and controlling divine revelation; the difference between the word of God and man's subjectivism thus disappeared'[44] This is the major problem of African nativism. It is in opposition to this development that classical prophecy is directed – for example, Isaiah says that they believe 'they can give correct guidance when their senses are befuddled with wine' (Is. xxviii. 7, 9). Jeremiah also reacts against this abuse of God's word, which is properly something extraneous to man, and objective (Jer. xxiii). Yahweh's task could only be fulfilled in continuous self-judgment (Jer. xxiii. 15, 18) and in absolute obedience (Jer. xxiii. 21 ff., 32). Presumptuous confidence desires control of Yahweh's word (Jer. xxiii. 18) and is blind to God's true nature (Jer. xxiii. 23 ff.). God's word is darkened by obscure dreams (Jer. v. 31, xxiii. 26 ff., 32),[45] and there is no criterion to distinguish it from natural desires (Jer. xiv. 13 ff., xxiii. 14; cf. Ezek. xiii. 3, 6 ff., 16). Deuteronomy, for example, subjects the prophet to the authority of the Word with which he has been entrusted (Deut. xviii. 20). The exclusive relationship of Yahweh with Israel, not signs and wonders, constitutes the axiomatic standard of the prophetic message; this is borne out in Deuteronomy xiii.[46] Nothing, not even wondrous dreams ,[47] can take the place of man's obedience to the central will of God (Jer. xiii. 5). The attitude of the prophets to ecstatic conditions is one of marked reserve, and a prophet's genuineness was not judged from psychic experiences. In the pre-exilic days, the Temple police kept a watchful eye over recalcitrant ecstatics (Jer. xx. 1 ff., xxix. 26), but later the Israelites did not even tolerate 'the form of preaching in independence of the Law'.[48] Nabism had degenerated because of the intermixing with loyalty to Yahweh of national preservation, implying acceptance of the *status quo*. Only by putting his messengers 'outside their people' could God give a clear interpretation of His purpose 'in the form of a purified salvation hope'.[49]

The later prophetic movements are to be distinguished from nabism. Here the ecstatic and visionary element is diminished when compared with the early period. Those elements are found in the prophets' call, but very seldom later – Ezekiel is the only exception. There is no question of mass hysteria in the case of the classical prophets, nor with Elijah and Elisha, great leaders of the Nebiim.[50] Later, as the prophets developed, ecstatic feeling was considered as only of very relative significance. Jeremiah stresses the 'utter worthlessness of all dreams and visions' when the sense of truth and justice has been lost.[51] Not only did abnormal psychic states recede with time, but the proper instrument of prophetic activity became the spoken and, gradually, the written word. In the earliest times the prophet was believed to have been entered by the spirit deity physically when in ecstatic trance, but with Amos the word of Yahweh, uttered through the mouth of inspired men (cf. Amos iii. 8), so far received precedence that it was preserved *in written form*. Through the centuries the conception of the Word of God evolved, starting possibly with Isaiah and certainly including Jeremiah, both of whom edited their utterances in books,[52] which became par excellence the media of their public activity. They subject themselves to the existential demands of God; in this way also they were freed from human ties.

This later prophetic movement had mainly to do with spiritual issues. 'Their guidance of the national life was framed on a coherent principle . . . what stands in the way of Yahweh's supremacy is no longer this or that error or imperfection, but a perversion of the whole conception of the divine-human relationship.'[53] What they had been hiding behind their own inadequacy and self-centred spirituality, had to receive renewed attention, namely a new understanding of the all-embracing will of Yahweh. They had to testify to the word, the experience of a new reality. They underwent a great change, out of which came a new certainty of God. In this new light, they predicted the end of the nation and the people. Man in his mighty self-assertion will be shaken, especially in his self-assertion towards God, whom he wishes to bind to his own selfish interests, and to the here and now. All Israel's outward achievements, their sacred images and symbols, their respected priesthood associated with a magnificent Temple, their special names used in invoking God, all this is nothing but 'huge misconceptions of the real nature of God, good for nothing but destruction'.[54] Human activity of whatever nature does not affect God: it is futile (cf. Amos v. 5; Hosea iv. 15, v. 8, x. 5; Is. xxix. 1 ff.). The prophet rejects all mediation through the Spirit or an angel: he sees God's action in all events of this world, (in Africa, this should receive emphasis.) God is seen as the exalted One. It was not a new doctrine of God that was given, but a new ethic and a new and purified understanding of God.[55] The prophets have given attention in their preaching to the whole of human life in a new focus of unity. They saw as the true divine goal for the universe the necessity that it should be morally ordered.

The real presence of God in the midst of the people is so real as a result of signs and wonders, that it becomes associated with a holy place. Both Isaiah and Ezekiel emphasise Yahweh's dwelling in

Zion (Is. viii. 18, xxxi. 9; Ezek. viii–xi; cf. Zeph. iii. 5). The historical character of the revelation gives the here and now a specific significance. Jerusalem becomes the place of God's perfect revelation, and this was a mighty factor against all syncretistic tendencies; there was a deep inner relationship which was opposed to any form of magic.

The prophetic conception of history is of great significance. God directs history, which is 'the real workshop of God'.[56] History is the locus of revelation, and with this concept of history is inevitably bound up the certainty that revelation will be finally broken off in the new age. 'The prophets' radical critique of the *status quo* rules out any optimistic belief in progress, which might hope that opposition would be gradually overcome.'[57]

The Abuse of the Old Testament in the African context. Although the Old Testament has only recently been published in some of the major and most influential languages of Africa (such as Kikuyu, Fang and Gabon in about 1950),[58] and although it is virtually unknown in many Churches, there nevertheless has been great interest in it through the years.[59] The Old Testament is easily understood in Africa because of the atmosphere it breathes, 'the nomadic and pastoral life, man's frank and outspoken longing for offspring, the experiences of seed-time and harvest; the concreteness of all that is said about God and man'.[60] All this and much more explains the popularity of the Old Testament in Africa: some maintain that its atmosphere is sympathetic to polygamy.[61] The stories are often like those of Africa, the sacrificial system is very much the same, circumcision is widely practised in Africa, some ritual prohibitions are similar, agricultural feasts have parallels in African life, much of the old law with regard to 'servants, cattle, the *lex talionis* and the attitude to other tribes, can be paralleled in Bantu life'.[62] Allegorical interpretation is another outstanding common characteristic, as well as literalism and legalism. 'Legalism comes naturally to the African, who finds it difficult to accept teaching as binding unless it is supported by outward sanctions.'[63] Justification is found in the Old Testament for much of their ritualism. The traditional religion itself is strongly ritualistic. Ritual is for the traditional African the continuation of an act which started outside him but which he reproduces. Rites are to him nothing less than myth, which is the 'beginning' of the holy act, in action.[64] The rites localise the 'beginning' so that a special place is often chosen which is the centre of the nativistic movement, a place where these rites are most effective. Here history is mythologised and myth historicised. The ritual was always considered to be necessary for the continuation of events of nature. These rites are life itself and without it the fixed givenness

169

could not be repeated. The acts of Jesus Christ can only become those of their community in the nativistic movement through the ritual acts of their leader and in their service. The traditional mind reproduces while the modern mind creates. The independent Churches and Christian sects have much less ritualism than the nativistic movements.

Much African preaching derives from the Old Testament, and there are, as Sundkler indicates, 'European tutors who are genuinely perturbed by the incessant interest in the Old Testament'.[65] Baëta maintains that 'where reversions to African traditional practices have taken place . . . the reason has been the authority of the Old Testament rather than the fact that the customs were African'.[66] Sundkler's observation about the Zionist Churches can however not be generally applied. He states that 'obviously the Old Testament forms the foundation of the belief of these Churches. A common argument in all *materia theologica* is: The truth is to be found in *uDutelonom* or *uLevi*.'[67] Hodgkin speaks about the 'evident relevance of Jewish Christian tradition to the situation of colonial Africa'.[67] The theme of people who felt themselves oppressed appealed to the African under colonial rule, and 'the identification of British, French or Belgians with Egyptians, Philistines or Romans, and of one's own African community with the children of Israel or with the early Christians, is natural and inevitable'.[68]

Paul himself gave the Jewish Old Testament to his converts as an inspired book and used it as his text, and 'seems to have left his newly founded Churches with a simple system of Gospel teaching, two sacraments, a tradition of the main facts of the death and resurrection, and the Old Testament'.[69] The Old Testament thus had a significant place in Christianity from the very beginning, as was also the case in Africa, even though in many Churches it was not accessible in the vernacular. Scripture, especially the Old Testament, has always supplied 'religio-political texts' for oppressed people. Chilembwe on occasions preached fanatical anti-European sermons which were rich in Old Testament imagery.[70] Harry Thuku in Kenya often referred to the exodus of Israel from Egypt, that White and Black are all sons of Adam and alike before 'Jehovah our living God'.[71] Followers of Chilembwe said that 'he got his inspiration from the Old Testament . . . and preached to many hundreds every week sermons in which the example of the Jews in their national struggle with Egyptians, Philistines and others was held up for their admiration and imitation'.[72] Roland Oliver refers to one Malaki, an ex-teacher of the Anglican Church in Uganda, who gained the support of ex-chief Kakunguru, and who in 1913 started to preach and quote Old Testament texts in support of polygamy. He opposed all forms of medicine and started to baptise independently; his following was estimated in 1921 at 91,000.[73] The movement of Enoch Mgijima – *The Church of God and Saints of Christ* – maintained a mixture of the Jewish and Christian ritual, accepted the Jewish calendar, the Sabbath and Passover, adhered to the Prophet and considered itself to be the elected of God. Polygamy was introduced after their conflict with government forces in 1921.[74] The *Memeneda Gyidifo* (The Saviour Church) or "Saturday Believers', was founded by Samuel Brako, who received messages from God in dreams in 1924; these messages had revealed to him that Saturday is the special day set aside for worship.[75] The emphasis on Saturday is an indication of how strongly they feel about reproducing the past. Adultery and drunkenness were due to disregard of the Sabbath; the ten commandments had to be strictly observed.[76] The founder of the *Apostolowo Fe Dedefia Habobo* (Apostolic Revelation Society), K. N. Wovenu, heard God speak to him and 'the phraseology of these utterances is assimilated as much as possible to that of Old Testaments prophecies'.[77] He also maintains that 'our food taboos are those stated in the Old Testament'.[78] In the Aladura Church or Church of the Lord, the feast of *Tabbieorrah*, or Feast of the Tabernacles, is held.[79] Many of the ritual objects used in the nativistic movements, such as the prophets' staff, cymbals, drums, trumpets and so on, are based on Old Testament texts.

The 'Church of the First-born' among the Tlhaping, an important section of the Tswana tribe, uses the Old and New Testaments as evidence for circumcision.[80] African doctors are rejected by this Church on the basis of Deut. viii. 10–12, and Rom. xiii. 1 is used to justify their going to European doctors: 'One should honour those placed in authority.' Opposition to the use of tobacco is based on Ezek. viii. 17, where the putting of the branch to the nose is listed as one of the abominations found among the house of Judah. Pauw says that 'this kind of literal application of fragments of the Bible is very common among Separatists'.[81] The 'Churches' in the Tlhaping area do not give the same preference to the Old Testament as Sundkler's Zionist and Ethiopian Churches; neither does The Church of the Lord (Aladura)[82] in West Africa, nor those with which the author came in contact in South Africa. Nevertheless much of their ritual is based on this part of Scripture.

Legalism is natural with the African as a result of the outward sanctions or ritual prohibitions in African religion itself. In this Church the legalistic stage is considered necessary, otherwise it may end up in antinomianism as in the second century.[83] Most of the

171

independent movements carefully observe details from Mosaic legalism. Pauw shows that a number 'of the portions used from the Old Testament deal with fulfilling the law in general, keeping the Sabbath, pure and impure animals, evils of wine and tobacco'.[84] The latter texts are mostly used in Sabbatarian and Pentecostal Churches. Ritual avoidance has a bearing on a person's spiritual purity and is related to the purification rites.

Frazer calls ritual avoidance negative, magic and sorcery positive. 'The aim of positive magic or sorcery is to produce a desired event, the aim of negative magic or taboo is to avoid an undesirable one.'[85] The most numerous and important ritual prohibitions are those related to food. He states that, just as the African eats 'many animals or plants in order to acquire certain desirable qualities with which he believes them to be endowed, so he avoids many other animals and plants lest he should acquire certain undesirable qualities with which he believes them to be infected'.[86] Others again interpret ritual avoidance as belonging only to the magico-religious sphere, having at the back a sanction which is a suggestion of some kind of mystic punishment if the rule is broken. In one's dealings with whatever has mystic power, there is a certain amount of indefinite risk associated with it, and ritual avoidance is an implied resolution that no unnecessary risks of this indefinite nature will be taken.[87] According to Shropshire, 'the essence and strength of taboo are rooted in the sacredness of life and custom'.[88] The sacred and all that is connected with it are dangerous and should be approached with sincerity. Ritual avoidance implies a sanction, which may be a definite one carried out by the community concerned; although generally it is indefinite, it may be definite and indefinite simultaneously, while the taboo breaker is punished and 'left with the curse of Cain, and it is automatic'.[89] Being so closely connected with the sacred, it must be treated with respect. It is thus easy to see how salvation depends in the independent movements on obeying ritual prohibitions. With the ancestors the ritually prohibited is connected with the sacred. The divine chief is a tabooed person. The powerful religious and social prohibitions stabilise the tribe or family. Some anthropologists maintain that the moral sense and intuition is prior to the ritual prohibition, but, according to Shropshire, 'there has been influence and interaction between the two'.[90] In Gen. xii. 10–20, xx. 1–18 and Lev. xviii. 24, it is stated that breaches in ritual prohibitions associated with marriage bring down on the community public calamities of the most serious nature.[91] Frazer says: 'On the taboo were grafted the golden fruits of law and morality.'[92] But moral intuition is deeper than taboo.

Pauw's experience amongst the Tswana is that ritual avoidance does not refer only to the Old Testament; for example, a leader referred to a list contained in Gal. v. 19 ff. together with Deut. xiv. Pork is avoided on the basis of Matt. viii. 25–34, the justification for this interpretation being that a swine is the habitation of evil spirits, apart from Old Testament references. Avoidance of tobacco is based on Ezekiel viii. 17 but also on 1 Cor. iii.16.[93] Pauw maintains that, as far as what he calls separatist Churches are concerned, the 'Old Testament ritual, which is usually no longer adhered to by Christians, has been revived in these Churches, as is the case with the use of ashes as a purificant, the slaughtering of animals as sacrifices, and some rules of avoidance'.[94] The literal and fragmentary interpretation of Scripture, together with the moralistic and legalistic approach to it, obscures the meaning of the Gospel message, with the result that outward formalism takes precedence. Beacause of the background, and because of the disintegration of society, moralistic and legalistic features receive a new emphasis, and the teaching is considered to be binding if it is supported by outwards sanctions which have a magical effect. 'Having this background of magic, new doctrines attaching a magical interpretation to the modes of behaviour with which they are concerned will have a stronger appeal than doctrines that are strictly non-magical.'[95] Beside the function of these prohibitions, namely to keep a society together, the legalistic approach of missionaries, the emphasis on a set of rules as a means of salvation, the disciplinary action in the Church exercised on the same basis as the traditional court session, all this has inculcated the idea that Christianity has to do with a set of rules to be executed meticulously in order to obtain salvation. Nothing will suit the traditional African mind better; his supernatural relationships depended on the observance of ritual prohibitions. This accounts for the legalism prevalent also in the established Churches in Africa. This legalism, the basis of which is magic, has led to much literalism.[96] It is also undeniable that the break-up of society causes the legalistic aspect of life to be over-emphasised by those who wish to maintain the *status quo*, and Christianity itself is seen as a 'new law' sanctioned by the notion of future judgment. The important point is that, as soon as the old takes precedence over the new, i.e. as soon as the traditional becomes prominent, the new is interpreted in the light of the old with its emphasis on ritual avoidance – only on thus can a sense of community be built and salvation obtained. As the strict observance of ritual prohibitions created the right relationship with the supernatural forces, so moralism, with its legalistic emphasis, ensures salvation for the individual. This is the only way in which he can overcome the demands of the supernatural world. Christianity is based on grace, and works are expressions of gratitude. But the doctrine of good works is a doctrine of magic: through his works, man attempts to influence the supernatural. Magic enters into the Church also by way of ritual avoidance, emphasising right behaviour and purification. Holy water becomes a new powerful magic in the hands of the prophet, the magical personality, and plays a great role in baptism as a purification rite. Food taboos, sexual taboos – for example, those forbidding menstruating women to attend Holy Communion – and medicine taboos are found all over Africa.

All these ritual prohibitions refer to a religion which does not concentrate on grace, faith and individual conviction, but concentrates instead on magic, moralism and legalism, anthropocentrism and man's own achievements. The Old Testament has an essential role to play in the sound growth of the indigenous Church and it should take its rightful place in theological training, with a thorough study of exegesis and Old Testament theology.

REFERENCES

1. J. Blauw, *Goden en Menschen: Plaats en betekensis van de heidenen in de Heilige Schrift*, Groningen, Niemeijer, 1950.

2. H. Kraemer, *Religion and the Christian Faith*, Lutterworth, 1958[2], 270.

3. Ibid., 270. Idolatry is rejected very strongly in the Old Testament. Barth says: 'It is consistently maintained, e.g. in Jer. x. 1–16 and Is. xliv. 9–20, that in all heathen religions man himself is originally the creator of his own god.' Karl Barth, *Church Dogmatics I*, transl. T. & T. Clark, 1956, 303.

4. G. E. Wright, *The Old Testament against its environment*, SCM, 1960,[7] 87. Wright adds: 'The surprising thing is not that the cult of magic and divination was known in Israel but that it should be so definitely forbidden in the law . . . so perfectly is the Old Testament on this point that it seems strange to me its resources together with those of the New Testament are not more vigorously used by the modern church to combat our modern superstitions which ultimately go back to the same pagan environment as that of Israel.' Ibid., 87, 88.

5. Kraemer, *Religion and the Christian Faith*, 270; Wright, *The O.T. against its Environment*, 78. 'Israel's life is, at least in ideal, astonishingly free from a world of demons, and magic with its prelogical conception of reality and divination.'

6. Cf. G. C. Aalders, *Sporen van animisme in het Oude Testament?* Kampken, Kok, 1914.

7. Paul D. Fueter, 'Theological Education in Africa', IRM, Oct. 1956, 389.

8. G. E. Wright, 'The Old Testament: a Bulwark of the Church against Paganism', IRM, 1951, 272.

9. Cf. G. E. Phillips, *The Old Testament in the World Church*, Lutterworth, 1948[2], 142.

10. Wright, *The O.T. against its Environment*, 26.

11. William D. Reyburn ('The Message of the Old Testament and the African Church'—I, *Practical Anthropology*, Vol. 7, No. 4, July–Aug. 1960, 152) says: 'Some have refused to translate the Old Testament, feeling that the embryonic life of the new Christian community would be endangered, finding in the Old Testament scriptures sanction for pagan ways of life.'

12. Cf. E. Brunner, *Die Unentbehrlichkeit des Alten Testaments für die missionierende Kirche*, Basel, Evang. Missionsverlag, 1934, 5. 'We have no Jesus Christ without the Old Testament.' Th. C. Vriezen (*An Outline of Old Testament Theology*, Oxford, Blackwell, 1962, 9), states. 'Christ's Messianic office cannot be confessed without the Old Testament.'

13. The call to prophecy came to Kimbangu from his reading of the Bible, especially the Old Testament. Andersson, 48. Schlosser, *Propheten*, 393, indicates clearly the prominent place the Old Testament receives in these movements.

14. Sundkler, *Ministry*, 285.

15. Ibid., 284.

16. J. Barr, 'Hebrew language in theological education', IRM, Oct. 1961. See especially Th. Boman, *Das hebraïsche Denken im Vergleich mit dem Griechischen*, Göttingen, 1954²; also J. Barr, *The Semantics of Biblical Language*, OUP, 1961.

17. IMC Theol. Report II, 60.

18. Barr, IRM, 438; C. H. Dodd, *New Testament Studies*, 1952; W. D. Davies, *Paul and Rabbinic Judaism*, SPCK, 1962.

19. Ibid., 438. Cf. Reyburn, 'The Message of the Old Testament', op. cit., 153, 'The desire to diminish the importance of the Hebrew background of the Christian message often creates a lack of appreciation and understanding of much of African culture which stands in close formal relation to it. . . . African life and thought share in many ways the cultural life of ancient Israel.'

20. IMC Theol. Report III, 45–46.

21. Barr, 439.

22. James Muilenburg, *The Way of Israel*, Routledge, 1962, 76.

23. Ibid., 85.

24. Vriezen, *An Outline of Old Testament Theology*, 1962, 99.

25. Wright, *The O.T. against its Environment*, 26.

26. Cf. Kraemer, *Religion and the Christian Faith*, 129.

27. Wright, *The O.T. against its Environment*, 100.

28. Ibid., 107.

29. Ibid., 108.

30. Ibid., 111–12.

31. K. Barth, *Church Dogmatics*, I, 2, T. & T. Clark, 1955, 280–325.

32. Kraemer, *Religion*, 243.

33. Wright, *The O.T., a bulwark* . . ., IRM, July 1951, 269.

34. Vriezen, *O.T. Theology*, 249.

35. Cf. J. H. Scheepers, *Die Gees van God en die Gees van die Mens in die Ou Testament*, Kampen, J. H. Kok, 1960.

36. Cf. Vriezen, *O.T. Theology*, 250.

37. Ibid., 250–51.

38. Vriezen, ibid., 257–58. See also G. von Rad, *Theologie des Alten Testaments*, Vol. II, Munich, Kaiser, 1960, 75. These phenomena were not considered to be important. Only Joel iii. 1 ff. expected that the whole of Israel will acquire this charisma.

39. Ibid., 258–59. G. von Rad (Vol. II, 93) states that with all the prophets of the Old Testament the 'Word of Yahweh' is in the centre. This Word is the content and very basis of their existence.

40. Eichrodt, Vol. I, 289, 291.

41. Cf. H. H. Kraus, 'Prophetie und Politik', *Theol. Existenz heute*, N.F. 36, 1952.

42. Vriezen, *O.T. Theology*, 263. Cf. N. H. Snaith, *The Distinctive ideas of the Old Testament*, Epworth, 1955[6], 118: 'The prophets were the first to be sure that the sins of their own people must meet with a just and terrible retribution.'

43. Eichrodt, Vol. I, 332.

44. Ibid., 333.

45. Cf. G. von Rad, *Theologie des Alten Testaments*, Vol. II, Kaiser, 1960, 211.

46. Eichrodt, Vol. I, 335.

47. Cf. E. L. Ehrlich, *Der Traum im Alten Testament*, bei. z.a.w., 155 ff.

48. Eichrodt, Vol. I, 337.

49. Eichrodt, Vol. I, 338.

50. Ibid., 341.

51. Ibid., 341.

52. R. H. R. Pfeiffer, *Introduction to the Old Testament*, A. & C. Black, 1945, 32–33.

53. Eichrodt, Vol. I, 343.

54. Ibid., 346.

55. Cf. J. Blauw, *The Missionary Nature of the Church*, London, Lutterworth Press, 1962.

56. S. Mowinckel, *The Old Testament as the Word of God*, Oxford, Blackwell, 1960, 35.

57. Eichrodt, Vol. I, 385.

58. Sundkler, *Ministry*, 214.

59. Cf. IMC Report, Part III, 1954, 45–46.

60. G. E. Phillips, *The Old Testament in the World Church*, Lutterworth, 1948, 6.

61. Phillips, 7.

62. Ibid.

63. Ibid., 9.

64. G. van der Leeuw, *De Primitieve Mensch*, 102–07.

65. Sundkler, *Ministry*, 214.

66. Baëta, 128. The *Apostolowo Fe Dedefia Habobo* maintains 'Our food taboos are those stated in the Old Testament', ibid., 82. In the Ngunza-Khaki movements, menstruating women may not, on the basis of the Old Testament, enter a place of worship, and are forbidden to give food to Ntangu, the leader. Andersson, 180. The 'rules of life' of the independent groups discussed by Monica Wilson are 'avowedly based on the Old Testament' (Wilson, *Nyakyusa*, 190).

67. Hodgkin, 97.

68. Ibid. R. Buell (*The Native Problem in Africa*, II, ch. 94) writes: 'At the trial Kimbangu and his followers defended themselves in a dignified manner. Questioned as to why he thought he was a prophet, Kimbangu quoted a verse to the effect that "thou hast hid these things from the wise and prudent, and hast revealed them unto babes". When the President asked what "these things" were, Kimbangu replied by repeating the Ten Commandments. When he started to repeat the seventh he was ordered to stop by the captain, whose native concubine was present in the court room.'

69. Cf. Roland Allen, *Missionary Methods, St. Paul's or Ours?* Dominion Press, 1927[3], 123.

70. Ibid., 285.

71. Ibid., 427–28.

72. Cf. Ibid., 428.
73. Oliver, 281.
74. Schlosser, *Eingeborenen*, 157.
75. Baëta, 68. Phillips, 9: 'Such people also consistently observe Saturday as their Sabbath instead of Sunday.' Andersson (181) states that in the Ngunza–Khaki movement, however, Wednesday was the day of rest – the day Kimbangu was sentenced to death. The Ngunzists are not allowed to work on a Saturday because it is considered to be the beginning of the Lord's Sabbath. Andersson, 108.
76. Baëta, 69.
77. Ibid., 93.
78. Ibid., 82.
79. Ibid., 125.
80. Pauw, *Religion*, 83. Sundkler, *Prophets*, 163. Shembe has introduced circumcision for men in his Nazarite Church, a system abolished by Shaka. They are forbidden to shake hands with the unclean and uncircumcised.
81. Pauw, 83.
82. Cf. H. W. Turner, *Profile through Preaching*, Edinburgh House Press, 1965.
83. Phillips, 9. Barth states: 'Even the New Testament seems to have a kind of *nova lex* alongside the Gospel. It seems that the Gospel's appeal is not only to faith but to man's free decision. On the one hand we have to believe, on the other we have to love and do good works. The second, the *nova lex*, becomes most important. The NT centres everything in Jesus Christ and faith does not mean merely the superseding but the abolishing of man's self-determination. It means that man's self-determination is co-ordinated into the order of the divine predetermination. . . . The only ultimate and really serious determination for the believer is that which proceeds from Jesus Christ.' Barth, op. cit., 313.
84. Pauw, *Religion*, 141. Phillips, 9. 'We hear of some Christians of this type, who are deprived of an important part of their diet such as scaleless fish or pork, because of prohibitions in Lev. xi. 7–10.'
85. J. G. Frazer, *The Golden Bough*, Macmillan, 19.
86. Frazer, 21–22. Cf. Franz Steiner, *Taboo*, London, 103, 156.
87. Shropshire, 311–12.
88. Ibid., 312.
89. Ibid., 312–13. A. R. Radcliffe-Brown states (*Taboo*, CUP, 1939, 9): 'A ritual prohibition is a rule of behaviour which is associated with a belief that an infraction will result in an undesirable change in the ritual status of the person who fails to keep to the rule. This change of ritual status is conceived in many different ways in different societies, but everywhere there is the idea that it involves the likelihood of some minor or major misfortune which will befall the person concerned.' The word *religio* which comes from *relegere* (to take into consideration), the opposite of *neglegere* (to neglect), indicates the relationship between man and God, which consisted in the observance of ritual prohibitions; cf. G. van der Leeuw, *Inleiding tot de Phaenomenologie van den Godsdienst*, Haarlem, Erven F. Bohn, 1948, 126.
90. Shropshire, 318.
91. Ibid., 319.
92. J. G. Frazer, *Psyche's Task*, Macmillan, 1909, 27. The idea of becoming like the swine when eating it is strong in this case. Cf. Franz Steiner, *Taboo*, London, Cohen & Part Ltd., 1956, 103.
93. Pauw, *Religion*, 171.

94. Ibid., 211.

95. Ibid., 195.

96. The Sabbath (Saturday) becomes a magically loaded day: Shembe I states in Isl. 188:

> *We all have been invited*
> *We have been invited by the Lord of the Sabbath*
> *that we may be saved*
> *through this Sabbath.*
> *Amen, Amen, Amen.*

In Isl. 24: 5 he says:

> *Today rejoice ye,*
> *Ye keepers of the laws,*
> *You are going to be anointed to sufficiency*
> *through having accomplished (fulfilled) the laws.*

7

SOME FEATURES OF THE INDEPENDENT MOVEMENTS

(i) POLYGAMY

Parrinder maintains that polygamy is not the root cause of the formation of independent movements in Nigeria.[1] In an area investigated in the Congo, among polygamists 37% were Catholics, 27% Protestants and 56½% animists.[2] What the missionary taught in this connection was so often not related to the African way of thinking, and the Old Testament with its polygamous outlook – at least as it appeared superficially – made a far greater impression. Price says that 'against that background, the missionary insistence on monogamy tended to seem merely a foreign fad'.[3] The Levirate marriage, common in much of Africa, finds a close parallel in the Old Testament. It was on this type of marriage that the 'Israelities' based their approach to polygamy after the Bulhoek tragedy mentioned above, when the widows had to be cared for.

Polygamy is an economic and social institution, although it is attacked by missionaries as originating from sinful lust. But Price rightly says that 'polygamy is the one reprobated act by which the sinner cannot effectually repent at his own cost alone. The relation once entered into brings its own loyalties which demand respect.'[4] Some maintain that many Africans have not yet developed to the stage where they can accept monogamy,[5] which is why some missionaries took the extreme approach to polygamists by baptising some of them with all their wives. The results were most often far from encouraging.[6] In many parts of Africa, however, it is still a case of many wives or many prostitutes.[7] Amongst those who have risen to professional or middle-class status, polygamy is limited to a small percentage.[8]

It is often 'The Spirit' that directs people to a polygamous life. A prophet may tell his congregation of two beds that have been shown to him by the spirit in a dream, which is an indication that he has to take a second wife.[9] The Musama Disco Christo Church

G 179

practise controlled polygamy, and maintain in No. 18 of their set of beliefs: 'We believe [as an African Church] that polygamy is not a moral sin.'[10] Others again maintain that 'polygamy is allowed, according to the Scriptures, but not loose living in sexual matters'.[11] Polygamy has its own ethical standards which are to be observed meticulously.

The entrance of a pagan into Shembe's 'Church' presents no difficulties, because the polygamist need not get rid of his extra wives.[12] The independent 'Churches' amongst the Nyakyusa (who live north of Lake Nyasa), although they read the Gospels at their services and recite the Apostles' Creed, base their rules on the Old Testament rather than on the New, and approve of polygamy. The Constitution of the African National Church states that 'members of the Church shall be people of good character according to the Native traditions, laws and customs, as contained in the *First Five Books of the Christian Bible*, whether polygamists or not'.[13] In their sermons there is continuous reference to polygamy.[14] Amongst the Tswana, while the established Churches oppose polygamy, the independent movements are quite favourably disposed to it. They are also in favour of *Bogadi* (bride price).[15]

When 'Spirit Visions' began to take the place of the Bible as the source of revelation, Ngunzism was open to new developments, and to the influence of the pre-Christian religion especially. The Puritan moral code was slackened, and 'spiritual marriages' became customary. The African Salvation Army in the Congo considered polygamy no sin, and stated that those who practise it 'will also go to Heaven', with the result that chiefs with large harems were favourably inclined to the Army.[16] Polygamy is practised in the Ngunza-Khaki movement, as well as 'spiritual marriages', which are based on African polygamy and Paul's words in 1 Cor. ix. 5.[17] The leaders in this movement select 'young and beautiful girls' and tell them 'Nzambi has told me that you are to serve me, it is no sin to serve God's servant'.[18] In this movement, sexual intercourse is even permitted within forbidden degrees of kindred.[19] The example set by the leaders had a demoralising and degenerating effect, as they maintained that 'to fornicate is no sin. God's spirit declares that the prophets must have female servants.'[20] The relationship between morality and polygamy has thus broken down, and this is undoubtedly the result of the breakdown of African society itself.

Polygamy is practised in the nativistic movements throughout Africa. As well as the movements just mentioned, it is allowed in the Zion Christian Church of Lekganyane,[21] and it was a live issue in the *Joswa Kate Mugema* (The Society of the One Almighty God).[22]

The Bamalaki justify polygamy on the basis of the Old Testament. The Kikuyu Independent Schools Association and the African Orthodox Church find polygamy un-Christian, but are forced by circumstances to condone it. The African Greek Orthodox Church discourages it, but 'admits that a young Church may have to condone polygamy in its circumference'.[23] On the other side, however, the modern economic situation counteracts polygamy – a harder task-master than religion. Also the women of an urban polygamous family feel their position as a liability, not as an asset;[24] in the city it is considered uncivilised.

The United Native African Church in Ibadan is polygamous; so also are the 'Prayer Church' and the 'Fishmonger Church' (Eleja).[25] The last-named Church maintains that polygamy is 'nowhere forbidden in the European rules of Methodism, but only in rules invented for Africa'.[26] The main idea here is that Christian ethics should be adapted to the African social setting. Polygamy is tolerated in most nativistic movements, and monogamy is frequently regarded not as a Christian institution so much as a specifically European one, lacking scriptural sanction.[27] Together with the emphasis on a national Church and a national hierarchy goes that of a protest against rigidity in moral and social theory. Amongst the prayer healing Churches in Ibadan, the 'Apostolic Prayer Church' and the 'Prayer Church' permit polygamy to members and pastors, and maintain that 'some of the Prophets who have been responsible for great revivals have themselves been polygamists'.[28] While the leaders of clergy here adhere to monogamy (cf. 1. Timothy iii. 2–12) the members are allowed to be polygamous. The Church of Christ in Africa, which is recognised, has the majority of its members in Kenya but also thriving congregations in Tanzania and Uganda. With regard to the sacraments, they base their teaching on baptism on Matth. xxviii. 18–20. People are baptised not for what they *are* but because they *believe*. If polygamists believe, they are baptised. Christ called all sinners, even though monogamy is the Christian teaching.[29]

Bishop Colenso, who was deposed in 1864 from his episcopal see in Natal, was in favour of the baptism of polygamists.[30] Because the established Churches prohibited polygamy, men left in order to join the African independent movements.[31] The question of whether monogamy is essential to Christianity was raised at the IMC Conference at Tambaram in 1938. The status of women was in any case affected in polygamy: some Churches are strict, others not, as to whether the women from a polygamous marriage become communicant members of the Church.[32]

181

The powerful development of the worldly mind and ungodliness among the Cainites is clearly seen in the life of Lamech, who is of the sixth generation. Cain and his descendants have left the fellowship of the Church, and Lamech in his self-rule becomes an unrestrained polygamist.[33] Of him it is told that he had two wives, showing that he was the first to leave the beaten track. With him, instead of the original monogamy (cf. Gen. ii. 21–23), polygamy appeared, a new sign of degeneration as a result of sin.[34] It is clear that the function of the poems in the book Song of Songs is to help man to have fuller communion with God, and that the love which culminates in marriage is the deepest and holiest element in human physical nature. 'Sex is capable of extreme abuse, but that is because it is capable also of the greatest heights of earthly experience. What this book has to tell us, more than anything else, is that this element in mankind is not outside the range of God's interest in us, that it may be and should be employed in accordance with His will in the concentration for a lifetime on a single human object. "Three score queens and four score concubines and virgins without number ?" No. "My dove, my undefiled, is but one." '[35] The problem of polygamy becomes acute if even Christians from the established Churches like Asamoa doubt whether the New Testament is monogamous. Even if there is no direct evidence, yet the whole spirit of Scripture points to monogamy, as the marriage of the first couple was monogamous, as was that of the parents of the Son of Man.[36] The problem, however, becomes complicated when the alternative to polygamy, with its strict sanctions of ritual prohibition – by which the African way of life is ordered, is in many cases today not monogamy but the pursuit of promiscuous relationships with its many tragic social consequences. The moral theology of the Church must accept its special task in this field. Polygamy, which has primarily to do with economy, with status, with abstinence between birth and weaning, needs to be approached with a theology of marriage.[37] The great danger in Africa, however, is the impression that is often given that monogamous marriage is automatically good – in spite of immoral developments within it in modern urban society.

(ii) SACRED SITES

Sacred sites where the deity reveals himself were characteristic of Old Testament religion. The idea is that God 'reserves to himself the right to decide where men are to call upon him'.[38] During Israel's trek, there was not only the Ark or the Sacred Text, but the Israelites could also draw near to God at Sinai, the Mount of God, and the sacred spring of Kadesh. After the occupation of Canaan there

182

were places like Shiloh and Mizpah, which were to be superseded by the Temple of Zion, the centre of Jewish worship after the exile.[39] The danger here is that the Godhead may be localised and limited to a specific people and place. Although the cultic worship of Yahweh was possible only at definite places, yet He would nevertheless hear the prayer of worshippers everywhere when they called upon His Name.[40] With the Canaanites, cult sites, sacred springs, stones and trees, as well as the temple building at Shechem, were important. After the occupation, Israel also maintained that God is inseparably connected with the holy places; temple buildings were erected in Shiloh, Jerusalem, Bethel, Dan, Ophrah and Mizpah. The Yahwist Zealots saw in this a destructive innovation as well as an 'irruption of the usages of Canaan, Phoenicia and Egypt'. The more the foreign element was assimilated – namely the Canaanite *bāmōt*, 'on every high hill and under every green tree'[41] – the more the covenant of God was localised and limited. Even with the Ark of God the connection between Yahweh and the cult object is so close that it 'almost amounts to identification'.[42] Eventually, however, there came a reaction against the Canaanite influence which associated divine temples with the divine presence. The prophets maintained that God is transcendent, and that his presence at the holy place is an act of condescension made in order to reveal himself. The Deuteronomic school went further and substituted for the pagan conception of the personal presence of God at the holy places that of the presence of His Name.[43] The priestly writings maintained that Yahweh was only present in the sanctuary from time to time, and then veiled in his *kābōd*;[44] He is, however, present there in a special sense in that the cultic activities are carried out 'before the face of Yahweh', *lipnē yhwh*.[45] Even the prophets saw the future importance of Jerusalem as a place where God reveals himself.[46] Jerusalem became the place where the concrete historical revelation found its emphasis, where it was established and whence it reached out to people. This prevailed until the revelation took place which was independent of a holy place, the fulfilment in Jesus Christ who could say 'One greater than the Temple is there'[47]

Such special places where God is active in a special way through his Spirit are a characteristic of the nativistic movements. Such a place is the home of the prophet or messiah and does not belong to ordinary, earthly localities. It has cosmic meaning, it is a centre of power, a piece of the other world in this world. Shembe's High Place or *Ekuphakameni* (meaning 'the high and elevated place') is the centre of the great July festival, and Nhlangakazi became the only mountain of the Nazarites for the annual January festival. Ekuphakameni is the earthly Jerusalem. Shembe I says in Isl. 50. 7: 'Leave ye the earth, come ye to Ekuphakameni.' A large number of Shembe's hymns praise the beauty and splendour of Ekuphakameni; in the hymnal it receives many 'heavenly' names. There is a close relationship between Ekuphakameni and heaven. The pools in Zululand receive Biblical names such as Bethesda because of the association of Bethesda with healing; the kraals of the faithful also receive Biblical names. The African's approach to the Bible is without the notion of geographical locality, as his main interest is in the event; thus any locality could be Jerusalem, Bethlehem or any other Biblical place.[48] His mythical thinking is not bounded by time and space; this again is a general characteristic of the enthusiastic.

In one instance, the Musama Disco Church made a 'covenant' and removed to a new site; the removal was 'planned and carried out in such a manner as to be reminiscent of the Exodus of the Israelites from Egypt'.[49] The place where they finally settled, and which became the sacred place, was called the New Mazano.[50] Healing took place there, which they based on Ex. xv. 26 and Mark xvi. 15–18. They built the 'House of the Holy Well' and the 'Holy Place'; from the first came the 'holy water', and in the second, also known as 'Sanctum', were to be found 'the Ark, the Book of the Holy Covenant, and the "Holy See" '.[50] The final rites, both for the ordination of ministers and the consecration of the prophets, are carried out here. The Ark (a sacred box) contains the Ten Commandments.[51] This, together with the 'Book of Holy Covenants', which contain promises made to the first leader and vows take by him, together with prophecies, may be carried round Mazano 'in a holy procession at any time of crisis, such as earthquakes, disease epidemics, or civic upheavals, whereupon God would avert extreme disaster'.[52] Healing is generally more effective if carried out at these sacred places.

Nkamba (Congo), the birthplace of Kimbangu, became the centre of the Ngunzist movement.[53] This place is now called Nkamba–Jerusalem. Pilgrimages are even made there at the present time, and have increased since the prophet's ashes were brought there in 1960.[54] Pilgrimages to Nkamba have been made since the beginning of the Ngunzist movement; indeed, they were made before Kimbangu had any idea of seceding. According to Andersson, the transmutation from pure Christianity to Ngunzism began with these pilgrimages.[55] (The administration received information that the dead were taken to Nkamba, that newborn babies had died there through lack of care and that women had given birth to children unattended.[56]) After the prophet had been deported, pilgrims still made their way to Nkamba and knelt before his house (*lumpangu*).[57] Again, Pendele is the gathering place for all those interested in the Congolese Khaki movement, and singing, praying, confession of sins, healing, raising of the dead, communication of the spirit and teaching of Khaki doctrine are carried on there.[58] At Pendele, moral rules are strict, because it is chiefly visited by those from Protestant missions, while at Ngetesemane, the holy of holies of the movement, immorality is practised openly.[58] The essential background of these holy places is the idea not only of having a specific centre, but also of having a place where revelation is vividly experienced. There is a close connection between the magical personality and his holy place, which becomes the centre of this magico-religious acts.

(iii) WATER

Water is important, not only in baptism but also in purification rites. It must be 'prepared by prayer in order to make it efficacious'.[59] According to Sundkler's Zionists the Spirit is best experienced in the pool.[60] The terms used by Zionists for the right kind of Bethesda-pool or Jordan-stream, which gives the spirit, are 'living water' and 'much water'. The depth of the pool is important so that the baptised may be totally immersed, and Paul's Romans vi. version of baptism, namely signifying death with and resurrection in Christ, is very real to the Zionist Church.[61] Baptism, which takes the place of a purification rite, means a literal washing away of sin[62] and therefore the whole body must be immersed and not only the forehead, 'as in the mission'. For others, the pool must also be associated with rapidly flowing water which is an assurance 'that the water is efficacious in washing and rapidly removing sin, sickness and pollution'.[63] Such a pool is even more efficacious if it is below a waterfall, where the most difficult cases will be assured that they will be filled with the Spirit.[64] Immersion also drives away sickness. Baptism, the washing away of sins, and healing are closely associated. This usually takes place with total immersion, which recalls much of the traditional ritual practices in streams, lakes and pools, where the old water cult was widely practised. Ritual washing before battle, for example, often took place in rivers, streams or pools after the confession of wrongs done against the society. This provided strength for the battle and enhanced the sense of community.

'Holy water' has an important function in healing services. Usually it is water that has been 'prayed for' by the leader or office bearer, which gives it magical value. This water is either consumed in the church or is taken home, where the patient takes it when he does not feel well. In the St Paul Apostolic Faith Morning Star in Taung drinking of water takes place after laying on of hands during the

Sunday worship. Referring to Rev. xxii. 17 and Christ's 'praying for' the water at the wedding at Cana, the minister explains that it is their medicine. Most of the people in this Church 'go through the water' after baptism.[65] Purification is effected by immersion. After a funeral, which defiles a person, purification is also required. On such occasions, only the hands are washed, a custom strictly adhered to by members of the established Churches. This is done as a result of the influence of African tradition, according to which even the milk of cows is affected by death and should not be touched for some time. The hands are washed so that the grave dust is not carried to their homes, as it may cause the death of somebody else. Just as sin is an evil negative mystic entity to be washed away from the body, so is death. To the traditional mind, death is never natural. The magic of death in the polluted grave dust has to be removed.

In the St. Paul Apostolic Faith Morning Star, members pass through the baptismal pool for health purposes, and after a death they perform a ritual similar to the Mosaic ritual, all present at the funeral being sprinkled with water, together with newly bought articles which they bring to the church services.[66] Baptism by immersion is also considered among the Tswana separatists as a rite of purification.[67] The emphasis on adult baptism as initiation into Christianity has been interpreted in the traditional context with its purification rites. As a *rite de passage*, purification takes place especially during the transition from one stage of life to the other. The 'dirt' of the old stage has to be washed away. Such purification also takes place in order to establish contact with the supernatural. At the completion of the initiation period the neophyte washes himself in a dam, pool, stream or river. Here again African traditional religion has been ready soil for the spiritualistic type of Christianity. The sacrifice that takes place after an important event takes the form of a gift but it brings the supernatural forces under obligation. He who sacrifices develops power which he directs towards his God or ancestor. Because sacrifice means the same as exercising power, it takes place through the magically strongest person in the family, clan or tribe or, in the nativistic movement, through its leader or elders.

Water that had been 'prayed for' was used in the pre-Christian pagan ritual, e.g. in the case of Tolonyane. Prayer here means the expression of magically loaded words. Tolonyane made the people drink water over which he had prayed.[68] Baptism amongst the Baganda in Uganda and Kikuyu in Kenya is not associated with purification or immersion, except in the Mengo Gospel Church where total immersion is European in origin; here ritual naming

186

has been important.[69] The Musama Disco Christo Church at Mazano in Ghana has the 'House of the Holy Well' the water of which is used for baptismal ceremonies as well as ceremonial ablutions. The water is fetched in bottles by those that live away from Mazano and drunk in order to restore and maintain health.[70] As Appiah, the son of the prophet Jehu and Nathalomoa, was born 'in the spirit', 'the water in which he was bathed became a very potent medicine for curing sterility in women, and septic sores'.[71] In the Transkei, a visiting Anglican bishop's bath water was used for healing – of course, without his knowing it. In *Memeneda Gyidifo* (The Saviour Church) baptism 'is by total immersion three times in a running stream'.[72] Both adult and infant baptism are practised – the infant's whole body, except for the head, being dipped into the stream and the head and face washed separately.[73] In Ghana, the religious significance attached to water is borne out both in ceremonial washing and healing.[74] The Church of Christ's People in Ibadan, Nigeria, have bottles of holy water which contain wooden crosses.[75] These crosses – fetishism in the form of Christian symbols – are the bearers of supernatural energy, as in the case of amulets, and add to the efficacy of the water. Much is made of holy water in the prayer healing sects in Ibadan.[76] Water also played a part in the Ngunzist Movement, where those seriously ill received special attention from Kimbangu but 'those who were not seriously ill went from the prophet's presence to a door on the left side of the enclosure, opening on the path to the water in which they bathed before going home again'.[77]

In the Khaki movement of Mavonda Ntangu, water is used as a catalyst in finding out whether the participants in the service, where there is much shaking and singing, have the spirit or not.[78] During these trials, song after song is sung and the members shake violently. The water is also used in this movement in connection with healing,[79] and baptism is performed in a stream.[80] Ancestor worship appears in connection with baptism, the newly baptised person having to go to the graves after the baptism ceremony to pray.[81] As regards sin, they believe that the missionaries have a special pond of purification (*Siloa*) where they bathe and their sins disappear. Mavonda Ntangu looks forward to the day when they also will have such a pond of purification, since divine justice must be applied to them also. Self-assertion and magic rather than grace form the emphasis, even in obtaining forgiveness of sins. The Cross of Christ is pushed into the background and man's attainments and secrets, his higher gnosis, his magic are now in the forefront. The magical personality creates his own world in which he reigns – and where the

Cross, being interpreted only magically, is superseded. The desire is to have their own god and their own religion, which 'will gain the victory and become the religion of the Congo when all the others have been driven out'.[82] This will be a religion without a Cross. Here the Churches are called to give a completely new call to the Cross of Jesus Christ.

(iv) THE CONCEPT OF SIN IN THE NATIVISTIC MOVEMENTS

Perfectionism, as found amongst Bible Christians such as the followers of Bhengu,[83] has a long history in the Church in Africa, and took many forms, of which antinomianism and legalism, or moralism, are the main types. Montanism was the great perfectionist movement of Africa. The perfectionist may discard 'the external law', or may 'be intent on polishing itself to an ever greater brightness, and therefore becoming ever more introvert and dull'.[84] The 'Brethren of the Free Spirit', whom Calvin met in Paris in 1534, maintained that the principle of evil has no real existence – 'If we fall into sin, great good may result. . . .'[85] The Ranters held very much the same views, as is evident from a tract written in 1650, which states 'that there is no occasion for them to read the Scriptures, nor to hear sermons, because Father, Son and Spirit are all in them, therefore they are above all commandments whatsoever. That there is no such thing as what men call sin. That sin and holiness are all one to God.'[86] 'Enlightenment by the Spirit', or being the personification of the Spirit, received the priority above Scripture as an external norm.

In the independent movements in Africa, we see that such people eventually become 'incapable' of sinning. The Anabaptists believed this of themselves, and Bullinger speaks about a sect of 'Holy and Sinless Baptists'. The 'Free Brothers' maintained that 'women did sin in having intercourse with their husbands who were still heathens, but they did not sin in having intercourse with the brethren'.[87] In Ngunzism, girls accompanied the prophets because 'God's Spirit declares that the prophets must have female servants'.[88] Adultery and profligacy were the result. Such a theology, which isolates itself from the norms of Orthodox Christianity and Scripture, and in which the inner light and subjectivism are paramount, is bound to result in immorality and a comparison between God's love (*agape*) and man's love (*eros*). In traditional African society, where sin is regarded as formal rather than ethical, grave difficulties arise.[89] For those truly initiated in the Khaki movement fornication and adultery are not considered as sins, because God Himself commanded 'Multiply and replenish the earth'. 'From Moutombo to

188

Kimbedi, it is thought that adultery is not a sin.'[90] Sundkler refers to the 'Salem Church', the teaching of which was originally ascetic. They practise the 'heavenly marriage'; theoretically, this implies a celibate state, but in this movement both asceticism and license are evident.[91]

The perfectionist looks at sins as temptations, while remaining 'inviolably attached to God in the centre of this soul'.[92] The problem here is that men put themselves on the same basis as Christ, in whom the union of the Divine and the Human is a hypostatic union, while the highest human possibility effected by God himself is a mystic union by which the human personality remains unabridged.[93] Wesley himself believed in the doctrine of sinless perfection,[94] a doctrine which was much in the forefront in the nineteenth century, and which came to Africa via the Pentecostal movements and Baptist Churches. With some it had a legalistic, moralistic approach, while with others it was antinomian in principle and in fact. After yielding themselves to the Holy Spirit they believe that they will never sin again and are free from all law – the Ten Commandments and the law of the land – according to which many believed that they are free to yield to their impulses, because whatever they do is done under the guidance of the 'Holy Spirit'. Some historians of the evangelical movement in England in the nineteenth century maintain that it combined 'fierce revivalist fervour with shameless immorality'.[95] Perfectionism often went together with extreme sex-consciousness. Knox says 'the danger is notoriously present in all revivalism; even in mysticism'.[96] Polygamy in some form or other has not only been a difficulty of the independent movements in Africa, but also in similar movements in Europe and the United States. The American Perfectionist Noyes, like some Anabaptists, had committed himself to a 'communist doctrine of sex relations'[97] within the community of the perfect (practised also in independent movements in Africa) as well as to 'spiritual marriages'. This is the tendency in most enthusiastic movements. Knox distinguishes between the mystical and evangelical enthusiast, and concludes that the mystic is 'tone-deaf, as a mule, to theology'.[98] As in Nestorianism, they see Jesus Christ not as God-Man but as a man somehow deified so that a second incarnation is not unthinkable.[99] This is their greatest christological heresy, and in the African context the position of the chief makes it easier for such a heresy to flourish.

It is thus clear that subjectivism which develops out of a wrong conception of the Holy Spirit and the work of Christ easily leads to antinomianism, which is most clearly to be discerned in attitudes to

189

marriage and sex. African ideology stresses the social nature of sin – 'the identification of the kinship group with the offender, and the need for social expiation'.[100] The worst consequence of sin is the destruction of one's corporate existence in society. This has been a deterrent in the past but, with the disintegration of the social structure, this aspect has steadily been broken down. Where it is still maintained, the anti-social concept of sin (without a sense of guilt) is made very obvious, as when, for example, sin is compounded by payment of money.[101] It is excellent to build the Church, the Household of God, round the family, but family ties are very strong and each family wishes to have as many candidates accepted for christening as possible; the Church is reluctant to apply its discipline to members of the congregation and exclude those who continously fall into gross sins. This affects the whole moral standard of the congregation and the Biblical concept of sin.

At the beginning of the Ngunzist movement, forgiveness of secret sins could only be obtained if they were confessed. In traditionalist African society an act is only sinful when discovered or when it spells evil for the society. Open confession is quite general in Africa, and goes together with purgation, ritual vomiting and ritual washing, healing and testimony. In varying degrees it also found a place in the Revival movement in East Africa. With the Ngunzists oral confession did not suffice, as the sins had to be recorded on a piece of paper the sinner held in his hand while he was in the presence of the prophet. If during the prayer and the 'laying on of hands', by which forgiveness was imparted, the paper did not move in a certain direction, the confession was considered incomplete. The paper often moved in the wrong direction, so that the penitents had to confess further transgressions or think of new ones.[102] Here is a reversion to the ancestors, who show their satisfaction or dissatisfaction in this and other ways – such as, for example, how dice fall. In spite of all these confessions, the puritan moral code of the Ngunzists degenerated as a result of reversion to pre-Christian ideas, which were now interpreted in a post-Christian context. A person would now be mostly aware of his sin through sickness, misfortune and his conscience.

'Prophesying' – in the sense of the prophet's ability to tell the innermost secrets of his members – has become an important factor in the independent movements. For example. a prophet can tell whether the Communion service is attended by a person with unconfessed sins, and 'in this way prophesying also becomes the means of watching over and safeguarding the chastity of young and old in the congregation'.[103] 'Spiritual marriages' became customary, and lewd scenes took place by day and night. The young married women taken by Congolese prophets have no connection with traditional polygamy, in which morals were strict. In this post-Christian nativistic movement, however, 'not only is free promiscuity practised, but also sexual intercourse with women with whom relations were forbidden on account of degree of kindred'.[104]

Sin and guilt in the early Ngunzist movement are regarded by some as having Christian features, but Andersson rightly has his doubts. Sin here tends to be formal and ceremonial, as is the case in all naturalistic religions, because ritual washing and vomiting can take it away. Andersson remarks that 'grave ethico-religious sins are often tolerated while the main stress is put upon proscriptions of a purely ritual character'.[105] Amongst the nativistic movements baptism has become a purification rite, accompanied by confession of sins, among which sexual transgressions have precedence. Confession is accompanied by ritual vomiting in order to get rid of the evil spirit and be cured.[106] Andersson has also pointed out that the procedure followed among the Ngunzists is that 'used for the native act of divination, not that used in the Christian confession of sins'.[107] Confession is given a special part in their service, and is indispensable in baptism.[108] It is interesting to note that in the modern liturgical development of the Western Church, confession of sin has taken a more prominent place; here, however, it is done by the congregation responding to the *leitourgos* or leader, or by singing a relevant hymn. In Africa, confession of sin is required at important moments in the life of the individual: for example, when a youth is to be initiated, he has first to confess his sexual sins; and in many places, a wife has to confess her unfaithfulness in marriage when she experiences difficulty in the delivery of a child.[109]

As sickness is associated in the African mind with sin, public confession of sin naturally plays an important part at healing ceremonies or in faith-healing Churches. One's soul is strengthened by adhering to the rules of society, which means good behaviour and the performance of special rites and sacrifices in honour of the ancestor spirits. Sickness is the result of oneself being anti-social, or of having an anti-social act performed against one by way of sorcery, which is considered equal to sin. 'Health is considered evidence of one's power of soul to ward off evil influences or of one's personal integrity and living in the community.'[110] In African society, as in old Israel, one lives according to a covenant, the breaking of which has negative effects and results in magical power being exercised on the offender. This explains why moralism has magical power, as it sustains the covenant, and the observation of outward laws is rewarded by certain divine benefits.

There is a great difference between the nativistic movement and the Revival movements in East Africa, which brought about a radical change in many lives. Revival adhered to Scripture as its objective norm, and not to subjectivism by way of injunctions of 'the Spirit'. Here again the background of African traditional religion gives the explanation. Lévy-Bruhl states that 'Seen from one aspect, to be "unclean" is a kind of essentially mystic quality, which makes a person find himself in the power of an evil influence and in imminent danger of disaster. From another aspect, it is a material defilement, a blemish that adheres physically to the unclean person or object, which can be transferred, or communicated through contact, or removed by cleansing, etc. The primitive mind does not choose between these two representations.'[111] In ritual prohibition, the solidarity of the group is maintained, and being unclean means being anti-social.[112] The only way to counteract such uncleanness is by way of purification rites.[113] (Baptism is often administered weekly on the same person if he or she claims to be unclean). Morality thus does not depend on inner conviction but on outward adaptation. The 'danger of disaster' is the main motive for compliance with ritual prohibitions. In many cases the moral standard in established Churches is not what it should be; on this point Taylor says that 'at present the majority in the Church have not progressed beyond the attitudes of the traditional morality, and appear to concentrate on preventing or punishing what they pretend are exceptional lapses from the moral standard'.[114] There are, however, the few clergy and teachers who give sympathetic guidance to youth on questions of morality, and many succeed in their fight for chastity. Adultery is considered to be the prime sin, on account of its anti-social character, and the seventh commandment receives special attention.

In the Khaki movement the prophet decides the penance to be imposed on the offender or sinner – thus showing Roman Catholic influence. This takes place in the service. The type of sin determines the number of times forgiveness has to be asked, and the number of prayers depends on the sin's heinousness. After the number of times has been decided upon, the sinner steps forward and begs forgiveness from the prophet. Grave sins require the sinner to kneel, not on the ground, but on sharp stones or palm-kernels. The prophet then forvives the sins, after asking the congregation whether they should be pardoned.[115] After this, the healing of the sick receives attention. This includes the driving out of evil spirits: forgiveness and healing go together.

Taylor describes this 'ordeal by confession' as something which may be peculiarly African. Confession has also been a characteristic of the Revival movement in East Africa, and is demanded of new converts or renewed Christians as a test of the reality of their salvation, and as an initiation into the fellowship. On these occasions it seems as though 'the element of "brokenness", humiliation and abandonment to the group, is more important than penitence or faith'.[116] Mutual confession of sin and failure was an important characteristic of the Revival; it 'solved the problems of fellowship'.[117] Bhengu in East London, for example, arouses guilt among the people and then heals them. He uses healing and open confession in addition to preaching.[118] The effect of public confession among Xhosas in crisis situations helped in restoring harmony within the tribe, and so strengthened their power to resist evil as well as to restore harmony with the ancestors.[119] For the African, open confession has much to do with the solidarity of the group; it is significant in the Pentecostal and nativistic movements, as well as in those Revival movements which are within the 'Orthodox' Churches. Taylor rightly says: 'The African concept of group solidarity may demand some form of "open" confession within the fellowship, as well as private confession in the presence of a priest in order to satisfy the troubled conscience and reinstate the penitent.'[120]

The placing of a curse on somebody is considered by the African to be a grave sin, unless there is an adequate explanation for it. Just like sin, it weakens and devitalises the soul. This is also the case in the Old Testament,[121] where, however, sin has to do with impurity of heart and the violation of conscience, and not in the first place with ceremonial defilement or anti-social activities. For Israel, all life was upheld by covenant; the essence of sin was breach of that covenant, and sins against others were violations of it.[122] However, all sin is a violation of God himself, who is the soul of the Covenant.[123] In the later prophets, sin had more and more to do with disobedience and rebellion against God. The indigenous gods of Africa are not only far away, and in general unconcerned, but they are capricious and have no fixed norm of what is right or wrong that could affect the whole concept of sin.

The African Holy Communion is turned into a purification rite, as well as baptism. Strict rules of ritual prohibition are observed, for example no menstruating women may take part, tobacco must not be taken into the church, and so on. Most of the nativistic movements do not observe the essential sacrament of Holy Communion, while baptism, as a purification rite, is prominent. All the moralistic prohibitions in the movements' teachings, which push the Bible into the background, have strengthened the place of magic, which, in the new context, takes the form of moralism. In some movements, where divination, witchcraft and protective charms are ruled out in the name of Christ, Christ may even be presented merely 'as a superior magic';[124] this is the case in the Lumpa Church. The Communion administered by the missions is considered to be 'negative'; according to Mavonda Ntangu, the leader of the Khakists, it is 'false and cannot wash away sin'.[125]

The *ex opere operato* approach to the sacrament is basic to animism. For the primitive mentality, 'symbol' means the coming together of the two realities: the bread and wine and the body and blood of the Lord participate in one another.[126] This means to the animist that vital force is imparted through the elements, with the result that not only are sins forgiven but secret wisdom and vital force are imparted. In the Roman Catholic formulation, the sacrament *contains* grace; it transmits it; it is the 'vehicle' or 'channel' of grace.[127] This interpretation is in line with the animist approach. But grace is not dependent upon a physical reality, because it is of an entirely different order. In the sacrament it is Christ who acts, which means that sacramental grace is personal grace produced by Christ even though physical instruments are used .[128] It is important to concentrate on this problem in the Church in Africa, where the bread and wine, the apostle's staff, amulets and charms, and baptismal water convey power and health in a magical way. Holy Communion is considered to be loaded with magical power, and the missionaries are suspect to the Khakists, who believe that they have their own communion which is able to wash away sin, as well as to give secret wisdom and the gift of prophecy.[129] Other movements again consider the Holy Communion as a 'filthy' invention of the Whites and have replaced it with the Passover. The Cross has lost its centrality, and thus Holy Communion is discarded or pushed into the background. Here again the tendency towards a *theologia gloria* instead of a *theologia crucis* is obvious. If 'holy' does not mean 'having magical power', it falls for the African animist in the same category as the profane and has no value. This may be the main reason why the Holy Communion has been discarded in the Lumpa Church and neglected in others.

The movement which succeeded the Salvation Army in the Congo, and which was composed of Ngunzists, Salvation Army members and Khakists, celebrates the Communion, but with water and bananas. Other attempts have been made to use indigenous ingre-

194

PLATES

1. This man, photographed at Rorke's Drift, Natal, worked in the coal mines until 'miraculously' cured of chronic headache through laying-on of hands. Where the Holy Spirit touched him, its fingers 'burned through' his head-covering. He travelled alone, preaching, apparently not attached to a congregation.

2. Healing is the main attraction of these movements to many people. Women frequently seek help, especially for barrenness or death of their children.

3. The use of 'holy water' that has been 'prayed over' is common. 2 and 3 were taken on the outskirts of a white suburb of Johannesburg.

4. Foot-washing before 'holy communion', near Johannesburg.

5. The pointed end of the brass rod casts unclean spirits, *oMoya aBabi*, on to victims; the rounded end confers benefits, such as (supposedly) the ability to conceive children.

6. A drummer in one of the many groups that gather along the Umgeni river on Sunday afternoons.

7. For the Holy Spirit to come into their midst, worshippers must work themselves into an ecstatic state. In white suburbs, services are commonly held in garages, but these are cold during winter on the Witwatersrand; thus here the men dance to receive the Spirit in the open sunshine.

8. Of the two drums, the large one is called *indoda* (man) and the smaller *umame* (mother). Note that, beside the prophet at right, only women are present. The 'holy' staffs are characteristic.

9. Dancing to get the *uMoya* (Spirit). 8 and 9 taken at Rorke's Drift.

10. The ritual cleansing, common to all syncretistic movements, is at times dramatic. Here the woman vomits into a large crack in the rock, from which she said it would not be able to come back, because of its depth.

11. A service outside Rosettenville, Johannesburg. Lacking a suburban house or garage for worship, the people gather round a cleared space on the ground, called in this area *isiguqo*, the 'place where one kneels'. They act as if the space were an enclosed hut.

12. A prophet on Eshiyane mountain, Rorke's Drift, warding off lightning. He wears special dress for the purpose. In Zulu life, this is an important event

13. The Bishop's gown is specially important. It reflects his authority, which in turn spells power that may be interpreted as magical. (Johannesburg.)

14. A group on their way to worship in Zululand, Natal. Most groups are small and intimate, and they walk singing and dancing. Note the Bishop and the star (as followed by the wise men) on his garb.

(*Acknowledgments:* 1–3 and 5–12, Rev. Dr. A. I. Berglund; 4, 13, Rev. D. van Zyl; 14, Dr. W. Bodenstein.)

3

4

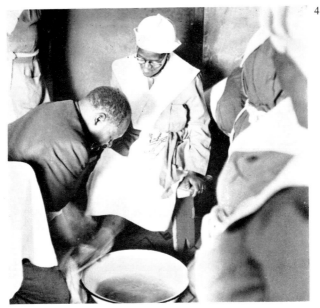

8

9

10

11   12

13

14

dients, for example *maza ma Nzambi,* which is 'water with ad-
mixture of grave-earth, and according to a number of unproven
rumours also with corpse juices'.[130] Mavonda Ntangu punished those
who used indigenous ingredients; he allowed the members of the
lower grade to take Holy Communion at the mission station, while
this was forbidden for the 'enlightened'.[131] That it was possible for
members of these movements to receive Holy Communion at the
mission station reflects the type of discipline and control that prevailed at these stations. This apparently hypocritical practice was
not considered cheating, because the missionaries, as foreigners,
were regarded as 'people who do not understand', an 'out group' to
which in Africa one need not be honest. Because in many Protestant
Churches and especially in the Pentecostal movements, the role of
Communion has been a minor one, with baptism taking precedence
and the Cross and suffering of Christ relegated to positions of
unimportance, there is thus very little understanding of what sin
actually means. According to African philosophy, Christ's death –
his 'weakness' – reflects negatively on his vital force, whence it is
natural that this aspect should not receive emphasis. A leader is
the symbol of vital force and not of suffering which, in the African
context, spells weakness. Sundkler observes that 'Communion is at
the very most held three times a year, at the Passover, Pentecost,
and Christmas. In other organisations again it may not be celebrated
over a matter of years,'[132] and in yet others not at all.[133] Holy Communion has no equivalent in African religion, while baptism is
related to the name-giving ceremonies, and the 'holy water' used in
baptism is associated with the purification rites.

Any suggestion that the pre-Christian African has no sense of sin
is superficial:[134] the confessions, ritual vomiting, and purification
rites refute any such view. Tempels says: 'The Bantu . . . rejects lies,
deceit, theft and adultery, on the same fundamental grounds as the
destructiveness inherent in them.'[135] The anti-social effect of such
deeds is, however, the main concern. Every act that 'militates against
vital force or the increase of the hierarchy of the *muntu* is bad',[136]
and implies a destruction of life. In spite of what has been said,
there is, however, in Africa the attitude that God, as well as the
ancestors, is not concerned about private and, to a great extent,
public morality.[137] Godfrey Lienhardt concludes that 'Since there
is no single sovereign god like Job's, one cannot feel entitled to
rewards for following a code of conduct pleasing to him, or deserving
of punishment for knowingly transgressing it. One lives according
to one's mundane rights, guided by the jural and moral sanctions of
society, knowing that the ancestors dispense justice by their own

standards and that one cannot please all of them at the same time'.[138]

In the *Confessio Africana* the Church in Africa should state clearly what sin is in its religious ethical context.[139] Anthropologists agree that the supreme Being in African religion is not concerned with a moral code; he is rather the *Creator*. He may be a person, but it is hard to believe that He is good; nevertheless, with some tribes, 'He watches the conduct of mankind'.[140] Willis observed that the Supreme Being is regarded as beneficent or malignant according to good or bad fortune, His character is unknown, and His personality is 'an open question'.[141] According to Prof. Idowu, the Yoruba think of *Olodumare* 'as both ritually and ethically holy . . . as absolutely clean and pure. He is never spoken of as being involved in anything immoral.'[142] But here again His transcendence is emphasised to such an extent that little could be said about His immanence.[143] Amongst the Zulu the *Unkulunkulu* is completely withdrawn into transcendence,[144] even though people have him daily in their minds. In the African myths, however, it is frequently said that 'men had talks with God and He with them; and that He was living among men'.[145] With the Tswana, again, their cult has hardly anything to do with God (*Modimo*) but rather with the dead.[146] Amongst the Tswana there is confusion as to what activity should be ascribed to God and what to the ancestor spirits.[147] The Tswana have given to the ancestor cult less prominence, while Ngunzism reverted to the old concept of the Supreme Being who withdrew from the world, so that the ancestors again acquire a prominent position.[148] The concept of God is thus a great theological problem, and Danquah's plea for a 'realistic' approach to this concept needs to be heeded,[149] but then this realism should be that of Scripture. Divine involvement through the ancestors, the mediators, where representation means identification, was always very real in Africa, in spite of the concept of the Supreme Being, who is to be seen more as unapproachable in a hierarchical system, than actually distant. This concept nevertheless explains why He is little known.

With such a vague concept of the Supreme Being, a Being whose immanence is doubtful, the onus for the norm of one's actions is thrown, not on God, but on the society with its ritual prohibitions sanctioned by the ancestors. The Supreme Being is not really the guardian of the moral order. Taylor rightly says that 'the primal world-view belongs to a "shame culture" rather than a "guilt culture" '.[150] The 'shame' is due to the fact that the offender is in a position of trust in the community and has forfeited the trust placed in him – he has broken the covenant relationship with his fellow men.

196

In a society like the African where the communal aspect is emphasised, individual responsibility, and hence personal guilt, count for little. Taylor remarks that 'a sense of sin seems to be felt not so much as guilt before God, but as being lost, cut off and destroyed'.[151] Since it is the sense of community against which the offender has sinned, personal destruction, rather than guilt, is what he has to face. In the African religion, wrongs are expiated by way of a curse, which leads to the total loss of power and possessions.[152]

Here witchcraft comes most clearly into the picture, defined by Taylor as 'the active embodiment of that brooding anger which is the essence of sin.[153] It has such a hold on the African that even Christians are charged with it.[154] The definition given by Nadel for Nupe witchcraft may be generally applied. He says: 'The specific concept of witchcraft is the idea of some supernatural power of which man can become possessed, and which is used exclusively for evil and anti-social purpose.'[155] Loyalty to the group, which the Church preaches, may easily take precedence under such circumstances over examination of the conscience. This makes Church discipline very difficult. Morality is seen as a function of society, so it is difficult to see sin in its Scriptural meaning of being 'godless', missing the mark, falling short of God's glory, lacking faith in Jesus and His redemption. There is thus no question of moral absolutes; and in the nativistic movements, as in the original African society, where 'the spirit' with its own subjectivistic interpretation prevails, one lives according to one's own standard. Under such circumstances God's tolerance and His pity are emphasised, while His wrath over sin is hardly mentioned. In this theology, man does not receive a clear understanding of what sin actually means, because the Cross has no place.

Monica Wilson states that 'the pagan universe is just and orderly'.[156] Good physical health depends, as we have seen, on good social relationships. According to Field, when a sick child is brought to the shrine the priest invariably tries to discover first whether there is any conflict between the parents.[157] In this society, the Kingdom of God 'is a community of the living and the dead, that is purified of all destructive antagonism'. [158] The most serious conflicts are experienced in the family, thus right relationships are of the greatest concern. In the African religion, 'the highest wisdom consists in recognising a unity in the order of beings in the universe. . . . This world order is the essential condition of wholeness in human beings. The Bantu adds that this order comes from God and that it must be reverenced.'[159] Sin is thus the rejection of or disrespect to authority and to the structure of the community, and for this reason witchcraft and sorcery are rejected in most of the nativistic movements in a very drastic way.[160]

Those, like Reyburn, who maintain that sin in the Old Testament sense is very similar to the African concept failed to analyse the Old Testament concept thoroughly; there sin may mean either 'deviation from the right way' (*ht*') or 'iniquity' ('*awon*), 'error' (*shagah*) or 'wickedness' ('*wl*). It may also mean 'perverse'. *Rasha* is used of the guilty and *asham* with regard to guilt or guilt-offering, *pasha* (*pesha*) signifies unfaithfulness.[161] All sin, however, is direct apostasy, violation of God and rebellion against Him. Confession of sin is essential [162] and should be done 'not only in the cult but face to face with God'.[163] The Old Testament always emphasises the sinfulness of particular actions – 'the personal spiritual attitude from which transgressions of law and morality arise'.[164] The divine–human relationship touches the very depth of the human personality, and sin is portrayed as 'at bottom a wanton jeopardisation, nay dissolution of this relationship'.[165] To Hosea sin is ingratitude,[166] and antipathy to God's very nature and will.[167] Right conduct again is described by such terms as Love, Faithfulness and Knowledge of God, whereas in African society fear, legalism and an ontologically based morality have precedence. In the Old Testament, man's sin consists in the desire to be like God.[168] As against the African concept of sin as being anti-social, Isaiah will answer that it is rebellion against God.[169] In the Old Testament the tabuistic and juridical-moralistic evaluation of sin is overcome.[170] The moral responsibility of the individual is emphasised as well as the *personal* quality of sin. What deepens and broadens the concept of sin is the way in which the prophets 'carry the concept of judgment to its logical conclusion'.[171] The rejection of God's sovereignty forfeits the very right to exist, and various descriptions are given of this divine punishment. The Old Testament must be a corrective to the African concept of sin – in theological terms their respective concepts are quite dissimilar. Add to this the deeper understanding of sin in the New Testament where it is described as rebellion against God in all its variations, whether individual or social, and which caused the death of Christ on the Cross. Here is the *theologia crucis*, the only remedy for sin which, in its final analysis, is separation from God.

The following is important in respect to the whole problem of sin: 'Abstract, disembodied and history-less sinners do not exist; only very concrete sinners exist, whose sinful life is determined and characterised by all sorts of cultural and historical factors: by poverty, hunger, superstition, traditions, chronic illness, tribal morality, and thousands of other things. I must bring the gospel of

God's grace in Jesus Christ to the whole man, in his concrete existence, in his everyday environment. It is obviously then a great error on my part if I do not take a person's culture and history seriously.'[172] The Christian Gospel has indeed brought into the African situation 'an extremely disturbing message concerning Sin (as understood in the Bible)'.[173]

REFERENCES

1. Parrinder, *Religion in an African City*, 108. Fritz Raaflaub ('Probleme von Kirche und Mission in heutigen West Afrika', EMZ, Jan. 1955, 6–7) maintains, however, that polygamy is the main problem in West Africa. See also R. T. Parsons, *The Church and Ghana Society*, 72. He maintains that most cases of exclusion from the Church were due to polygamy. In a report prepared for the Christian Council of Nigeria entitled *Christian Responsibility in an Independent Nigeria* (1962), it is stated that one Church, which permits associate membership of those practising polygamy, reports that out of a membership of one thousand, less than thirty couples can partake of Holy Communion. The report of another denomination states that practically all in a position of leadership have been disciplined for marital irregularities, while another disfellowshipped nearly one hundred men because they took more than one wife. (76)
2. Balandier, *Sociologie Actuelle*, 192.
3. T. Price, *African Marriage*, IMC Pamphlet No. 3, SCM, 1956³, 10.
4. Price, 11.
5. P. Scheibler, 'Polygamie und Taufordnung in der Mission-kirche von Kamerun', EMZ, May 1947, 69.
6. H. Henking, 'Die Polygamiefrage in Borneo und auf der Goldküste', EMZ, May 1947, 91.
7. Cf. CMS News-Letter, Feb. 1961.
8. Cf. *Special study on Social Conditions in Non Self-Governing Territories*, UN, NY, 1950; see also Parsons, 98–115.
9. Sundkler, *Prophets*, 167–68.
10. Baëta, 154. The following texts are quoted to support the statement: 1 Cor. vii. 28, 36; Matt. xxii. 30; Gen. xvi. 2–3; 2 Sam. xii. 8; Hebr. xiii. 4; 1 Cor. vii. 7–9; Matt. xix. 10–11. Paul is being criticised for having invented monogamy – cf. Sundkler, *Prophets*, 277. The Israelites maintained that marriage is a European affair – Adam and Eve just took one another. Ibid., 277, cf. Willoughby, 122 ff.
11. Baëta, 82.
12. Schlosser, *Eingeborenen*, 253.
13. Wilson, *Nyakyusa*, 190.
14. Ibid., 198.
15. Pauw, *Religion*, 83.
16. Andersson, 80, 133.
17. Ibid., 221.
18. Ibid., 182.
19. Ibid., 184.
20. Ibid., 112.
21. Schlosser, *Eingeborenen*, 196.

22. Welbourn, 41.

23. Ibid., 184–85. Welbourn says 'Polygamy in the AGOC is different from polygamy in the tribal African culture, because there is an express intention to develop towards monogamy' (ibid., 185). 'While monogamy is recognised as an ideal, which is practised faithfully by its leaders in Buganda, it is not regarded as a rule which can yet be imposed on a young Church in a polygamous area. It is not impossible that the Orthodox are here on sounder theological ground than the immigrant Churches from the West' (ibid., 185). In Lango (East Africa), the AGOC is popular because polygamists are admitted to baptism (ibid., 95). In some parts like North Nyanza, the Church is 'openly polygamous' (ibid., 98). This poses a problem for the Anglican Church, which has fraternal relations with the Orthodox Patriarchate of Alexandria, and whose ministry and sacraments are recognised (ibid., 101–02). 'Of all the problems that confront the Church in West Africa, polygamy is the most difficult with perhaps the least light. Like an ominous dark cloud it seems to haunt the Church in all areas. Out of about one thousand members in a congregation which allows polygamists as associate members, only twenty to thirty couples practise monogamy.' Cf. *Christian Responsibility in Independent Nigeria*, Report, 1962, 76.

24. Taylor & Lehmann, 85–86; Thunberg, 147. The social and economic development here made polygamy impossible.

25. Parrinder, *Religion in an African City*, 113, 119.

26. Ibid., 113. E. A. Asamoa ('The Christian Church and African heritage', IRM, July 1955, 299) says 'It is a controversial question whether the New Testament has anything to say against polygamy as such, even by implication.' See G. Parrinder, *The Bible and Polygamy*, SPCK, 1950. He has given in this important booklet a clear indication of the Biblical concept of monogamy.

27. Cf. Hodgkin, 103. Baëta maintains that 'polygamy is allowed on principle and is not intended as an attraction. In view of the apparent approval of the Old Testament, and in the absence of any definite prescription of plural wives anywhere in the Bible, the teaching of monogamy is considered by these groups (or by many other African Christians) to be based on European usage and custom, with no religious significance whatsoever . . . monogamy is held responsible for much hypocrisy . . .' Baëta, 133. All the groups discussed by Baëta, except the Etodome Prayer Groups, practise polygamy.

28. Parrinder, *Religion in an African City*, 119.

29. Cf. F. B. Welbourn and B. A. Ogot, *A Place to feel at Home: a Study of Independent Churches in Western Kenya*, OUP, 1966, 70. No polygamist can hold office in these independent Churches, on the basis of Titus i. 6 and I Timothy iii. 2.

30. E. H. Brookes, *A Century of Missions in Natal & Zululand*, 1936, 25.

31. I. W. C. Dougall, *African Separatist Churches*, 258.

32. Ed. Arthur Phillips, *Survey of African Marriage and Family Life*, London, OUP, 1953. A summary by T. Price, *African Marriage*, SCM, 1954.

33. C. F. Keil and F. Delitzsch, *Biblical Commentary on the Old Testament*, Vol. I, Eerdmans, 1951, 117.

34. G. C. Aalders, *Het Boek Genesis*, Kok, 1949, 165.

35. T. H. Robinson, *The Poetry of the Old Testament*, Duckworth, 1952², 209.

36. E. A. Asamoa, 'The Anglican Church and African Heritage', IRM, July 1955, 299. Cf. Ernest Gray, 'Some Present-day Problems for African Christian Marriage', IRM, July 1956, 267–77 (209): 'In seeking the minimum definition of Christian marriage I think we should agree in the following points: Christian marriage is monogamous . . . it may be likened to the union between Christ and

His Church; Christian marriage presupposes the intention of a life-long union; Christian marriage presupposes faithfulness on the part of both parties to the marriage vows; Christian marriage is a binding contract made before God.'

37. See G. Parrinder, *The Bible and Polygamy*, 43.
38. Eichrodt, Vol. I, 102.
39. Ibid., 103.
40. Gen. xxiv. 12; Judg. xvi. 28; 1 Sam. xxvii. 1 ff., xxx. 23, 26; 2 Sam. xv. 8.
41. Eichrodt, Vol. I, 105.
42. Eichrodt, Vol. I, 105. 1 Sam. iii. 10, iv. 7.
43. Deut. xii. 5, 21, xiv. 23 ff., xvi. 2, 6, 11, xxvi. 2; 2 Sam. vii. 13; 1 Kings viii. 16, 18 ff.; Jer. vii. 12.
44. Ex. xi. 3, 4 ff; Num. ix. 15 ff., x. 11; Lev. ix. 23 ff.; Num. xiv. 10, xvi. 19 ff., xx. 6.
45. Eichrodt, Vol. I, 107.
46. Is. ii. 2–4; Micah iv. 1–3; Is. lii. 9 ff., Is. xix. 23; Zech. viii, 3, 22 ff.; Is. lvii. 7, lx. 10 ff.; Zech. xiv. 5–9, 16 ff.
47. Eichrodt, Vol. I, 107. Matt. xii. 6.
48. Parrinder, 121. The Sacred Cherubim and Seraphim Society periodically visit the hills outside Ibadan, especially the one which is called Mount Tabor.
49. Baëta, 37.
50. Ibid., 37.
51. Ibid., 48.
52. Ibid., 49.
53. Andersson, 69.
54. Charles-André Gilis, *Kimbangu – Fondateur d'Eglise*, Brussels, La Libraire Encyclopédique, 1960, 107 ff.
55. Andersson, 83.
56. Ibid., 62.
57. Ibid., 69. The Church of the Lord (*Aladura*) maintains that 'a promise of the settlement of "spiritual Jerusalem" was pronounced unto our said Primate and Founder'. Baëta, 121.
58. Ibid., 164, 182.
59. Sundkler, *Prophets*, 206.
60. Ibid., 207. 'If a person is not filled with the Spirit any longer, we first bring him to the pool. There the spirit (*uMoya*) will re-enter Him, and with new force.'
61. Ibid.
62. Shembe I states in Isl. 93[4]:
*We praise you beautiful lake
for washing away our sins.*
See also Oosthuizen, *The Theology of a South African Messiah*, 114.
63. Sundkler, 207.
64. Ibid., 208.
65. Ibid., 186. In some movements water baptism is regarded as unnecessary as this has been superseded by the baptism of the Spirit. Cf. Welbourn and Ogot, 103.
66. Ibid., 192–93.
67. Ibid., 194.
68. Ibid., 30, 37, 149, 196–97.
69. Welbourn, 186. In Kimbanguism baptism is considered not to be a John the Baptist affair 'as is the case with that of the missionaries' but that of the Bangunza is a 'baptism of the Holy Spirit'. Andersson, 169.
70. Baëta, 48.

71. Ibid., 37.

72. Ibid., 78.

73. Ibid.

74. Ibid., 131. H. W. Turner, who writes on West Africa, maintains that the old magical practices in healing have replaced magic but admits the new danger is that holy water may be a new magical power. Cf. 'Pagan features in West African Independent Churches', *Practical Anthropology*, July–Aug. 1965, 146.

75. Parrinder, *Religion*, 124.

76. Ibid., 130.

77. Andersson, 54. Andersson relates the story that an emaciated man suffering from sleeping sickness was carried to Nkamba, laid at Kimbangu's feet and told by him 'in the name of Jesus, to stand up and walk to the water, which he did' (ibid., 55). A medically trained person however maintained that he had 'found no genuine case of faith-healing' (ibid., 55). Others, however, did see such healing being performed. Andersson, 79.

78. Andersson, 173 ff.

79. Water obtained from graves is used as medicine, 'to restore the Spirit, as a kind of Communion, as consecrated water to besprinkle the people, or as medicine against *bandoki* and so forth' (ibid., 174).

80. Ibid., 190.

81. Ibid.

82. Ibid., 192.

83. Schlosser, *Eingeborenen Kirchen*, 25 ff.

84. Kraemer, *Religion*, 409.

85. Cf. Knox, 173.

86. Cf. ibid.

87. Ibid., 136.

88. Andersson, 112. In the teachings of the Khaki movement of Mavonda Ntanga it is stated in Point 21 that 'sisters and brothers do not need, when they are together in this work, to feel shame at each other' (ibid., 184).

89. Cf. W. C. Willoughby, *Race Problems in the New Africa*, OUP, 1923, 258.

90. Andersson, 182.

91. Sundkler, *Prophets*, 154.

92. Knox, 258.

93. Ibid., 159.

94. Clark, 55.

95. Cf. Knox, 566.

96. Ibid., 570.

97. Ibid., 571.

98. Ibid., 583.

99. Ibid.

100. G. Quick, 'Some aspects of the African Watch Tower Movement in Northern Rhodesia', IRM, April 1940, 224.

101. Andersson, 45. Adultery was considered to be the main sin which has to be rectified by way of restitution. Cf. Paul D. Fueter, 'Theological Education in Africa', IRM, Oct. 1956, 386. See also W. C. Willoughby, *The Soul of the Bantu*, SCM, 1928, 387 ff. As long as one is not discovered, one has no sin, has done nothing wrong. Sin is merely a wrong, done against society not against God. Ibid., 393.

102. Anderson, 80.

103. Sundkler, 259. Andersson, 70.

104. Ibid., 221.

105. Ibid., 220. In the basis of instruction of the Lumpa Church specific sins are mentioned which emphasise the anti-social aspect of sin even more than the other separatist movements. Cf. Taylor & Lehmann, *Copperbelt*, 253. Legalism and moralism is a general tendency, cf. Pauw, *Religion*, 218. After describing the different reasons for the formation of sects and independent movements, the Rev. S. A. Mbatha concludes that 'African sects are results of failure to bear the Cross' (cf. *Marangu Report* 1956, 84).

106. Shembe I states in Isl. 87[3]:

> *I confess it* (vuma = vomit, bring out) *and*
> *put it before thee you redeemer of sinners.*

For his concept of sin see Oosthuizen, *The Theology of a South African Messiah*, 119–26.

107. Andersson, 220.

108. Shembe I states in Isl. 118[1]:

> *All ye nations be converted and be baptized.*

109. Sundkler, 220–21.

110. William D. Reyburn, 'Sickness, Sin and Curse: the Old Testament and the African Church—II', *Practical Anthropology*, Vol. 7, No. 5, Sept.–Oct. 1960, 217.

111. Lucien Lévy-Bruhl, *Primitives and the Supernatural*, 242–43.

112. Shembe I often repeats 'run away all ye sinners'. One reads in Isl. 155[5]:

> *The angels are expelling them,*
> *those who watch at the gates*
> *of Kuphakameni*
> *on account of their sins.*

113. Shembe II states in Isl. 227[2]:

> *Where is that stream*
> *Through which I can wash?*
> *The dirt will disappear.*
> *I am then beautiful and complete* (perfect).

114. Taylor, *Buganda*, 165.

115. Andersson, 166. A special formula is followed: 'In the name of God the Father and the Son and the Holy Ghost I say: witness in heaven and witness on earth, forgive me all the sins I have committed.' The prophet now proclaims in the name of the Father, Son and Holy Ghost that 'that which is bound in heaven is bound on the earth, that which is absolved in heaven is absolved on the earth' (ibid., 166).

116. Taylor, *Buganda*, 101.

117. Sundkler, *Ministry*, 72.

118. Mayer, 194–50.

119. M. Hunter, *Reaction to Conquest*, OUP, 1936.

120. Taylor, *Primal Vision*, 194.

121. Reyburn, 'Sickness, Sin and Curse', 222. Cf. Ps. cix. 6–15.

122. Cf. Gen. 1. 17; Amos i. 6, 9, 11; Gen. xxxix. 9; Lev. xx; Deut. xxiv.

123. 2 Sam. xii, xiii.

124. Taylor, 'Saints or Heretics?' in *Basileia*, 308–10.

125. Andersson, 190–91.

126. Van der Leeuw, *De Primitieve Mensch*, 41.

127. O. Cullmann and F. Leenhardt, *Essays on the Lord's Supper* (trans. J. G. Davies), Lutterworth, 1960, 79.

128. Cf. ibid., 79, 80.

129. Andersson remarks that the missionaries, considered to be foreigners and thus not part of the congregation, run up a long list of sins which according to the African 'needs a source of purification of extraordinary power'. Andersson, 192.

130. Ibid., 191.

131. Ibid., 191.

132. Sundkler, *Prophets*, 215.

133. Welbourn and Ogot, 103.

134. Taylor, *Primal Vision*, 174.

135. Tempels, 77.

136. Ibid., 79.

137. Taylor, *Primal Vision*, 174. William Reyburn ('The Transformation of God and the Conversion of Man', *Practical Anthropology*, Supplement, 1960, 16) raised the point whether a man can be converted to Christianity 'without the transformation of his idea of God to conform to a Christian concept of God?' There is a tremendous distance between the non-Christian and the Christian's concept of God, and this is very definitely related to the concept of sin and morality.

138. *Divinity and Experience*, 54, quoted by Taylor, *Primal Vision*, 174–75.

139. Oosthuizen, *Theological Discussions*, 254.

140. E. Johanssen, 'The idea of God in the Myth and Proverbs of some East African Bantu Tribes', IRM, 1931, 535.

141. J. J. Willis, 'The interpretation of Christianity to Primitive People', IRM, 1915, 384.

142. E. Bolaji Idowu, *Olodumare, God in Yoruba Belief*, Longmans, 47. About theistic ideas among the Yoruba and Ewe, see G. W. Dymond in *African Ideas of God*, edited by E. W. Smith, Edinburgh House Press, 1950, 137.

143. Idowu, 47.

144. Andrew Burgess, *Unkulunkulu in Zululand*, Augsburg Publishing House, 1934, 13.

145. Oosthuizen, *Theological Discussions*, 258.

146. I. Schapera, 'The Tswana', *Ethnographic Survey of Africa, Southern Africa*, Part III, London: International Africa Institute; Pauw, *Religion*, 12.

147. Pauw, *Religion*, 28.

148. Andersson, 108.

149. Cf. J. B. Danquah, *The Akan doctrine of God*, Lutterworth, 1944, 17.

150. Taylor, *Primal Vision*, 175.

151. Taylor & Lehmann, 297. Shembe I states in Isl. 131[2]:

> All haters of it (i.e. Ekuphakameni)
> let them not be written
> in the Book of Life,
> let their names be destroyed.

152. Reyburn, *Sickness, Sin and the Curse*, 221.

153. Taylor, *Primal Vision*, 190.

154. Cf. H. W. Debrunner, *Witchcraft in Ghana*, Presb. Book Depot, 1961, 139.

155. S. F. Nadel, 'Witchcraft and Anti-Witchcraft in Nupe Society', *Africa* VIII (1953), 424.

156. Wilson, *Nyakyusa*, 160.

157. Field, *Security*, 113, 118, 119.

158. Taylor, *Primal Vision*, 188.

159. Tempels, 78.

160. Taylor, *Primal Vision*, 194. Cf. Tempels, 79: 'Objective morality to the Bantu is ontological, immanent and intrinsic morality. But moral standards depend essentially on things ontologically understood.'

161. Some nativistic movements give a perfectionistic impression, but an analysis of their concept of sin indicates a somewhat superficial approach. The hymns of Shembe I bear out this statement. For him sin is (i) weight; (ii) dirt to be washed off, an 'unclean' mystic quality; (iii) the works of darkness such as witchcraft; (iv) bonds that bind the 'free spirit', the seat of a person's authority as against the 'bodily soul' which has to do with personal salvation, and (v) sin as anti-social. 'Anti-social here means primarily to be against his movement. The Sunlight Soap Church use Sunlight soap effectively to wash off sin, and the Castor Oil Dead Church kills the evil with castor oil, hence the use of the word 'dead'.

162. Ps. xxxii. 5, xxxviii. 18.

163. Ed. Alan Richardson, *A Theological Word Book of the Bible*, SCM, 1962[7], 226–28.

164. Eichrodt, 375.

165. Ibid.

166. Hosea ii. 10 ff., iv. 1, v. 4, ix. 17.

167. Hosea vi. 4, 7, vii. 14, viii. 11, ix. 8, xii. 11, 14 ff.

168. Vriezen, *An Outline of the Old Testament Theology*, 205.

169. Isa. i. 2, 4, ii. 6 ff., v. 12, 21, 24, ix. 8 ff., xxviii. 1, 10 ff.

170. Dr. John Mbiti from Uganda maintains: 'Many, if not all, African languages have no word for sin.' Cf. 'African concept of Sin', *Frontier*, Autumn 1964, 182. This is, for example, clear in Zulu. Shembe I uses words such as those for wrong, dirt, spoiled, injured, unclean, etc. Cf. Oosthuizen, *The Theology of a South African Messiah*, 119.

171. Eichrodt, 378.

172. J. H. Bavinck, *An Introduction to the Science of Missions*, Philadelphia, The Presbyterian and Reformed Publishing Co., 1960, 81.

173. Mbiti, 184.

8

THE ETHNOCENTRIC 'ECCLESIOLOGY' OF THE MOVEMENTS

Many objections could be raised to the heading of this chapter. To use the terms ethnocentric and 'ecclesiology' in one breath, and to bring ecclesiology into relation with post-Christianity may seem anomalous. The true Church could never be ethnocentric. It has to be Christ-centric, otherwise it ceases to be the Church. The Church is judged from the viewpoint of scripture, and if it is grounded firmly in Christ (*Christus-ständig*), i.e. if the word of Christ is the only content of its message, if it is indigenously rooted in the native soil of the word of God, then its future is guaranteed[1]. Keller says: 'The Church which is rooted in the word of God (*Wortständige Kirche*) is *eo ipso* indigenous, for genuine loyalty is already presupposed in the Ten Commandments. It is the Gospel which through its inherent creative power moulds the potential forms of the people.'[2] A true Church, following the inherent principles of the Word of God, will make contact with the soul of the people, regenerating their innermost being, and here the process of indigenisation will be on firm ground.

In the nativistic movements the Bible has taken second place; with most of them it has been superseded by the words of the prophet, inspired by 'The Spirit'. Even when the Bible is used by them, its exposition takes place in the magico-religious context of their world. Here basically is the reason for the African return to ethnic religion. These ethnic institutions are not the only ones in which the original African religion has its influence; this influence is also felt within the Churches. The difference is that while the ethnic institutions are founded on the African religion, the Churches are founded on Jesus Christ and His Word. Africa has clearly shown that while formally a system may have been submerged, existentially its influence continues to be very much present. Practically every Church in Africa has contact with some aspect of the creed of the African religion, the most common of which is that concerned with the ancestor spirit, as discussed above. The forms in which *official* Christendom sometimes presents itself as the 'Church' of Christ are late fruits from non-Christian roots growing in Christian soil, the so-called Church of Christ eventually ending up as nothing other than an ethnic cultic institution. In Europe, the 'German Christians'[3] during the Hitler period, against whom the 'Confessing Church' waged a struggle for the sake of the inherent truth of the Gospel, were an example of this kind of development. In the nativistic movements in Africa, the reversion to the African religion has been consciously achieved through the prophet who becomes the leader of a new cult.

Most African Christians live spiritually on two levels; because of the foreignness of the 'established' Churches, many of them prefer their own, which they understand and which satisfies their whole being; the result is that they easily become followers of the prophets. Others remain in the Church, but their interpretations, of, say, the sacrament and the Church itself, are made according to their background. The African in his pre- or post-Christian stage sees himself as part of a cultic community which embraces his whole life: life is massive, concrete, it has no 'gaps' and no individualism; this is true of all animism.[4] He thinks not analytically but synthetically, all his experiences being gathered together in one great totality. Thinking is not an intellectual function but an existential one, performed by the whole man in connection with another totality.[5] The final totality is the community, which again is incomplete without the supernatural world. This whole system, based on magic and religion, is the institution from which he receives his 'salvation', not in the Biblical sense of an inherent regeneration, but as a result of fixing himself harmoniously into the whole and enjoying in this way social, economic and spiritual benefits. Here is the perfect 'social gospel'. A religion which cannot bring material benefits for the whole community is of no value. The African Christian is not really helped by religion if it does not cater for his social and economic needs; neither is he helped if his fellow men are not cared for. The difficulty here is that the social and the economic take precedence. For the African all religion is judged by these criteria and because of his strong sense of community, its success depends on building up good human relationships.[6]

There is here no divorce between heaven and earth, and the Christian ideas have not 'modified the belief that Man, Nature and the Unseen are inseparably involved in one another in a total community of which it might be said that all is here and all is now. A man's well-being consists in his belonging to, and being in harmony with, this totality. . . .'[7] 'Material well-being is equated with "a state of grace" ',[8] whereas misfortune is a sign of having lost contact with the whole and thus being in disharmony. Contributions of

207

money to the leaders in the syncretistic post-Christian movements are aimed at realising this 'state of grace', which is a sign of prosperity; the prosperity of the leader satisfies the aspirations of his followers. He is the personification of the state of grace, and in this way the popularity of the movement is enhanced. It is a sign of success, and thus an evidence of blessing.

All this is expected from the community on which the individual is dependent. Part of this community is the supernatural world with its ancestor spirits, which are the guardian spirits of their descendants,[9] exercising great influence on them because of their direct relation to their well-being, their health, happiness and harmony in the tribe. They also satisfy the need for a living contact with the unseen and they sanction ritual prohibitions. A hierarchy among the spirits is accepted, since the spirits of chiefs and royalty possess enhanced vital force, and are thus 'the source of communal well-being and prosperity'.[10] Prayers and sacrifices are offered to them,[11] and the nativistic movements have the doctrine of 'the Spirit' as the basis of their cult community. Tylor says: 'On the continent of Africa, *manes*-worship appears with extremist definiteness and strength.'[12] Both material benefits and adversity come from them, with the result that the living have continuously to be in a diplomatic relationship with their ancestors, to whom they perform sacrifices, which are not reconciliatory in the first instance, but are signs of subjection. So important a part does ancestor-worship play in the ritual of these movements that they develop into ethnic cultic communities following the traditional lines of African religions.[13]

The role of magic needs further consideration. The magical person creates a world of his own in which his will reigns. The religious person *struggles* with the forces, spirits or gods, while the magical person *accepts* them and tries to get the forces into his hands in order to rule them.[14] But the two can never be separated, with the result that we can only speak of a religious person. We have seen how grave water, rings, and special crosses, and photographs of André Matswa, Shembe and others, have magical power. In the same way baptism can be magical in character when the rite has a specific influence on account of the water used, which has been 'prayed over' or 'prayed for'. This is also the case with the holy communion, the elements having magical power.[15] No healing is considered to be natural in primitive religion; this is clearly reflected in the attitude to healing in the nativistic movements. Healing comes about as a result of counteracting forces.

In magic the person acts as an individual *over against* his world, refusing to be merely *a part* of it. It is essentially reaction *against*, refusing to accept the *status quo*, and taking extraordinary measures. Magic is a means of making *this world* into *my world*.[16] It is the technology of the traditional man of Africa to overcome external forces in his way. This is the main reason why magic is one of the main aspects of the nativistic movements. Magic is modern in the sense that it objectifies the given world making it into an object which can be manipulated.[17] Because of this great need to control the external world, it plays an intense role in the modern city. However, it is primitive in the sense that it tries to control the objective world, not by natural forces, as is the case in science and modern technology, but by means of supernatural forces. Formulae are used, the words of which are considered to have mysterious intrinsic power. In magic, man controls everything; it is a way of self-assertion, the non-religious approach in a religious world. It cannot, however, be separated from the religious life, where there is a struggle for power. This is the reason why a theology of grace is so repugnant to the believer in magical power. Synergism is the motto of the magical approach, which explains the ritual richness of a cult community.

A cult community is so-called because blood relationship, membership of the tribe or community, is the only way whereby its benefits can be received. One becomes a member by birth, and in the name-giving ceremonies one receives the blessing of the family and tribe, and in initiation that of the tribe.[18] Through its sacrifices, the tribe demonstrates its power, in which every member has a share if he lives in harmony with it. The family and tribe also provide the necessary safety – this community is a man's only haven of peace. On a simple analogy with tribal practices, the prosperity of White men is ascribed to the fact that they have their own type of religion which they withhold from the African; they have their own Bible, their own Holy Communion, and their own purification rites, which carry within themselves material and other benefits. These strengthen the African's motives for the formation of his own movement, through which he will obtain these benefits in his own way. This is his concept of the Church. Learning to read and write were considered to be introductory rites to Christianity.[19] This strengthened the idea that the mission was an institution conferring material benefits alone. As such it resembles the cult community, although the mission is considered to be more successful, having more effective magic and knowing the secrets better. Only when disappointments arose did the reaction come, giving a strong boost to independentism. Worship is considered to be the means of participating in the power of the tribe, from which none should be excluded. This traditional disposition is reflected in the large gatherings of independent movements during

209

special festivals, when, for example, healing is considered to be more effective than at any other time.

It is on to this ground that the seed of the Gospel is sown. The only way to counteract syncretism here is to build a community of the reborn in Christ,[20] where man's works do not take precedence, but rather God's grace with which a quality of life is lived of which the New Testament gives sufficient evidence. A thorough knowledge of Scripture is necessary, as well as the building up of a strong, actively interested group which is steeped in the main tenets of the Christian faith. Furthermore, thorough knowledge and understanding of the environment are necessary.

The Church is based on Christ and not on its own achievements. When Scripture moves to the background, Christ moves there with it, and the Church becomes something which man possesses instead of his being possessed by Christ. The Church is no human achievement, but it is established through the working of the Holy Spirit. At Pentecost we are confronted with God's activity. The Hebrew *Kahal*, the Greek *ekklesia* are words for an assembly, as Calvin calls it a company, literally of those 'called out'. The whole possibility of this *ekklesia* lies with God. In the nativistic movements, as in the old cultic community, the ultimate possibilities of life lie with the community and its activities. Its sacraments are approached in this light, so that baptism signifies that the child is accepted into the fold of the movement as was the case in the traditional name-giving ceremony. The Church's first task here is to indicate that not birth but rebirth makes a person a member of God's kingdom. Although the Church is not the kingdom of God, it is an instrument for the establishment of that kingdom, and thus has nothing to do with the 'blood and soil' relationship of ethnic thinking. For many, even in the established Churches, baptism is significant as a sign of the washing away of sins, while Holy Communion is either relegated to the background, or it is understood as a sacrifice whereby its participants come into the deepest relationship with the Deity. In the nativistic movements, because of its apparent concentration on the weakness of Christ, Holy Communion is either seldom or never observed; it is thus easy for the prophet as a magical figure, to take the place of Christ.

The Church can never give the kind of assurance that is given by the tribe. Christ cannot be bound up into an organisation, otherwise we do not have Christ, but a cult personality. The institution regulated by man, with all the dangers of anthropocentrism prevailing, becomes ethnic-oriented, with supernatural power held in man's own hands.[21] This attitude, of course, is possible not only in the nativistic move-

210

ments but also in the Church. Perhaps it is necessary to state here that the Church itself has given the impression of ecclesiastical tribalism. Not Church-planting but the proclamation of Christ should be the missionary aim. The Church *alongside* Christ is ethnic,[22] but the Church living in and through Christ is Christian.

In Protestant theological thinking today, the Church has become central mainly as a result of the activities of Karl Barth and the World Council of Churches. This development is also discernible in missionary thinking, in spite of the fact that it was only at the International Missionary Council Conference at Jerusalem in 1928 that the missions and the Churches came together to discuss their common difficulties. It was, however, only at Madras in 1938 that 'mission and Church had found one another'.[23] All the discussions on the latter occasion were related to the Church, and those who assembled at this Conference were conscious of the fact that they were 'members of the Church – of that one Church which exists within the Churches'.[24] At the IMC Conference at Whitby, Canada, in 1947, it was fully accepted that mission and Church are 'insolubly bound together'.[25] It was at Willingen, Germany, in 1952, that Hoekendijk made his criticism of the Church-centred orientation of the missionary enterprise,[26] although this criticism from him had received attention earlier.[27] Mission understood as the planting of the Church[28] – such as was advocated by Voetius, although he sometimes corrected it to *conversio gentium* – means that missions are seen as 'the road from the Church to the Church'.[29] The interest of the first generation was always in christology; ecclesiology became important only in the second generation. Hoekendijk made the point that 'evangelism and churchification are not identical, and very often they are each other's bitterest enemies';[30] the idea that the whole surrounding world should not be defined merely in 'ecclesiological categories'[31] was evident already in the missionary thinking of Warneck,[32] and has exerted an influence ever since. It is only through mission, i.e. being in the world, that the Church can fulfil its task. Karl Barth rightly states that mission is the Church,[33] and that through her apostolate the Church is called to stand in the world. The Church cannot be conceived of as having a mission and alongside this her Church life – the mission is at the same time her life.[34] The once prevalent idea that the Church is the object of mission[35] results in the relationship between the Church and the kingdom of God, which has to be established in the world, being obscured. Hoekendijk's warning is also very timely for Africa, although Hoekendijk has directed his attention too one-sidedly on the Church's task without giving adequate attention to its being.[36] Lesslie Newbigin emphasises that the Church is more than a mere instrument to manufacture Christians, it is the community of the Holy Spirit.[37] But Hoekendijk's statement should not be analysed merely dogmatically, as his firm purpose was to pull the Church out of its ghetto-type of existence into the world, to which it is sent. Ecclesiology is for Hoekendijk merely a part of christology, a part centred round the Church's messianic relationship to the world. He rightly objects to the nineteenth-century 'bourgeois sociology' whereby every social environment was defined in terms of *Volk* (nation, peoples), so that the people's Church became the 'exact opposite of the pietistic congregation of the elect'.[38] We have already referred to Gutmann in this connection. Hoekendijk's reaction against the negative aspects of taking the environment into consideration, and his emphasis on the apostolate have led him to oppose these two concepts to each other; these two concepts should, however, both be accepted as important in the matter of communication, which we discuss in Chapter 9. Indigenous development and the apostolate need not oppose each other, but should be seen together as the most effective means of communicating the Christian message. One fully agrees when he maintains, however, that 'Church-centric missionary thinking is bound to go astray, because it revolves around an illegitimate centre'.[39] Is the difficulty not that the Church round which missionary thinking centred was a foreign entity? It is the world and the kingdom for which Christ came which should occupy the mind of the Christian, and the Church is his instrument. Its essential definition lies within Christ.

The ideology of the *corpus Christianum*, from which the Church suffered in the West, is even more dangerous in the African context, where the family and indeed the tribe expect to be accepted *in toto* into the Church. Is independentism in Africa not an effort in this direction? Hoekendijk sees the Gospel and the world as belonging intrinsically together, but his reaction against churchification misled him into overemphasising this point; God has called together his believers into the fold of the Church, where they exist as an organised community, not only for the world's sake, however important that aspect may be, but also for their own sakes – to receive its benefits through faith. Andersen's criticism of Hoekendijk is important, namely that 'the Church, for all its wretchedness and inadequacy, is the bridgehead' of the kingdom of God, which the Holy Spirit Himself has brought into being in the world.[40]

Apart from the danger of ecclesiastical tribalism in Africa, there is the further danger of complacent acceptance of a weak level of spiritual life, which results from routine and legalism. Stephen Neill

212

says: 'In three generations a Church can pass through all the stages of Church history, from martyrdom to a placid conformism, in which the goodwill of non-Christian neighbours has been purchased by the total failure of the Church to prove disturbing at any point of their way of living.'[41] Neill warns against the false development in the minds of the adherents, namely that 'the Church exists for its own sake . . . the Church becomes a closed shop'.[42] The main factor contributing to this is the impression given by the mission board or society that it is not a servant; it appears rather 'in the demonic guise of usurped Christ and spiritual authority, based on financial direction and control'.[43]

The Methodist 'class' system has worked most effectively in Africa. According to this system, the congregation is divided up into classes or cells of not more than twelve members, each with its own 'class leader'. Here person-to-person contact is maintained, and in this way the Church is not only adapted to the village, with its emphasis on the family, but also to the urban areas where the need of true brotherhood and fellowship, or *koinonia*, is felt. Many secessions among independent movements are due to the fact that they become too big, and the sense of fellowship is lost. This class system gives 'vitality to local village groups and authority to responsible local leaders'.[44] The meaning of fellowship became clear to many in the revival movement in Africa,[45] where small sub-groups were formed, co-operating in the great task of evangelism, and in which 'strong ties between leader and followers' were formed.[46] These strong ties between leader and adherents are not strange when seen in the perspective of the African background, with the chief and his tribe. It has its dangers however, for the leader easily becomes autocratic. Smaller units or cells should be the aim in the Church in Africa, and Paul's idea of house congregations is of value everywhere that Christianity is called upon, especially in the cities of the world, to form new brotherhoods. These house congregations have proved to be most effective in Japan with its web society.[46] The family-centredness of African thought could be purified and used effectively in the Church. Primitive Christianity built up its congregation from nuclei of families and relatives.[48] J. Spencer Trimingham maintains that one great weakness of Christianity in the face of Islam is that the place of working of Christianity is the Church, where as that of Islam is in everyday life – the workshop, the market, the home.[49] While the Church needs to be developed in terms adapted to the African background, the aim should, however, be to establish not a Church *of* Africa but a Church *in* Africa. Indigenisation applies to all the forms of worship as well as to the ministry.

213

In Africa the pastor receives a central place, because of the African idea of mediatorship. He is the representative, or the mid-man as Sundkler calls him.[50] But on the side of the corporate fellowship of the Church, the Christian community, although it belongs to the new age, and although made up of strangers and pilgrims,[51] has to relate itself to the environment, without becoming nationalistic and isolated – otherwise it ceases to be a Christian community. The solution lies in the formation of smaller cells, which will act as spearheads of the Church, and here the African background must be considered, where 'the great Biblical terms for the Church – the People of God, the Body of Christ, the Household or Family of God – find a vibrant sounding board in the structure of the African social patterns, particularly of the clan'.[52] The priesthood of all believers should receive its rightful place, with the leader tending to receive special authority over his flocks, and with a tendency to clericalism, which springs from the African paternalistic background.

Finally, in the liturgy and the sacraments, and through the festivals of the year, the Church in Africa is called upon to recover what Africa could have given to the Church and what it should give.

REFERENCES

1. Oosthuizen, *Theological Discussions*, 26.
2. W. Keller, *The Younger Churches in their Struggle to become Indigenous*, Morrison & Gibb, 1938, 24. Sundkler said at Marangu: 'The Church in various parts of Africa was too often an ark built according to the blue-prints in the White man's shipbuilding office, brought out ready-made from Swedish or German or British or New England shipyards.' B. G. M. Sundkler, 'The Church and its Environment', *Marangu Report*, 117.
3. Kamma, 'De ethnologische 'Kerk' en de Kerk van Christus'. *De Heerbaan*, May 1949, 113.
4. G. van der Leeuw, *De Primitieve Mensch*, 31.
5. Ibid., 33.
6. Taylor & Lehmann, 152: 'It appears from the studies of social anthropologists in many parts of the continent that it is common for African people to judge the practice of religion by its results in terms of material good fortune and social status, and particularly by its efficacy in maintaining happy personal relations.'
7. Taylor & Lehmann, 276.
8. Ibid., 277.
9. Here it is a matter not of *resurrection* but of continuation after death. In traditional religion the spirits of those who had positions of authority in the family, clan or tribe are put into office some time after death.
10. Eiselen–Schapera, 'Religious Beliefs and Practices' in Schapera (ed.), *The Bantu-Speaking Tribes*, 251.
11. Cf. J. G. Frazer, *The Golden Bough* (abridged ed.) Macmillan, 71–72.

12. Tylor, Vol. II, 201.

13. Shembe I in Isl. 148[4] states about the ancestors, with whom the living are in a symbiotic union:

> They have been called out of the graves,
> they are already out, we have seen them,
> they have entered the city that is holy.
> May Jehovah be praised.

14. Van der Leeuw, De Primitieve Mensch, 77.

15. Pauw (Religion, 147) states that 'when it is believed that a rite or an object may have a particular effect but that the outcome ultimately depends upon the decision of a spiritual being in which that being decides according to his own free will, it is non-magical. Ritual is also non-magical if it is merely a symbolic representation of a mystical belief, but as soon as such symbolic ritual is thought of as necessarily having a particular effect, it bears a magical character.'

16. Cf. Van der Leeuw, De Primitieve Mensch, 78.

17. Ibid., 80.

18. Cf. Kamma, De Ethnologische 'Kerk', 118.

19. Andersson, 44.

20. Group dynamics which is basically related to the Christian koinonia is a most effective way of evangelism. Cf. J. W. Pickett, Christian Mass Movements in India, Lucknow Publishing House, 340. Only when the laity receive their full share in the koinonia can it be this evangelising factor. See also J. W. Pickett (ed.), Church Growth and Group Conversion, Lucknow Publ. House, 1937.

21. Cf. Jamma, De Ethnologische 'Kerk', 125.

22. Ibid., 125.

23. Cf. W. Andersen, Towards a Theology of Mission, IMC Pamphlet No. 2, SCM, 1956, 20.

24. Ibid., 21.

25. Ibid., 35.

26. J. C. Hoekendijk, 'The Church in missionary thinking', IRM, July 1952, 324.

27. 'The call of Evangelism', IRM April 1950, 162–75. See J. C. Hoekendijk, 'Mission in der Krise', AMZ, May 1949, 3, 7. See further by this author Die Zukunft der Kirche und die Kirche der Zukunft, Stuttgart/Berlin, Kreuz-Verlag, 1964. Max Warren sees the aim of evangelism as 'preparation for the coming of the King and the triumph of His Kingdom'. Cf. The truth of Vision, The Canterbury Press, 1948, 56.

28. Cf. H. A. van Andel, De Zendingsleer van Gijsbert Voetius, 1912.

29. Hoekendijk, The Call to Evangelism, 170.

30. Ibid., 171.

31. Ibid.

32. Cf. G. Warneck, Evangelische Missionslehre, Gotha, Berthes, 1897–1903.

33. Karl Barth, 'Die Theologie und die Mission in der Gegenwart', Zwischen den Zeiten, 10th ed., No. 3, 1932, 189 ff.

34. I.P.C. Van 't Hof, Het Zendingsbegrip van Karl Barth, Hoenderloo, 1946, 19.

35. A sudden shift came in the discussions on Faith and Order since the third World Conference on Faith and Order at Lund, Aug. 15-28, 1952, where the departure was not ecclesiology but christology. Cf. Hans Jochen Margull, Hope in Action, Muhlenberg Press, 1962, 33 ff.

36. H. Berkhof, 'De Apostoliciteit der Kerk', Nederlandsche Theologische Tydschrift, II (1947), 201.

37. Newbigin, Household of God, 23. See also S. C. Neill, Unfinished Task, 21 ff.

215

38. Hoekendijk, *The Church in Missionary Thinking*, 328.
39. Ibid., 332.
40. Andersen, 49.
41. S. Neill, *Creative Tension*, Edinburgh House Press, 1959, 77.
42. Ibid., 78.
43. Ibid., 89. Cf. M. Hollis, *Paternalism and the Church*, OUP, 1962, 46. The people of the land did not see the missionary 'as an example of self-sacrifice and of humility. *He* did not see himself as a servant'.
44. Sundkler, *Ministry*, 298. The class system of the Methodists is democratic but in the independent movements 'these democratic principles are realigned and transformed into autocratic categories'. Sundkler, *Prophets*, 138.
45. Cf. Warren, *Revival*, 78.
46. Sundkler, *Ministry*, 72.
47. Cf. Oosthuizen, *Theological Discussions*, 242.
48. Cf. I Cor. i. 16; in Philemon, verse 2, Paul speaks about 'the church in your house', etc. Households and families were the smaller units from which the congregations were made up. Paul speaks about teaching from house to house. Acts xx. 20.
49. *A History of Islam in West Africa*, OUP, 1962.
50. Sundkler, *Ministry*, 303 ff.
51. I Peter ii. 11.
52. Sundkler, *Ministry*, 298.

9

THE CHURCH AND THE
ROAD TO THE FUTURE

(i) RELIGION VERSUS REVELATION

In Western Europe, Christianity almost became a folk religion. The idea developed that a whole population can be conceived of as *corpus Christianum*. Owing to the breakdown of Christendom in Europe, the Church was compelled more and more to define itself, both in theory and practice, as a body distinct from the community as a whole.[1] The Church is in a proper and genuine sense an institution. Because man is social, God entered through the Incarnation into the life of man, which He endeavours to redeem, 'a life lived out in an inescapable network of relations'.[2] The Church has a sociological and organisational aspect, but this is only secondary, because what the Church is in its deepest sense can only be described in relation to Christ. The sociological and organisational aspects of the Church have taken precedence in theological thinking, and this has distorted the real issue, which is the true relation of the Church to the living Christ.

Syncretism started very early in Christian history. The culture of Rome exerted a great influence on the Gospel, with the result that the world entered the Church in an impure way. The antithesis provided by the Reformation, although in many respects not ideal, was a necessity, and a necessity of principle. Unfortunately, however, the view evolved that contact with the world can only be dangerous, so that the Church has to be in opposition to environment in non-Christian countries. This view had a very negative influence on African culture, and the missionaries, where they did feel that there were elements of this culture which could be 'baptised', thought the African insufficiently educated for the task.[3] This is one of the main reasons why the Church of the Reformation has remained foreign in her outreach. Furthermore, the Church in Africa gives the impression that everything has been thought out in Western terms, as if the Church has outlived its old vitality of thought. The Church will only

217

rediscover her missionary consciousness, in Africa, as elsewhere, in the face of Islam and the fast-expanding independent movements, if it starts to think about the essence of Christendom. The desire to keep and cherish what you have sought and found is quite human, but the Church has to lose itself in the world if it wants to be effective in its outreach. Instead of being closed in order to preserve, the Church should be open in order to receive.

Form and content are interdependent. The Church as the Body of Christ must take note of the people amongst whom it moves as an institution.[4] This was most clearly stated at the IMC Conference at Willingen in 1952. No tribe or nation is an artificial collection of individuals; because of historic growth, it is an organism. The Church in the non-Christian countries has only been negatively aware of the very solid unity of tribal life, which led to a 'confrontation' between it and everything indigenous, and debarred the peoples from contributing from their own genius. The primary fact is that the Church must be the Church; it must be founded firmly on the Rock, Jesus Christ, to whom it owes all its loyalty, and not to any people. The Church must maintain her prophetic character in the face of the strange and pagan views of the people. Excessive respect for the people is apostasy from God; the new root of the Gospel message can never be grafted on to infected trunks. One cannot accept the view that the non-Christian religions have been a *preparatio evangelica*. Paul Tillich misses here an important truth when he says: 'One might call this preparation, which we find in all nations, the "Old Testament" for these nations.'[5] Barth, however, treats these problems under the significant heading *The Revelation of God as the abolition of religion* (Gottes Offenbarung als Aufhebung der Religion).[6] Religion, construed as man's reality and potentiality, denies God's revelation, as has been obvious in our previous discussions. To regard God's revelation as a religion among other religions is according to Barth 'basically the plain question whether theology and the Church and faith are able and willing to take themselves, or their basis, seriously'.[7] Both the act of revealing (*a parte Dei*) and the experience of revelation (*a parte hominis*) are from God, and have nothing whatsoever to do with man's potentiality. Man's religion, in the light of revelation, is unbelief.[8] All religions are endeavours to self-assertion by way of self-justification, self-sanctification and self-redemption, pushing God into the background and not accepting Him as He really is according to the revelation in Christ. Revelation has nothing to do with this, but 'is God's self-offering and self-manifestation'.[9] Man's own attempt to know God is utterly futile, because the truth comes to us only in an activity which corresponds to revelation, namely faith. Man thus establishes in his own way his own religion with his own energy.[10] In this religion, he gropes for God; however 'a grasping religion is the contradiction of revelation, the concentrated expression of human unbelief, i.e. an attitude and activity which is directly opposed to faith'.[11] Revelation is the active, redemptive self-offering and self-manifestation of God to which man can add nothing. In faith we accept that everything has been done once and for all in Jesus Christ.[12] Religion puts a human product in the place of God's word; man wishes to justify and sanctify himself – as in the case of the prophetic movements. Thus the Cross of Christ and Scripture are pushed into the background, and only used as a kind of fetish in man's hands. Even Israel's zeal to fulfil the Law is futile (Rom. ix. 31). The law given to Israel by God is a spiritual law (Rom. vii. 14), and Christ is the end of this law, providing justification for everyone that believes (Rom. x. 4). The law works wrath (Rom. iv. 15), and kills (2 Cor. iii. 6; Rom. vii. 5, 13). Pharisaic legalism is another form of old lawlessness: 'Thou gloriest in the law and dishonourest God by transgression of the law' (Rom. ii. 23). The righteousness of works is at the root of the old idolatry, which is self-assertion against God.[13]

Religions are dependent upon historical circumstances and have to change continuously not to become fossilised and obsolete. They have to fight for their lives because they are 'acutely or chronically sick'.[14] Religion is not only weak, but it leads man astray from God. Only through revelation can the magic circle of religion be broken.[15] The strength of Barth's point of view lies in the fact that revelation in Christ is our sole standard of reference. There is no theological point of contact between the Christian and the non-Christian religions.[16] The only point of contact lies within the sphere of communication, which depends 'on the love, the sensitivity, the spirit of humble service and solidarity, the straightforward clarity and frankness of thinking, which the ordinary bearer of the Gospel message of the Church or the theological thinker displays, when encountering non-Christian fellow-beings or particular manifestations of spiritual reality'.[17] It is impossible to permeate another religion by colouring certain concepts with Christian ideas. The nativistic movements have sufficiently proved by assimilating 'Christian' ideas 'that non-Christian religions build up a stronger frame of resistance against Christianity and the preaching of the gospel'.[18]

In the nativistic movements discussed above men have stopped living by the grace of God. The emphasis is on man's self-assertion; man is also dependent upon the forces nearest to him. For these people a thorough explanation of the Incarnation, with Christ as the firstborn among men, seen in connection with the position of the chief, could be most important.[19] Much independentism has resulted from uncertainty with regard to the theological approach to these issues. This uncertainty is due to theological training that has taken place in a vacuum.

The religion of the Nazarites, Kimbanguists and others usurps the place of Christ, and in this sense it is post-Christian. Barth rightly says: 'As a "Christianity without Christ" it can only vegetate. It has lost its only *raison d'être*.'[20] The Church cannot look even for one moment away from Jesus Christ without ceasing to be the Church; only in Christ, according to the Scriptures, can we have the true religion. The structure of Christianity is completely different from that of any other religion. This is due to the work of Jesus Christ, of which the major aspect is the divine justification of sinners. Man's forgiveness is only in Jesus Christ, and thus faith should only be directed to him. He is the first-born of those whom he calls his brethren, and who are forgiven on the basis of his merit.

The Church in Africa has to give renewed attention to the question of the sacraments. Freytag maintains unequivocally: 'All walling-up of Church life in confessional tradition, in a blind alley of self-satisfied self-assurance, is constantly challenged by the Sacrament.'[21] In many of the young Churches, 'the sacrament has much more significance than in the West, is more humbly received, is palpably proven forgiveness and proven mercy, giving a clear understanding what the Church of Christ has in the Sacraments. A Church which has lost its sacramental life dies.'[22] The idea of *ex opere operato*, with its magical connotations in the independent movements, should receive close attention. Baptism, associated by the prophetic movements with name-giving ceremonies and purification rites, must receive its rightful theological place in the Church, and the Holy Communion, abolished in some of these movements, should, together with baptism, be thoroughly explained in all catechetical work.

Speaking about the Churches in Asia, Manikam and Thomas hold that they are not only minority churches but are *alien* Churches: they imported their architecture, music and theology, wholesale from Western Christianity, with the result that their forgiveness has 'repelled rather than attracted' people to Christ.[23] Islam and Buddhism on the other hand have fully penetrated the culture of the Asian countries, and become domesticated. The Churches must be rooted in Christ before they can be related to the soil, and they will in this sense be foreign to the world, but they must live and spread in the new climate. In the process of detribalisation in Africa, many look to the Church for guidance, but Christians are often disillusioned because of its foreignness and its unsympathetic attitude to their deepest and most sincere desires. There lies one of the main reasons for the formation of independent movements. For a movement to become creatively indigenous involves a process of organic growth, and in this the Church is rightly cautious, as there should be no direction, hurrying and pushing from without. History has continually shown how a Church may become typically expressive of national genius but still remain rooted in Jesus Christ and His teaching. Theologically, the Church is called upon to digest the relation between God and the concrete world; this should be done dynamically and positively. Theology is the intellectual work, to be undertaken by devoted Christian thinkers in the Church, and having as its aim 'to explain the Church's basis and spiritual experiences in such a way that it satisfies the desire for clearness and cohesion of the believers.'[24] Although theology is not Christianity, the demand for a systematic intellectual explanation of what it believes in its existential situation comes at all times and ages. For various reasons, a theology in Africa, which takes the African situation seriously, is desperately important. Theology has first the negative task of confronting anti-Christian streams of thought, concepts, etc., but it has the very positive task 'of discovering new treasures from the Bible and the stating of these in a language comprehensible to the people concerned'.[25] The tendency to imitate should be overcome in the Church in Africa. Now that Africa is on the way to a discovering of herself, the Church must do the same and help the African to rediscover himself. In separatism there is a desire for a Church less alien, which takes the traditional background seriously.[26] The missions did little to develop indigenous forms of self-expression in liturgy, in music, in theology and in pastoral work: mission is not propaganda, a platform for ideas, but 'When I help somebody else to give his own response and his own form of obedience to the message, it is mission . . . when I proselytise, it is propaganda. Whenever the "indigenous" function of mission occupies the foreground, the caricature of mission vanishes – that reproduction of what we are ourselves or, what is much worse, what we should like to be and do not quite attain.'[27] The first converts reacted violently against the old traditions because they knew how the old religion had penetrated every aspect of their lives.[28] It is thus not just the missionaries that are to blame. The Church should be one all the world over, and yet be naturalised in each different land and amongst each people. The desire for less elaborate institutions 'to revive the comparative simplicity of the Church of the first two centuries' should not take the form of a desire to abolish but 'to give them indigenous form'.[29]

There is, of course, danger that the Church can become so embedded in the indigenous culture that it loses its prophetic voice. The Ethiopian Church, for example, has 'accommodated the Gospel to the Hamitic culture, an assimilation so profound that it has completely lost its prophetic voice to change the lives of its people'.[30] The Church should in a certain sense be supranational – even Christians can be led astray by the nationalist outlook; this means that it should exist, not above the nation, but within it. The Church should be indigenously democratic by taking up its position within the people's own life and history. Both Tambaram and Willingen have given special attention to this fact – that the Church, rooted in Christ, should be related to its specific setting.[31] There is a tendency among theologians to speak of the Church as something that exists in a realm of its own, a sacrosanct entity. Stephen Neill says: 'The Church is undoubtedly a divine society, but it is also a society immersed in history, and must live perpetually in action and reaction with the societies by which it is surrounded.'[32] The identification of the Church with the kingdom of God has been one of the great sources of misunderstanding. Each ethnic group has its own angle of vision – the group is not merely a collection of individuals in the Hobbesian sense but an organism. Smalley rightly says that 'an indigenous Church is precisely one in which the changes which take place under the guidance of the Holy Spirit meet the needs and fulfil the meanings of that society and not of any outside group'.[33] The New Testament's idea of an indigenous Church is where the Holy Spirit has worked its transformation within the society. The Greek Church differs from the Jewish one; however, the message of Christ is supranational and supracultural because the theme of the message is that God in Christ reconciles the whole world to Himself.[34] An indigenous (*bodenständige*) Church is Word-centred (*wortständige*) Church. Since Zinzendorf emphasised one-soul conversion (*Einzelbekehrung*), the concept of indigenisation has been neglected to the detriment of effective communication. This 'pietistic' method, advocated by him and others, saw the aim of missions as the gathering of souls into *ecclesiolae*, which had to be isolated from the world as the first-fruits of the kingdom.[35] The other extreme – the view that the aim of mission is the conversion of the whole people[36] – was embraced after men realised that a change was necessary. The followers of this view emphasise the 'blood and soil' aspect and, on the basis of Luther's theology, maintain that racial and national individuality is part of the natural order created by God. But this theology has not faced adequately the Scriptural basis of the relationship between nation and Church; it leads to 'ethnic Churches', rather than Churches in the Biblical sense. Together with men like Edwin Smith, Westermann and others previously mentioned, they helped to change the climate of opinion with regard to Africa's heritage. Gutmann, with his emphasis on the primordial social ties of the African tribe and kin, insisted that the individuality of peoples has to be respected by the Church, and allowance made for its unfettered developments; in this way the *Selbstbewegung der Gemeinde* (spontaneous expansion of the congregation) was to be achieved, and the *völkische Weltanschauung* purified and regenerated; but he has *over-emphasised* an important principle of method which has often been neglected elsewhere with no little effect in the Church in Africa. The theological basis of indigenisation should be sound, and Gutmann has missed this point – he takes, rather, a stand in the group or tribe instead of in Scripture. 'Nation' came to have a special theological significance. But Christianity poses many difficulties to the African who wants his life to be 'African', because it has caused such radical disruptions and made little effort to show the way out of the impasse that has been reached.[37]

Because of the strong link between the living and the dead in African society, Sundkler maintains that it is of vital importance for the new African theology to concern itself with the dead and with 'the meaning of their after-life or death'.[38] Family ties are so strong that ecclesiology in Africa will concern itself more and more with the family and the Church as the Great Family.[39] It was Hoekendijk who advocated an 'ecology' which should take serious note of man's concrete *oikos* (house, concrete social milieu): 'Instead of making the existing, established local congregation the focal point of a missionary Church, the human being in his *oikos* must become the focal point. The Church must grow through house congregations. . . .'[40] If this is true for our Western society, it is even truer in African society and will serve as a buffer against much of the independentist tendencies prevalent in a situation of rapid social change. The dangers in this approach are numerous; for example, many will expect that the whole family or tribe should enter the Church, a characteristic of independent movements, and also of the Churches. The African tribal affiliation is so strong that, in spite of the formation of new types of social personalities, the old tribal loyalties – and factions – are maintained and often extraordinarily emphasised in a new context. The Church can easily become tribal in such a situation, and this carries within itself the germ of nativism. The Church should work continuously for the 'reintegration' of the African community. At the same time it must be related to the emerging world-wide culture, although it cannot be identified with

223

this or any culture. It was this aspect that received special attention at the International Missionary Council at Willingen in 1952, when a report was produced significantly entitled *The Indigenous Church – the Universal Church in its Local Setting*,[41] in which the implications of the tension between the 'indigenous' and the 'universal' were brought out. The Church is called upon to take 'a positive yet national attitude to the cultures'.[42] The Church has to realise and proclaim that it is not tied to any particular social structure 'but subjects every structure to the judgment of God'.[43] This indigenisation should be done by the nationals themselves,[44] otherwise it will be superficial. It is not merely a matter of self-government, self-support and self-propagation. Many self-governing Churches in Africa are not indigenous even today, but reproduce Western patterns of leadership and organisation. A truly indigenous Church, as Reyburn puts it, 'is a group of believers who live out their life, including their socialised Christian activity, in the patterns of the local society, and for whom any transformation of that society comes out of their felt needs under the guidance of the Holy Spirit and the Scriptures'.[45] The Church is truly a society aware of the presence of the Holy Spirit, transforming individual lives, as well as the life of the society. Many missionaries have given the impression that they would prefer the Church *not* to be relevant to its local setting, but rather reflect their own culture and personality exactly. In the most essential field, the formulation of theology in indigenous terms, scarcely anything has been done. The African will interpret the Gospel in terms of his own symbols, and with his own poetry and song.

In Africa the danger of an ethnic Church will always be present in the background if not in the forefront. Many of the traditional aspects of African religion will still have influence, such as the relationship between the living and the ancestors or gods, which is not based on faith or trust but on diplomacy, which can only be countered by means of the power of the community. In the tribe, religious life especially, but in fact life in all its aspects is the struggle for power, and sacrifice is a diplomatic and symbolic gift. Combined ceremonies demonstrate the power of the tribe. Here the Church can learn that the religious is not isolated from life as a whole; it is only the highly sophisticated African who has adopted the Western disposition of separating life and religion. This expression of our faith in terms of wholeness is needed today the world over. 'In the endeavour', says Stendahl, 'we have no need to look upon the thinking of Africans as a threat. It can rather be a means of helping Christians in the West to acquire a new and more adequate understanding of the witness of the Bible for our time.'[46]

224

Analysis of the independent movements has shown that greater attention needs to be given to the working out of a liturgy suitable to the Church in Africa.[47] The Church as the *communio sanctorum* is involved in the relationship of man with his neighbour, which affects liturgy. No Church can discard liturgy, because in it the public worship of the congregation finds expression. Vilmos Vajta defines liturgy as 'the form in which the congregation receives God's word in Word and Sacrament, and in which it, at the same time, clothes its prayer, its praises, and its confession'.[48] The relation between theology and liturgy is of vital importance, because liturgy is not autonomous, but must be based on sound theological presuppositions. The theology on which worship has to be based therefore needs a thorough study before the formation of liturgy can be sound and effective. Amongst the Churches in Africa we find a legalistic and formless liturgical order, and an imported and badly adapted liturgy. Liturgy is not a fixed form applicable everywhere under all circumstances; it is only a form, an earthly vessel, which may differ and change. It is not a gift to be accepted in a certain form as from God Himself – an impression left by many missionaries. 'The liturgical creativity of the spirit in the contemporary congregation dare not be disregarded. It is therefore always dangerous to enforce forms upon a congregation which were produced in another era.'[49] Legalism in this respect 'forces the Gospel from its throne and places the earthly vessel in the place of the eternal'.[50]

Liturgy has much to do with love of one's neighbour, because the gathering together of people for worship demands an external order. It does not just exist for the sake of the congregation: it is a means of proclamation. 'Liturgy is the proclamation of the glorious deeds of God. Where liturgy is understood as something other than proclamation it has lost its heart.'[51] Because it has to do with proclamation, all genuine Christian liturgy must have a christological centre.

The word liturgy has apparently lost its original meaning. It was used outside Scripture in a political-technical sense, and as a cultic *terminus technicus*. It entered the Church and received a cultic priestly content via the Septuagint.[52] Etymologically, the word is made up of *leitos* ('the people', the community of the people) and the root *erg-* (noun *ergon* and verb *ergō*, 'work'). The composite *leitourgō*, *leitourgein* means 'to render a service' – not a private one, but a service to the people. It was eventually used in connection with the cult, sacrifice and carrying of cultic objects. It was a people's affair, because the political and the cultic community were the same. In the New Testament the word is changed, although something of the original meaning is maintained. It receives its most characteristic meaning in Philippians ii. 17, where the faith of the Philippians is seen as an offering brought to God. Paul as a missionary performed this priestly sacrifice by giving his life. In liturgy the priest also offers something of himself, and in this sense it has to do with proclamation. But, in its emphasis on the neighbour, liturgy is bound up with community, an important characteristic of African society. Scripture, symbols, poetry, song, dance and pictures have all to be specially interpreted in the African context. The problem in Africa is that the Gospel has often been reduced to a Western ideology, a packaged Christianity instead of naturalised relevant Christianity.[53] Periodically the liturgy has to be examined because, as practical theology, it is a vitally important means of communicating the Christian message. Thus, not only because of the different existential situation but because of the Church's responsibility to the world,[54] the liturgy must fit in with the specific genius and characteristics of the environment in which the Church finds itself. This in itself involves a missionary task, as many congregations developed out of an animistic background where the ritual is rich – for example, with regard to childhood and youth, marriage, death, and many festivals and sacrifices.[55] Such congregations may be visited by illiterates, who are able to discover immediately through the liturgy what is taking place in the service, and what it is endeavouring to represent. Prof. Bavinck relates how in Java a minister carried the Bible reverently at a level with his breast when he entered the Church, because it was a custom there when somebody of lower rank had to carry a letter from the ruler, that he carried it in front of him above his heart, as a sign that the letter and its message are of more account than he is. In liturgical expression, the smallest things are important.

Traditional forms which have no spiritual significance whatsoever, and which the indigenous peoples accept as part and parcel of the Gospel, should be evaluated and if necessary discarded or replaced. These forms have no value if the emphasis is only on the act of doing them and the satisfaction of having complied with tradition. They may have magical effects, which help to distort the message of the Gospel, instead of proclaiming it. The difficulty here is that many of the simpler Church members cannot distinguish between the essentials in the worship service and what is accessory. The task of liturgical expression in Africa does not fall to the Westerner but to the indigenous peoples themselves. Westerners can have their attention drawn to this in the theological education they receive in

226

the seminaries; they can learn to distinguish between what is essential and what is accidental, what is Scriptural and what is specifically Western. What does it mean to gather round the Word of God? What does the worship service imply? What is the double function of the minister speaking to the people on behalf of God, and speaking to God on behalf of the people? What are child and adult baptism? What is Holy Communion? What are Christmas, Easter and Pentecost? Does the Congregation understand Holy Communion, as it is served in Western forms? Is there something magical in the bread and wine or in the baptismal water? Each Church should ask itself the question, What have we done to explain all this in its real context, taking into consideration the African background?

The concept *holy*, for example, needs intelligent explanation. 'Holy' to the traditional African, means 'loaded with mysterious power.' If the magical element for the animist is taken away, the concept *holy* loses all its value and is included in the profane. A holy life is a life which has to fulfil many legalistic prescriptions and observe various ritual prohibitions. Even in the Bible-centred Pentecostal Church, legalism is intended to give holiness in a magical way. The observation of legalistic prescriptions results in a moralistic, 'holy' life based on the magic of man's works. The Holy Communion is associated with Church dues and becomes something you buy. Only with difficulty do they see baptism and Holy Communion as holy. If the water or the elements have nothing magical about them, the rites are considered to be profane, and anything but holy – they are indeed considered *ordinary*, without danger and therefore without power.[56] 'Holy' in the Biblical sense is totally different. There is an element of danger, but it is quite different from what is considered to be magically dangerous: there is nothing dangerous or magical in the minister or in the elements, but if the communicant eats and drinks in sin, he exposes himself to judgment.

Liturgy must in the first instance speak to the people, and secondly it must give expression to the holiness of it all, which is different from taboo holiness.[57] Liturgy should not be ethnocentric, as in the syncretistic movements, but Christocentric, and the Word must speak to the conscience of the congregation and not be pushed into the background. It is important that those in the so-called young Churches should learn to what they must give liturgical form, and this knowledge requires sound theological understanding. Only when those in the young Churches have ceased to copy the Westerner or what is Western, will they stop living from psychological and ethnic motives, and only then will liturgy have to do with their faith, and mean more than acting on a stage. For liturgical understanding

227

the close connection between theology and liturgy has ever to be stressed. It is of the utmost importance in Africa that liturgy should receive its proper serious attention. Much of what is practised in the Churches today is outmoded, irrelevant, superfluous and insignificant—no wonder that this evokes strong negative reactions from many Africans.

REFERENCES

1. Lesslie Newbigin, *The Household of God*, Friendship Press, 1953, 3.
2. Max Warren, *The Christian Mission*, SCM, 1951, 81.
3. Cf. R. T. Parsons, *The Churches and Ghana Society*, 32–33.
4. Cf. Freytag, *Mission zwischen Gestern und Morgen* (World Missionary Conference in Willingen, 1952), Stuttgart, 1952, 8.
5. Paul Tillich, 'The Theology of Missions', *The Occasional Bulletin*, Vol. V, No. 10, Aug. 10, 1954, 5. He adds: 'It was the reality of the Divine, preparing in paganism for the coming of the manifest Church.' Such an attitude is basically syncretistic. Kraemer, surprisingly enough, underestimates the strength of the African religion in this respect (cf. *Religion*, 405–06). What happens to Islam may easily happen to Christianity. Trimingham states: 'The new culture which emerges as a result of this process may be compared to an embroidered textile. The basic fabric is the animist culture. Upon this is embroidered the Islamic pattern. In time this pattern is woven into the very texture of the background. The actual structure of the ground is no longer discernible, but it remains firmly rooted and provides the variation between different ethnic cultures. Religious life rests on a double foundation, the animistic underlayer and the Islamic superstructure.' *Islam in West Africa*, 43.
6. Karl Barth, *Church Dogmatics* I², T & T. Clark, 1956, 218–325.
7. Ibid., 283.
8. Ibid., 297.
9. Ibid., 301. The Christian revelation as the record of God's self-disclosing revelation in Jesus Christ is absolutely *sui generis*. H. Kraemer, 'Continuity or Discontinuity', Tambaram Madras Series, I.
10. Barth says: 'The image of God is always that reality of perception or thought in which man assumes and asserts something unique and ultimate and decisive either beyond or within his own existence, by which he believes himself to be posited or at least determined and conditioned.' *Church Dogmatics* I, 2, 302.
11. Ibid., 302–03.
12. Ibid., 308.
13. Ibid., 311.
14. Ibid., 316.
15. Kraemer in his article on 'Continuity or Discontinuity', in the *Tambaram Madras Series*, Vol. I, 23, concludes: 'Fundamentally speaking, we have in regard to our problem only to choose between two positions, to start consciously or unconsciously, from a general idea about the essence of religion and take that as a standard of reference, or derive our idea of what religion really is or ought to be from the revelation in Christ, and consciously stick to this as the sole standard of reference. To my mind the choice of the second of these alternatives is inescapable.'
16. H. Schärer (*Die missionarische Verkündigung auf den Missionsfeld*, Basler

Missions Buchhandlung, 1942) maintains that Gutmann has not studied the very essence of the non-Christian. He rejects Gutmann's 'primordial ties' and 'unity of life' or 'sense of community', which is no preparation for the Gospel, but rather a falling away from God. Primitive collectivity spells collective self-divination and it is thus not a question of accommodation but of regeneration. Cf. J. H. Bavinck, *The Impact of Christianity on the Non-Christian World*, Eerdmans, 1949, 29.

17. Kraemer, *Religion*, 364.

18. Ibid.

19. Cf. Harry Sawyerr, 'The basis of a Theology for Africa', IRM, July, 1963, 279–71. Tempels, 42, maintains 'The true chief . . . is the source of all zestful living, he is as God himself'. Taylor, *Primal Vision*, 135: the Chief or King's person 'is the sum and substance of the whole community'. In spite of the fact that the position of the chief is in many places precarious, his historical setting could nevertheless be helpful. Paul D. Fueter, 'The African Contribution to Christian Education', *Practical Anthropology*, Vol. II, No. 1, Jan.–Feb. 1964, p. 10.

20. Barth, *Church Dogmatics*, I², 347.

21. W. Freytag, 'Missionary thinking in Germany in recent years', IRM, 1946, 395.

22. Oosthuizen, 19. Cf. G. F. Vicedom, *Die Taufe unter den Heiden*, Kaiser, 1960; G. F. Vicedom, *Das Abendmahl in den jungen Kirchen*, Kaiser, 1960.

23. Winburn Thomas and Rajah B. Manikam, *The Church in South East Asia*, Friendship Press, 1956, 164.

24. Oosthuizen, 24.

25. Ibid., 28. C. G. Baëta, 'Deutsche Evangelische Weltmission', *Jahrbuch*, 1954, 65. 'The task of the Mission is to help build up a real African Christianity and not to demonstrate what a powerful personality can do.'

26. Paul D. Fueter states (in 'The African Contribution to Christian Education', *Practical Anthropology*, Vol. II, No. 1, Jan,–Feb. 1964, 8) 'Those of us who have been able to compare a group of Africans at work, at a dance, at a traditional funeral and then in church are often startled by the contrast. It is as if there were two persons at war in them.'

27. Jan Hermelink, 'The New Africa and an Old Imperative', *Lutheran World*, March 1959, Vol. V, No. 4, 361.

28. S. Neill, *Christian Partnership*, SCM, 1952, 16–17.

29. Godfrey E. Phillips, *The Transmission of the Faith*, Allen & Unwin, 1946, 110.

30. Cf. T. S. Johnson, *The Story of a Mission*, SPCK, 1953, 50.

31. On the supranationality of missions, see the statements issued by the IMC, Whitby, 1947.

32. S. Neill, *The Unfinished Task*, 9.

33. William A. Smalley, 'Cultural Implications of an Indigenous Church', *Practical Anthropology*, Vol. 5, No. 3 (1958), 56.

34. Cf. Smalley, 'Culture and Superculture', *Practical Anthropology*, Vol. 2, No. 3 (1955), 58–71.

35. Cf. J. C. Hoekendijk, *Kerk en Volk in de Duitse Zendingswetenschap*, 51.

36. Cf. Bruno Gutmann, *Gemeinde-Aufbau aus dem Evangelium*, Leipzig, 1925. S. Knak, 'Bantuvolkstum, Evangelium, Pietismus', *Evangelische Missions-Magazin*, 1932, 143. S. Knak, *Zwischen Nil und Tafelbai*, Heimatdienst Verlag, Berlin, 1931. E. Johanssen, *Geistesleben afrikanischer Völker in Lichte des Evangeliums*, Munich, 1931.

37. Cf. P. Abrecht, *The Churches and Rapid Social Change*, SCM, 1961, 16.

38. Sundkler, *Ministry*, 289. Sundkler ('Response and Resistance' . . . op. cit.,

145) maintains 'any study of church life and Christian belief in Africa which fails to lay emphasis on the whole complex of ideas centering on death, burial and after-life misses something essential. In fact, this complex of ideas acts as an index to determining where we stand in the process of Christianization in Africa.'
39. Sawyerr, 267.
40. Hoekendijk, 'The Church in Missionary Thinking', IRM, July 1952, 324–36. Cf. also H–R. Weber, *The Marks of an evangelising Church in the Missionary Church in East and West*, ed. C. C. West & D. M. Paton, SCM, 1959, 111.
41. Cf. Ed. N. Goodall, *Missions under the Cross*, Edinburgh House Press, 1953, 195.
42. Ibid., 196.
43. Cf. *Dilemmas and Opportunities: Christianisation in Rapid Social Change*, Report of an International Ecumenical Study Conference, Salonika, Greece, 1959.
44. R. Pierce Beaver, *The Christian World Mission*, Calcutta, Baptist Mission Press, 1958, 13.
45. William A Reyburn, 'Cultural Implications of an Indigenous Church', *Practical Anthropology*, Vol. 5, 1958, 55.
46. Krister Stendahl, 'The New Testament and the Preaching', *Lutheran World*, Vol. VI, No. 1 June 1959, 112.
47. E. C. Parker ('All-Africa Christianity', *The Christian Liturgy*, May 22, 1963, 670) writing on the All-Africa Conference held at Kampala April 20–30, 1963, states that, apart from elimination of missionary control, the identification of the church with the African struggle, 'We want a Church that is African in philosophy and practice . . . development of an African theology, an African liturgy, African translations of Scripture and literature, African forms of worship and administration.' Prof. A. Mulders, director of the Roman Catholic Missiological Institute, Nijmegen, Holland says: 'A missionary Liturgy celebrated in great form should directly give to the neophyte a consciousness of having found in the church of Christ not only the true faith, but also the possibility of encountering God and of rendering to Him true worship – worship in which the genuine aspirations of His cultural heritage find their fulfilment.' Cf. *Liturgy and the Missions*, ed. I. Hofmeyer, Kenedy & Sons, 1960, 19.
48. Vilmos Vajta, 'Theological basis and nature of the Liturgy', *Lutheran World*, Dec. 1959, Vol. VI, No. 3, 234.
49. Ibid., 239. Pauw, *Religion*, 128, refers to 'the informal and familiar manner' in which services, even those of 'strongly liturgical character' are conducted, which illustrates 'the intimacy of relation within the Church group'.
50. Vilmos Vajta, *Theological Basis*, 240.
51. Ibid., 245.
52. Cf. G. Kittel, *Theologisches Wörterbuch zum neuen Testament*, Vol. IV, Stuttgart, Kohlhammer, 1942, 221–38.
53. Sundkler, *Ministry*, 299, maintains that the 'new and radical group expressions found by Separatist Churches in the South and in the West are indications of the fact that the really indigenous African Church in the future will orientate itself away from Western intellectualism and show a sense for the rich and generous orchestration of African emotional life'.
54. J. H. Bavinck, 'Liturgische vormgewing op het Zendingsveld', *De Heerbaan*, Nov. 1948, 315.
55. Cf. G. F. Vicedom, 'Die Liturgie der jungen Kirchen', EMZ, Sept. 1951, 134: 'The heathen is in his cult very rich. He has for all life's circumstances, for the whole year his sacrifice, feasts, festivals according to very fixed prescriptions.'

Pauw (*Religion*, 220) states: 'Traditional magico-religious practices did not include long sermons, they did include prayers, but they included more action. Sacrifices (which meant sacrificial meals), sprinkling or washing with medicines in rites of purification and observing the fall of the dice in divination provided the opportunity for seeing, feeling and actively participating in the magico-religious sphere.'

56. Cf. Bavinck, *Liturgische Vormgewing*, 319.
57. Ibid., 321.

10

COMMUNICATION OF THE CHRISTIAN FAITH IN AFRICA

(i) THE WORD

The Church's greatest difficulty in Africa lies within the field of communication. The late Prof. J. T. Jabavu often repeated that only an African truly understands an African. In the mission, communication has been taken for granted. Christianity has suffered set-backs in communicating the Christian message not only to those who live in indigenous African society, but also to those in the cities where the advance of Western civilisation, industrialisation and urbanisation has been in many respects rapid and revolutionary. All efforts to relate Christianity to the 'soil' in Africa are overdue, and the faith must be freed from its ghetto mentality. Our basic task should not have been to communicate Europe or Great Britain or America to Africa but to communicate Christ. The good news in Christ is the *content* of Christian communication. The Church often spoke 'in tongues' because of its unwillingness to study the African mind and way of life.[1] Methods worked out in the West cannot automatically be applied in Africa. If Christianity carries with it the stigma of being just another imported item from the West, it will remain sterile in communication and thus in mission. There is a difference between *form* and *content* of Christian communication. The content remains the same, but the form changes. Eugene Nida has indicated that the Church is perilously afloat upon a sea of words, with the encoding and decoding of messages, with their sources, receptors and feed-back, and with the idiosyncratic cultural and experiential 'grids', which 'skew' messages and produce 'noise' instead of the effective identification which is the ultimate purpose of communication.[2] Christian communication must be intelligent in form as well as faithful in content. Taylor even says that the missionaries preached from within the culture of the last century – Evangelical Protestantism or Roman Catholicism – while the Baganda heard it from within his own background. He adds:

232

'Historically and sociologically, the communication of the Gospel is a matter of culture contacts. . . . The convert . . . hears (the Word of God) . . . from within the "auditorium" of his world, as he sees and knows it.'[3] It is a 'mystery of preaching' that the Word of God is ever heard.

In the Genesis story, God takes the initiative to approach fallen man, and eventually in Jesus Christ we find the 'decisive and authentic' act of communication. Man's fallenness from the right relationship with God has 'affected all other patterns of communication',[4] but in Jesus Christ the possibility of effective communication has been restored. When we analyse the Old Testament, it is clear that the emphasis is on the word of God as the means of communication. The Jew was always alert to listen, as 'the channels of sound were for him the all-important channels of communication.'[5] Yahweh could not be seen, but He could be heard, with the result that the emphasis is on verbal communication, which finds its culmination in the Incarnated Word, Jesus Christ. All other means of communication were subordinated to what the Old Testament Jew considered to be the primary means of communication.

In the New Testament, communication by sight comes more clearly into the picture, and here it is Word and Image, although the Word remains basic. The Person of Jesus, which communicated itself to the eye, and the work of Jesus, which communicated itself to the ear, were indispensably bound together. The Bible is God's great picture book, because Christ, who has been incarnated, is actually a picture of God. This leads Weber to say that 'God does not reveal the deepest mysteries by word . . . but through signs: immersion at baptism, the breaking of the bread, the cross'.[6] In the liturgy of the Roman Catholic Church, communication was made mainly through the eye; this is especially the case in the Eastern Orthodox Church, where the service is a great drama, in which all the senses take part.

The Reformation gave the Word once again its central place, after it had been in the background for centuries, with the result that preaching, teaching, hearing and reading the Word were *over*emphasised, to the detriment of all other means of communication. In indigenous African cultures, where religion is acted out, this 'idolisation' of preaching has, if anything, a negative effect. The root of the problem lies with our translation of the Greek verb *kēryssein*, in which all the emphasis is put on preaching; 'to proclaim' is the correct translation, which implies something much broader than preaching, because what has to be proclaimed is an all-decisive event, not doctrines and truths or Bible lessons. The term *kērux* is very seldom used in the New Testament, and, when it is used, it has a wider meaning than mere preaching, referring rather to proclamation, because 'proclamation, in the Bible, always has a dialogue and dramatic character'.[7] The history of redemption is a great drama, which cannot be communicated merely by means of words. Proclamation comprises both the pictorial and the symbolic: Paul pictures to us the crucified Christ, and the sacraments proclaim what is 'unutterable' in this drama of redemption, while the 'utterable' parts of the drama are proclaimed by the preaching of the Bible. Intellectual exposition in preaching and the symbolic proclamation by the sacraments go together.[8] The ritual must thus receive a wider scope in the Church in Africa as is evident from the success of the independent movements.

The all-important question is, How is this message to be communicated to the new cultures, each with its own, in many ways, distinct presuppositions, its own myths and its own social patterns? If this is not taken into consideration, not only do we fail to communicate the message, but services will be plain boring. To give an example of a happy 'marriage' of foreign elements, Max Warren relates how the collection in a Sierra Leone 'Independent African Church' is taken to the accompaniment of song, drums and dance.[9]

The psychological distance between two cultures is a difficult issue. The first major transposition, at the start of Christianity, took place from the Jewish cultural milieu, where the Word is predominant, to that of the Greek world, where the image is central. The Greek world of mystery cults, which promised salvation in their own way, held many dangers in store for the Church.[10] Jesus became half a god and was at most a teacher and example. This heresy has been confronted, although not yet adequately, because our christology today still suffers in many ways from another heresy of that time, docetism. Paul used the language and imagery of the late priestly Judaism as the bridge by which the Gospel should enter the Greek cultural world.[11] The process was not so easy because, in the Jewish world view, a religious principle, namely the *Torah*, was in the centre, whereas the *Logos*, a rational principle, was in the centre of that of the Greeks. Paul, well versed both in Rabbinic Judaism and in all aspects of Hellenism, was in the centre of this transposition. The first Christian evangelists used the images, ideas and verbal symbols and language patterns of the Hebrew tradition, already adjusted to the Hellenistic world in this process of translation and transposition.[12] The Gospel, with its prophetic and historical background, could thus be transposed into the Greek language which was characterised by symbol and myth. Dillistone rightly says: 'The symbolic and mythological had to be evangelised, and perhaps the greatest wonder

234

of Christianity is that the central place in each was claimed for Jesus the Christ. The New Testament ends with Christ at the centre of the covenant community and of its history, at the centre of the Divine organism and of its myth.'[13]

The immediate question is: Why did this not happen in Africa, where Christianity had its greatest opportunity to influence the masses?[14] The fact is, of course, that Africa had no Paul. What Africa needs today is men thoroughly versed in the Bible, in contemporary theology, in world trends and social conditions, and in the African world and its thinking. Nida repeatedly indicates that the accomplishments of indigenous Christian movements must be ascribed to the use of the people's own language and indigenous media, and that Bible texts were explained in the cultural context. The independent movements accept the fact that they have to do with their own world and world view, and this is in contradiction to many missionaries whose motto was 'You must become like us'. The new rush of Western civilisation does not affect the urgency of this matter – it merely emphasises it. In the Middle Ages, when the Christian truths were translated into the Latin language, the Christian revelation was pressed into its static moulds which unconsciously thwarted the 'immense vitality of the new faith to regenerate both language and life.'[15] Immediately the Gospel was translated into the vernaculars, it became again a great missionary factor.

(ii) LANGUAGE

A brief reference to the problem of language is necessary. In our context, language, the chief though by no means the sole instrument of communication, is less a psychological and social phenomenon than a theological and philosophical one.[16] Language is not a natural function of man, and speech varies from one group to another because it is a historical affair of that specific group.[17] Speech is not instinctive but an acquired 'social' function, and it is related to a universe of its own. Three statements about semantic correspondence should always be remembered; Nida adequately puts them as follows: '(i) no two people mean exactly the same thing by the same word; (ii) no two words in any one language ever have exactly the same meaning; (iii) no two words in any two languages ever have exactly the same meaning.'[18] The problems of communication implied here can only be met by those who have a thorough knowledge of the African world view; i.e. by the man of Africa himself. In religion, only the vernacular can convey the deepest in man, in spite of the fact that every language has its limitations in this respect. But the danger is that the African Church may fail to communicate the

Gospel to its *own* society, because it has learned the Gospel in loan words from the West. Loan words can be understood by the intelligentsia, but they do not speak to the heart of the nation. They do not reflect its own spiritual struggles and, because of this, they fail to communicate the word of God.

The Westerners in Africa have largely attached the stigma of primitiveness to the indigenous languages. But when the so-called primitive and the so-called civilised languages are compared the one can be seen as a planed block of wood; the other as an unplaned one; the difference is limited to a very thin layer on the surface. *Linguae francae* are important, and in African higher education they may be an absolute necessity. In matters of religion, however, there is no other language that speaks to the human heart as does that learnt at the mother's knee. There is no such thing as a primitive language in the sense of an inferior languge. If we compare, for example, Attic Greek with one of the most beautiful languages of the world – Zulu – the same complicated grammatical principles are found in both. The language of the South African Bushman is a rich system of symbols which, according to Sapir, is in essence comparable to the developed French language.[19] Although abstract concepts are limited in the languages of Africa, their fundamental bases, their differentiated system of sounds, their specific association of speech elements with concepts, the subtle rules for the rendering of all kinds of relations, are fully worked out in a systematised form. In forms and modes of expression, these languages surpass in wealth many of the so-called 'civilised' languages, which are so readily accepted in Africa as status symbols. Unfortunately, the wealth of these languages has not been utilised in the Church in liturgy and theology, as one would expect from an indigenous Church, but this is largely due to the ignorance of too many missionaries and the reluctance to build up an indigenous leadership. Those languages which emanated from what were considered to be centres of civilisation have received priority above those that really speak to the heart and mind of Africa. The so-called civilised languages help to put on an outward veneer, make superficial emphases, and give the impression that Christianity is a civilisation. There is an intense psychological relationship between race, language and civilisation, which is well-nigh impossible to break, and the new civilisation will not succeed in outliving the indigenous languages in Africa. The vernacular is the language used in the services and hymns of the independent movements.

Language is much more than a transposition of ideas – it gives expression in the form of symbols to our innermost feelings. The

236

peculiarities, limitations and potentialities of one language are not reproduced exactly in another. Here difficulties in translation work arise.[20] In the languages of Africa the words have concrete meaning; for example, it is difficult to find a generic word for a tree because allowance is only made for specific types of tree. The Bavenda in South Africa have no general name for rain, but for every kind of rain they have a separate word, as they have for each type of grass. The fact that abstract conceptual words are so few indicates that the abstract is often made concrete. Another problem in translation is that word-meanings are as circumscribed as possible; all the characteristics of an object are concentrated in a single word, hence these languages are extremely complicated.[21] Furthermore, in these cultures the dominant features are particular images and concrete symbols – to see is the normal quality of those with this background.[22]

Very few people are ever fully bilingual. Those experiences one had as a child can never be adequately translated in one's mind. But it is also a fact that the knowledge acquired later in another language can only be translated with some difficulty into the mother tongue. Mother tongue education should be advocated with discretion. Although it is a fact that a scientific truth is never coloured by the specific language medium in which it is expressed, and thus its message can be easily transposed into another language which possesses an adequate vocabulary, the point is that the vocabulary of the indigenous languages is not adequate. Because, in a certain sense, science is 'the set of symbols that scientists use to communicate their knowledge to other scientists',[23] the necessity of transposition is not so acute as in literary expression, which is personal and concrete. There is no temperament or feeling in science, and thus it can be studied more fruitfully by African students in an international language. Our technological, universal society gives preference to such languages in matters which are of common concern in the technological and scientific fields.

In many parts of the world, linguistic variety has decreased since the beginning of historical records; for example, in North Mexico the indigenous languages have been reduced by about 40% since Europeans arrived.[24] Yet in Africa, as in other continents, indigenous languages have become important *linguae francae*, such as Hausa in West Africa and Swahili in East Africa. In the Church, an indigenous language should be accepted as a *lingua franca* where it is not possible to use the vernacular (which should take precedence where possible). Where multi-racial Churches come into being, the Western languages find their place.

The problem of language is much more acute than can ever be

imagined by those who know only one language, because translation means 'imaginatively moving from one universe to another' and, says Kraemer rightly, if we do not realise this we may end up by 'speaking in tongues'.[25] The mother tongue is the language in which people hear the deepest lessons of life.[26]

So far we have tried to indicate the importance of the vernacular in the Church, in spite of the importance of a *lingua franca* or international languge in some subjects in secular education. Language, however, is also a theological problem. We have already referred to the Genesis story where the breaking of the dialogue between God and man, and thus between man and man, is vividly described. In Acts, this broken dialogue in all its dimensions is restored through the power of the Holy Spirit. Kraemer concludes: 'Fall and Redemption, Babel and Pentecost are hidden factors behind language and communication.'[27] Only in Christ can there be real communication between God and man and between man and man, and this is effected through the working of the Holy Spirit, who transcends the isolationist tendencies of a language. The necessity of a universal language does not arise – apart from being impossible, it would also be impractical. This contradicts not only 'the actual, living reality of language' but also the inability of man to achieve wholeness.[28] The broken dialogue between God and man is at the centre of our problem of communication – which makes communication thus a theological problem.

(iii) CULTURE

Although the judgment of God is upon all culture, Christianity cannot be divorced from it. The Christian message takes on colouring from the medium through which it is conveyed, as we have seen in the independent movements. This is seen in Matthew's Gospel which is directed to people with a Jewish background, and Luke's Gospel, which is directed to people in the Greco-Roman world. For example, Matthew uses the phrase 'Kingdom of Heaven' thirty-three times, and 'Kingdom of God' only four times, because the name of Yahweh was ritually avoided amongst Jews, and used only by the High Priest in the Holy of Holies; whereas Luke uses only 'Kingdom of God', as 'Kingdom of Heaven' would not have been understood by the Greeks. Among the Kaka in the Cameroon, reconciliation can be solemnised by eating with a person, so that the Holy Communion symbolises for them reconciliation with *Njambie* (God), when members have sinned. This reconstruction of the Christian communion in the Kaka's own terms has missed the Biblical meaning.[29]

The breaking up of our world culture has shown that even modern

238

man is not merely an intellectual being, but that abstract ideas have to be translated for him into concrete forms. It is thus important for the Westerner to take note of the richness of African culture in ways and means of communication; he will benefit from studying the channels through which African illiterates communicate. This study is also important with regard to the communication of the Gospel *to* illiterates, who will be with us for at least the next generation. We have already maintained that the Bible message should not be communicated merely through man's intellect and words, because the 'Word' has never been important in African religion, which has always been acted out. Our Western conditioning has stunted our non-intellectual receiving organs;[30] the Reformation, reacting against Roman Catholicism, affected the fullness of divine worship as it is found in Scripture, and as it is also found today in Africa. The ritual of the animist is rich and varied in expression, and could be utilised with great profit in the expansion of Christianity; yet every indigenous form of expression has been discouraged rather than studied. Should these forms not be studied in a situation where thousands flock to these independent movements? 'Dancing before the Lord' and 'repetitive singing', two expressions of worship indigenous to Africa, are abolutely alien to the European;[31] but the sacred rhythm of the hymn wants to find expression in sacred dance, as seen in the Shembe movement, where special days are set aside for dancing, and different groups – old men, young men, married women, girls – dance separately. 'Just as at the Feast of the First-fruits of old, a quiet stately dance with accompanying songs was performed, so today the Nazarites dance at their "July" festival and on similar occasions in a dignified and quiet manner.'[32] In praying, singing, drumming, dancing and shouting, religion is acted out in many of the independent movements, and in this tense, emotive atmosphere 'the spirit is mightily shed abroad'.[33] Rhythm in the African religion is, according to Senghor, 'the architecture of being, the inner dynamic, which gives it form; the pure expression of vital force: it expresses itself through material means like lines, colours, forms in architecture, painting, accents in poetry, music and move-ment in dance. Rhythm is indispensable for the word; it makes the word active. In rhythm the word finds its full expression.'[34] Many a sermon of the African preacher in general concentrates on 'one leading idea, image or sentence or story and turns this over and over again, savours it this way and that way, describes it in various emotional terms and metaphors, and repeats it *ad infinitum*.'[35] The hymn-singing also concentrates on repetition of a phrase until they absorb it fully. Hymns with choruses are very popular. Much of the singing

239

has a trance effect, and is suspect to many Churches because of its old association with spirit possession.[36] Our Western-dominated liturgy, transplanted whole into the African world, gives very little scope for rhythmic movement or colour.[37] Wherever this aspect of rhythmic movement has been discussed, controversy has resulted, and even the benevolence of European Christians has been tempered with suspicion.[38] Nketia, after emphasising the concreteness of expression in indigenous worship in West Africa – by way of libation, the blood sacrifice, food and drink offering, the sacramental meal shared with the gods at sanctuaries and homes, and dancing images – indicate that there is 'greater freedom of movement, more spontanaeity and gaiety in indigenous African worship than in the Churches where formalism prevails and movement has little place'.[39] Baptism by immersion encourages them to look for a religion which is sensually, emotionally and vividly experienced.[40] Weber says 'simplicity in itself does not make worship more sincere, any more than ritual necessarily makes for complexity and unreality'.[41] All this is an indication that ritual should receive more attention than it has done up to the present.

Music also has been neglected in the Church in Africa, where it should have received a major position.[42] The protest of the African against his experiences in contact with the White man finds expression in the vernacular hymns. Hymns used in the Churches are mostly translated and the tunes are European. Sundkler says 'one of the most disturbing examples of the White man's dominance, even in spiritual matters, over his Zulu co-religionists is this fact that Zulu Christians have not felt led to express their new faith in the composing of songs and hymns of their own'.[43] The 'Israelites' sing Bible verses to some well-known Zulu tunes. There is nevertheless an outstanding collection of hymns published in Zulu, namely Isaiah Shembe's *Isihlabelelo*[44], from which we have already quoted examples. Andersson has gathered a number of so-called 'heavenly songs' of the indigenous movements in the Congo.[45] Hymn writers and composers emerged in Africa, who composed sacred songs and tunes expressing the 'feelings of their heart'; these were not imitations or feeble translations of American and European hymns given to them by missionaries.[46] Nketia maintains that 'Western metrical forms are foreign to African languages', because 'the African traditional poetry is not based on a fixed number of syllables per line' and 'Western tunes ignore two principal features of African songs: (*a*) the close imitation of the natural rhythm of speech, and (*b*) the close imitation of the intonation of the words in the melodic line of the song'.[47]

The composition of songs and hymns is quite common in the Church in East Africa, and the singing of hymns and canticles had a deep effect upon their growth.[48] East Africa was fortunate to have Pilkington's beautiful Luganda hymns, but the first hymns in Luganda were printed by Mackay, and Swahili translations were made of these by Bishop Steere. As in the other indigenous movements, singing was important in the worship of the Lumpa movement: 'The most important medium in the Lumpa congregations is not the spoken but the sung word . . . and everybody recognised the peculiar Lenshina tunes.'[49] The rhythmic element found overwhelming expression in the singing of *tukutendereza*, and partly in dance, during the Revival in Africa.[50] Lesslie Newbigin describes how the original *Kummies* in India (a dance accompanied by song) took on a completely new meaning after being Christianised.[51] But missionaries have been, generally speaking. little concerned with the development of hymnody.[52]

Pauw mentions that, in the separatist Sabbatarian Churches he has investigated, the music to which portions of Scripture are sung 'had originated within the Churches, but were reminiscent of traditional Bantu Music'.[53] In the *Memeneda Gyidifo* (Saviour Church), there is much hearty singing 'of African lyrics, begun by one person and joined in by the whole congregation'. No foreign melodies were sung.[54] A study group of the Methodist Church in Ghana in 1949 agreed that one of the African forms that could be included in the Christian form of worship was the use of lyrics.[55] Research has been undertaken more recently into African music in its ecclesiastical connection,[56] and this subject needs the closest attention of the Churches, and of indigenous Christians who have a background in music.

Special attention also needs to be given to the drama. Indigenous public worship has often been combined with it;[57] however, there are dangers. Non-Christian drama, for example, does not differentiate between form and content. Nevertheless, as most forms of communication have a strong dramatic character, closer study should be made of this phenomenon in indigenous African worship. The festivals, for example, are nothing else but dramatic presentations of great and small events.[58] The study of African ritual, drama and indigenous dance has been taken seriously in West Africa. Taylor poses three lines along which African drama could be developed as an educational and evangelistic medium; to be varied only according to the indigenous forms of an area: 'There are the narrative-song, with chorus and interpolated actions by a few leaders; the free-dialogue rendering of short plays by a small cast; and large-scale dance-pageants with very little speech.'[59] Spectators become part of the drama. With regard to the narrative song, Taylor mentions the Dinka of the Southern Sudan who, after conversion, went through the villages singing the Gospel message in traditional style.[60] A most interesting aspect of this development has been the bringing of songs from the market places into the churches, and a collection of these songs now forms the first hymn book of the Dinka Church. Taylor refers also to the Jeanes School, Kabete, Kenya, where they experimented before the Second World War with religious propaganda plays, based on folk tales, which were a great success. The dialogue, according to Taylor, does not appeal so much 'as the portrayal of character by pantomimising gesture and by costume', and he concludes: 'How hard it is for Europeans to learn that in Africa the heart of a dramatic performance does not lie in the dialogue, but in the "externals" of movement, mimicry and the bodily expression of emotion.'[61] Much scope must always be given here for freedom of expression because Africans are not in these respects puppets as Westerners so often are, but real creative artists.

The large-scale dance pageant, condemned by the missions, is, according to Taylor, the 'most natural form that developing indigenous drama could take'.[62] Unfortunately, only the baser elements, appealing to man's baser instincts, have been kept alive in dance, 'while other types of dance commonly used in the old days have practically died out because they were too innocent for the beer-parties to be interested in them'.[63] The neglect of group dynamics – concrete experience in pictorial and dramatic form – has handicapped the presentation of the Gospel message in Africa. There is much in the African dance according to Taylor, which could be redeemed and utilised by Christian usage. 'It may be', he says, 'that in various places the African Church will be courageous enough to work out some great liturgical drama, similar to that of the Middle Ages, making use of the dramatic traditions of the great mystery religions of Africa.'[64]

Another form of communication – story telling – could be used most effectively among illiterates. Bible stories could be told with a Christocentric emphasis, and could be most effective in the communication of the Gospel message. Abstract ideas about the eternal are foreign to them; only visible symbols have appeal. Pictorial and symbolic vision, the one direct, the other drawing on inner resources or meditation, are well suited to illiterates and would meet their need to concretise what is abstract. Theological problems exist here, but the story-telling technique could be wisely used without overstepping any theological boundaries. Pictures are much used today in evangelistic work amongst illiterates, but new Christian symbols could be created, and a new interpretation could be given to non-Christian symbols; a combination of the two could take place, while the non-Christian ones are completely 're-baptised'.[65] Symbols, according to Weber, must have a central position in worship; the sacraments are symbolic representations of the drama of redemption. Drawings on the board, 'talk and chalk', should be used as a method also, and this is more important even than looking at artistic pictures.[66] Visual aids, such as films, film strips, slides, etc., could be used with great effect in 'educated' or literate congregations. Audio-visual aids have their limitations, and can never be substitutes for Christian witness, but they can make it more effective. The radio is still an effective means of communication but, as Nida says, 'the trouble is that in mass communication we must make the message more and more generalised in order to make it fit more and more people, until at last it is often abstracted out of all contact with concrete reality'.[67] Mass communication lacks the individual, personal aspect and is mere information or religious propaganda. It could be profitably used for instruction, but personal communication is of vital importance.

Symbolic colours play a great role in African religion. For example, white is the diviner's colour, and the whiteness of the dress helps her to 'see' more clearly and so become fully spirit-possessed.[68] A white dress is worn by many an independent neophyte. The colours to be used for uniforms, robes, sashes and holy sticks are supernaturally revealed by the 'Holy Spirit' or an 'angel' (these two concepts are used indiscriminately) and in healing they vary according to the illness which has to be cured.[69] (They are then put on the heads of the patients, and transfer numinous power from the prophet.) White is throughout Africa the colour of priesthood, although among some groups green clothes are considered the proper dress of the Spirit, while black, the colour of death, and red (because Jesus was given a red dress) are taboo.[70] The banner used in the Khaki movement as a sign of power for the prophet, to cure disease or to confer spirit and power, may be either of red, black and yellow together, or a single colour such as red.[71] Apart from the colours used, uniforms, badges and other insignia are important in the nativistic movements, which points to the symbolic nature of their thinking. The symbolic colours of the dress of the Methodist Manyanos – black for sin, red for the redeeming blood of Christ, and white for purity – have had great effect. The robes of the traditional Churches are considered to form an integral part of Christianity. A teacher in Ghana who wore the traditional Ashanti *Kente* cloth

I

in the pulpit was asked to resign, but was permitted years later to preach in it.[72]

There is a profound difference between the primitive Church and the Church today, in that the primitive Church was a small minority group in a non-Christian world, while the Church today has a great history behind it – yet the world which it influenced has emancipated itself from it.[73] This process is to be discerned in the cities in Africa, where a person may move from animism straight to secularism, without having been in real contact with Christianity. In the days of the Roman Empire, external conditions were favourable to the growth of Christianity, whereas today conditions are becoming less and less so. Yet in many ways the Church today meets the same opposing forces as were experienced by the first Church. But this first Church acted in love, and Christian fellowship was extended even to slaves – so radical a departure lending great force to the communication of the Gospel message. When Christianity became a state religion, under Constantine, the effect on the Christian faith was negative because, as Kraemer points out, 'the *symphonia* of faith and empire, of Church and State, take the inherent and necessary tension away . . . here lies the root of the marriage between nationalism and Christianity'.[74] The relation between Church and State in Africa has altered considerably in the course of time, and it is to be hoped that the necessary tension between the two will generally remain. Nationalism and Christianity have always merged in Orthodox countries,[75] (nowhere more plainly in recent years than in Cyprus), with the result that the Church loses its prophetic voice. In such circumstances, rigid doctrines are formulated and intellectualism prevails within the Church. The Gospel means a living encounter and not the inculcating of objective knowledge. Christianity developed, during Constantine's time and later, into a cultural, social and religious system, and so lost its transforming power. So, among the accretions of the institutional Church of today, are the strong impressions it gives of confusion within its own ranks and association with the privileged bourgeois interest or class – impressions that it must do its utmost to live down.

It is with the man who has moved into the industrial cities of Africa that the Church most urgently needs to communicate. He has changed from the organic to the technological pattern of life, in which the unseen, the personal, the ethical have little significance any more in face of the mechanical and its concretisation of everything. The new world view looks upon the Bible not only as naïve but also as out of date, with the natural result that for many both the Bible and the Church lose their authority. This greatest mission field in the world has also become the most difficult thus far experienced, for science is worshipped with unquestioning faith. Few of the new arrivals in cities have the ability to make decisions, which were previously, as it were, made for them by the power of the community.

Loneliness and individualism prevail in the cities where communication within the family is often forcibly broken down, and for this very reason many independent movements build up new communities in cities, like the brotherhoods of Islam. The sense of community, brought from the traditional surroundings but now frustrated, finds expression in non-personalist philosophy. This is a disaster. Communism has been in the past more effective in satisfying this longing for belonging, with the result that whole classes of people have become alienated from the Church. Many feel that the Gospel preached by the Church is isolated from their deepest needs and thus utterly irrelevant. There is a breakdown of communication between the man in the pulpit and the man in the pew, not only because of secularism but because the pulpit has lost touch with the world. Not only do many feel that the Gospel preached by the Church leaves their deepest needs untouched, but in many cases those in the pew quite simply have a much higher education than those in the pulpit; hence the intelligentsia receive very little spiritual nourishment. Bultmann tried to make the New Testament acceptable by demythologising it,[76] but can one take away the mythical concepts of the New Testament because they need to be replaced, in an age when there is so little with which to replace them? Dietrich Bonhoeffer[77] speaks about the adultness (*Mündigkeit*) of modern man, who is irreligious in principle and in fact. The approach of evangelism to this type of man has hitherto been based on the presupposition that man has a *sensus divinitatis*, a *semen religionis*. But Bonhoeffer maintains that we can only relate the spiritual presuppositions of the Christian faith if we speak religionlessly about God, and if we live in the world as if there were no God. He accuses Barth, who makes a distinction between religion and faith, of positivism, because he does not show the way out. Only through solidarity with our religionless world can we indicate that religion and faith are quite different realms. Bonhoeffer maintains that our world lives today without God, but Barth reacts by saying that it only thinks it can, while in truth it does not.[78] The modern world, according to Kraemer, is the 'most prolific producer of new religious, cults, pseudo-religions and idolatries there ever was, demonstrating thereby that man has an ineradicable religious appetite. . . .'[79]

After having discussed the question of the indigenisation or relevance of the Church in Africa, one finds it necessary to emphasise the vital importance of Christian fellowship in spite of cultural differences. One should ask in this connection what the relation was between the mother congregation at Jerusalem, constituted mainly of Jews, and the daughter congregation constituted mainly of Gentiles. It is difficult to know precisely how the Church was organised in the beginning; the Jerusalem congregation, which took more or less the position of a mother congregation, disappeared in the post-apostolic era as a result of its increasing conservatism. Antioch became the first Gentile Church and the mother of all the other Churches.[81]

The problem of culture and race soon made itself felt in the Christian Church. At the first general assembly in the history of the Christian Church the question of Church and race was fully discussed. According to the believers of the party of the Pharisees (the word Pharisee means 'one who separates'), Christians of other races had to become Jews. Paul's condemnation of Peter, who had a vision in this respect[82] is fully justified. In this vision one finds a sign of the undivided felowship in the Church – all those who are called and regenerated out of every nation are added to the one Holy Catholic Church. Peter, Barnabas and Paul, who came from Antioch, emphasised the unity of the Church in spite of racial differences. In Acts xv. 14, Peter says God 'first visited the Gentiles, to take out of them a people for his name'. (*Ex ethnōn laon*, translated 'a people from the nations'; the 'people', here contrasted with nation, means – as in the Old Testament – God's people, His Church.) The Pharisees refused to have communion with the uncircumcised, whereas the emphasis in the New Testament is on the one undivided Church. Paul, Peter and Barnabas agreed with James at this assembly that the Church should not get involved in national prejudices, especially with regard to its unity,[83] the final obedience of the Church lying with Christ. James however compromised, and the *status quo* was maintained for the Jewish Christians. Intolerant Judaism rejected his tolerance towards the Gentiles and, according to Eusebius,[84] Ananus, the high priest, persecuted James and his party of Jewish Christians, who had to flee to Pella, where they became a small sect, insignificant not only in the life of the Church, but also in the life of Jesus. James's compromise would have limited Christianity to a nationalistic religion, instead of it being a universal faith. The Church had to decide whether to remain a Jewish sect, or to become the bearer of a world faith. The flight over the Jordan meant a definite separation between the Law and the Gospel, Sinai and the Cross, Moses and Christ. They could not have both; the one excluded the other, and Christianity included people from every race on a different basis from the Jewish social order.

James himself maintained that God has gathered for himself a people out of the nations, an argument which he based on Amos ix. 11 ff. in the Septuagint. The remnant of Israel and the believers from the Gentiles will be one people of God whose fellowship will be based, not on *eros* but on *agape*, the power that unites the fellowship. John x. 16, says Calvin in his Commentary, refers to the 'calling of the heathen' to be *one body* with the Jewish people. The unity of the Church is not based on unanimity, consensus of opinion or any similar factor of the kind that unites human organisations, but it is *given* in Christ. Paul speaks about the unity of the faith[85] and the unity of the Spirit.[86] Calvin maintains in the *Confessio Gallicana*, Articles 25 and 26, that nobody should separate himself from the body and be satisfied with his own person, but that all believers should together preserve and maintain unity. Calvin's distinction between the two aspects of the Church,[87] the visible and invisible, should never be an excuse for a division in the visible Church. We cannot maintain that, because we have invisible unity, it is not necessary for unity to be seen in the visible Church. Dr. W. Jonker says: 'all true believers belong visibly to Christ and thus also to the Church. If you will, they all belong to the invisible Church. But the visible should be as far as possible nothing else than the visible form of appearance of the invisible Church.'[88]

Koinonia in Scripture is a dynamic and organic concept, which Paul described as 'the communion of the Holy Spirit'. This is the existential unity in Christian fellowship. Unfortunately the *locus* of Christian unity has been shifted from *koinonia* to the institutional form, which has naturally led to division, strife and disruption. Where different Churches came into existence because of linguistic and cultural differences, the existence of which can be fully justified, the shifting of the *locus* of Christian unity has been so final that there is hardly anything left of *koinonia* between some of these Churches. Doctrine, organisation and tradition became more important than Christian fellowship, and this was fatal, because only in *koinonia* have we a category big enough to include the whole concrete reality of Christendom.[89] Believers belong to the same *koinonia*, which has been preserved through the centuries in spite of divisions, because it is not based on man but on the work of the Holy Spirit. Nations and races can never break this unity – they only put obstacles in the way of its external realisation. In Christ there are always Jew and

Greek or man and wife, but they are called upon to receive one another as members of His body. Scripture never advocates uniformity, but neither does it condone racial and class discrimination.

The indigenisation of the Church can mean an enrichment in the body of Christ, in spite of its dangers, but the development of indigenous Churches should be based on purely practical considerations. People of different languages, culture and social classes belong to the one Church of Jesus Christ, and thus to the one fellowship; hence, denominationally speaking, Africans, Asians, Coloureds and Whites should all belong to the same Church connection in spite of indigenisation.[90] In many places in Africa, not only in South Africa by any means, good reason could be made out for multi-racial congregations, but indigenisation should ever be based in sound theology. Tribal loyalties and tribal clashes are an everyday phenomenon on the African continent today.

The boundaries that divide people who are outside Christ vanish 'when they come together in Christ'. A slave becomes a beloved brother,[91] and Paul urges Philemon to accept Onesimus 'both in the flesh as well as in the Lord' (kai en sarki kai en kuriō). Here is a question not of paternalism but of full brotherhood.[92] Ephesians ii. 11–22 describes how the Jews and Gentiles were separated at the Jewish temple, where the loyal Jews had a wall built between the inner and outer court, but in the same chapter, vv. 14–19, we read: 'For he is our peace, who has made us both one, and has broken down the dividing wall of hostility . . . [and] reconciles us both to God in one body through the cross, thereby bringing the hostility to an end . . . for through him we both have access in one Spirit to the Father. So then you are no longer strangers and sojourners, but you are fellow citizens with the saints and members of the household of God.' There is in Christ no question of superiority or inferiority.

The Christendom of the New Testament would have been impossible had it not broken radically with the existing social order of the Jewish community, which felt that only isolation could save it from extinction.[93] Christ left the orthodox closed circle and went to the lax Jews, Samaritans and Gentiles, eating and drinking with publicans and sinners, and showing solidarity with them all. It was this that made Christianity become a world religion. Christ accepted no closed circles. The Church of the New Testament never discriminated against either Jew or Gentile. The resolution of the Church assembly (Acts xv.) had a great influence on the future of Christianity (cf. Gal. ii. 1–10). No psychological distance was established between the Church and those outside. At Pentecost, the chaos of Babel was restored to harmony in principle. The dividing wall of language was broken down, and the people at Pentecost did not lose their identity, but only their separateness. They experienced full spiritual and social communion.[94] True *koinonia* has more evangelising power than any number of missionaries and sermons. The Church's task in Africa should be reconciliatory also and race prejudice, which has been shown not to be the prerogative of one race, and which has played a great part in stimulating separatism, must disappear in the Church. Indigenisation and unity in the Church must co-exist.

REFERENCES

1. The question 'Can the White man understand the Black man?' – asked at Marangu where the All-African Lutheran Conference was held in 1955 (cf. *Marangu Report*, LWF, Geneva, 1956) – comes into the picture here. Max Warren remarks that at this conference a 'tremendous gap was discernible between the thinking of Europeans and the thinking of Africans' (CMS *News Letter*, Feb. 1956, 3). In Africa the largest religious groups are those that adhere to the traditional African religion. Out of a population of 110 million in West Africa, 65 million are in this group, 36 million are Muslims, 4 million Protestants, 5 million Catholics. Cf. *All-Africa Church Conference Bulletin*, Oct. 1965, 12. An important document entitled 'An Advisory Study' published by the United Presbyterian Church in the USA in 1961. In it are analysed the Scriptural basis of the Church; the concept of indigenous Church as the only effective instrument of the Holy Spirit; the Church as a charismatic community, which in its institutional structure constantly changes and is renewed; lay and ministerial training; the colonial mentality within the Church; and the ecumenical approach to missions (as stated at the Faith and Order Conference held in Lund, Sweden, 1952): 'We should do together all things which our Christian conscience does not compel us to do separately.' See also *New Delhi Speaks*, SCM paperback, 1962.

2. Eugene A. Nida, *Message and Mission*, Harper & Bros., 1960, 88.

3. Taylor, *Buganda*, 253.

4. H. Kraemer, *The Communication of the Christian Faith*, Lutterworth Press, 60, 212.

5. F. W. Dillistone, *Christianity and Communication*, Collins, 1956, 7 ff.

6. H. R. Weber, *The Communication of the Gospel to Illiterates*, IMC Pamphlet No. 4, SCM, 1957, 21.

7. Weber, 64.

8. Ibid., 64, 65. Parsons, *The Church and Ghana Society*, 82, speaks about two cultural systems – the African and Christian, meaning by 'Christian' Western.

9. Max Warren, *Great Pan is not dead*, CMS *News Letter*, July 1957. In traditional society, the ritual dance is part of the whole cosmic movement, and it has power in itself so that without it the cycle of the year could even stop. In many nativistic movements, special dance festivals take place and dance here is a way of receiving power, vital force and also of saying 'thank you' to the supernatural forces. The traditional person acts in this case also collectively. These festivals take place during specific periods.

10. Kraemer, *Communication*, 35.

11. Cf. W. D. Davies, *Paul and Rabbinic Judaism*, 1–16.

12. Dillistone, 70.

13. Ibid., 78. On the Westernness of the Church as far as denominations, culture and civilisation, history, theology, liturgy, denominations and resources are concerned, see D. T. Niles, *Upon the Earth*, Lutterworth, 1962, 194–220.

14. J. S. Trimingham, *Islam in West Africa*, 42, states 'Islam in Africa has developed cultural patterns that are at one and the same time African and Islamic. But the Christian community, especially where formed by converting individuals, comes into being in the midst of the animist community in such a way that it is in conscious opposition to it.' It is of utmost importance that a new Christian African culture develop, according to C. G. Baëta; cf. 'Christianity and African Culture', Report of Proceedings of a Conference under auspices of the Christian Council of the Gold Coast, 1955, 58–60.

15. Ibid., 80. The insistence on Latin in the worship service has been criticised by Roman Catholics like Hans Küng. The second Vatican Council wisely decided on the use of the vernacular in the service.

16. Kraemer, *Communication*, 65.

17. Cf. Edward Sapir, *Wat is Taal*? Transl. by Sötemann, Amsterdam, Noord Hollandsche Uitgewers Maatskappij, 1949.

18. Nida, *Message and Mission*, 88.

19. Sapir, 23.

20. The Church in North Africa limited itself to the Latin Bible; in the Abyssinian Church, the Bible was only in classical Ethiopian, and has only recently been translated into living Amharic. More than 80% of the languages and major dialects in Africa, of which there are over 500, have the Bible or parts of it in the vernacular. Cf. Groves, Vol. IV, 317–18.

21. Dillistone, 135.

22. Cf. Frank C. Laubach, *The Silent Billion Speak*, Friendship Press, 1945, 1–3.

23. George A. Miller, *Language and Communication*, McGraw-Hill, 1951, 1.

24. Cf. Edgar H. Sturtevant, *An Introduction to the Linguistic Science*, Yale Univ. Press, 1956, 5, 41–42.

25. Kraemer, *Communication*, 74.

26. Cf. IMC *Theol. Reports* I, II, III. One should also read H. von Sicard's article in IRM April 1955, 147–52, entitled 'Language and Theological Training in Africa' – with certain reservations, however. See also J. H. Nketia, 'The Contribution of African Culture to Christian Worship', Report, All Africa Church Conference, 1958, 61.

27. Ibid., 65, 66.

28. Ibid., 71.

29. Nida, 88.

30. Weber, 29.

31. Max Warren, *Revival*, 30; see also Gerhard Günther, *Erweckung in Afrika*, Stuttgart, Evang. Miss. Verlag, 1959. E. Louis Backman (*Religious dances in the Church and in Popular Medicine*, Allen & Unwin, 1952) states that it was accepted in the Church that heavenly bliss consists of a never-ending dance. These conceptions were prescribed through the centuries. Hymns accompanied these heavenly and sacred Church dances and the choristers' dance was popular up to the last century.

32. Sundkler, *Prophets*, 197. R. R. Marett (*Threshold of Religion*, London, 1909, XXXI), like others, states that traditional 'primitive' religion is 'not so much thought out as danced out'.

33. Sundkler, *Prophets*, 198. The Musama Disco Christo Church, in a summary of what it believes, states 'We believe in Drumming and Religious singing as part of Christian worship. Ps. cl., Ps. cxlix. 3, Ps. lxxxi. 2–4, Eph. v. 19.' Baëta, 153.

34. Senghor, *Der Geist*, 226.

35. Mia Brandel Syrier, *Black Women at Prayer*, Lutterworth, 1962, 35–36.

37. Ibid., 295. Cf. Sundkler, *Prophets*, 184; Andersson, 172. At Pendele, the prophets of the Khaki movement walk and stand on the fire accompanied by the singing of the congregation. In the Kimbangu movement, the singers played an important part in the healing of the sick. Ibid., 52.

38. In a paper read at the All-African Youth Assembly, Nairobi 1962, entitled 'Evangelisation in Africa', Jean Kotto said: '. . . nearly all the customs were condemned; it was said that this was done in the name of the Gospel, but in fact it was done to implant a new way of life and this itself was to the detriment of the Gospel'.

39. J. H. Nketia, *The Contribution of African Culture to Christian Worship*, Report, All African Church Conference, 1958, 61. See also Nketia's article in IRM, July 1958, 265–78, entitled 'The Contribution of African culture to Christian Worship'. The Aladura sect which seceded from the Anglican Church and spread from Nigeria to Sierra Leone has produced and published its own, so-called 'The Holy Litany', which has an indigenous character. See H. W. Turner, 'The Litany of an Independent West African Church', *Practical Anthropology*, Vol. 7, No. 6, Nov.–Dec. 1960, 256 ff.

40. Pauw, *Religion*, 228.

41. Weber, 29. Cf. The Roman Catholic view as stated by J. van Cauwelaert, *Local Custom and Liturgy*, ed. Hofinger, 202 ff.

42. Sundkler, *Ministry*, 229. 'In thirty or forty years' time there may possibly appear some African church leader or theologian who will claim that the approach through African Christian music is the key and the organic principle of teaching of Christian theology as a whole in Africa. Such an attitude could very well appear, by way of reaction to a supposedly sterile Western intellectualism in the approach to theology.' Cf. *The African Music Society Newsletter*, Roodepoort, South Africa.

43. Sundkler. *Prophets*, 193. Prof. K. A. Busia maintains the African drinks from his own cup, incomparable with any other. (*Christianity and African Culture*, ed. by Christian Council of the Gold Coast, 1955, 23.)

44. Published with several printing companies in Natal. First published in 1940.

45. Andersson, 270–87.

46. Ibid., 84. The three Separatist Churches of Sabbatarian persuasions discussed by Pauw (*Religion*, 44) 'sing only unrhymed portions from Scripture to original melodies'.

47. Nketia, 62.

48. Taylor, *Buganda*, 76, 220.

49. Taylor & Lehmann, 255.

50. Warren, *Revival*, 30, 63–67.

51. Lesslie Newbigin, *A South India Diary*, SCM Press, 1951, 63.

52. Cf. James M. Riccitelli, 'Developing Non-Western Hymnody', *Practical Anthropology*, Vol. 9, No. 6, Nov.–Dec. 1962, 241. See also in the same issue Mary Key, 'Hymn-writing with indigenous tunes'; John D. Ellenberger, 'The Beginnings of Hymnology in a New Guinea Church'; Louis L. King, 'Indigenous Hymnody of the Ivory Coast'; W. I. Wallace, 'Hymns in Ethiopia'; Herbert C. Jackson, 'Some old patterns for men in Missions'.

53. Pauw, *Religion*, 135.

54. Baëta, 71.

55. Parsons, *The Churches and Ghana Society*, 83.

56. H. Weman, *African music and the Church in Africa*, Uppsala, 1960; A. M. Jones, 'Hymns for the African', *Books for Africa* (27), Sept.–Oct. 1957; see also K. P. Wachsman, 'An Approach to African music', *Uganda Journal*, Jan. 1939, 149. He states 'the significance of the vernacular in a song can hardly be exaggerated according to native opinion'. On indigenous music, see Nketia, 64.

57. Cf. Nketia, 61.

58. Ibid.

59. John V. Taylor, 'The Development of African Drama for Education and Evangelism', IRM, July 1950, 293. For the dangers of the identification or representation with what is represesented, see K. Th. Preuss, *Der Unterbau des Dramas* (Vortr. der Bibl. Warburg, 1927–28). See also Janheinz Jahn, *Muntu*, Eugen Diederichs Verlag, 1958, 65–94. Cf. Max Warren, 'Communion through Drama', CMS *Newsletter*, July 1962.

60. S. G. Williamson, ('The Lyric in the Fante Methodist Church', *Africa*, Vol. XXVIII, No. 2, Apr. 1958, 26, 132–33) maintains that the Methodist Church here is Western. Among the illiterate Fante Christians the lyric is very popular and has been successfully transplanted to Ashanti, where it has been influenced by Ashanti indigenous forms. In the rural areas, it has displaced to a large extent the Western type of hymn even though their hymn book is in the vernacular. The Methodist Church had appointed a Fante Religious Lyric Committee in 1954, in order to collect indigenous songs amongst the Fante, who showed great interest in indigenous music and song, which had a marked influence on surrounding tribes. Parsons, *The Churches and Ghana Society*, 113.

61. Ibid., 295.

62. Ibid., 298.

63. Ibid., 298. E. Louis Backman (*Religious Dances in the Christian Church and in Popular Medicine*, George Allen & Unwin, 1952) refers to the Greek writer Lucian who maintained that 'one cannot find a single mystery induction not associated with a dance'. There is probably not a single advanced religion in which the dance has not been, or still is, a more or less essential part of the divine service or of the drama of the mysteries. 'This is true not only of the ancient, pre-Christian religions, it is also true, in a very high degree, of Christianity itself' (ibid., 1). The Jewish cult was influenced by those people who regarded dance as an essential element of their cult and the 'Jewish dance ceremonial determined in a high degree the development of Church dances . . .' although Backman detects also influences from the pagan mysteries in this respect. In the summary of this interesting book Backman states 'Even in pre-Christian times the dance was a means of influencing the invisible powers and of establishing contact with them. This was also the fundamental belief of the Christian Church' (ibid., 328). Sundkler (*Prophets*, 22) states that much time is given at the initiation of a diviner to rhythmical dancing. Singing and dancing take place to the tune of the special song which each diviner has 'in order to please and materialize the spirit in whose honour the song is composed'. In the Christian Church dances served different purposes; e.g. the Church dance in fear of God, the churchyard dances for the martyrs were 'an act of Grace and signified a triumph' (Backman, 328), the dance for the dead, etc. During the fourth century these dances showed signs of degeneration. The dances were not only to comfort the dead for their resurrection but also as protection against evil spirits (ibid., 329, 330). As in the case of the Nazarites, religious processions during the fourteenth century and later were dance

processions. In the independent movements of Africa, as was the case in the Church in Europe, dance plays a mighty role in healing. From the earliest times religion and medicine have been closely associated and during the Middle Ages healing was primarily an activity of the Church. Religious dance played a major role in the expulsion of devils considered to be the main cause of disease (ibid., 335). Dancing and singing round a prophet is not an unfamiliar scene with the independentists.

64. Taylor, *African Drama*, 298. 'Ritual' is contrasted with 'ceremonial' in the sense that in 'ritual' people believe that if they perform certain actions they will influence the course of events while in 'ceremonial' there are no mystical notions attached to actions. Cf. Max Gluckman, *Customs and Conflict in Africa*, Blackwell, 1963, 119.

65. Cf. Weber, 54. Also D. J. Fleming, *Christian symbols in a World Community*, Friendship Press, 1940. Here again great caution is needed because in the pre-Christian African mentality 'symbol' is what it expresses. In the image of their God, for example, the God takes part in the image and the image takes part in the God it 'represents'. (Cf. A. Bertholet, Das Wesen der Magie, Nachr. der Ges. der Wiss. Göttingen, Gesch. Mitt. 1926–27, 9.) It is thus easy for the traditional mind to accept that the bread and wine in Holy Communion are the body and blood of Christ. They are 'symbols', i.e. their reality meets the reality of body and blood. (Cf. Van der Leeuw, *De Primitieve Mensch*, 41.)

66. Weber, 84 ff. Cf. Ed. Frör, *Das Zeichnen im kirchlichen Religions–Unterricht*, Munich, Kaiser, 1954, 2.

67. Nida, *Message and Mission*, 177.

68. Sundkler, *Prophets*, 22. M. Gluckman, 'Zulu Women in Hoecultural Ritual', *Bantu Studies*, 1935, 263.

69. A missionary who had some medical knowledge states: 'When converts were won, I found I had not merely to examine them in doctrine and life, but I had to examine them with my stethoscope too.' Cf. R. H. W. Shepherd, *Children of the Veld*, London, James Clarke, 1937. The stethoscope is for many part of the healing process. Injections are often preferred to oral medicine because of its immediate contact with the blood, which is magically more effective.

70. Sundkler, *Prophets*, 214. The 'royal robe' in Acts xii. 21 evokes much interest in nativistic movements, as does the healing of the sick woman who touched the dress of Jesus. In some movements, handkerchiefs, cloth, etc., over which the prophet has pronounced the benediction, are taken hundreds of miles away to be laid on a sick person.

71. Andersson, 158.

72. R. T. Parsons, *The Churches and Ghana Society*, 113. A kente is the national dress of the Ashanti which leaves the left arm and shoulder free and is snowy white with red border like a Roman toga.

73. Adolf Harnack, *The Mission and Expansion of Christianity* (Theological Translation Library), 1908.

74. Kraemer, *Communication*, 43.

75. In Africa, Orthodoxy and political nationalism have also gone hand in hand. Cf. Roland Oliver, quoted by E. G. Parrinder, 'The Religious Situation in West Africa', *Africa*, Vol. 59, No. 234, Jan. 1960, 41.

76. Cf. R. Bultmann, *Theology of the New Testament*, Vol. I (1952), Vol. II (1955) SCM; *Jesus and Mythology*, Charles Scribner, 1958; *Jesus and the Word*, Collins, 1958.

77. Ed. E. Bethge, *Letters and Papers from Prison*, SCM, 1953. See also Bonhoeffer's *Sanctorum Communio*, Kaiser, 1960.

78. Cf. T. J. J. Altizer, *The Gospel of Christian Atheism*, London, Collins, 1967. See T. W. Ogletree, *The 'Death of God' Controversy*, London, SCM, 1966.

79. Kraemer, *Communication*, 103.

80. Material in this connection, taken from an article by the author in the SA *Outlook*, Oct. 1962, is used by kind permission from the editor.

81. Cf. James Strahan in Hastings's *Dictionary of the Apostolic Church*.

82. Cf. Acts x.

83. See also 1 Peter ii. 9, 10. See Everett Tilson, *Segregation and the Bible*, Abingdon Press, 1958.

84. *Ecclesiastical History*, III, 5, 2–3.

85. Ephesians iv. 13.

86. Ephesians iv. 3.

87. Cf. *Institutes* iv. 1. 7.

88. W. D. Jonker, *Die Sendingbepalinge van die Ned. Gereformeerde Kerk van Transvaal*, Potchefstroom, Herald Press, 1962, 21.

89. Cf. J. C. G. Kotze, *The Divine Charge to the Christian in the Church*, Stellenbosch and Johannesburg, SCA Booksellers, 1951.

90. Taylor & Lehmann, 196. 'If the integration of two races in one Church means that those deep emotions, which ought to be voiced and offered and purged in prayer, have to be left in the church porch, while worshippers allow themselves only the lowest common denominator of passion in the polite deference of a multi-racial club, that Church will die, either from boredom of mediocrity or because all its most vital members, black and white, have drifted into the sects.'

91. Cf. Philemon 15, 16, 17.

92. See also Colossians iii. 1–11.

93. Davies, *Rabbinic Judaism*, 61.

94. H. R. Weber, *The Communication of the Gospel to Illiterates*, 21.

11

THEOLOGICAL TRAINING IN THE AFRICAN CONTEXT

IF the Church in Africa does not make a drastic change in its theological training, and accept the fact that its greatest immediate challenge is relevance, then it will be an even greater instrument in creating post-Christianity than it has been hitherto. Furthermore, whenever the term 'theological education' is used the great mistake is made of thinking only of the training of ministers. Theological education covers a much wider field, and the sooner it is restored in Africa to its fundamental meaning in the Church the better, because theological education is perhaps the main focus in the development of the young Churches today. The unhealthy disposition in the Church towards the view that theological training is something only for the 'ministry'[1] is due to Western influence. The present associations of the word 'ministry' indicate how clericalised the Church is. There is no such thing as an elected few called to the 'ministry'. The correct Scriptural approach is that of the *ministry of all believers* – all who profess Christ are in the ministry, just as all share in His service (*ministerium*).

The Church in its modern renewal has made a 'discovery' of this fact, and realises that theological thinking, as well as theological judgment, is of the greatest importance for the so-called laity. The modern believer is called upon to give justification for his faith at every point, and to make theologically important decisions. Lay theological education has received very little attention, but the time for its working out is overdue. Laymen in secular vocations should be able to relate the Gospel truths to their work, and their divine vocation should receive a new emphasis.

The Church will become an insignificant factor in African society if it does not seriously study the question of the lay apostolate, and give efficient leadership in that direction. No Church can be an evangelising Church without its two forms of existence, namely *ecclesia* and *diaspora*. The excessive emphasis given to the former

255

has led to the narrow conception of the ministry, so that the priesthood of all believers, by far the most important aspect in the Church, has been neglected. This is one of the major emphases in the nativistic movements. The reason for the Church's very existence is to live in the *diaspora*. This is the true work of the laity, which is in the front line of the Church's confrontation with the world. The strength of the Church in Africa is mainly due to the fact that it has become a lay movement. Thus it is vital that closer attention be given to the training of the laity, and this can only be done on an ecumenical basis.[2]

In many cases the African Christian has to rediscover himself. As a Christian he does not cease to be an African, and the acceptance of Christianity should not make him a foreigner to his own people. Some theological seminaries in Africa, especially those in remote rural areas, give the impression of being remnants of the monasteries of the Middle Ages, living far away from the real issues of life; most seminaries have predominantly non-African theological teachers, many of whom appear altogether uninterested in studying the African situation. Furthermore, the aim should be not just to produce academically well-trained theologians, but men who will be able to launch an inspired evangelisation activity on the world. The institution of an African Studies department is essential,[3] as theological institutions must introduce students thoroughly to the problems they have to face, whether it is the hitherto neglected but vital task of *effective* communication, or whether it is religiously orientated nationalism, materialism, resurgent animism, communism, industrialism, or Islam. All these need to be studied and theologically confronted. The frontiers are hardening, and the ordained minister is often bewildered because he cannot grasp things, and he compensates by absorbing himself in the organisational aspect and tradition of the Church.[4] In the present circumstances the pastor should be a confident leader, well grounded in his subject, and should be able to train the laity.[5]

Kraemer proposed three indirect ways of counteracting syncretism: (i) to build up a community, reborn in Christ, in which the spirit is that of 1 Cor. xv. 57, 58, and where the Bible with its prophetic apostolic message is taken seriously; (ii) to bring about the right understanding of the Biblical message and drama, which never leads to a closed mind but to the world; and (iii) to establish a strong minority that knows the main elements of the Christian faith, and can give an account of that faith.[6] This strong minority needs the help of the pastor by way of special training in the congregation, which presupposes a solid training of the pastor himself, whether

256

this training is done at university level or at seminary level. Welbourn argues in favour of the university faculty or department of divinity,[7] which training should be followed by seminary training. One can argue however for a three-tier training, namely, the diploma and certificate training at a seminary and the degree course at a university.[8] Theology must have its rightful place as an academic discipline at a university, and in this way be at the centre of the intellectual life of a nation, and on a dialectical footing with the other academic disciplines. The Church must have a say in such a faculty, and for this a *modus vivendi* could be worked out to avoid appointments being made which are unacceptable to the Church. The university, however, should have the final authority in such appointments.

Theological faculties or departments of religion have been established at several university colleges in Africa, for example at Legon in Ghana, Ibadan in Nigeria, Yaounde in the Cameroons, Fort Hare in South Africa, Makerere in Uganda, at the University College in Salisbury, Rhodesia and at the University of Lesotho, Botswana and Swaziland. After university training, at least two years should be spent on vocational training. Welbourn's arguments in this connection are most convincing, namely, that (i) only at the seminary can the future minister fully dedicate himself to his life's task; (ii) the university faculty being interdenominational, the particular denominational approach can only be given at the seminary; (iii) pastoralia and liturgy belong really to the theological seminary and not to the university faculty; and (iv) real commitment to the truths can only take place at the seminary.[9] Church organisation also can only be studied there. Both at the university and the seminary, each discipline should take note of the existential theological problems.

The course of Protestant theology in recent years has not produced any real stimulus towards the religious life. It rather represents the interesting phenomenon of the restoration of the autonomy of theology.[10] In the last decades efforts have been made to reinterpret the task of theology, but in many ways it remained static as before, and in the witness of the Church it had only superficial value. But in Africa this must change. Nobody should teach theology on this continent unless his teaching takes note of the Church's existential situation.[11] Theological training should take place in the 'field'. The younger generation claim that they are fed up with the preaching of the older generation, but it is a fact that even those with advanced degrees often do not understand the existential situation. Digestion and assimilation of material and its application is what counts in education.[12] Years spent abroad, out of Africa, by ordinands can mean very little to the Church in Africa. The best theological centres for Africa must be in Africa. An analysis of the thesis themes of most theological students from Africa who study abroad will reveal very little relevance to the vast theological problems in Africa. A Church is only truly independent when it comes forward with its own theology in its own environment, and has not only outward independence but also inner freedom to meet its problems theologically. Theology can only be exercised when students are theologically well trained, do research, bring forward their own theological answers, defend what they believe in, counteract syncretism and, in their life of faith, live in communion with God and devote much time to the study of the Scriptures.[13]

A critical sense has not yet been developed in the Church in Africa; nor, as is so obvious in sermons, has an analytical approach. It can be called a pre-scientific congregational theology, which has as centre the blood of Christ. So will the Church in Africa be able to steer clear of all the rocks of syncretism? The nativistic movements are sufficient evidence of what may happen if the Church is not attentive to what Scripture teaches. Latourette states that these movements 'can be interpreted as a foretaste of what an indigenous African Christianity will be, deprived of the steadying influence of missionaries from the older Churches'[14] – but one need not be as pessimistic as Latourette in this respect. Well-trained indigenous leaders and men of spiritual integrity in Africa have a great task to fulfil. Stephen Neill says: 'What matters above all else is that he should be a saint. Given that, nothing else matters nearly as much.'[15] At the centre of his life and teaching, however, should stand the Cross, so often overlooked.

But, as Neill goes on to say, 'saintliness is not enough'. Africa has many saints but few who can meet the situation. The Church has to be well guided.[16] It may expand at the circumference, but the problem is often what happens at the centre. It is sometimes astounding to hear how, for example, Church members look at the sacraments, Church offering and Church attendance, and how confused they are and how deeply caught up in the syncretistic web.

But the selfhood of the Church in Africa is important.[17] Africa needs its own *Confessio Africana*, in which the young Church takes notice of its own existential situation. The independence of a Church does not lie in its organisation but in the way it answers Christ's question, 'Who do you say that I am?'[18] No evidence in Africa exists of independent confessional development – it has either been transplanted or prepared by Westerners.[19] Arne Sovik, a Lutheran, rightly maintains that 'Lutheran theology in Africa needs to get its cue for its application from the African environment. . . .'[20] It is surprising to see that, with all the difficulties the Church has to face in matters of Christology, ecclesiology and pneumatology, nothing has actually been done to put forward a well worked-out theological exposition of these issues, taking into consideration the African background and the difficulties it poses. The proposed department of African Studies, or Missiology, will be of great help, and its findings must be brought into relation with the deepest meaning of the Gospel message.

Sundkler speaks about the 'search for an integrated curriculum'.[21] In the study of the Bible, it is necessary to do thorough exegesis and to relate words such as sin, blessing, grace and others to the African understanding of them. At the higher levels of training, the Biblical languages, Hebrew and Greek, should receive close attention and the principal Hebrew and Greek terms should receive attention at the lower levels. The study in Africa of the Biblical languages will make the whole theological training much easier.[22] Hebrew, which is closer to the African mind than Greek, should be in the curriculum, and the Old Testament world view needs clear interpretation, especially because of its superficial similarity to the African world view. Hellenistic or 'New Testament' Greek should be studied rather than Attic, and the translation work from the New Testament can be of great help in understanding the meaning of the text. It has been proved that the African has a natural proficiency in languages, and that it is within the reach of every student of average intelligence to pass the examinations in these languages. Apart from sound exegesis, the Old Testament should be taught without a legalistic or moralistic bias and without texts being used as if they have magical power. The attitude to the Old Testament is often not a theological but a pastoral problem, which makes even more intensive exegesis necessary. In Africa the need to distinguish between Law and Grace presents a fundamental problem.[23]

Systematic theology is the core of theological education, and this should be related to the African world view. As far as ecclesiology is concerned, the Church is a pilgrim Church and cannot safeguard all the sentiments of a tribe – it has a higher authority and aim. According to Raaflaub, the African is not concerned in the first place with dogmatics and dogmatic formulations, but rather with the Gospel as 'the way', which may be an indication that Africa's first contribution will be in the field of Ethics.[24] Such questions as ancestor worship, magic and fetish should find an adequate theological confrontation during the period of theological education.

259

Church history occupies a very uncertain place in the curriculum in Africa, according to the IMC *Theological Report*, Part III, and the situation has not much improved since the *Report* was published. Whenever it was taught, the emphasis was mainly on the history of the denomination. Some theological tutors, according to this *Report*, even maintained that the African has no conception of history. Although the historical perspective of the African is shorter than that of the Westerner, and he thinks more in terms of personal relationships, it is unjustified to say he has no conception of history; rather, his conception and that of the Westerner are different. The one is more factual, the other more personal. Here we need to select and, in discussing outstanding personalities, the African must see that the Church in Africa has its own history, which should not be taught from the European point of view. The authors of the IMC *Report* (*Report III*, 47) state: 'In our opinion the two foci of a good theological course are: (i) Bible studies, with doctrine related as closely as possible to these studies, and (ii) church history.' If it is true that 'historical narrative proper arises when a people experiences the historical process by which it is shaped into a nation or a state',[25] Africa will become even more aware of its own history. Church history should not be studied from a distance, so that the impression is created that all the major events in Church history took place somewhere else, especially in Europe; it should be taught in such a way that not only are theological developments seen as within the Church, but that, as far as Africa is concerned, the dynamic of the growth of the Church is seen on the African continent. The dichotomy that exists in the African mind about many things, because of what has been given to him by the missionaries and his own interpretation, should be overcome in relating Christian teaching to African life.[26] A well-balanced Church history book for the Church in Africa, as well as for theological schools and faculties, is desperately needed.[27] Names should feature prominently in Church history for Africa, where the person takes precedence over anything else.

Islam, nationalism, the relation between the Church and African independent states, materialism, the developing urban society and all its implications, communism – all these aspects need to be studied in theological education in Africa, as well as all the implications in pastoralia. The Church is today a highly political factor in Africa, whether it wants to accept this description or not. Should the Church take part in politics? Certainly not in party politics, but it should exercise its prophetic voice over all political issues. Questions such as the political responsibility of the Christian and the relationship of the Church to the state all have to be worked out theologically.[28]

Religion in Africa must be related to the total life of the people, without degenerating into a social Gospel.[29]

The Bible School, where the laity can receive inspired well-balanced short courses related to the existential situation is important. If such schools could be established on an ecumenical basis, the wealth of experience that could be fruitfully used would be very great. Compared to the rest of Africa, South Africa is still in a backwater in this respect. These Bible Schools can be of great value to the young, who would like to serve in and through the Church more effectively. The effort to train leaders of the independent movements should be encouraged.

The language medium of institutions is a controversial subject. The leading languages spoken in Africa are Arabic (74 million), Hausa (13 million) and Swahili (10 million). In Africa south of the Sahara, there are more than five hundred languages and dialects classified into twenty-one major language groups.[30] French and English are mainly used in the Protestant theological seminaries as media of instruction, although quite a number of these include the vernacular. (The French discouraged the study of the vernacular in their colonies.) The variety of languages represented by the trainees, however, calls for *linguae francae*. At a Theological Institute refresher course held near Stutterheim, South Africa, during January 1963, the vernacular was stressed, notably by the Africans, but it was generally agreed that in a situation where men from different backgrounds undergo common training, a *lingua franca* is an absolute necessity. If the Gospel has to be preached in a vernacular surrounding, students should learn to think about the encounter of the Gospel with that environment in the vernacular. Theological literature in the vernacular is, however, the great difficulty, and for this reason both African and non-African languages should be used as language media. The African language brings the student into contact more realistically with his own world, and the European language brings him into contact with the riches of theological literature. In the lectures, concepts should, however, continuously be translated into the vernacular.

In many respects the training of the Roman Catholic clergy is far ahead of that of other Churches in Africa, with regard both to the indigenous priesthood and to the quality of education. Prospective candidates are chosen for the priesthood when they are still very young, and there is no distinction in the quality of training between the indigenous priesthood and their expatriate fellow-priests.[31]

Raising of standards will mean very little if the aims and methods pursued at a training centre are not adequately worked out. The emphasis should be on a 'theology of missionary encounter'. Trust between teachers and students must be established, and the lectures presented in the form of discussion and dialogue. Paul's theological encounter carries with it the marks of the hearer of his time. In Part III of the Survey on Theological Education in Africa, the authors wrote: 'It often occurred to us that the whole process of "teaching" theology to Africans needed less rigidity in time-tables and subjects, and far more free discussion between teachers and taught on the basis which would make the teacher as much a learner as his students. . . . Probably the ideal class would constitute not a number of students receiving instruction from a teacher (and laboriously taking down notes), but a group of people – some European, some African – together wrestling with the central doctrines of Christianity and their bearing on African thoughts and conduct.'[32] Memorising should make room for independent judgment, and theological instruction must be related to the actual practice of the ministry.

The following recommendation was put forward by the IMC *Theological Report*, Part II (1954): 'We believe that not less than one-fourth of missionary personnel and effort should be wholeheartedly directed to the training of ministers and of lay workers in the Churches. . . .'[33] Expenditures of selected mission boards for theological education abroad indicate that, as far as the American boards are concerned, the highest expenditure of any of these is 11% and the lowest 2%; the highest expenditure in Britain is 1·96% and the lowest 0·45%.[34] In Africa the position has improved during the last few years – a revolution has taken place both in expenditure and in the number of staff,[35] but there is still a great lack of insight in the importance of a well-educated relevant ministry. The importance of theological training must be seen in the light of the fact that the average period of service of a minister is around thirty years, during which time thousands of people may be served well, or may be done measureless harm.

Attention should be given to recruitment. The shortage of new recruits is due to quite a number of factors: (i) the spiritual condition of the Church; (ii) 'the decreasing respect for the African minister within his own community';[36] (iii) the difficulty experienced by Churches in supporting their present number of ministers; (iv) the low stipends paid to African ministers; (v) the growing nihilism amongst the intelligentsia as a result of the failure of the Church to relate the Gospel message to the contemporary problems of society; (vi) conservatism of the old clergy under whom the young clergy have to work; and (vii) the African Christian community seldom sees the office of the ministry as an integral part of the life of the

Church itself.[37] The Pentecostal and Adventist Churches have the highest precentage of ordained ministers and unless attention is given to this factor it will still be true that 'flocks without shepherds, shepherds who have not learned how to care for the flocks, are dangerously numerous in Africa today'.[38] Many of these make themselves at home in the nativistic and the independent movements. Dr. C. H. Hwang has summarised the main difficulties as follows:

(i) The pattern imported by the missions is 'church-directed' – the need is for theological training in world-directed ministries.

(ii) The imported pattern of the ministry is denominational – the need is for ecumenical encounter in theological education.

(iii) The imported pattern of the ministry is 'mono-tary' – the need is for theological education for a variety of ministries. The emphasis on the 'male' pattern of the ministry should be reconsidered in the light of the emancipation of women, also in Africa; the 'mono-tary' pattern of the ministry is too static in a dynamic society.

(iv) The imported pattern of paid ministry; the set-apart ministry is necessary but not necessarily identical with the pattern of paid ministers which is a heavy burden in Africa.[39]

A most interesting article appeared some years ago in a Roman Catholic periodical, which is of great significance in the interpretation of Church history.[40] The author's starting-point is the encyclical *Mystici Corporis* and he presents the thesis that Church history should be understood as an organism which develops and matures – and does not merely expand. The Church is thus not just something that is inherited – that the coming generation can simply take over and safeguard and pass on to its successors; but new treasures and insights are discovered with each generation. This is what is expected of the Church in Africa, which has so much to give to the universal Church. The question is, however, whether Africa could ever become a continent won for Christianity without a more united Christian Church, and whether religious liberty will be honoured. It is only when the Church in Africa becomes truly missionary that unity at least will be accomplished. Max Warren writes: 'It is no accident that it is where the faith advances on the frontiers that the Body of Christ is most visibly becoming one.'[41] Whether this will be true of Africa depends on how the Church here meets the challenge. If independentism is an indication that the challenge is not being met, then the Church in Africa must seriously reconsider its very nature, especially when, as a result of its foreignness and aloofness from the African approach, it is itself co-responsible for the development of post-Christianity.

REFERENCES

1. Cf. H.-R. Weber, 'The Marks of an Evangelising Church' in the *Missionary Church in East and West*, ed. by C. C. West & D. M. Paton, SCM, 1959, 101–03. See also *The layman in Christian History*, ed. by S. Neill and H.-R. Weber, SCM, 1963. See also H.-R. Weber, 'Der Dienst der Laien in der Missionarischen Verkündigung der Kirche' (EMZ, Sept., 1956, 160). Cf. also A. T. Hanson, 'The Pioneer Ministry', SCM, 1961, Laity Bulletin, WCC, Geneva. Ed. J. Specker and W. Buehlmann, *Das Laienapostlat in den Missionen*, Schöneck–Beckenried, 1961. The Roman Catholic Church has grown remarkably in Africa South as a result of the building up of a sense of community and belonging, indigenisation of the Church, building up a new African Christian culture, and the emphasis on the lay apostolate. Cf. Cecil Northcott, *Christianity in Africa*, SCM, 1963; also P. Beyerhaus, *Theological Training in Southern Africa*, Johannesburg, 1964.

2. F. B. Welbourn, 'The Church and the Faculty', IRM, April 1955, 141.

3. Reyburn, 'Africanisation and African Studies', 102.

4. Cf. Ed. N. Goodall and E. W. Nielsen, Survey of the Training of the Ministry in Africa, Part III, *Report*, London, IMC, 1954.

5. F. G. Welch, *Training for the Ministry in East Africa*, Mercury Press, 1963; Sundkler (*Ministry*, 304) sees here a tension between the teaching of the priesthood of all believers and 'the African propensity for representative leadership'. To aid in popular religious instruction, Luther prepared in 1529 two catechisms, of which the one for the laity, 'the short catechism is one of the noblest monuments of the Reformation' (Williston Walker, 319). The laity need such a document in which the faith is expounded on an ecumenical basis in the African context.

6. Ibid., 102.

7. Welbourn, 'The Church and the Faculty', 141.

8. Cf. Oosthuizen, 'Theological Education in South Africa', IRM, July 1963, 283.

9. Welbourn, *The Church and the Faculty*, 143.

10. Cf. Krister Stendahl, 'The New Testament and the Preaching', *Lutheran World*, June 1959, 722.

11. Cf. G. C. Oosthuizen, *Theological Education in South Africa*, 285. Christian ethics should be carried into the sphere of society and help establish a wholesome social, economic and political life. Cf. Parsons, *The Churches and Ghana Society*, 181 ff.

12. The Roman Catholics give attention in their 'Lay Apostolate' programme to social, political and cultural problems of the new Africa. The Mindolo Ecumenical Foundation and the All Africa Conference of Churches are doing much in this direction.

13. Georg Vicedom, 'Von der Theologie einer jungen Kirche' in *Das Wort Gottes in Geschichte und Gegenwart*, ed. Wilhelm Andersen, Kaiser, 1957, 104. An important meeting took place in East Africa at the Limuru (Kenya) Conference Centre in April 1964, when 140 theological students from nine colleges met and discussed the task of the Church in East African society. Cf. mimeographed report entitled *Christ and Culture*. Seminars such as those held at the University of Edinburgh will be fruitful, especially in Africa itself. Cf. mimeographed lectures of the April 1964 meeting, entitled *Religion in Africa*.

14. K. S. Latourette, *The Christian World Mission in our Day*, Eyre & Spottiswoode, 1954, 104–05.

15. S. Neill, IMC *Theological Report* I, 59. See also the other IMC Theological Reports, namely Part II by N. Goodall and E. W. Nielsen, London and New York, 1954, and Part III by F. Michaeli and B. G. H. Sundkler, Paris, 1954.

16. Cf. H. Scholten ('Afrikas Weg zur Theologie', EMZ May 1952, 17), after referring to the difficulties confronting an African minister, concludes 'Nein, der Afrikanische Geistliche muss ein wissender sein'.

17. Cf. E. Bolaji Idowu, *Towards an Indigenous Church*, OUP, 1965.

18. Cf. Paul D. Fueter, 'The All-African Lutheran Conference', Marangu, 1955, IRM, 1955, 289. Two-thirds of the 165 representatives were African. See also Heinrich Mayer, 'Das Wagnis von Marangu' in *Deutsche Evangelische Weltmission Jahrbuch* 1956, 22–28. The emphasis on a *Confessio Africana* is also given by Heinrich Waltenberg, 'Probleme der Afrikanischen Christenheit', *Lutherische Missions* Jahrbuch, 1957. For a Lutheran discussion of confession and unity see V. Vajta and H. Weissgerber (ed.), *The Church and the Confessions*, Philadelphia, Fortress Press, 1963.

19. Cf. Oosthuizen, *Theological Discussions*, 270 ff.

20. Ed. Arne Sovik, 'Confessions and Churches – An Afro-Asian Symposium', *Lutheran World*, Vol. V, No. 4, March 1959, 366.

21. *Ministry*, 210; see also Max Warren, CMS *Newsletter*, May 1959, 3 ff. For the most recent discussions on 'Confessing the faith in Asia Today', see *The South East Asia Journal of Theology*, July–Oct. 1966 and Jan. 1967.

22. African concepts should constantly be 'juxtaposed and examined along with the Biblical meanings. If this is not done one runs the risk of teaching isolated and abstracted information unrelated to anything known, felt and practised.' Reyburn, 109.

23. Jean Kotto has written in the above-mentioned paper: 'Most sermons are expositions of moral precepts, negative preaching, résumés of the Godly maxims, proclamation of God's judgment on sinners. As prophets of ill omen, we have made religion a dry moralism.'

24. F. Raaflaub, 'Afrika sucht seinen Weg', EMZ, 3, 1961, 110.

25. R. Bultmann, *History and Eschatology*, Edinburgh University Press, 1957, 14.

26. Cf. W. Cason, 'The Teaching of Church history in Liberia', *The Ghana Bulletin of Theology*, Vol. 2, No. 3, Dec. 1962, 36–43.

27. Sundkler, *Ministry*, 221.

28. Cf. Heinrich Mayer, 'Politische Verantwortung und Afrikanische Theologie', *Jahrbuch Evangelischer Mission*, 1961, 18–24. Cf. Seppo A. Teinonen, *Missio Politica Oecumenica*, The Finnish Society for Missionary Research, 1961, 67.

29. Cf. J. V. Taylor, *Christianity and Politics in Africa*, Penguin, 1957, 20; cf. Max Warren on 'Marangu', CMS *Newsletter*, Feb. 1965, 5–7.

30. Yorke Allen, Jr., *A Seminary Survey*, Harper & Bros., 1960, 247–8.

31. Welch, *Training for the Ministry in East Africa*, 86–88. See also Adelrich Morant, *Die Philosophisch-Theologische Bildung in den Priesterseminarien Schwarz-Afrikas*, Schöneck-Beckenried, 1959; ed. J. Beckmann, *Der Einheimische Klerus in Geschichte und Gegenwart*, Schöneck-Beckenried, 1950. Louis and André Retif, *The Mission of the Church in the World*, Burns & Oates, 1962.

32. IMC *Theological Report*, Part III, 44.

33. Ibid., Part II, 1954.

34. Yorke Allen, 549, 550.

35. Welch, *Training for the Ministry in East Africa*, 89–90. Christian Stewardship has often been neglected in the young Churches and needs serious attention.

36. IMC *Theological Report*, Part III.

37. Cf. Ibid.

38. Cf. M. Searle Bates, 'The Training of Christian Ministers in non-British Africa', IRM, July 1954, 289.

38. C. H. Hwang, 'A Re-thinking of Theological Training for the Ministry in the Younger Churches today', *The South East Asia Journal of Theology*, Oct. 1962, 20–25.

40. Richard Kleine, 'Philosophisch-Theologische Erwägungen zur Kirchengeschichte im missionswissenschaftlichen Gesichtsfeld', in *Zeitschrift für Missionswissenschaft und Religionswissenschaft*, 1, 1951.

41. M. A. C. Warren, 'The Missionary Obligation of the Church in the present historical situation', IRM, Oct. 1950, 400.

INDEX OF NAMES

268

Primianus, 1
Priscilla, 150

QUICK, G., 43

RAAFLAUB, F., 259
Raum, O., 138
Reyburn, W. D., 198, 224
Rogatus, 1
Ross, W. M., 49

SARILI, Chief, 85
Schlosser, K., 30, 80
Schmidt, G., 2
Senghor, L. S., 239
Shaka, 123
Shembe, I., 35, 36, 37, 74, 75, 78, 90, 91, 92, 93, 95, 96, 97, 98, 119, 120, 123, 149, 150, 157, 184, 208, 240
Shembe, J. G., 125
Shibe, S., 33
Shropshire, D. W. T., 3, 89, 136, 172
Smith, E., 3, 223
Sovik, A., 10, 258
Spartas, R., 47, 49
Stendahl, K., 224
Stumpf, H., 49
Sundkler, 34, 71, 72, 77, 88, 91, 97, 120, 123, 128, 130, 134, 135, 163, 170, 171, 185, 188, 189, 214, 223, 240, 259

TANI, G., 56
Taylor, J., 5, 7, 43, 44, 45, 47, 126, 135, 138, 158, 192, 193, 196, 197, 232, 241, 242
Tempels, P., 195
Tertullian, 4, 150

Thomas, W., 220
Thuka, H., 49, 51, 170
Tile, N., 32
Tillich, P., 218
Tlapane, 84
Tolonyane, 125, 137, 186
Trimingham, J. S., 8, 213
Troeltsch, E., 15, 156
Tucker, 3
Tunolashe, M., 53
Turner, H. M., 33, 71
Tylor, 208

UMHLAKAZA, 84, 85
Umlanyeni, 84

VAJTA, V., 225
Van Wing, J., 87
Venn, H., 3, 31, 33
Visser 't Hooft, W. A., 13
Voetius, G., 211

WALLACE, A. F. C., 76, 77
Warren, M., 82, 234, 263
Weber, H. R., 233, 240, 243
Welbourn, F. B., 46, 49, 257
Wesley, J., 153, 154
Westermann, D., 3, 223
Wickham, E., 16
Wilberforce, W., 2
Willoughby, W. C., 3
Wilson, M., 88, 140, 197
World Council of Churches, 211
Wovenu, C. K. N., 59, 171

ZINZENDORF, N. L. von, 222
Zwemer, S., 19

INDEX OF SUBJECTS

271

Kereke Ea Moshoeshoe, 39
Kerygma, 13
Khaki Movement, 187, 188, 192, 194
Kikuyu Independent Schools Association, 181
Kitawala, 32
Koinonia, 213, 247, 249

LANGUAGE, 235 ff.
Last day, 85
Lay Christians, 15, 255 ff.
Laying-on of hands, 59, 185
Leadership, 9, 42, 60, 81
Legalism, 61, 131, 169, 173, 174, 225
Liturgy, 8, 60, 225 ff.
Love Feast, 57
Lumpa 'Church', 41, 136, 194

MAGIC, xi, 31, 41, 89, 97, 102, 169, 174, 209
Magical personality, 75
Magical technology, 76
Magician, 80
Malakites (*Bamalaki*), 45, 181
Mahdism, 19, 20, 21
Manyanos, 243
Marcionism, 161
Marriage, 60
Matswa Movement, 40
Mau Mau, 51, 100
Medicine, 41, 98, 122
Medicine man, 80
Mengo Gospel Church, 186
Mennonite Baptists, 152
Menstruating women, 174
Messiah, 7, 32, 75, 76, 79, 84, 93, 96, 102, 126
Messianic Movements, 75, 79
Methodism, 156, 181
Methodist Church, 241
Miracles, 92
Monogamy, 182
Montanism, 188
Moravian Movement, 153
Munkukusa Movement, 153
Musama Disco Christo Church, 135, 184
Music, 8, 240, 241
Myth, 35, 90, 96

NATION, 223
National Baptist Convention, 80
Nationalism, 5, 6, 32, 47, 48, 80, 244
Native Anglican Church, 136
Native Economic Commission, 77
Native Labour Regulation Act, 34
Native Land Act, 34
Native Trust and Land Act, 34
Nativism, ix, 75, 79
Nativistic Movements, xi, xii, 73, 74, 75, 76, 79
Nazarites, 35, 36, 183, 220
Nestorianism, 189
New Testament Sect, 47
New Zion, 41
Ngunza Khaki Movement, 180, 184, 190, 191, 194
Ngunzistic Salvation Army, 152, 180

OLD TESTAMENT, 59, 84, 161 ff.

PAN-AFRICANISM, 34
Parousia, 84, 95, 100, 104
Partnership, 9
Passover, 47, 171
Paternalism, 5, 31, 52, 60
Pentecostal Holiness Church, 140
Pentecostalism, 72, 120, 121, 127, 128, 135, 137, 140, 189
Perfectionism, 188, 189
Political consciousness, 5, 31, 33, 60, 80, 82, 83
Polygamy 42, 48, 51, 56, 60, 87, 92, 169, 170, 171, 179 ff.
Polygyny, 14, 59
Post-Christianity, 9, 102, 207, 263
Praise songs, 139
Prayer Church, 54, 181
Prayer Healing Churches, 53, 59
Prayers, 38, 57, 60, 86, 186
Presbyterian Church of Africa, 72
Prophecy, 1, 190
Prophet, 54, 79, 80, 83, 84, 86, 91, 93, 99, 102, 126, 127, 133, 180, 181
Prophetic Movements, 75
Prophetism, 92

QUAKERISM, 152, 156

272

273